Understanding and Representing Space

Understanding and Representing Space

Theory and Evidence from Studies with Blind and Sighted Children

SUSANNA MILLAR

Department of Experimental Psychology
University of Oxford

CLARENDON PRESS · OXFORD
1994

Oxford University Press, Walton Street, Oxford OX2 6DP

Oxford   New York
Athens   Auckland   Bangkok   Bombay
Calcutta   Cape Town   Dar es Salaam   Delhi
Florence   Hong Kong   Istanbul   Karachi
Kuala Lumpur   Madras   Madrid   Melbourne
Mexico City   Nairobi   Paris   Singapore
Taipei   Tokyo   Toronto
and associated companies in
Berlin   Ibadan

Oxford is a trade mark of Oxford University Press

Published in the United States
by Oxford University Press Inc., New York

A catalogue record for this book is available from the British Library

Library of Congress Cataloging in Publication Data
Millar, Susanna.
Understanding and representing space : theory and evidence from studies with
blind and sighted children / Susanna Millar.
Includes index.
1. Space perception in children.   2. Mental representation in
children.   3. Children, Blind.   I. Title.
BF723.S63M55   1994   155.4' 13752—dc20   94–10299
ISBN 0 19 852142 1

Typeset by Footnote Graphics, Warminster, Wilts
Printed in Great Britain on acid-free paper by
Bookcraft (Bath) Ltd, Midsomer Norton, Avon

To Fergus

Preface

This book is intended for psychologists and for all who are interested in questions of the development of spatial skill and knowledge, whether as students, specialists in the field of blindness, fellow researchers in other fields, or from sheer curiosity. The book aims to contribute to answering the question of how visual experience relates to spatial knowledge, what information needs to be restored in its total absence, and what this tells us about developmental processes.

My gratitude is due to a number of people and institutions. Foremost is the Department of Experimental Psychology of Oxford University and the colleagues who provide the stimulating intellectual climate without which it would not have been possible to write this book. I particularly want to thank Professor Weiskrantz for having created an atmosphere in which independent work can flourish, for his support of my research over the years, and for useful criticisms of the book. I am very grateful also to Professor Iverson for continued support of my work. I have greatly enjoyed St Hugh's College, both as a Senior Research Fellow, and in teaching undergraduates as Director of Psychological Studies. Of my former doctoral students I would like to mention particularly Dr Rona Slator whose findings on young children's memory for locations with different input and output conditions were novel and exciting and Dr Lucy Henry for her meticulous work on young children's memory for auditory inputs, and I should like to refer also to Dr Ittyerah who greatly helped in carrying out the experiments on mental practice during her post-doctoral Fellowship. Dr John Stein and Dr Adrian Moore were kind enough to read various parts of the manuscript and I am greatly indebted to them for their valuable comments. The mistakes that remain are my own. To Dr Carl Sherrick I owe a very fruitful term as Visiting Fellow at Princeton University and what knowledge I have of vibrotactile devices. Dr Tobin of Birmingham University has been an invaluable and kind colleague in the field of visual handicap who could be relied on for support, sympathy, and a wide variety of information, always accessible and generous with his time.

The Economic and Social Research Council, formerly the Social Science Research Council, needs particular mention. The Research Council supported all the experimental work which I undertook over many years on the questions discussed in this book. The research could not have been carried out without that support.

Finally I want to record my gratitude and my affection for the blind and sighted children and young people, and their teachers and head-teachers who participated in the research, for their unfailing welcome and cooperation.

Oxford   S.M.
June 1994

Contents

1

Introduction: questions and terms

A little girl, who was skipping confidently ahead of me on our way to a familiar room in her school, remarked casually: 'Oh, you're wearing your blue dress today, Miss'. Her confident walk and what she said would be quite unremarkable, except that the child was totally blind and had been so from birth.

The anecdote highlights some of the questions which are central to the theme of this book. How important is vision to the notions we have about space? Is visual experience crucial? Or is it as irrelevant to the ideas we have about perception and representation, as it may seem if we consider the blind little girl's confident walk along a familiar route, and her quite correct use of the colour word for a dress she had touched and heard about before? More generally, the question is about the relation between the sensory modalities and spatial representation.

It may seem paradoxical to write a book on spatial development from the point of view of the blind. Books on space perception are mostly synonymous with studies on vision. But it was done quite deliberately. The reason is very simple. We do not really know what role vision plays in understanding space. Its importance is usually taken for granted, and other sense modalities, and particularly touch and movement, are rarely considered in that connection.

But suppose we take the opposite view, that we do not take the role of vision for granted, and do consider movement, touch and sound as sources of spatial information? That is the standpoint taken here. To understand the role of vision, I am asking what, if any, information is missing in its absence and, if so, how it can be substituted. Furthermore, sound, as the main other distance sense we have, is often regarded as the only substitute for vision. But investigating information from touch and movement is equally, if not more, important because, as I hope to show, it can yield knowledge about relations between extended surfaces in a way that hearing alone cannot do.

It should be said at once that this book is not about spatial ability or disability. There is no reason whatever to suppose that the blind differ from the sighted in their potential for spatial understanding (Millar 1982a, 1988a). The question is about the role of the sense modalities in spatial coding.

There are both theoretical and practical reasons for studying spatial coding in blind as well as in sighted conditions. The theoretical question turns on the role of sensory modalities in the informational and cognitive systems during development. It asks what, if any, role vision plays in spatial processing. Evidence from conditions of short-term, as well as long-term, total deprivation of sight is essential if we are to understand what and how vision and other sense modalities contribute to spatial coding.

The obvious practical question which is connected with the theoretical concern is about the means and procedures that are needed to compensate for absence of sight. Practice is almost always based on quite definite ideas and assumptions. But they are rarely, if ever, made explicit. The fact that the assumptions are tacit means that they are not questioned. But we need to understand precisely what aspects of information the different perceptual systems contribute, and what aspects of information are missing when sight is excluded, in order to provide adequate substitute information. It is a mistake to assume that we already know what that information is, or how it is best substituted. We do not. The present book is intended as a contribution to that quest.

Given that the form in which we ask questions is crucial, questions which demand answers in terms of the 'nature versus nurture' dichotomy should be avoided, in my view, for a number of reasons. The dichotomy does not correspond to what is known already. It is theoretically stultifying and mischievous in practice. It is neither true nor useful to assume that spatial knowledge must either be inborn or that it can only be acquired through vision. In practice, both views lead to inaction. For theoretical understanding, both lead to asking the wrong questions.

The questions that need to be answered are about the processes that underlie performance. The answers depend on looking at the conditions that produce and change processing. The point of looking at spatial processing in blind conditions is to understand what information vision, and modalities other than vision, contribute to spatial processing. The purpose of comparing performance by blind children with that of blindfolded sighted children is precisely that. It allows us to compare the effects that lack of vision has in the long and short term.

A similar point applies to the study of development. The question whether children have or lack spatial ability is not, as such, particularly useful for understanding behaviour. Ability tests are often necessary for practical purposes, but they do not tell us what processes underlie performance. For that, we need to probe the conditions which produce or change performance.

The temptation to think in terms of a dichotomy of abilities and disabilities stems to a large extent from the legacy of older 'innate ideas versus blank slate' philosophical theories, which still colour our notions about the development of spatial coding and representation. The following section looks briefly at some of the background for the nature/nurture question which that legacy has produced, and why it had better be discarded.

I Some origins of the innate/acquired controversy

Questions about vision were considered central to our understanding of ideas about space long before psychology existed as an experimental science. The great British empiricist philosopher, John Locke (1689), reported the now famous question by Molineux. Molineux asked whether a man who had been born blind, but later recovered sight, would be able to recognize, by sight alone, objects and shapes which he had formerly experienced only through touch.

For John Locke the question was important because he held that concepts of space derive from sensory experience. The mind, according to him, is initially like a blank tablet on which experience writes.

The contrast was with rationalist philosophers. Plato, among the ancient Greeks, taught that the soul before birth knows concepts in their pure form; they merely have to be uncovered afterwards. Kant (1781) argued (rather differently) that perception of the world is impossible except in terms of *a priori intuitions* of space, time and causality. The precise meaning of Kant's *a priori* intuition of space is still debated (e.g. Kitcher 1990; Waxman 1991); and does not correspond exactly with current meanings of concepts of space.

The philosophical arguments for the empiricist and for the rationalist views are themselves highly controversial, and no factual implications follow from them in any case (Strawson 1989). Nevertheless, the philosophical controversy, or how it has been perceived by others, has had an enormous influence on psychology. Particularly in the study of child development, the influence is still present in the form in which questions are often asked today. The influence has not been entirely beneficial. The reason is that the controversy is often wrongly taken to imply an empirically based division between what is inborn and what is acquired. The dichotomy, even if it was misperceived (Evans 1985), carried over directly into what has almost become the main question in the study of child development, namely the 'nature' versus 'nurture' issue.

Scientific studies of psychology in English-speaking countries initially followed the empiricist view, with interludes that concentrated on motivation by trying to count the number of instincts we were supposed to possess. But learning was described entirely in terms of increments in the strength of connections between items which occur together frequently.

From about the middle of this century, the influence of ethology from the continent combined with other factors to change the balance in favour of explanations in terms of inborn abilities and knowledge. Ethology, which used systematic observation of animals in combination with experimental methods, showed that many animals respond innately to quite specific constellations of stimuli (e.g. Tinbergen 1951). There was a renewed interest in the study of very young infants for that reason. Instead of viewing the newborn baby as a total blank, with everything yet to learn, the infant came to be considered as already endowed with innate responses to preselected stimuli.

Another line of argument came from linguists such as Chomsky (1957, 1965). Chomsky argued that it must be assumed that there are inborn universal rules of syntax, and that it would be impossible to acquire language without these. Specific languages merely instantiate these universal rules. Chomsky made the useful distinction between competence and performance. Errors and failures occur, not because people do not have the necessary competence (do not know the rules), but for other reasons. They may be tired, or may have forgotten or have misunderstood the question or forgotten some of the information in the first place. The view of development became that of a process of maturation which uncovers the competence that is present from the start.

Like all sciences, psychology uses current technology as models for explanatory theories. Computer technology initially helped the assumption of innate knowledge systems, by making a new analogy possible. The hardware wiring of computers provided a literally solid model for the otherwise somewhat vague notion of innate knowledge and innate concepts; the software could be analogous to less fixed functions. The notion of innate wiring of specific domains of knowledge was also strengthened by advances in neurophysiological methods which showed that there is considerable specialization in the brain (see Chapter 4). Neuropsychological and physiological findings, especially on patients with cerebral damage, suggested that different aspects of knowledge could operate relatively independently. This gave rise to the notion of 'modularity' of mental function, and a model of functionally separate innate systems (Fodor 1983). However, interrupting a flow system may isolate components that do not normally operate in complete isolation. The modularity question will be considered further in Chapters 4 and 7.

In fact, computer and computational models can be used for either side of the nature/nurture controversy. Recent advances in computer technology permit the simultaneous processing of several lines of information in parallel. Means of modelling parallel processing of information from different brain regions are thus available. Moreover, connectionist models have suggested how empiricist, associationist notions of learning could be implemented computationally. Rules, including those of language, could be learned incrementally (Rumelhart & McClelland 1986), rather than having to be wired-in, as rationalists argue. Computer analogies have contributed greatly by forcing theoretical descriptions and assumptions to be made clearer and more precise in attempts, for instance, to write programs which can reproduce some of the known facts about human perception, thinking and problem-solving. Moreover, in principle, theories which prove impossible to implement can be weeded out as inherently improbable.

Similarly, the revival of interest in performance by very young infants has produced ingenious methods in an area where experiments were previously considered impossible. However, even ingenious methods do not justify the notion of an initially totally blank system or the notion of innately totally specified competence. The findings on infants (Chapter 2) make it improbable that there is a dichotomy between genetic determination and learning or experience. Hence, neither the metaphor of a '*tabula rasa*' (blank tablet), nor that of a repository furnished with complete innate concepts which maturation will uncover, are useful models for psychological enquiry.

Psychologists and philosophers often appear to be asking the same question. In fact, they look for different types of answer, and base these on a different form of evidence. The philosophical debate about rationalist and empiricist notions is about logical priorities, not about empirical evidence (Millar 1982b, 1988a). The question whether the notion of perceiving the world involves the notions of space, time and causality is a philosophical problem. It cannot be resolved by empirical test.

The nature/nurture dichotomy is particularly misleading in looking at developmental questions (Millar 1988a; Morgan 1977). Even the toned-down version that admits the involvement of both nature and nurture seems to imply that the main job of scientific enquiry is to ascertain 'how much' there is of each. It carries with it the tacit assumption that genetic and environmental effects are additive. That is almost certainly incorrect. It is important to examine these misleading tacit assumptions. Otherwise they perpetuate useless controversies. The continuing, fruitless debate about 'how much' of intelligence is innate is a case in point. As a basis of empirical enquiry, the innate/acquired controversy drags on precisely because it stems from asking the wrong question. It will be argued that a closer look at empirical evidence on the interplay between the sense modalities and cognitive skills shows the dichotomy to be unjustified. With that, the additive question how much is genetic and how much is acquired, becomes theoretically meaningless.

The Molineux question, on the other hand, is of interest to psychologists, because it is relevant to empirical enquiry about how perception relates to knowledge. The answer depends on empirical results. Evidence from conditions of congenital total blindness is therefore relevant to understanding the role of vision in spatial knowledge and processing.

The viewpoint from which the present book was written thus deliberately challenges the common tacit equation of vision with spatial experience. This is not because vision is here regarded as unimportant. On the contrary, it is precisely because there are no easy or obvious answers to questions about the role of vision in spatial development that performance without vision is of interest. Blindness is not equivalent to merely closing one's eyes. The interest is in what happens in the total absence of visual experience. The spatial performance of the congenitally totally blind formed the basis of much of the research on which this book is based. It is reviewed here and compared to evidence on visuospatial development. The emphasis is on the conditions which determine performance

One advantage of considering evidence from performance without sight as well as with vision is that it highlights some aspects which are often neglected. The most obvious one is the fact that vision is not the only sense modality which conveys spatial information. Sense modalities other than vision do so also. The need to consider what information is available when a sensory source is absent, as well as what it provides when it functions, raises questions about similarities and differences between information from different senses, and how their contribution to knowledge should be described theoretically.

Another useful consequence of the shift in emphasis is that terms which are usually taken for granted have to be clarified if we are to make sense of the evidence.

Almost inevitably, whenever one raises questions about the nature and development of spatial coding, especially in connection with the blind, it is assumed that the question is about spatial abilities or their absence. Empirical findings are often misconstrued accordingly. It is necessary to examine the usually rather vague abstract terms from the outset to avoid such confusions.

A distinction that needs to be clarified further is between the notion of *a priori* knowledge of concepts, and the quite distinct idea of innate potential for acquiring knowledge of concepts. The book is thus not at all about spatial abilities. It is about the effects of informational conditions on the manner in which we determine and remember locations, directions and distances.

In the sections that follow I look at the terms 'ability', 'competence' and 'space' in some detail in order to clarify their use here.

II   The notion of ability

When Mephistopheles impersonates Faust as tutor (Goethe 1808) he tells his student not to worry if he lacks good ideas. Ideas are quite unnecessary.

A well sounding word will do instead. Mephistopheles might have added that such words are almost always abstract nouns.

The danger of reifying abstract nouns is well known. Nevertheless, the mistake of thinking that nouns necessarily refer to some real substance is actually quite common, and very easily overlooked. That can have quite serious consequences for the questions we ask and the models we use to represent the answers.

Take the word 'ability'. It is really an adverbial prediction. To say that a person 'has ability' is to use a very convenient shorthand label to predict that the person will perform some task satisfactorily or well, if and when the occasion arises. The forecast is usually made on the basis of past evidence that the person has performed a similar task, or solved a difficult problem, uncommonly quickly or well. The word ability is therefore a label for an adverb, or adverbial phrase, elevated for convenience into an abstract noun. It is not the name of an object for which it is profitable to look in the hope of finding it residing at some location, not even in the brain, although there is no doubt that efficient cognitive performance is highly correlated with anatomically intact and well functioning neural systems and brain (Chapter 4).

There is no doubt either that valid and reliable ability tests predict future efficiency of performance successfully from current performance. Such predictions are extremely valuable in practice. Individuals differ reliably on such tests. But that does not make test scores into a clue to some mysterious substance which some people possess in a greater degree than others. The scores simply show that some people are more efficient at solving difficult problems than other people.

The phrase 'having ability' also has overtones of approval. It refers to the potentially high quality of an activity. Such evaluation is not relevant to understanding what is going on. The very fact that tests of intelligence or ability are extremely important in practice makes it particularly easy to forget that nouns like 'ability' and 'intelligence' are labels for test scores. As such, the terms are useful as a shorthand, to refer to the fact that scores from the tests predict the quality of future performance on similar activities. The invention of intelligence tests illustrates this. Binet (Binet & Simon 1908) was asked by the French government to devise some means to detect children who would not be able to benefit from education, which had recently been made compulsory for all. Binet did this brilliantly. He selected a variety of short questions which a majority of children at a given age could answer without special teaching or training. Correct answers at, or above or below these age norms, were found to predict how well the child was likely to perform at school in the future. Tests of spatial, verbal, and numerical ability, and a host of others constructed since, have been invaluable precisely because they can predict, with high probability, how efficiently people will, on average, carry out tasks of that nature in the future.

Problems arise only when people ask what 'it' is that is being tested. The 1920s saw a solemn debate on that point. Not surprisingly, it was inconclusive. Spearman (1927), a founding father of factor analysis, a method based on matrix algebra that analyses sets of test correlations, vainly insisted that the factor 'g' that his formula extracted was a mathematical factor. It has been identified with intelligence ever since, and people ask how much of 'it' is innate and how much acquired, as if the concept were a piece of processed cheese which consists of eighty per cent cheddar, and twenty per cent other products.

The point is not trivial. It is no accident that the innate/acquired controversy has been interminable, and shows no sign of being resolved. The lack of solution stems from asking the wrong sort of question. An abstract noun is used as if it referred to a divisible object.

Psychology, like all experimental sciences, rightly looks for quantitative descriptions. But mathematical descriptions are only as good as the assumptions that prompt them. Simple dichotomies invite simple additive models. Mathematical models that make more reasonable (non-additive) assumptions can be useful to test genotype/environmental assumptions (e.g. Eaves *et al.* 1977). For psychological enquiry, dichotomies are often not so much a first step, as a step in the wrong direction.

The reification fallacy has to be borne in mind, because otherwise the relations between genetic factors, anatomical structures, and the physiological and psychological functions of an organism lead to needless confusion.

It would clearly be impossible for people to raise even a finger in salute or in protest, to point to a culprit, or to a direction, let alone to understand a story from a page of print, or a route from a map, if they were not genetically endowed with appropriate structures and the potential to develop the appropriate functions.

The genetic predispositions of cells and the environment in which they flourish, mutate, or are assailed operate from conception, not merely from birth. But 'how', not 'how much', is the question for the psychologist who looks at behaviour after birth, as it is the question for the molecular biologist who looks at cells in yeast or humans.

The important discoveries on genetic coding and advances in the field of molecular biology, which demonstrate the very close link in molecular structure of genetic materials between humans and other animals, clearly make it important to understand precisely what is involved at molecular (biochemical and physiological) levels. It is equally necessary to ask questions about the conditions under which overt behaviour occurs, and what information a person needs to perform successfully. Questions about the genetic endowment of a person and questions about his or her understanding of the cuneiform alphabet or market forces demand answers at several different levels.

There is ample evidence that damage to the brain impairs performance, and that particular interconnections of neurones (see Chapter 4) are concerned in spatial skills. Such evidence makes it especially important to bear in mind that the term 'ability' is an abstraction which designates the quality of performance. As such it does not 'reside' in the brain (or anywhere else), nor are spatial skills identical with the neuronal functions on which they depend. Abstract terms such as ability are very useful. But one has to be suspicious of them because they usually have too many functions, often at quite different levels or domains of enquiry.

Questions on the same subject can be asked from the point of view of philosophy, physics, genetics and biochemistry, physiology, or psychology. Nevertheless, what is apparently the same question demands answers that depend on quite different forms of evidence. Clearly, evidence which comes from questions and studies at molecular and at behavioural levels has to be compatible. But neither reduces to the other. It is certainly of interest to look at the relation between the different levels or domains of enquiry, to ask, for instance, what parts of the brain are involved in spatial behaviour and vice versa. Similarly, findings from biochemistry and genetics are of interest as important components of an eventual complete description. But results from different domains complement rather than reduce to each other.

From the point of view of biology, the most important argument against a nature/nurture dichotomy is that it implies that the genetic structure of an organism, the medium in which that structure is expressed, and the environment in which the organism develops are independent of each other. At present, all the evidence points the other way. Despite its venerable tradition, the dichotomous notion that spatial concepts are either inborn or acquired needs to be discarded also for that reason.

The view taken here is that the nature/nurture dichotomy about ability should be discarded. It stems from a philosophical debate about empiricist and rationalist concepts and does not address an empirical question. The next section suggests that the term ability is equivalent to the notion of potential rather than competence.

III Potential and the competence/performance distinction

One consequence of discarding the nature/nurture dichotomy as far too simplistic is to reduce the temptation to reify the notion of ability. This is particularly important because the tendency is to confuse ability with competence. Competence needs to be distinguished from the potential ability which an individual has before competence is established.

The terms competence and ability both refer to latent dispositions to behave in certain ways, rather than to actual performance. But they are not synonymous. Competence refers to a skill or knowledge which a person can be shown to have, even if he or she is not exhibiting it at this moment. Errors in performance can stem from a lack of competence in the particular skill or knowledge, or they can be accidental, for reasons that are irrelevant to the skill.

To take an example, a master craftsman may make a 'performance error'. He may make mistakes when he is tired, or momentarily inattentive, despite the fact that he is normally competent and knowledgeable. Chess grandmasters may make stupid moves when they are drunk. That does not mean that they lack competence in chess.

Such 'performance errors' have long been distinguished from incompetence. But it is also necessary to distinguish latent competence from the ability to acquire competence. In Jane Austen's *Pride and Prejudice* (1813), Lady Catherine asserts confidently that her daughter would have been a highly accomplished pianist, if her frail health had allowed her to learn to play. But even Lady Catherine does not imply that the girl could play, if only she opens the piano. The girl's current lack of competence was not in question. Her mother's assertion was about her potential for acquiring competence.

Chess players must, even as infants, have had the potential or ability to learn chess. But they clearly did not then have the competence to play chess which they have as adults, even when asleep. The baby Einstein did not have the competence to invent the theory of relativity in his cradle, but he must have had the potential for doing so. It has to be assumed that people must have had the potential for grasping the concepts that they acquire. That applies to the potential for the concept of Euclidean space, but also to the potential for any other (e.g. multidimensional) concept of space. Human newborns have a potential for solving crossword puzzles, playing chess, cricket, and tiddlywinks, to which not even the most astute of porpoises can aspire. But they do not, in the cradle, have the competence to do these things better than a porpoise.

The distinction between competence as latent mastery and ability as the potential for acquiring that mastery is important in considering developmental processes. It is even more important when looking at differences in performance which stem from differences in information.

It will be argued that the nature of coding is influenced by long-term as well as by short-term informational conditions. It should be clear that lack of information does not imply a lack of 'ability' to do otherwise; nor does it imply an inability to acquire the relevant competence.

IV   The concept of space and spatial coding

There is no point in consulting a dictionary about the notion of space. The word has too many meanings for that to be useful. From the viewpoint of this book, we are once again dealing with an abstract noun; that is to say, with a useful label for performance on a number of different tasks. Instead of puzzling about the concept of space, I shall consider performance on spatial tasks. By these I mean all tasks in which we need to know *where* something is.

Typical spatial tasks are to locate objects in relation to oneself and to other objects, to move from one place to another, to point to a location or to represent these actions in terms of measures of distance, direction, turns and angles, or by points on a shape. To test spatial skills in children and adults means no more than to get them to perform tasks which, by common consent, we label as 'spatial'. Looked at like that, some of the more intractable pitfalls of the concept of space disappear.

It is necessary also to distinguish between solving a spatial task and solving it my means of spatial coding. By spatial coding I mean that the location of an object is determined by reference to at least one other cue or anchor point, and is remembered as such. Spatial coding, as I use the term, depends on reference information. A single eye, suspended in an unstructured universe (assuming this were possible) without the presence of any other object, could not specify even its own position spatially. There must be at least one other object or anchor which can be used as a reference, if the eye is to relate to the other object spatially. Two separate objects or points are needed for a distance or extension to be defined. Even that is not enough if the task is to specify directions. At least a third separable object or point is needed.

The main characteristic of spatial representations is that they involve the use of reference. To code a location in terms of Euclidean geometry is to determine the location in terms of coordinate extensions or projections. They apply to the real world. But Euclidean relations are strictly logical relations in that they necessarily follow from the propositions that define them. The definition of right-angled triangles implies that the hypotenuse must be longer than either of the other sides. The length relation can be inferred from Euclidean geometry. However, coding locations and directions strictly by reference to Euclidean coordinates and geometric principles is by no means the only useful form people have of representing information in spatial tasks. The argument of this book is that the manner in which people code locations, directions, and distances depends crucially on what information they have in terms of both prior knowledge and the information that the task conditions afford.

There are, for instance, important differences in information between small-scale and large-scale space, even in vision. Small-scale space can be viewed from a single vantage point. In large-scale space, at least when some one is moving through a built-up environment, the field of view is limited by walls and buildings, and prevents people from seeing round the corner until they get there (Acredolo 1981; Slator 1982). But the environment still provides continuous updating cues.

In the normal course of events, people are unlikely to be aware that they are using information for reference as they move about the house or go for walks. We circumvent tables and chairs and other obstacles, avoid colliding with walls, reach for objects, and otherwise move in a direct line to the place in the room or garden to which we want to go, without feeling the need to calculate either distances or directions deliberately. In other words, we continuously take account of the changing information we receive from the environment as we move about, and update our movements accordingly, without being in the least aware that is what we are doing.

We also take it for granted that quite young toddlers do the same. They may be less steady on their feet, and topple over, or hold on to a support on occasion for that reason. But they do not walk into the furniture, and need no guide to understand the direction in which they have to move in order to get to where they want to go. This all seems so obvious that we quite fail to be surprised. The reason is that toddlers as well as adults can see the obstacles and the place to which they wish to go. Nevertheless, toddlers differ from adults in their knowledge of the environment, in their means of remembering landmarks and routes, and on tasks that require them to update or reorganize their spatial knowledge. That raises questions about the role of longer-term knowledge in processing, and about possible changes in coding with development.

Questions about spatial coding in the *absence* of vision look at the problem from a perspective that concentrates on the kind of information that is available in that condition. The interest centres here on what possible influence the modalities have on coding processes, in addition to effects on the 'quantity' of knowledge. It is clearly not the case that total absence of vision means the total absence of reference information. Information from other modalities can be used. The question is whether and how that affects the nature of coding inputs in spatial tasks.

I have argued that the question whether concepts of space are innate or acquired is misleading. In so far as the term 'spatial ability' labels a potential for action and thought, we can assume in principle that the very young, and the congenitally totally blind, have the potential to acquire the relevant competence. The question is how.

V   Aim and layout of the book

The role of the sense modalities in spatial coding and representation has been a central question in my research over many years. The aim of the book is to argue for the theory of spatial coding and development that has resulted from this work.

The evidence centres largely on my own studies. But it is by no means confined to them. My aim has been to consider how my findings relate to the results of other studies and explanations of spatial coding and development. Developmental factors as well as modality are therefore among the variables which are of interest in most of these. But relevant findings with adults are included.

I want to stress that findings in conditions of complete congenital blindness need to be considered if we want to understand the role of perceptual inputs in spatial thinking. That has not always been taken sufficiently into account. In fact, total deprivation of sight is very rare indeed. The majority of blind people have had some sight earlier on. Even blindness from birth often leaves residual light perception. That is important. Minimal light perception, even if it is not sufficient to discriminate shapes, can be useful for orientation, if it signals a change in the external world. Similarly, very early vision in the first year of life, even if it cannot be recalled, has lasting effects. It is to be hoped that future research will look at the way in which residual and early vision can be made useful in all cases (Barlow 1975).

The aim in my studies was to look first at information in the total absence of sight. I was therefore careful to distinguish between findings based on early or residual vision, and results based on conditions of total congenital blindness. My main studies were conducted with two carefully screened groups of children whom I followed over the years. The groups changed somewhat in composition as some left the schools and others entered them. The ages in the groups ranged from pre-school to late adolescence. Their ability on standardized tests (e.g. Williams 1956) varied from low average to very superior, with means at the average level. In all cases, I had access to medical as well as to school records, and records of my own of control tests. The children were thus known to me to be blind from birth or, in one case, totally blinded at the age of five months after her congenital (glaucoma) condition had been recognized. A few had some pupil reaction from light shone directly into the eye, but these reactions could not be used in any way. In studies which compared performance by these children with sighted subjects, the latter came from the same school intake area and socioeconomic backgrounds and were carefully matched not only on ability and verbal tests, but also on specific tests that tapped similar cognitive skills in a different medium (e.g. backward digit recall for backward recall of spatial locations). Such matching is necessary, because standardized tests differ for blind and sighted populations (Millar 1982a), and is all the more necessary because numbers are bound to be small. Unfortunately, comparisons based on unselected small groups of people who happen to be available, and conducted without matching controls, are still sometimes reported. Control of extraneous factors is necessary for interpreting what findings mean.

Looking at coding strategies in spatial tasks under different informational conditions is not, of course, the only possible level of enquiry. One could ask questions in the contexts of geography, architecture or environmental issues. Alternatively, questions could be at physiological, anatomical or molecular levels. These fields of enquiry are equally valid. But they do not reduce to each other. One kind of phenomenon is no more 'fundamental' than the other, nor do findings at one level of enquiry explain all the others. However, findings and explanations in different areas of enquiry do need to be compatible with each other. I am including a brief chapter on some neuropsychological evidence, because it is relevant to the question that I am asking. But I have, quite deliberately, not started with sensory systems, and then worked up to 'higher' functions.

In the chapter which follows, I consider first two types of theories about how the modality systems relate to each other. One assumes that inputs are quite separate and mediating schemata have to be acquired. Other theories suggest unitary processing. Findings that relate to these explanations are described.

In the third chapter, I argue on the basis of previous experiments that the different sense modalities actually provide complementary, convergent and overlapping information (Millar 1981a). The point is illustrated by other empirical studies, particularly on reaching, sitting and standing by infants, with and without sight of the spatial environment. Chapter 4 shows that the neuropsychological evidence strengthens the case for considering spatial coding as dependent on the integration and organization of multimodal inputs.

Processing information about the shape of objects by touch and vision is considered in a separate chapter from spatial coding. That is partly because the neuropsychological evidence strongly suggests that processing information about the identity of an object and about its location needs to be distinguished. But the comparison between shape recognition by touch and vision is also important in its own right in the present context.

Both touch and vision code shape. But in touch, unlike vision, the contribution of active movement differs with the size and depth of objects. I argue that the different types of complementary information for different types of object must be taken into account in theories of haptic coding.

Spatial coding of small-scale layouts is discussed next. Chapter 6 looks at developmental theories and findings on spatial coding in infancy and childhood and in blind conditions. I argue against the assumption that spatial development consists in a change of reference frame. Modes of coding depend on the salience and accessibility of relevant information, and become faster and more accurate with practice and experience.

The representation of large-scale space is considered in Chapter 7. This chapter looks particularly at orientation and route knowledge in geographical space, and its representation in terms of configurations. The evidence shows that memory of actually moving through space, and representing this in terms of maps, requires some form of symbolic translation. The question is taken further in Chapter 8. Modality-specific imagery is considered in the context of emergent symbols for actual representation, by drawings and maps. It is argued that covert coding of movement output can mediate non-visual spatial representation in memory.

Some practical implications of the evidence are considered in the penultimate chapter. In the final chapter I propose a theory of spatial representation which I believe best explains the findings we have at present. I have called it the 'Convergent Active Processing in Interrelated Networks' (CAPIN) model, for reasons that will, I hope, become clear later. The assumptions of the theory are briefly outlined in the next section of this chapter.

VI   Theoretical assumptions of the CAPIN model

After a family car ride years ago, one of my young children lay on his back and waved his legs from side to side, because he was being a windscreen wiper. That seemed to me to be a rather nice example of the repetition with variations which characterizes the overt play of children and the covert ruminations of adults (Millar 1968). The nature of the representation was also intriguing. The apparent translation from vision to movement raised questions about crossmodal coding, and the nature of representation without vision.

Later experiments on crossmodal coding suggested a view of the relation between the modalities (Millar 1981a) that is still part of the theory that I am putting forward. It is the first of the assumptions that I am listing below.

What I proposed, and still believe to be a good description of the evidence, is that the sense modalities are sources of specialized, but complementary and convergent information. The senses do not operate as completely separate systems; nor do they all convey precisely the same information. It is the convergence and overlap of complementary inputs that is important in coding and organizing apparently disparate inputs.

I now argue further that the integration of convergent multimodal information, particularly (not solely) from systems concerned with gravitationally (internal and external) specified inputs, is a major factor in spatial coding. Spatial coding demands reference information. The redundancy that results from the convergence and overlap of complementary inputs provides that. The integration is served by a number of specialized but interconnected cortical and subcortical structures.

It is assumed that (other things being equal) there are genetic predispositions for all forms of selecting, analysing and coding inputs to the system. It is also assumed that the systems cannot function or develop without constant environmental inputs. The conjunction of endogenous factors and experience constantly modifies processing and connections in the systems, and determines rates of change. Development depends from the outset on the combined action of endogenous and environmental conditions.

Development is explained by the reduced need for redundancy and saliency of inputs, due to the combination of maturity and knowledge. Moreover, processing difficulties, which occur when normally convergent inputs fail to coincide, are also reduced with experience.

There is more than one form of coding (representing) information in spatial tasks. The nature of coding depends on task demands, the salience and redundancy of current information, and the effects of longer-term (stored) knowledge.

Coding is assumed to be an integral part of storing information in memory and is present from the outset. Simple spatial coding occurs relatively early because of the redundancy of multimodal inputs about gravitational directions. For tasks that demand complex spatial reorganization, familiarity (stored, accessible knowledge) with all other aspects of a task is needed, to allow processing resources to be concentrated on relevant task components.

Complete absence of one sensory source has specific effects on coding. No single sensory system, including vision, is either necessary or sufficient for spatial coding. Nevertheless, complete absence of a sense modality eliminates a specialized output. It also reduces redundancy (overlap with other convergent inputs). This biases inputs, and modes of coding based on these, towards the remaining sources of information. In the complete absence of vision, inputs from proprioception and movement tend to be more prominent, but are less readily connected to relevant sounds, than with vision. The normal redundancy and overlap between inputs thus has to be restored when substituting missing information by other means.

It is argued that representation in short-term memory can be derived from most modes of input, not merely from vision or hearing. But to mediate short-term memory adequately, some form of output organization is needed. Movements can be used symbolically both for directional and configurational representation. Such symbolic representation can be used to sustain non-verbal temporary memory, and provides an alternative coding system also in the absence of vision. Such means of coding are spatial if the information is organized in terms of references.

The assumptions that I am making can be represented formally by convergent, constantly active and changing processing in interrelated networks of processes. These converge in a number of different combinations. I am calling the convergent active processing in interrelated networks, the CAPIN theory for convenience. It assumes that the interrelated networks are not confined to functioning hierarchically in up or down directions, but are influenced also by lateral interconnections.

The theory is considered in more detail in the final chapter. The evidence and justification for the view occupy the rest of the book.

2

Modality and cognition in developmental theories and the evidence

The manner in which the sense modalities operate in spatial performance is central to the questions which are explored in this book. The theories that have dominated developmental thinking in the past differ typically in how they conceive the relation between the sense modalities, and how these relate to cognitive processes.

The chapter briefly reviews evidence in relation to empiricist explanations and Piaget's theory in so far as it relates to the problem, and then looks at the phenomenalist view of the modalities as a unitary system.

I Empiricist assumptions of separate senses

In the extreme empiricist view, vision, hearing, touch, taste, and smell are separate senses from which we get all the information we have about the world. The association between them is learned. Intuitively, it seems obvious that feeling something rough is not the same as smelling it, or seeing its shape, or hearing it squeak. So, *prima facie*, the idea that these are initial sensations and we have to learn to associate them seems quite reasonable. It would also follow that there must be some repository for progressively learned associations to mediate between sensory modalities— a memory store from which we can retrieve the learned associations when necessary. Some theories of perception conform to that prescription. They differ mainly in what type of mediation is assumed.

One solution has been to argue that one particular input system serves as the basis for connections. The assumption that touch and movement are necessary for three-dimensional space perception to occur, was made by the eighteenth-century philosopher, Bishop Berkeley. A similar claim in this century was made partly on the grounds that the retina of the eye produces flat, inverted pictures of what is seen, and also because perception certainly requires change in stimulation and this involves moving (Zaporozhets 1965). Thus touch was assumed to 'teach' vision.

It is certainly the case that nothing is seen if the eye is immobilized and nothing felt (but see Sherrick & Cholewiak 1986) if contact with the skin is maintained without change. However, the notion that 'touch teaches vision' cannot be sustained. There is now ample evidence, excellently reviewed by Gibson and her colleagues (Gibson 1969; Gibson & Spelke 1983), that infants discriminate the shape, size, depth, and distance (within limits) of objects by vision from birth or soon after.

There is also clear evidence from studies which compare vision with touch and movement directly that young children actually find it much more difficult to recognize shapes and distances by touch and movement than by vision (Abravanel 1981; Goodnow 1971; Millar 1971, 1972a,b, 1975a; Rudel & Teuber 1964).

The converse, that vision is the main basis for integrating spatial information (Hatwell 1978; Revesz 1950; Schlaegel 1953; von Senden 1932; Warren 1974, 1977), has been somewhat more difficult to counter. Vision seems to be specifically linked to spatial skills. Some researchers have therefore assumed that this could constitute an almost insuperable difficulty for the blind (Worchel 1951).

Revesz (1950), on the other hand, suggested that spatial organization is different, rather than lacking, in the total absence of sight. According to him, the sighted organize space mainly in terms of external spatial coordinates. The congenitally totally blind rely instead on haptic (touch and movement) space. In that organization, spatial reference is centred on the body (self-reference) rather than externally. The studies that bear directly on this question will be discussed in more detail later.

Evidence which apparently supported the view that visual experience is essential for visuospatial understanding came from findings that monkeys who were blindfolded from birth did not learn visuospatial skills when restored to sight (Riesen 1947). A retrospective survey by von Senden (1932) of people who had congenital cataracts removed in adulthood showed that many of them had difficulties in seeing and in recognizing objects. It is now known that it is impossible to restore vision if there has been complete blinding from birth which has continued for a considerable period of time. Unless there is some visual stimulation, anatomical, peripheral and cortical structures that are involved in vision deteriorate irreversibly (Rapin 1979).

The evidence on anatomical and physiological changes is reviewed in Chapter 4. Here it is sufficient to note that this solution will not do. Vision is neither necessary nor sufficient for processing information across modalities, or for understanding external space, but it does facilitate such understanding (Gregory & Wallace 1963; Millar 1981a, 1988a).

Another solution of the empiricist problem was to suggest that information from different sensory sources is integrated by means of verbal mediation (e.g. Ettlinger 1967). Learning the same verbal tag for disparate items is obviously useful. But naming is not necessary for intersensory matching. Apes, monkeys (Davenport & Rogers 1970; Davenport *et al.*

1973; Weiskrantz & Cowey 1975) and even young infants who cannot yet speak (e.g. Bryant *et al.* 1972; Bushnell 1986; Gibson & Spelke 1983; Meltzoff & Borton 1979; Starkey *et al.* 1983, 1990; Streri, 1987) have sufficient appreciation of similarities and differences to match what they have seen to what they only feel or hear.

The theory that crossmodal matching requires a specific mechanism which improves with age and learning cannot, of course, be rejected solely on the grounds that infants show some crossmodal effects. Some initial anatomical and physiological substrate for intersensory connections must be in place at birth or soon after. However, such a substrate might function to support the learning-specific equivalence rules (Goodnow 1971). Alternatively, it could consist of an increasing long-term store of non-verbal translations, served by modality-specific temporary memories. That was proposed by Connolly and Jones (1970).

Two lines of evidence show that learned translations are not the main basis for crossmodal coding. One is that young children are not necessarily worse at crossmodal than at intramodal tasks (Millar 1971, 1972a; Rudel & Teuber 1964). Moreover, direct tests (Millar 1972a, 1975a) showed that neither age, nor delay, nor task difficulty relate specifically to crossmodal performance. Such connections should be found if crossmodal coding depended on learned associations. The view that crossmodal coding depends on a growing pool of learned associations predicts that crossmodal performance improves differentially with age. Crossmodal coding would also be impaired more than intramodal coding with more complex and difficult task stimuli. That is not so.

The study (Millar 1975a) showed that crossmodal performance as such does not relate to age. Moreover, in some conditions, differences between crossmodal and intramodal performance were, if anything, in the opposite direction to what would be expected if there were age improvements in crossmodal performance as such (Millar 1975a). That is important. The assumption that there is a single factor or 'mechanism' which underlies crossmodal performance is neither necessary, nor, indeed, likely to be correct.

Millar (1975a) argued that the younger children in the study actually showed less difference than older children between intramodal and crossmodal conditions, because they used a simpler or more general criterion as the basis for matching within and across modalities. The older subjects took more facets of the task into account in matching, and so used more specific criteria which were not necessarily the same in all conditions.

Children certainly become more efficient at most tasks and cope better with difficulties as they grow older. But there is no evidence of a progressively narrowing gap specifically between matching across modalities, as compared to matching within the sense modalities.

II Separate senses and Piaget's logical model

Jean Piaget (1896–1990) assumed that the newborn baby is incapable of logic and perceives sensory inputs as belonging to separate spaces. Logical concepts of objects and space develop in stages. For these reasons, he is often treated as a pure empiricist.

However, Piaget's theory cannot be assigned securely to the empiricist camp. To do so misconstrues his main objectives. Piaget's initial training as a zoologist (Flavell 1963) ensured a biological bias. But he was also a dissatisfied philosopher—dissatisfied that is with both rationalist and empiricist accounts of logical concepts. This psychologist/philosopher and erstwhile zoologist entitled his theory 'genetic epistemology' quite deliberately. His intention was to demonstrate how logical ideas develop within biological constraints.

There is little doubt that Jean Piaget was the most prominent figure in child development this century. Piaget's theory and, perhaps even more, the ingenious empirical paradigms which he invented have generated an enormous amount of subsequent research.

The literature on Piaget is vast, and critical appraisals abound. It is not intended to add to these. There are two reasons why the theory has to be considered nevertheless. One is that most current studies on spatial development were originally provoked by it. It is impossible to understand the findings without considering the implications of the paradigms on which they are based.

The second reason is perhaps more important, because it is very often ignored. Piaget's interest was in the development of logic, that is to say, the development of concepts as strictly logical ideas (Piaget 1953). Further, he specifically assumed that the formal description of performance in terms of logic is, *ipso facto*, its psychological explanation.

Both these points have an important bearing on what we make of the empirical evidence in relation to his theory and his views about the development of the concept of space. Not all followers or opponents of Piaget have fully taken into account the important observation by Flavell (1963) that Piaget's interest was as much, or more, in epistemology (the philosophical theory of knowledge) as in children (Flavell 1963; Piaget 1953).

Piaget's theory does not escape completely from the rationalist/empiricist legacy. His theory is an attempt to solve it. In Piaget's view, logical concepts are neither innate nor learned through accumulated associations. They develop through biological forces and are limited by ceilings set by these.

Briefly, his theory assumes that the sense modalities initially function quite separately. Combined schemata develop later. Logic, including logic about space, is first absent and then (after development) present.

Logical concepts about objects and space are achieved in a series of invariant, sequential, biologically-limited stages. From birth until the age of about two years, the baby is in the 'sensorimotor' stage. During this period the infant develops action schemata with regard to objects and the world. In the next period, the previously achieved action schemata are internalized. This 'representational' stage lasts until the age of seven or eight years. The child's thinking is still pre-logical ('pre-operational'), because the internalized action schemata are not yet divorced from actual actions in space and time. The internalized schemata become progressively divorced from actual action sequences. By the end of the representational period, they have become reversible, logical operations. But only concrete logical operations are possible until the age of about thirteen or fourteen. The final major 'formal operational' stage is then achieved, and abstract logical thinking (formal operations) can now take place.

Piaget's explicit aim was to apply formal symbolic logic to psychology as a method of analysis (Piaget 1953). It was innovative and led to interesting new empirical paradigms. The astonishing fertility of Piaget's paradigms stems, at least in part, from the intention to produce concrete problems which can only be solved correctly by applying logical principles.

The rationale of the paradigms is unexceptionable. Logical concepts have implications which cannot be violated without self-contradiction. Clearly, therefore, if a particular type of behaviour violates a self-evident implication of the logical concept, the behaviour cannot have been mediated by the use of the logical concept.

But Piaget went beyond this. He assumed that, if a child's behaviour consistently violates the logical concept that the concrete instance exemplifies, it can be inferred not only that he or she did not use the concept, but also that he or she does not have that concept. That is not a logically justified inference.

Piaget proposed that development occurs on the basis of 'assimilation' and 'accommodation'. The names have an attractively biological flavour. Assimilation is analogous to food intake by unicellular organisms. The organism changes edible particles into protoplasm, thus assimilating them. By analogy, the organism changes incoming information so that it conforms to action schemata that have been developed already. Accommodation is the opposite process. The unicellular organism literally changes shape or posture to get round obstacles. By analogy, the baby changes current action schemata to get around unavoidable external facts. Intelligent adaptation and progress to the next stage occur when the two processes of assimilation and accommodation are in 'equilibrium'. The metaphors are nice, but they are assumed to represent biological causes, and that would be difficult to validate.

Sensory inputs are initially construed in terms of separate spaces. The spaces are then united into a single action schema. Integrating the different spaces occurs at a relatively early stage, as a prerequisite for developing the object concept. However, the findings reviewed earlier suggest that even newborns recognize some characteristics of inputs across modalities.

Piaget's paradigms had two aims. One was to demonstrate that the infant's behaviour violates the logical assumptions implied by the object concept. The other was to show how the infant, during the first eighteen months of life, progressively achieves action schemata which no longer violate the logical characteristics of the object concept.

I shall look at the paradigms first as they were intended, namely as evidence for Piaget's theory of logical thinking. In fact, findings from the paradigms are of interest also for questions that do not concern the logical status of the infant's concepts. In my view, these are more interesting than to view the development of spatial thinking as if it solely concerned the possibility of making inferences from strictly logical propositions. But that is the basis of Piaget's theory.

The evidence that relates to Piaget's theory of logical knowledge will therefore be considered next. The implications of findings for spatial coding by infants will be discussed later.

III   Evidence from search paradigms on the logical object concept

Piaget used search for hidden objects by infants before the age of two years as a method to test whether they know the logical implications of the concept that objects exist in space and time, independently of the observer.

Piaget called this the sensorimotor period and divided it into six stages. At each stage, the baby achieves action schemata that deal progressively with specific logical implications of the object concept.

The newborn infant receives sensory inputs that are unconnected in space. She builds up separate schemata for space information from different modalities. She does not have a logical object concept, and therefore does not know that objects exist independently of herself.

Piaget's subjects were his own young infants. He showed the infant desirable objects, their feeding bottle at first, little toys later, which he then hid or displaced in various ways. The rationale was that, if the infant has a logical concept of objects, she would know that objects exist in space and time independently of herself. But the newborn cried when her bottle disappeared from sight, as if the bottle had ceased to exist. When she was slightly older, she looked fixedly at the spot where the bottle had disappeared: a first intimation of object permanence, but a permanence that apparently depended on her own perceptual (looking) activity.

At the age of six months the baby can reach reliably for an object at which she is looking. Infants fail to search for objects that are completely covered, thus apparently violating the principle that objects continue to exist even if they are not in view. The infant will look for the object, provided it is only hidden partially, and she can still see or touch parts of it. She thus still acts as if the object's existence depends on her actions. At about eight to nine months the infant does look for objects, even when they have been covered completely. She now understands that objects exist independently of her actions. But she does not yet understand that an object cannot be in two places at the same time. If a toy is moved from a hiding place where the baby has found it before, she will search for the toy at the original hiding place (the so-called 'A-not-B' error) even if she has just seen it moved from there, rather than looking elsewhere, thus violating the logical principle. It is not until towards the end of the second year of life that the child shows evidence of action schemata which adequately deal with objects as existing independently, through invisible displacements in space and time.

Innumerable experiments have been performed since Piaget's studies of his own infants early this century. If one may sum up the outcome very briefly, it is fair to say that Piaget's findings have been replicated again and again, not merely in Geneva, but in France, England, and the Americas.

It is equally important to note that Piaget's results have been replicated only when experimenters have repeated his test conditions exactly. When the experimental conditions were changed, often apparently quite marginally, the results differed. Babies responded as if they expected objects to behave as objects in the real world do behave.

In one of the first experiments which pushed Piaget's search paradigms further, Bower (1967) conditioned seven-week-old infants to suck a nipple at the sight of a distinctive red ball. The ball was then made to disappear either fast or slowly. When the ball was made to disappear fast, by a 'sleight of hand' (or rather, of mirrors) which made even adults assume that the ball was no longer present, the infants stopped sucking. But when a moving screen was drawn slowly across the ball so that it disappeared from view gradually, the infants continued to suck, even when the ball had become completely invisible. They thus behaved as if the ball were present but hidden.

Few experiments are so perfect that alternative explanations can be totally ruled out. Bower's (1967) babies could have stopped sucking simply because they perceived a change in the environment when the ball disappeared suddenly, and continued sucking when there was no sudden change, without this necessarily being evidence for a belief in the continued existence of the hidden ball. What does increase support for one explanation over another, or serves to reject an alternative hypothesis, is when findings from different methods converge. The hypothesis that infants necessarily fail to look for objects because they think that objects exist only when seen or touched can be rejected with some probability on these grounds. Hood and Willats (1986), for instance, showed that five-months-old infants reached for toys in the dark at the locations at which they had seen them before being plunged into darkness.

For babies who are too young to reach for objects reliably, the 'habituation' method is particularly useful. The method makes use of the fact that novelty catches attention. That is as true of babies as of all animals. Infants look longer at novel than at familiar objects and events. When an object is shown repeatedly, the infant looks at it less and less, and finally stops looking altogether, thus showing habituation. If the object is changed in some way on the next trial, the infant looks at it again. This form of dishabituation shows that the baby has not just fallen asleep with its eyes open, but is able to discriminate the change.

In a very interesting series of experiments, Baillargeon and her colleagues (e.g. Baillargeon 1986, 1987; Baillargeon & Graber 1987; Baillargeon *et al.* 1990) used the habituation method cleverly to test whether babies discriminate between possible and impossible spatial events. Six- and eight-month-old babies were habituated to the sight of a toy car rolling down a track (Baillargeon 1986). She then showed them the car rolling (impossibly) down the track, although the track was blocked by a box, and the car rolling down the uncluttered track, part of which was hidden behind the box. The babies looked longer at the impossible event. This suggests that they were surprised by the spatially impossible event, while treating the normal disappearance and emergence of the object from behind the box as unsurprising. In another study Baillargeon (1987) habituated still younger babies to a solid screen which rotated back and forth like a drawbridge. Three- and four-month-old babies looked longer when the bridge continued to descend impossibly past an object which should have stopped it. Similarly, five- to six-month-old babies (Baillargeon & Graber 1987) looked significantly longer at the impossible spectacle of a tall toy rabbit disappearing behind a screen with a cut-out which should have revealed it, than at the spectacle of a suitably small rabbit which the cut-out would hide. Neither short nor tall rabbits elicited surprise when they were hidden or emerged from solid screens. The findings suggest that these very young babies knew enough about space at this very early age to be surprised at spatially impossible events, and expected objects to exist even if they were hidden from view.

The methods and controls used in recent studies on babies are particularly impressive because they ensure objectivity in judging looking-time, or surprise and other dependent behaviours which can be measured. Independent observers monitor video-recordings of the behaviours without knowing the event which is presented to the baby. It has to be understood that testing very young babies is extremely difficult. The infants need to be awake, sufficiently well fed not to cry or fuss, but nevertheless alert and happy for long enough to take part in the study at all. Positive results are therefore important even when not all the babies, even when testable, show the required behaviour.

The fact that young infants have been found to show surprise at spatially impossible events and to look for partially or wholly hidden objects is clearly evidence against Piaget's assumption that they cannot do so. The findings also allow us to reject any hypothesis which predicts that infants necessarily fail to look for hidden objects.

But we have to ask also whether the findings establish the opposite hypothesis, namely that infants have *a priori* knowledge of the logical object concept. Can we deduce from the empirical findings that, before the baby has any experience of the world at all, she knows that objects exist independently of her actions in space and time, and also knows the implication that an object cannot be in two places at the same time? In my view there are several reasons why that cannot be deduced.

Piaget's assumption that the laws and structures of logic are identical with the laws and 'structures' of psychology (Piaget 1953, pp. 1 & 2) is misleading. Formal logical and/or mathematical descriptions of behaviour are certainly useful. The formal description of an error characterizes its logical status. But that does not explain how the error arose. If babies behave as if objects were dependent on their perception, it is clear that they are not using the logic of the object concept. That does not and cannot establish that they are 'incapable' of having the concept.

But the converse is also true. If babies behave as if objects continue to exist when they are not looking, their behaviour is certainly consistent with the logic of the object concept. But it does not establish that their behaviour was necessarily due to their using the concept, or having it innately.

The object concept is defined as the concept of something that exists independently of the observer in space and time. The definition logically implies propositions about object-permanence and the proposition that an object cannot be in two places at the same time. The implications of logical concepts are true by definition. They are necessarily true, because the propositions which define a concept are logically equivalent to the propositions which designate their implications. Their equivalence is exhibited if either proposition can be substituted for the other. We cannot deduce that, because she expects objects to behave as objects do behave, the infant's behaviour necessarily results from an (implicit) awareness of the logical equivalence of the propositions which define the object concept.

The question of whether or not infants have a logical concept of objects is circular, because the answer depends on how we define what is to count as having a logical concept. Logical propositions are formally-defined relations in a symbol system. Once the definitions are known, equivalences and implications of propositions are known also and can be demonstrated. But they are not learned in addition to the symbol system that defines them.

What we can assume, without any special investigation at all, is that infants have the potential for understanding logical concepts, as they have for contingent and probabilistic concepts. Human infants also clearly have the potential for symbolic processing.

In my view, the relevant question is only whether neonates have a coding or symbol system that is sufficient to hold more than one proposition in mind long enough to see whether two propositions are (or are not) the same. That is an empirical questions. It is not about the child's logic, that is to say, it is not in question whether she can see that identical propositions are identical. The question is about the nature of her symbolic representations.

Piaget's theory leaves it unclear whether action schemata are some form of 'thinking-in action' or whether infants are assumed to lack any form of coding in memory. Symbolic (representational) behaviour is certainly said to occur only after the age of 18 months. However, action schemata are presumably stored in some way; otherwise they could not function at all. If so, that must imply some form of 'internalized' coding.

The ambiguity is of interest because it shifts attention to the wider issue of rational thinking. People can, and usually have to, proceed on the basis of imperfectly defined events. Strict logical deduction, based on necessary propositional identities, is a limiting case. Propositions that are defined *a priori* in a symbolic (mathematic, algebraic, geometric) system can be applied to the 'real world'. But children and adults can solve everyday problems perfectly reasonably and rationally by analogies that are not strictly implied by events (e.g. Goswami 1988; Johnson-Laird 1983), and on the basis of expectations from experience which may be falsified. The question will be discussed further in Chapter 6.

Here it is important to note that recent evidence has shown that some form of learning and recognition occurs from very early on, and even in neonates (e.g. Bushnell *et al.* 1989; DeCaspar 1980; Walton & Bower 1993).

The fact that neonates can learn and remember shows that coding processes do not suddenly emerge at a given stage. Some form of coding for storing inputs in memory must be assumed from the outset. The question about the nature of coding in relation to emerging and acquired symbol systems will be discussed in Chapter 8.

IV   Some implications of object-search for spatial coding by infants

The fact that Piaget used infants' search as a research method has had important consequences for empirical research on spatial knowledge and development in infancy, if only because it stimulated a great deal of methodological ingenuity to test the validity of his observations.

The major advances which empirical findings on infant search have produced are threefold. First, we can infer with some confidence that babies act as if they expect objects to behave in the way that objects in the world do behave, although not all babies show the behaviour and the behaviour is found only in some conditions. It is an important if not, strictly speaking, surprising conclusion. It would be more surprising if babies behaved consistently as if the world were different from what it is. But the evidence contradicts the frequently held view that a baby's world is necessarily totally different from that of adults.

Another conclusion we can draw from the work on infant search is that the behaviour of even very young infants is influenced by past events. Again, it would actually be rather surprising if it were not so. But it has often been assumed that memory, and by implication learning and some form of representation, functions only at much later ages.

The findings, and particularly those reported by Baillargeon and her colleagues (1986, 1987; Baillargeon & Graber 1987; Baillargeon *et al.* 1990) are important. Whether or not one can infer from paradigms which use habituation and surprise that babies are actually aware of representing the information, is a moot point. But these results and others (Sophian 1985) suggest considerable continuity in the means of coding and representing information by very young infants and by adult humans.

Perhaps most important of all for future research and understanding is the variability which different task conditions produce (Butterworth *et al.* 1982). The fact that findings differ should be regarded as a growth point for knowledge. It is these apparently discrepant findings that allow us to identify the factors which produce positive and negative indications of search for objects that are not present to the infant's perception.

In almost all the experiments, the critical search behaviour occurs significantly only in some conditions rather than in others. Instead of dismissing negative findings as mere chance imperfections due to the hazards of testing young babies, a number of experimenters (e.g. Baillargeon *et al.* 1990; Diamond 1985; Harris 1983; Wisehart & Bower 1984) have rightly asked why such failures occur, and why it is that babies so often fail to look for hidden objects spontaneously, if they know quite well that objects continue to exist when hidden.

Typically, answers have differed in different studies. There are now almost as many theories as conditions which allow or prevent the infant from implementing what he knows. Some excellent overviews of these are available (e.g. De Loache 1989; Schuberth 1982; Wisehart & Bower 1984; Harris 1983), and they will, consequently, not be discussed in detail here. Here the interest is in the *conditions* which have been found to lead to discrepant results.

Bower (1967) showed a difference in reaction to fast and slow disappearance of objects. The tempo of object movement thus seems to be one critical condition. The salience of boundaries between objects may be important (e.g. Wisehart & Bower 1982). Another factor is the time sequence of events.

Significantly, Baillargeon's (1986) finding that babies looked longer at the impossible event was qualified by the order in which possible and impossible events had been shown. Only those babies who saw the impossible event immediately after habituation looked longer at the car hurtling impossibly down the ramp despite the obstacle on it, than at the following possible event. The babies who saw the possible event immediately after the initial habituating event did not look longer at the impossible event which followed. Baillargeon (1986) argued that maybe these babies had become bored. But we cannot be sure. Individual differences in habituation rates may be another limiting condition, especially at younger ages. Only three- and four-month-old babies who habituated quickly to the initial control event looked longer at the impossible event. The others did not show the critical difference in looking at possible and impossible events. The detailed findings thus suggest that the speed of object movements, the sequence of events which the baby experiences, and the baby's own 'state' are factors which need to be probed further.

The importance of specific task conditions will be even more evident in considering the further implication of Piaget's theory, namely that babies are egocentric. The assumption that babies are egocentric follows from the supposed lack of a logical object concept, namely the concept of an object that exists independently of the viewer (i.e. independently of the self). However, although Piaget uses the term 'egocentrism' very much more widely than this, the term does, *inter alia*, refer to body-centred spatial reference.

The implications of findings on search behaviour for spatial development and especially for the use of reference systems are the subject of Chapter 6.

V Perceptual systems as unitary: the phenomenological viewpoint

James and Eleanor Gibson (E. J. Gibson 1969; J. J. Gibson 1966, 1979; Gibson and Gibson 1955) came from a background of Gestalt theory (total configuration) of perception which implies a phenomenological viewpoint.

They argued that traditional models ask the wrong questions. Traditional models start with questions about light and colour, and answer by looking at the structure and function of the eye. The jelly-like substance (the vitreous humour) of the eye has a backdrop of complicated interconnections of nerve cells that form the retina. The retina consists of cones that are specialized for detecting colour and rods that are sensitive to much dimmer light. The transparent cornea and lens in front of the vitreous humour focus the light rays on the centre of the retina (fovea) where the cones are concentrated. Light rays transmitted to the back of the eye in that system produce an inverted and flat 'image' on the retina. The question was how we come to perceive the world as upright, three-dimensional and stationary although the retinal image is inverted and flat, and our eyes move over the scene.

The main concern was thus primarily with the peripheral sensory stimulation and its relation to 'central' (brain) organization.

The Gibsons considered that this is the wrong starting point. They (e.g. J. Gibson 1966; E. J. Gibson 1969) argued that we do not construct objects or shapes from sensations with the aid of memory or by means of inference. People see a three-dimensional, upright world, although the retinal image is flat and inverted. The world is perceived as static, although the eyes move. A circle is seen as round, even if part of it falls on the blindspot, that is the point where the optic nerve enters and there are no rod or cone end-organs to receive stimulation. Objects are seen as complete and separate wholes, even when placed in front of each other so that their boundaries are obscured and invisible. We also see contours that are indicated only by the perceptual context.

For the Gibsons, perception of objects and of spatial relations requires no mediation by retinal images. Perception is direct and present at birth (E. J. Gibson 1969). The senses do not provide isolated sense data which then have to be combined by means of past experience. Perception requires neither memory of past events, nor inference from sense impressions. The sense modalities are organized perceptual systems (J. J. Gibson 1966) which pick up change and invariance from environmental stimulation.

Perceptual development is seen in the same terms. It does not depend on memory or inference. The emphasis is on detection. Spatial relations are detected from birth, and infants simply get better at detecting higher-order, invariant spatial relations (E. J. Gibson 1969). Perceptual learning, according to James and Eleanor Gibson, depends on differentiation of distinctive features in the environment. Gross features are discriminated first. With greater familiarity more subtle features are distinguished.

In this view there is no problem about intersensory connections. All perceptual systems perceive higher-order 'amodal' relations directly. Spatial relations between planes and objects are detected in the same way by all systems. With development and experience, children pick up more detailed information than is possible at first and also get better at 'higher-order' coding.

It is assumed that the detection of higher-order spatial invariants improves with age and that invariant features are picked up better by vision than by touch. That makes it possible to explain any crossmodal errors in terms of inferior processing of higher-order invariants by the less proficient modality (E. J. Gibson 1969). The theory can account for findings which show that matching shapes from vision to touch or from touch to vision can be as accurate, or more accurate, than matching tactual shapes alone (e.g. Millar 1971, 1972a; Rudel & Teuber 1964).

A relatively simple further assumption can also deal with the fact that crossmodal comparisons are frequently found to be less accurate and/or slower than comparisons within the most difficult of the contributing modalities (e.g. Chase & Calfee 1969; Connolly & Jones 1970; Kress & Cross 1969; Legge 1965). E. J. Gibson (1969) suggested that such findings occur typically with stimuli that vary only along one dimension, such as length or distance presented by vision or touch, or brief light flashes and tones which can only vary in intensity. The idea is that invariant features are less easily picked up from these stimuli than from items which vary on a number of dimensions. Shapes, for instance, can vary in the number, angle and size of turns in the contour, and in whether they are round or pointed, as well as in overall size.

However, the theory that crossmodal matching depends on the pick-up of amodal features should predict that matching from vision to touch is equivalent to matching from touch to vision. In fact, however, errors are not necessarily symmetrical between the two crossmodal conditions (e.g. Connolly & Jones 1970). More recently, Hughes et al. (1990) found greater improvement in judging shapes presented either visually or through vibrotactile stimulation when the visual shapes came first. Similarly, the model does not predict that seen and felt length differ (Teghtsoonian & Teghtsoonian 1965, 1970).

Short-term memory differences between modalities have sometimes been invoked to explain such asymmetries. The proposal is that haptic (touch and movement) items are coded less efficiently. Memory for haptic standards therefore 'fades' more quickly (Goodnow 1971; Millar 1972a; Posner 1967), or is less accessible than for visual items (Hughes et al. 1990). Asymmetries between two crossmodal conditions have therefore been attributed to sequential presentation in touch. If the first item (standard) is presented by touch, memory for it fades more quickly than if the standard is visual. However, that could explain crossmodal asymmetries only if they occur consistently with delay.

The problem is that asymmetries in performance between the two types of crossmodal task are not consistent across experimental conditions, even when the standard input is the same (Millar 1972a). Millar (1975a) found that quite minor differences in the order of presentation determined whether matching across modalities was poorer than matching within the same modality.

In this experiment children had to compare visual and felt lengths, both of which were experienced sequentially. All lengths were presented in a dark box by means of a small joystick. For haptic inputs and responses, the children held the top of the joystick through a curtained opening and moved it to prepared or to remembered stops, respectively. In the visual conditions, they looked through a restricted viewing chamber which allowed them to see only the light point of a small recessed bulb at the top of the joystick. The visual lengths were presented by the successive movements of the joystick light to the same stops as at input, and were stopped by the subject's verbal 'here' in response. When the intramodal matching tasks came first, they were performed significantly more accurately than the subsequent crossmodal matches. But when crossmodal matches came first, there was no difference in accuracy (Millar 1975a). The simplest explanation was that how children coded the inputs was influenced by the conditions and context of the tasks, and not only by the inputs as such.

Bushnell (1986) suggested that, in infants, attention and exploration may also constrain crossmodal functioning. In all, the evidence strongly suggests that the manner in which subjects code the information across, and indeed within, modalities, can vary with the clarity (salience) of inputs, the mode (simultaneous or serial), and even the order of presentation.

The main problem with E. J. Gibson's (1969) formulation is the assumption that perception of 'higher-order invariants' is amodal and direct. The puzzle is what these 'higher-order' relations are, and why we need different senses if we perceive such relations directly and amodally with all of them.

Some characteristics of stimulation are indeed general and experienced via all modalities. The intensity of stimulation is one of these. But it is not clear in what sense this is 'higher-order'. Highly intense stimulations are noxious. They lead to avoidance, even by the most lowly unicellular organisms that have no differentiated sensory modalities. Nevertheless, the loudness of a sound is processed differently from the intensity of a light. If that is irrelevant, it becomes difficult to understand why we have more than one modality system.

VI The ecological approach

> Space is a myth, a ghost, a fiction for geometers ... if you abandon the dogma that 'percepts without concepts are blind', as Kant put it, a deep theoretical mess, a genuine quagmire, will dry up (J. J. Gibson 1979, p. 3).

Gibson's (1979) later, yet more radical, version of his theory gives an exhilarating kick to the old controversy. Associative learning had been rejected from the outset (e.g. Gibson & Gibson 1955). The newer formulation stressed the fact that animals and humans need to orient themselves in a world in which they move. Static visual perception, impoverished viewing of two-dimensional pictures, is the exception, not the rule. The organism and its environment are part of the same system.

There is no need for innate spatial concepts. Nor does the animal have sensory cues which the brain converts to perception of angles and distances. The animal perceives places and habitats directly and picks up environmental information about these by moving around and by manipulating objects.

The theory is expressed in terms of the ambient information, and can easily accommodate changes in performance with changes in the task. Asymmetries in performance between vision and touch, which change with task factors, do not require any special assumptions. Moreover, important advances were made by asking what optical information actually specifies the unbroken character of an object; or how people perceive the collision of two objects, and whether the bodies are hard or soft, when all that is presented is a pair of moving patches on the screen of an oscilloscope. Runeson (1977) varied the relative velocity difference between motions before and after contact. According to Gibson (1979, p. 181) that is the crucial information for perception of collision and the hardness of bodies.

Justly influential though it has been, there is a problem with the later formulation, in that it accounts for too much and becomes circular. Gibson uses the term 'direct perception' in several quite different senses. The central notion is that the environment offers what are called 'affordances' to the animal (Gibson 1979, p. 127). By these are meant simply all the potential uses of the environment that the animal or human picks up from invariant characteristics of the environment. 'Affordances' do not change. They are invariant and always there to be perceived directly (p. 139). The assumption is that what is perceived is the 'real world'. That takes us into the realm of metaphysics rather than of science.

Gibson (1979) also uses the term 'direct perception' to deny specifically that learning or experience and memory play any part in perception. It is at this point that the theory becomes circular. Gibson suggests that 'the affordance of an object is what the infant begins by noticing. The meaning is observed before the substance and surface, the colour and form are seen as such' (p. 134).

The justification is that even young animals and very young human infants respond, for instance, to 'looming' objects that project expanding optical flow patterns, by avoidance reactions which seem to anticipate an impact. This is similar to the adult's anticipation of a collision (e.g. Runeson 1977). However, the newborn presumably does not directly perceive the 'affordances' of a postbox. The adult perceives the postbox not only as an object that looms larger during her approach, but also as a receptacle for posting letters. The theory explains such change by the assumption that perception improves with practice and 'the education of attention'. The perceptual system becomes attuned to detect further affordances.

However, it is something of a sleight of hand to deny that past experience influences perception, at the same time as suggesting that experience alters the state of the individual. Phenomenologically, perception is, of course, 'direct' in the sense that the perceiver is usually not aware of past accretions. But it begs important questions about how this occurs. Similarly, the fact that we do not perceive the 'retinal image' is not, of course, a reason for neglecting research on peripheral processes.

Nevertheless, Gibson's (1966, 1979) insistence that the modalities should be considered not as separate senses but as perceptual systems, and that we do not already know what information is available to an organism, as well as his emphasis on the view that search for that information must start from the fact that animals and humans move, is important.

VII   Summary and implications

Findings on crossmodal coding suggest that there is more than one basis for recognizing information across modalities. Neither a strictly empiricist view, nor Piaget's notion of a constructed common schema will do. The results on very young infants, and better recognition of dual inputs from two modalities, show that information from different modalities normally converges.

The Gibsons (E. Gibson 1969; J. J. Gibson 1979) were clearly justified in assuming that the sense modalities are not separate 'channels' which can only be brought to substitute for each other by a long, slow process of associative learning. At the same time, there are also problems for the view that the modalities form a totally unitary system in which all sources convey exactly the same amodal invariant features, and that modality-specific information is unimportant. Further, the assumption that we perceive higher-order amodal relations directly does not actually explain perception or cognition.

Crossmodal paradigms typically separate, or even oppose, what are normally concomitant inputs. The extent of recognition thus depends very largely on task conditions, such as familiarity, restriction of constituents, coincidence in time and place, and even the order in which task conditions are presented. But inputs from different modalities cannot be considered as unitary either. The notion of modality systems, as suggested by Gibson's ecological approach, is suggestive. But the assumption of direct perception of invariant higher-order spatial relations presents difficulties.

In the present context, the notion of 'visual kinaesthesis' is of particular interest. J. J. Gibson (1966, 1979) argued that information from seeing and moving has to be investigated as a single system, rather than as two separate systems which have to be connected. Traditionally, the nerve endings in the skin, ear, or eye which are stimulated by the immediate external environment (change in touch, light, or soundwaves) are classified as 'exteroceptors'; while the nerve terminals in the muscles, tendons, joints and receptors in the inner labyrinth of the ear which give information about the movements and position of the body are classified as 'proprioceptors'. Gibson (1966) was concerned to show that visual perception is not purely exteroceptive, but also requires interoceptive (or proprioceptive) information (Gibson 1966).

Gibson's notion that 'exteroception and proprioception must be complementary' (Gibson 1979, p. 183) is amply supported by evidence on the role of vision and movement in the development of reaching, standing and walking which is considered in the next chapter.

The view advanced here is that the sense modalities normally provide complementary information which converges and partly overlaps (Millar 1981a, 1988a). It incorporates Gibson's point that sensory inputs are complementary. But it also implies that some of that complementarity, as well as modality-specific information, is lost in the absence of a particular sensory source. It suggests further that the fact that inputs normally converge provides important informational redundancy. The hypothesis is discussed in the next chapter and is illustrated by evidence from studies on reaching, search and motor skills in blind as well as in sighted infants and children.

3

The modalities as convergent sources of spatial information

My view of the relation between the sense modalities (Millar 1981a, 1988a) is that they are sources of complementary information which converge and partly overlap, and that the resulting redundancy of information is important.

The evidence that was reviewed earlier showed that the empiricist view will not do. At the same time, the bases of 'higher-order perception' are not entirely the same in different modalities. Further evidence for the view that informational redundancy results from the convergence of different inputs comes from the findings which are discussed below.

The complementary nature of visual and movement information in early sensorimotor skills is discussed first and compared with the relation between hearing and movement. Observations and results of intervention programmes with blind infants are considered next. It is argued that, in the absence of sight, there is some disruption also of the convergence and overlap of inputs.

Finally, experiments on the effects of bimodal and concomitant inputs are discussed. They show some of the conditions under which redundant information from different sources is an advantage.

I   The role of vision in standing, sitting, and reaching

An ingeniously simple experiment by Lee and Aronson (1974) looked at the control of posture in children aged just over a year, at about the age at which infants stand upright independently. Lee and Aronson placed infants in a room which was so constructed that the walls could be moved independently. When the wall in front was tilted gently towards the infants, they promptly lost their balance. The direction of the tilt determined the direction in which they fell.

It is not immediately obvious why vision should be important in standing upright. A lot of other conditions seem more necessary: a firm skeleton; adequate muscles for keeping its parts together and for moving these parts; muscles strong enough to resist the force of gravity; a central nervous system which continually processes information from the receiving organs including joint receptors in the hips and ankles, and from stretch reflexes from muscles in the back and legs, as well as from touch on the balls of the feet. Moreover, the organism has to have a central nervous system and brain which is so constituted that it initiates and monitors the execution of consequent adjustments by the musculature (Roberts 1978). It has been known for a long time also that the sense receptors in the inner (vestibular) ear, with its labyrinth of three-dimensionally arranged semicircular canals, act on the anti-gravity muscles together with joint receptors, and the other forms of proprioceptive (internal to the body) information, and that this plays a large role in maintaining balance (Howard & Templeton 1966; Roberts 1978).

It is of considerable interest to know that visual control (probably acting on eye muscles) was apparently more important for the postural balance of infants than their internal (anti-gravity) information. The visual tilt of the moving room determined whether and in what direction the infants fell over, although their internal anti-gravity information had remained the same.

Lee (Lee & Aronson 1974; Lee & Lishman 1975) followed Gibson (1966) in challenging the traditional view which divides sensory modalities into two receptor systems. It had been assumed previously that the proprioceptive (muscle, joint, and inner ear) receptors were concerned exclusively with providing information about internal bodily states. By contrast, exteroceptive sensory systems, such as vision and hearing, were considered to be sources of information solely about the outside world. The experiments of Lee and his associates (Lee & Aronson 1974; Lee & Lishman 1975; Lee et al. 1983) showed that vision also has proprioceptive functions and plays a part in the stability of posture and movement of adults. Visual information is integrated with information from other (e.g. joint) receptors (Brouchon & Hay 1970). Accuracy in aiming at a target drops considerably even after a few seconds of closing one's eyes (Lee et al. 1983).

The finding that infants fell over when there was a change in the visual frame which bounded their vision shows that visual information has an important role in the posture and balance of infants from the very beginning of standing upright.

More recent studies have confirmed these findings (Ashmead & McCarty 1991; Berthenthal & Bai 1989; Butterworth & Hicks 1977) and extended them to still younger babies. Butterworth and Hicks (1977) and Berthenthal and Bai (1989) showed that vision is also involved in being able to sit up. They tested infants aged five to nine months. The average age when infants first begin to sit up independently is about six months. The studies used similar conditions to the sort of moving room that Lee and his colleagues employed. Moving the front frame towards or away from infants caused them to sway and fall backwards or forwards, according to the direction of the moving frame. This occurred despite the fact that the infants' gravitational information and physical support remained the same. Berthenthal and Bai (1989) found that responses to the optical flow information became increasingly systematic in the second half of the first year. The relation between vision, posture and movement is thus not completely fixed initially, but becomes closer or more systematic as control over voluntary movement increases.

A still earlier movement skill also shows visual involvement. It is normally around the age of about four to five months that infants typically first reach out spontaneously and deliberately to touch and grasp objects at which they are looking (Halverson 1932; Gesell *et al.* 1934). Prior to that age, infants wave their arms back and forth, looking at their hands while they do so, and from their hands to objects that are placed within reach of the hand (White & Held 1966). It has been suggested that placing bright, moving toys within the view and reach of infants accelerates visually-directed reaching (e.g. White & Held 1966), although there is no evidence that this alters the sequence in which motor skills appear.

Some visually-directed reaching has been observed even in newborn infants (Bower *et al.* 1970). They move their arms in the direction of objects at which they are looking. According to some reports, that behaviour occurs only after a few days of experience of the world. Thus both full-term and pre-term infants show reaching movements to visual targets from a postnatal age of about five or six days, but they apparently do not do so in the first three or four days after birth (Bower 1989).

The basic channels of hand–eye coordination thus seem to be in place very early on, although some form of experience also seems necessary before there is any evidence of that. It takes another four months before there is decisive evidence of deliberate voluntary ('mature') reaching to visual targets (Granrud 1986).

One condition which has been considered important for the coordination of eye and hand is the systematic correlation and concurrent feedback between different sources of information. In vision, stimulation from self-produced movement normally correlates with visual feedback (Held 1965; Held & Hein 1963). In a now classic experiment, Held and Hein (1963) reared pairs of kittens in the dark, except for some hours' daily exposure to light to prevent permanent damage, until one of the pair of kittens was able to move around. The pairs were then given their daily hours of light in a cylindrical compartment which had vertically striped walls. The active kitten of each pair was free to walk as he wanted in the compartment. The other was seated in a cart which was yoked to the active kitten, so that the movements of the active kitten moved the cart in which the other one sat passively. Both kittens thus had the same visual stimulation and the same type and rates of movement. But for the active kitten the changes in visual stimulation resulted from, and thus correlated systematically with, his own movements. The passively moved kitten had no experience in which his visual perception systematically correlated with his own movements.

The pairs of kittens were given sensorimotor tests after some weeks of experience in the cylinder. The active partners were as accurate as normal kittens at placing their paws so as to land on the firm slats of a grid with visible gaps, at avoiding approaching objects by blinking, and at discriminating depth cues. The passive kittens were significantly impaired. After some days of normal visuomotor experience, the previously passive kittens also behaved appropriately on the tests.

Some learning is obviously needed. But it is learning of a different, or at least much faster kind, than the learning by slow, repeated associations of individual sights and sounds which was the typical assumption of how learning takes place in early associative models of learning.

Correlations between information from active movements and from systematically related environmental changes are clearly involved in the development of sensorimotor performance. Such effects were obtained also in studies of visually-directed reaching in monkeys (Held & Bauer 1967). The animals were, from birth, fitted with ruffs around the neck which prevented them from ever seeing their limbs and hands or paws, although they could move the limbs freely under the ruffs. The animals were trained to extend their hands, again without seeing these movements until the testing sessions. When finally tested with objects which they could see as well as reach, these animals spent a long time looking at their newly exposed limbs, and were inaccurate at reaching for the objects when they did so. In monkeys, eye closure during the first six months of life seems to have no effect on visual pathways, but does prevent the integration of visual with movement information (Hein & Jeannerod 1982). Control of eye movements in the monkey seems to be multimodal. So does the control of reaching (Jeannerod 1991).

Concomitant visual and vestibular information plays a major role in controlling upright posture and equilibrium in locomotion in human adults (Assaiante & Amblard 1992). Balance in human locomotion depends on stable head posture with regard to the body, and on gaze relative to fixed landmarks in external space. Assaiante and Amblard (1992) showed that there is a stable (adult) head position during locomotion by the age of eight years. They measured successive positions and orientations of the head relative to the orientation of the trunk, and derived indices for rotational head movements, head anchoring to external space, and a head–trunk correlation. Head (vertical) pitch and roll decreased significantly between the ages of three and eight years. Horizontal rotation varied relatively little. Interestingly, the results suggested that the four-year-olds controlled head stabilization with regard to external space when walking normally, and that, by the age of seven, there is integration between head position relative to the supporting surface, so that relatively free movement of the head during normal walking becomes possible. Below the age of seven to eight, there is also more rigidity when balancing is made more difficult by having the children walk along a beam.

The findings are not, of course, incontrovertible evidence for the strong hypothesis (Held 1963, 1965; Held & Bauer 1967; Held & Hein 1963) that normal sensorimotor development is impossible without the systematic correlation between visual experience and the stimulation produced by active movement, and the return information ('reafference', von Holst & Mittelstaedt 1950) which this affords. What the findings do suggest strongly is that systematically correlated overlapping or concurrent information from more than one source is an important factor in behaviour and development.

II Sitting, standing, and reaching in blind conditions

It must be emphasized again that useful conclusions about the need for vision can only be drawn from studies in congenital total blindness. As was noted earlier, the condition is extremely rare. Most people whose visual impairment is so severe that they are considered legally blind for the purpose of education or legal status actually have various degrees of residual vision.

Even people whose blindness is so profound that it prevents them from recognizing any shapes of any kind or size by sight can often discriminate between light and shade, or have had some perception of light from very bright sources, at least early in life. Unfortunately, many otherwise careful studies do not always distinguish sufficiently between complete absence of visual experience and blindness with residual, if minimal, vision.

The distinction is not only necessary for theoretical understanding. It is equally so for practical purposes. The blind child is not served well by the assumption either that nothing can be done, or that we know already what kind of information is missing, or how it can best be substituted. Only painstaking studies and careful consideration of the evidence can tell us what aspects of experience may serve in lieu of sight.

Two apparently contradictory pieces of evidence are of considerable interest in understanding the role of sight. First, there is no doubt that congenitally totally blind infants who are neurologically intact do sit up, do stand without falling over, and do reach for and pick up objects. At the same time, it is clear also that the spontaneous appearance of such reaching, sitting, standing, and postural balance is seriously delayed compared to that in sighted infants (e.g. Axelrod 1959; Norris *et al.* 1957; Fraiberg & Fraiberg 1977). The body posture of congenitally totally blind children is also often poor later on.

The Fraibergs and their associates devised an extremely interesting intervention programme for ten congenitally totally blind infants (e.g. Adelson & Fraiberg 1974; Fraiberg 1971). They showed that the intervention programme speeded up the appearance of motor skills, and brought most of them, except for self-initiated movements, to within (Bayley scale) norms for sighted children. The Fraibergs' programme was apparently not as successful in accelerating the appearance of 'self-initiated' as of 'passive' movement skills (Adelson & Fraiberg 1974).

The Fraibergs' reports make it very clear that their intervention programme was extremely complex. They quite deliberately concentrated on every means they could think of to accelerate the development of blind children (Adelson & Fraiberg 1974; Fraiberg & Fraiberg 1977). Sound was used extensively. But the programme was far more than a simple attempt to substitute sound for sight. It included encouraging close parent–infant relations within which sounds and touch could become meaningful for the infant. In the nature of the case, we therefore do not know precisely which elements of the programme were most important in contributing to progress, or how they worked together. They could have acted as lures, or as reassurance, or as means of giving significance to objects, or as information about spatial distances and directions, or all of these and more. But touch rather than sound seems to be important in alerting blind babies initially to the presence of objects (e.g. Bigelow 1986).

An obvious first question on the findings by the Fraibergs and their colleagues is why improvement was less for perceptuomotor skills than for passive movements. A possible answer is that eye–hand, and more generally eye–movement coordinations are more closely 'pre-wired', or mature earlier, than the coordination of movements with other sense modalities. That would fit in with observations on the early appearance of reaching to visual targets (see above). But to say that merely serves to rephrase the question. It does not actually answer it.

In fact, there are also instances of early coordination between movement and touch. For instance, loss of body support provokes movements of the arms and legs ('moro reflex') in newborn babies. Holding them upright with their feet touching a hard surface provokes stepping movements. The stepping pattern of the newborn tends to disappear after two months unless it is trained daily (Zelazo 1983). The pattern differs from the early phases of independent walking, and is gradually (over a period of years) transformed into the locomotor gait pattern of adults (Forssberg 1985). The early involuntary (reflex-like) movements seem to be organized at the spinal level, as are those of lower animals (De Vries *et al.* 1984). But independent (unsupported) locomotion in humans cannot be elicited by spinal organization, and is organized at higher (supraspinal and cerebral) levels which progressively inhibit spinal control (Forssberg *et al*. 1991). Physiological evidence as well as behavioural observation thus suggests that the first deliberate independent steps of the toddler differ from the initial stepping movements of the neonate in their dependence on 'higher' (more central) levels of control.

Visual perception is one factor, although by no means the only one, in the development to adult human posture and locomotion by what is probably a process of gradual reorganization by influences from cerebral levels (Forssberg *et al*. 1991).

Work on the coordination between vision and movement suggests that, when correlation between two sources is disrupted or does not occur spontaneously, coordinated information may have to be introduced, or fostered deliberately. It is probably not enough to use sounds as 'lures' to motivate movement in blind children, or even to use sounds initially at given locations in the belief that this will indicate the location of a goal to the infant. Conditions may have to be arranged so that they produce correlated feedback between sounds and self-produced movement (Bigelow 1986; Schwartz 1984).

The coordination of movement, sound and sight seems to follow a similar path to that of hand–eye coordination. It was shown long ago that newborn infants turn their head and eyes towards the source of sounds (Wertheimer 1961). Nevertheless, systematic coordination between sound and movement seems to lag considerably behind the coordination of sight and movement. The question is what conditions may accelerate the coordination between perception and movement at this early level.

That possibility has been explored with echo-location devices (Bower 1977). Blind babies were fitted with headbands which had a built-in electronic echo-location device. Whenever the baby moved, the device sent out sounds into the environment. The returning (echo) sounds were fed into the babies' ears via earphones. The babies' movements were thus correlated with sounds from objects and obstacles in the environment.

It is not entirely clear whether echo-location devices help in eliciting reaching, sitting and standing at normal ages, because the babies who took part in these trials were already somewhat older (Humphrey & Humphrey 1985). General developmental acceleration has been reported, although some blind adults suggest that the devices could also have detrimental effects on attention to naturally occurring sounds.

It seems likely that intervention programmes need to encourage attention to natural sounds as well as ensuring systematic feedback with movements. Practical reasons necessarily limit the extent to which effects of different types of intervention can be studied.

Clearly, simple 'nature versus nurture' models will not do. Reliable quantitative estimates of 'how much' learning is needed, will differ with the specific sensorimotor skill, the maturity of the relevant motor system and its relation to concomitant inputs from the sense modalities.

III   Redundancy and concomitant inputs from more than one source

Quite young children benefit by having simultaneous inputs from two modalities (Millar 1971). In this experiment three- and four-year-olds matched complex three-dimensional nonsense shapes to standards either by vision alone, or by touch alone, or with combined visual and tactual inputs. All children were able to match the shapes by vision alone, while matching by touch alone was much more difficult. Indeed, the shapes were too complex for the three-year-olds to recognize them by touch. But the four-year-olds benefited from the dual inputs. They were significantly more accurate at recognizing the shapes by touch when standards had been viewed as well as felt, while touching alone produced almost chance level responses.

Simultaneous hearing and vision also converge. In a well known experiment, McGurk and MacDonald (1976) dubbed a syllable that was heard through earphones, on to the lips of a filmed head that observers saw mouthing a different syllable. The results were startling. Instead of the sound fed into their earphones, what observers actually **heard** was some fusion of the spoken and dubbed (seen) syllables (McGurk & MacDonald 1976). The amalgam they heard was quite often totally different from either syllable. Interestingly enough, the illusion depends on the strict coincidence of the heard and dubbed syllable in time (MacDonald & McGurk 1972; Dodd 1983; Dodd & Campbell 1987). Even very young infants respond to bimodal specification of events (Gibson & Spelke 1983; Spelke 1979). The fact that there is a joint contribution from audible and visible speech, and more generally, integration of multiple sources of information has been confirmed repeatedly (Massaro & Friedman 1990). The findings strongly support the view here that convergence of simultaneous inputs from different modalities is the norm rather than the exception.

However, multiple inputs are not always better. One condition in which correlated information from another source facilitates recognition is when perception from one of the sources is difficult, or clarity is reduced. In Millar's (1971) study, dual visual and tactual inputs only benefited tactual shape recognition; visual recognition was as accurate for standards that had only been seen, as for standards that had been felt as well as seen. The advantage of visual over tactual shape recognition is, of course, well documented (see Jones 1981 for review). The finding thus suggests that benefit from additional input occurs particularly in conditions of uncertainty (Gollin 1960). Dodd (1983) found that seeing as well as hearing a word produced better repetition than only hearing it. Dodd (1977) used noisy conditions which impair hearing. This again suggests that the addition of seeing the mouth gestures for the words improved their being heard correctly, when there was uncertainty due to noise. The practical implications of this evidence are, of course, important. The use of lipreading by the profoundly deaf is an example (Dodd & Campbell 1987).

Vibratory stimuli have been used to boost poor hearing through touch in speech perception by the deaf (Cholewiak & Sherrick 1986; Sherrick 1991, 1992). That could be useful particularly for deaf people who are also visually handicapped. The stimulation comes from a rectangular matrix of vibrators. The matrix is attached to the skin, and the vibrators are activated in successive patterns.

Converting optical to vibrotactile stimuli has been successful in a device known as the 'optacon' (optical-to-tactile converter) for reading by touch. The forefinger rests on a small rectangular array of vibrators. A device with a matrix of photocells is held in the other hand to scan print and to translate the visual patterns into vibrotactile ones (Bliss 1978; Craig 1977; Craig & Sherrick 1982; Sherrick 1991, 1992). As mentioned above, in principle, vibrotactile information may also boost low-quality speech perception (Sherrick 1984). However, whether adding inputs from different sources will enhance, disturb (e.g. Sherrick 1976) or be ineffective seems to depend on specific aspects of the inputs and the kind of information that needs to be augmented. Sherrick (1991, 1992) reports that, for speech, multivibrator devices which lay out speech signals as spatial patterns that represent frequency-or-voice-formant relations are so far the most effective in conjunction with lipreading. It is not yet clear whether vibrotactile stimulation could also boost hearing, if the frequency, intensity, regularity and temporal pattern (interval organization) with which impulses are delivered could be made to be compatible; nor what aspects of hearing are best recruited as redundant cues to facilitate recognition by touch without vision (Sherrick 1992).

Millar (1986a) tested the hypothesis that redundant information could improve tactual recognition of otherwise difficult patterns. Raised dot patterns were used. These were similar, but not identical to braille cells. Dot patterns in braille derive from a single dot matrix. Differences between patterns depend on the presence or absence of dots in the matrix. Such patterns are difficult because they vary only along a single dimension. Millar experimented with the possibility of improving the tactual recognition of such patterns by importing additional texture information, using a Garner (1974) type design. I varied dot density, concomitantly with the size of patterns in one study, and with the outline shape of the patterns, in another. The findings showed that correlating easy-to-feel density differences with shape or size improved discrimination by both blind and blindfolded sighted children. The opposite manipulation, which made texture an unreliable cue for size or shape, produced worse shape recognition. Facilitation and interference effects could also be reversed, by making texture cues more difficult than shape. In this instance, the redundant information came from different aspects or 'submodalities' of what is usually labelled a single modality, rather than from two modalities.

Redundant information seems to be useful also more generally in conditions of uncertainty. It may be important in tactile perception (Schiff & Isikow 1966) for that reason. Gollin (1960) and Munsinger (1967) suggested that young children need more informational redundancy. Gollin (1960) showed that young children needed more connecting lines in pictures of objects than adults do in order to recognize the objects. Redundant cues from an easier dimension also facilitate difficult discriminations by adults (Garner 1974).

Difference in recognition difficulty is thus not the only condition in which two compatible cues are better than one. Millar (1986a) found better tactual recognition of dot patterns when shape and texture varied concomitantly, even when shape and texture alone did not differ in difficulty. Similarly, opposing shape and texture so that they varied unpredictably interfered with processing even in these conditions (Millar 1986a).

Some modalities and submodalities are more closely correlated than others. That does not mean that they convey the same information. The main distinguishing mark seems to be that they converge or covary under normal conditions. For instance, Jastrow (1886) showed that in touch the impression of extent is influenced by the type of movement that has to be used in judging it. Holding a small sphere between the forefinger and middle finger when these are crossed over each other produces the illusion that two objects are being touched (Gibson 1966). Errors are thus largest, and illusions typically occur, when the normal covariance of different inputs is deliberately disrupted or is rendered incompatible.

Converging inputs can, on the other hand, have advantages beyond a mere increase in recognition accuracy. Having two eyes is useful precisely because they each give rise to slightly different views. When the cues from the two views converge, the scene is seen in depth. If they do not converge, viewing is fragmented. When two different spoken syllables are heard and seen as if they emanate from the same location at the same time, they give rise to auditory illusions (McGurk & MacDonald 1976).

There has been some controversy as to whether the advantages of having two compatible sources of information depend on their perceptual specification or involve memory and cognitive contributions. However, these are not necessarily alternative explanations. The biological advantage of having several specialized sense modalities is presumably that this produces more and more precise information. Overlap and redundancy of converging information may add a further significant dimension, as in the case of depth perception by the two eyes. But dual inputs can also help to convince the organism that the information is reliable. The advantages are thus not necessarily due solely to perceptual coincidence in all conditions. Cognitive elements are likely to be involved covertly, if not overtly. Certainly, the close correlation between heard and seen speech must have been learned in the first instance, however 'automatic' it becomes later. The synchronicity of bimodal events is an important factor in such correlations (e.g. Dodd 1983; Massaro et al. 1993). But that is not evidence that the effects are due to either purely sensory or purely cognitive events. Both must be involved. That is evident also from a related phenomenon, known as the 'stroop' effect (e.g. MacLeod 1991). Recognition of the printed word 'green' is impaired if the word is coloured red. People may not be aware of retrieving the conjunction of word-meaning and colour-perception, nor of the coincidental cues which lead to the interference. That does not mean that covert central events can be ruled out. It is a mistake to believe that processing must either proceed in a top–down (cognitive to sensory) or bottom–up (sensory to cognitive) direction.

The 'fuzzy logic' model of perception (Massaro 1989; Massaro & Friedman 1990; Massaro et al. 1993) accounts explicitly for bimodal perception and the enhancement of inputs by the integration of multiple sources. 'Fuzzy logic' provides for evaluations along a continuum of relative values (relatively more like or unlike the prototype). In contrast with standard logical operations of negation, conjunction and disjunction, fuzzy logic operates in terms of evaluation, integration and classification. The model assumes that perceptual information from multiple, independent sources is continuously evaluated with respect to prototypical responses, using a multiplicative (rather than addition) rule. There is thus a common metric for contributions from sensory and contextual ('higher order') information. The model was designed to account for the bimodal effects of heard and seen speech (Massaro et al. 1993). In principle, it should apply also the effects of other multiple sources. That needs further testing.

IV Summary

To sum up, the behavioural evidence suggests that, far from constituting an added burden on processing, having more than one source of concurrent information can actually facilitate processing. Thus, although reaching, sitting, and standing by infants were found to occur in a developmental sequence that does not seem to require vision, because the behaviours certainly occur also in the total absence of sight, inputs from vision that correlate with movements are nevertheless important for eliciting and fine-tuning the motor skills. Experiments on concomitant inputs from different modalities and submodalities provided further evidence of advantages from correlated, redundant information.

The findings that were reviewed showed that we also know something about the conditions in which redundancy facilitates processing. Poor information from one of the sources is one condition in which two inputs are better than one. Conditions of uncertainty more generally also favour informational redundancy. A specific condition in which separating two inputs disrupts performance particularly is one in which inputs, including inputs from submodalities, normally covary.

It is, of course, the norm rather than the exception that more than one sense modality contributes to the perception of an object. We hear, see, smell, and feel the same object. That is not because all senses provide the same information, but because the contributions from different modalities converge and overlap sufficiently to be felt as 'same' rather than as 'different'.

Discrimination of change versus sameness, or unchanged conditions, must be regarded basic to perception by any organism. Even unicellular organisms respond to it. Babies certainly do.

The evidence shows further that facilitation and interference can occur between perceptual inputs and meaning, as much as between perceptual features. The findings suggest that information processing cannot be described in terms of unidirectional (either peripheral to central, or central to peripheral) processes.

It was argued that the evidence is consistent with the view that the modalities provide specialized but converging information and that this informational redundancy is particularly important in the absence of a major source of information. It was also suggested that the fuzzy logical model of perception (Massaro 1989; Massaro & Friedman 1990; Massaro *et al*. 1993) could provide a useful basis for testing this further.

4

Neuropsychological evidence on convergence

It is neither intended, nor within my competence, to give an account of the complex anatomical pathways and neurological functions that are involved in spatial skills. A brief review of findings from neuropsychological studies is, however, needed in order to show that they are consistent with the purely behavioural evidence. The behavioural findings suggest that spatial perception and skill depend on convergent information from a number of different sources. The neurophysiological and neuropsychological evidence suggests this view quite as strongly.

Even apparently quite simple discriminations have been found to depend on convergent information from different sources. For instance, monkeys can discriminate round from straight objects without vision, by grasping them in the hand. Sakata and Iwamura (1978), using single-unit (neurone) recording, showed that this depends on a combination of inputs from the skin and from the joints, which converge into single neurones in the parietal cortex. This is only one, albeit a typical, example.

In the first section I give a very rough outline of some of the relevant brain regions and sensory systems for reference by readers who do not know this area. The other sections concern hemisphere specialization, especially for spatial processing in parietal regions of the right cerebral hemisphere, effects of early experience, and the convergence of inputs in spatial functioning.

I   Brain regions and sensory systems

Some of the main shifts in descriptions of brain functions have concerned the relative specificity of function of different areas. The nineteenth-century phrenologists supposed that the mind (and brain) is composed of a number of different faculties which show in bumps on the cranium. Scientific studies suggested initially that much of the brain is equipotential in function. It was thought that the amount of brain tissue correlates with cognitive skill. However, recent advances in neurophysiological and neuropsychological methods leave no doubt that there is considerable specialization of function in different brain regions.

The cerebral cortex consists of two hemispheres which are connected to each other by a network of fibres known as the corpus callosum. In humans, the new brain or neocortex is a deeply convoluted outer layer with many deep sulci and fissures. These greatly enlarge the total surface area, which is proportionally much larger than in other animals.

The cerebral cortex can usefully be considered in terms of a number of functional regions. These are organized both in depth, connecting peripheral sense organs with the brain, and laterally, connecting different regions of the brain.

Looking at the outside of brain at the left hemisphere, the areas at the back of the head are known as the occipital lobes. The area in front of the occipital lobes, which extends to the deep central sulcus, is known as the parietal cortex. Below the deep temporal or lateral fissure lies the temporal cortex. Anterior to the parietal cortex and beyond the central sulcus is the frontal lobe, containing the motor cortical areas, and extends to the prefrontal cortex (Fig. 1).

The neocortex overlays phylogenetically older parts that are cradled beneath it. That includes the cerebellum, a smaller, bulging, phylogenetically old structure. There are large numbers of connections between the cerebral cortex and subcortical areas, the midbrain regions, and the cerebellum. Looking at the right hemisphere from the inside, without the outer left hemisphere, reveals the corpus callosum. Below it lie the thalamus, hypothalamus, hippocampus, and amygdala, which will be mentioned briefly later (Fig. 2).

Relays of nerve fibres connect the peripheral receptor organs of sensory

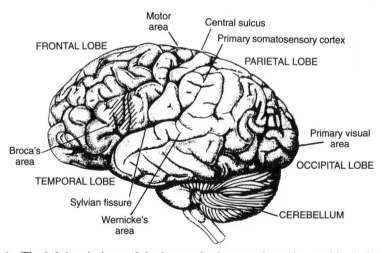

Fig. 1 The left hemisphere of the human brain, seen from the outside. Adapted from S. Zeki (1993). *A Vision of the Brain*. Blackwell Scientific Publications, Oxford (with permission from author and publisher).

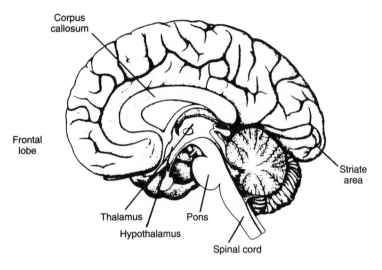

Corpus
callosum

Frontal
lobe

Striate
area

Thalamus   Pons

Hypothalamus

Spinal cord

Fig. 2   The right hemisphere of the human brain, seen from the inside (without left hemisphere). Adapted from S. Zeki (1993). *A Vision of the Brain*. Blackwell Scientific Publications, Oxford (with permission from the author and publisher).

modalities to the brain, along a variety of neuronal paths, connected via the spinal cord and subcortical centres. They finally reach designated areas of the cerebral cortex which, in higher animals, determine the final organization of inputs, and initiate responses via the motor output systems. Each neurone consists of a cell body with all its branches, including axons (e.g. in motor neurones this is an elongated structure that ends in smaller, branched terminals on the muscle fibres) and dendrites that sprout directly from the cell body. Neurones are separate cells. Impulses are transmitted from the end (axon) fibres of one neurone to the dendrites on the cell body of the next neurone across synapses. The synaptic connections are of crucial importance in brain function (e.g. Ashton 1992) and development (e.g. Spreen *et al*. 1984).

Most of the nerve fibres from peripheral end-organs cross over from one side to the other at various points, either in the spinal cord or at higher levels. Some, but proportionately far fewer, neuronal connections remain on the same side of the body from which they originated. In the main, information from the peripheral sense organs is relayed to the cerebral cortex via lower relay stations.

The connections were considered initially to form completely hierarchically ordered systems: the cerebral cortex as the 'highest' level of organization; the peripheral or end-organs of the sensory modalities as the 'lowest'; with the midbrain and other subcortical regions (and the cerebellum) as middle organizational and relay stations. That model is not an entirely correct description for all (e.g. motor control) systems (Evarts 1973).

In the visual system, the eyes and retinal receptors can be considered outcrops of the brain developmentally. The lens transmits light to back of the eye so that light from the right half of the visual field reaches the left half of the retina and light from the left half of the visual field reaches the right half of the retina. The retina at the back of each eye consists of cones and rods. The cones lie in the centre and provide high acuity and colour information. The periphery of the retina mainly consists of rods which detect peripheral motion and are light/dark sensitive. The rods and cones of the retina feed into the optic nerve. The point at which the optic nerve leaves the retina contains no rods or cones, and produces a 'blindspot'. The blindspot is not normally noticed. For instance, a circle is seen as complete even at the point which falls on the blindspot (see earlier).

The optic nerve contains bundles of fibres which meet at the level of the optic chiasm where they divide (Fig. 3). Nerve fibres from the right half of each eye project to the right geniculate body, and nerve fibres from the left half of each eye project to the left geniculate body. The geniculate nuclei are situated in the thalamus, a structure anterior to the midbrain. From there

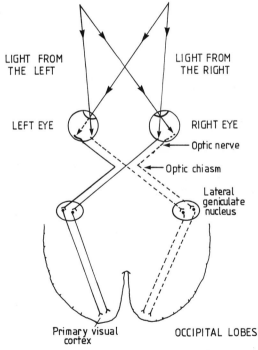

Fig. 3 Schematic outline of pathways from the eyes to the primary visual cortex, showing the crossover of fibres from the right and left half of the eyes, respectively.

they project to the visual area of the cortex, known as the striate area. So fibres from the right half of each eye go to the right half of the visual cortex (Fig. 3) which deals with the left half of visual space, because of the reversing optics of the lens. Similarly, fibres from the left half of each eye end up in the left half of the visual cortex. Some fibres also go to midbrain structures, known as the superior colliculi, and to the tectum. These latter function in regulating pupil size to light stimuli.

The striate cortex is the primary visual area. It receives stimuli previously analysed by the retina and by the geniculate bodies in the thalamus. The primary visual cortex contains neurones which are selectively sensitive to particular orientations of edges and contours (Hubel & Wiesel 1963, 1965, 1977) of visual shapes.

The striate cortex is surrounded by visual association areas. There are further anatomical and functional subdivisions in adjoining areas (Zeki 1992), in which cells are selectively sensitive to different aspects of visual inputs. Thus the cells of the prestriate area (V5) are responsive to moving stimuli, and most are selectively sensitive to the direction of movement, but not to colour. Cells in another area (V4) respond mainly to colour but not to movement. According to Zeki (1992), vision depends on an intricate relation between areas which mainly have specialized functions.

Another important contribution to vision comes from the oculomotor system which controls the eye muscles. Eye movements and corollary discharges from the system contribute to three-dimensional spatial (depth) information and to the fact that the visual scene is perceived as a stationary one which is being scanned by eye movements, and is not seen as a multiplicity of moving stimuli. Not all the contributing systems are fully mature at birth.

The vestibular system (Chapter 3) also relates importantly to visuospatial perception. The vestibular system is situated in the inner ear and is physically connected with the cochlea, a snail-like structure which contains the basilar membrane (see below). The vestibular system depends on structures that consist of three semicircular canals which are in a (roughly) right-angular (three-dimensional) relation to each other. They connect to the utricle and saccule which are two sac-like prominences on the vestibule. It is a sensory system which provides the central nervous system with spatial information about the position and movement of the head, and is important in posture and balance.

Hearing is primarily represented in areas of the auditory cortex in the temporal lobes and in areas buried in the temporal fissure. The inner ear consists of a number of small structures that convey sound-wave vibrations to peripheral end-organs in the cochlea. Briefly, the sound waves coming into the external ear press on the ear drum (tympanic membrane), and vibrations are transmitted via three small bones (ossicles) to a membrane at the end of the cochlear duct which is filled with fluid. The vibrations distort the basilar membrane in the cochlea, and so activate the haircells that vibrate to different frequencies. The basilar membrane has a register of fine haircell receptors which vibrate to different frequencies when the ear is stimulated by tones of different frequencies. The receptors are innervated by portions of the auditory nerve, which connect to the auditory cortex via a number of subcortical areas (e.g. cochlear nucleus, inferior colliculus, medial geniculate nucleus of the thalamus). Different sound frequencies register subjectively as 'pitch'. Information from different portions of the basilar membrane in the cochlea of the inner ear are represented by different regions in the auditory cortex (e.g. von Bekesy 1960).

The auditory system contributes spatial information about the direction and distance of external sources of sound. Interaural time-and-intensity differences (arrival of sound waves in the left and right inner ears) are the main cues that permit localization. One can also use changes in the intensity of sounds during locomotion, or if sounds move nearer or further away, as cues to distance.

Information from touch and somaesthetic sources is represented in the anterior part of the parietal cortex. Lesions in that area make it impossible to feel anything with the skin (Stein 1991). Touch is served by a variety of nerve endings in the skin which mainly differ in function. It has been suggested that the four types of organized nerve terminals for touch in the skin possibly form four types of tactile sensory units: Meissner corpuscles which are closest to the skin surface; Merkel cell complexes which lie below these; Ruffini endings which are located more deeply in the skin; and Pacinian (pressure) corpuscles and endings which are found in the deepest subcutaneous tissues (Vallbo & Johansson 1978). Fine, bare nerve endings convey pain and cold and heat. In addition, muscle spindle and Golgi tendon end-organs convey information from muscles. Two pathways convey cutaneous information to the cerebral cortex. The spinothalamic pathways carry mainly pain, temperature, and diffuse touch to the reticular formation, thalamus, and cortex. The lemniscal system carries information from tactile and kinaesthetic receptors via the spinal cord and dorsal columns and has synapses in the lower medulla; fibres from there cross over and ascend in the medial lemniscus tract and synapse in a thalamic relay nucleus, and from there project to the somatosensory areas in the anterior parietal cortex just behind the central fissure. There is also a trigeminal path from the face. Ascending systems cross over to the contralateral side in the brainstem, although there are also some ipsilateral fibres.

The posterior parietal cortex, especially of the right hemisphere, is important in spatial processing, and its functions and interconnections will be discussed later.

The motor cortex (MI) lies anterior to the central fissure; it represents body movements, literally in a head to foot direction. As in all systems, areas that serve the most important or prominent functions are largest. The regions can be stimulated to show this reliably. The motor cortex has interconnections with other areas of the cerebral cortex and with subcortical regions. The cerebellum (Fig. 1) is particularly important in sensorimotor activities (Evarts *et al.* 1971, 1973); so is proprioceptive information from sensory nerves in the joints, muscles and skin (McCloskey & Gandevia 1978).

Smell is represented in a structure (rhinencephalon) which is nearer to the older brain, cradled beneath the cerebral hemispheres in primates. Identification and differences in intensity of smells can be used to locate distant objects.

The phylogenetically older parts of the brain are part of what may be thought of as relay systems, and also exercise analysing and controlling functions for sensory inputs. Other areas are concerned with the bodily functions of eating, sleeping, temperature keeping, and digestion in 'lower' as well as in 'higher' animals. Areas below the corpus callosum contain important systems that are involved in arousal for emergencies, and alertness. These areas are connected with the systems discussed earlier, and with the prefrontal cortex.

The brief catalogue of sensory functions should not obscure the fact that normal perceptual functions are characterized by extensive interrelationships among various sensory and motor systems, and between cortical and subcortical areas. Intersensory communications take place not only at the highest cortical level. According to Fessard (1961, p. 585) 'the brain, even when studied from the restricted point of view of sensory communications, must not be considered simply as a juxtaposition of private lines'. The primary ascending pathways send large numbers of collaterals through which sensory signals of different origin also pass to subcortical areas. Fessard (1961) argued that regions of intersensory communications function through polyneuronic, networklike organizations.

Some recent work in cognitive neuropsychology, with individual patients who have presented very specific symptoms, has suggested that models should incorporate a much larger number of further subdivisions of the brain into areas with quite restricted functions. These specific 'modules' or processing systems, assigned to different regions of the brain, are assumed to be quite separate from each other (e.g. Fodor 1983), although they can interact. Examples are subdivisions which, it has been suggested, account for different forms of dyslexias (Coltheart 1987). Some dyslexics are poor at recognizing words spelt by regular (visual) letter-to-sound mapping, but can read some irregular words, while others show an almost opposite tendency. This was explained by assuming (neurological) damage to either an indirect route from the visual letter-string to recognizing word meaning via a phonological system, or damage to a direct route (Coltheart 1987). There are cases of people with brain injuries who exhibit even more specific damage and sparing of functions. In some cases, only words in a given category seem to be affected.

A recent shift in modelling the brain is a greater emphasis on the innumerable interconnections between different cortical systems. Although it had, of course, been known for some time that different cortical areas also connect with each other, evidence from more recent techniques has brought these interconnections into prominence. Advances in method are uncovering vast networks of connections between apparently quite separate areas of the brain at all levels.

It is becoming clear that descriptions of input processing in terms of a single-direction, hierarchical organization will no longer do. The current view is that many of these networks act in parallel at different levels, and not solely in a sequential, peripheral (sense organ) to central (brain centres) hierarchical fashion.

There is plenty of evidence for specialization of function in different areas of the cortical and subcortical structures. However, it is also clear that, far from operating in isolation, under normal conditions it is precisely the confluence of inputs from many different areas that leads to efficient and higher-order functioning (e.g. Arbib 1991). Symptoms that look as if they depended on a single, highly specific expert system could result from an insult which reduces or eliminates a contributing informational source. A similar view has recently been expressed by Ellis (1987).

II   Hemisphere asymmetries and functions of the right hemisphere

An important aspect of specialization is the fact that, in man, the left and right cerebral hemispheres tend to function asymmetrically, in language and spatial skills, respectively.

It is estimated that in the great majority (about 95%) of people the left hemisphere is specialized for language considerably more than the right hemisphere (e.g. Geschwind 1972; Geschwind & Levitzky 1968; Gazzaniga 1988). Two areas in particular are implicated. One, named after Broca, who first discovered it, is concerned with speech-output and lies in the anterior part of the brain, just by the premotor area and in front of the central fissure (Fig. 1). The other, situated in the temporal lobe (planum temporale), is named after Wernicke who first described it. The area is involved in speech perception and comprehension (Fig. 1).

The evidence that language processing is predominantly carried out in the left hemisphere comes from studies on split-brain functions, when the two hemispheres have to be divided by sectioning the corpus callosum, in the case of people who have sustained insults to the left side of the brain, either from gunshot wounds, strokes or the excision of tumours. There is no doubt at all from such studies that the left hemisphere is specialized for speech (e.g. Gazzaniga 1988; Rasmussen & Milner 1977). At the same time, some aspects of language are represented also in the right hemisphere (Zaidel 1985).

Left-hemisphere functions have also been investigated in normal subjects. The methods rely mainly on the fact that most receptor inputs are processed by the contralateral hemisphere. Two tasks in particular have been used. One is the dichotic listening task. In that task, information is fed separately (via headphones) into the two ears. As would be expected from left-hemisphere specialization of speech, there are right-ear advantages in listening to speech compared to non-speech sounds (e.g. Gazzaniga 1988; Geschwind & Levitzky 1968; Kimura 1964). A second test is to use the difference in the connections of the hemifields of each eye. The method involves presenting stimuli briefly to one or other visual half-field, while the subject is fixating a central point, and assessing which hemifield shows an advantage in recognition-speed for letters and words. An advantage similar to the right-ear advantage in dichotic speech recognition has been demonstrated for visually-presented verbal material, although there is less consensus about the visual studies (M. Annett 1985) than about the significance of right-ear advantages in language processing.

The right cerebral hemisphere, by contrast, is involved more in spatial processing (De Renzi 1978, 1982; De Renzi et al. 1977). The evidence comes from a large number of findings on people with neurological damage. This includes bisections (disrupting the corpus callosum) which isolate the hemispheres, and findings on patients with unilateral brain damage from gunshot wounds, strokes, tumours and the like (Cutting 1990; De Renzi 1982; Ratcliff 1991). Hemisphere function is also sometimes inferred from hand preference and advantages in skilled tasks.

The region of the brain that is involved more particularly in orientating oneself in the environment (Semmes et al. 1963) and in body-centred coding (Stein 1992) is the posterior portion of the parietal cortex. The areas in the posterior parietal cortex which lie at the junction of the visual and somatosensory areas are specialized for aspects of visuospatial processing (Duhamel et al. 1991).

There are cortical impairments which lead patients to ignore information from one side of their bodies. This occurs in the absence of damage to the visual system as such. The patients simply do not recognize any object that falls within that hemispace. Spatial neglect of one side is also more common with damage to the right than to the left parietal region (Ratcliff 1991).

Interestingly enough, Bisiach, Capitani, Luzzatti & Perani (1981) found that right-brain-damaged patients not only showed neglect of the left side, but were also unable to describe the left half of remembered images. Bisiach and his colleagues suggested that the association cortex of the posterior parietal–temporal–occipital junction was involved.

Right-hemisphere post-parietal lesions impair haptic as well as visual performance in spatial tasks. According to Stein (1991), it is not always easy to distinguish between primary loss of a sensory area and effects which depend on difficulties in directing attention to the sensory inputs. Right-hemisphere superiority has been reported for tactile pattern recognition, in cases of cerebral commissurotomy (Kumar 1977; Milner & Taylor 1972).

Findings which specifically implicate the right hemisphere in spatial processing vary to some extent with the type of performance that is tested. For instance, disorders of visually-directed reaching are predominantly associated with unilateral lesions in the post-parietal cortex of the contra-lateral hemisphere (Ratcliff 1991). Misreaching in the contralateral side occurs as often with damage to parietal areas of the left hemisphere as of the right hemisphere (Ratcliff 1991).

A number of simple dichotomies have been proposed to summarize functional differences between the left and right hemispheres. However, there is evidence against almost all exclusive disjunctions; for instance, that the right hemisphere is never involved in language, or that it processes inputs holistically as opposed to serially, or in terms of emotion rather than cognitively (e.g. Cutting 1990; Folstein *et al.* 1977; Zaidel 1985; Sperry *et al.* 1979). Cutting (1990) argues against such dichotomies. But he supports the suggestion by Kosslyn (1987) that the right hemisphere processes information in terms of spatial coordinates, while the left hemisphere processes inputs in terms of categories. However, confusion of left–right directions has been found with left-hemisphere damage. At present, this finding fits only uneasily into a strict dichotomy.

There is little doubt that the right hemisphere is specialized for spatial functions: performance is more often disrupted by right-hemisphere than by left-hemisphere lesions, and there is also further specialization within these regions. But the evidence makes it implausible that any simple dichotomy of function can form the basis of an adequate description. The two hemispheres are normally connected via the corpus callosum (Fig. 2) and function together in most tasks (Gazzaniga 1988). Too many areas of the cortex and subcortical systems (see later) are involved for the notion of an exclusive one-to-one mapping of different spatial tasks with one specific, restricted region of the cerebral cortex to be tenable.

The separation of the language and spatial functions in the left and right cerebral hemispheres respectively is not complete (Cutting 1990; Gazzaniga

& Ledoux 1978). The right hemisphere can be involved in language functions (Zaidel 1985; Gazzaniga 1988). There is also recent evidence that
the left hemisphere can be involved in some spatial processing. Thus,
Mehta and Newcombe (1991) found that left hemisphere damage can
result in deficits on spatial rotation and orientation tasks.

Hemisphere specialization looks like another example of the 'double-
but-different' principle, which seems to characterize central as well as the
sensory systems. The systems do not simply duplicate each other: they are
sufficiently specialized to provide additional functions, as well as forming a
basis for fail-safe multiple representation.

The specialization of various brain regions for primary sensory analysis,
as well as hemisphere specialization in association areas for more complex
language and spatial skills, respectively, applies too generally for such
specialization of various regions to be accidental. There is evidence for left
hemisphere asymmetry in the speech area (planum temporale) at birth
(Molfese & Molfese 1979) and perinatally, although asymmetries may be
modified by events during the perinatal and possibly also in postnatal
periods (Galaburda *et al.* 1987; Gazzaniga 1988; Geschwind
& Levitsky 1968; Previc 1991) Lateralization does not seem to increase
with age during childhood (Hiscock & Kinsbourne 1978).

It seems very likely that the parietal region of the right hemisphere is
predisposed from birth to process spatial information. Spatial processing
also involves a number of other regions, distributed over many parts of the
brain. These are specialized for slightly different aspects of spatial perception and performance (see later). At the same time, as Fessard (1961)
suggested some time ago, the brain cannot be regarded as a mosaic of quite
independent regions.

The question whether neuronal network organizations are complete or
unalterable at birth will be discussed in Section V.

III   Hand advantage and the right hemisphere

Another line of evidence for right-hemisphere functions in spatial performance comes from studies that show better input recognition by the left than
by the right hand.

Hand advantages in tactual recognition need to be distinguished from
the notion of 'handedness'. Left-hand tactual recognition for non-verbal
stimuli is akin to left-ear advantages for non-verbal auditory stimuli in
dichotic listening and to left visual field advantages in visual shape recognition. It refers to advantages for inputs that arise on one side of the
body; the inference is that such advantages characterize the processing
of the contralateral hemisphere in people who are assumed to have left-

hemisphere specialization for language and right-hemisphere specialization for spatial behaviour.

Handedness, by contrast, refers to consistent preference for one hand for executing more or less skilled manipulations. Typical tasks are writing, cutting with scissors, using a toothbrush, threading needles, picking up objects, throwing and hammering. People state their hand preference for such tasks in questionnaires, or preferences are assessed by observation. Speed of moving pegs on a peg-board is also sometimes used to assess skilled performance (e.g. M. Annett 1985). The point of such tests is to establish handedness. People are considered right-handed if they consistently prefer to use the right hand for skilled (dexterous) manipulations. Most people are right-handed by that criterion, although many are not completely consistent in their preferences across all types of tasks (M. Annett 1985). In short, handedness is based on assessing performance (output rather than input processing). In some cases, consistent sidedness is assessed by testing also for the preferred foot for kicking, and the preferred eye (i.e. the right or left eye, rather than the relevant hemifield). The relation of handedness to hemisphere lateralization will be considered in the next section. By contrast, left-hand advantages in recognition speed and/or accuracy do not indicate that the person is left-handed. On the contrary, the inference from a left-hand advantage is for spatial processing by the right hemisphere in a right-handed person.

The most consistent evidence for a left-hand advantage has come from various forms of non-verbal spatial tasks (Kumar 1977; Milner & Taylor 1972; Dodds 1978). Kumar (1977) used evidence from patients with commissurotomy (bisected hemispheres) and showed right-hemisphere superiority for tactual recognition. He also showed this does not exclude right-hand/left-hemisphere processing in such tasks.

The inference that left-hand advantages in tactual recognition tasks indicate right-hemisphere processing is reasonable on the ground that most impulses which arise from peripheral stimulation on one side of the body are first processed by the contralateral hemisphere. At the same time, direct inference from better recognition of haptic inputs to the left hand, to the function of the right hemisphere, does require some caution. Inference to hemisphere function which is only based on better performance by one hand is liable to some circularity. When a left-hand advantage is found, the temptation is to consider the tasks which produced it as spatial and to use the finding as evidence for right-hemisphere spatial functions. Conversely, when the right hand produces better recognition, this is more likely to be ascribed to left-hemisphere function, and consequently seen as due to some verbal element of the task for that reason. External validation of the criteria for considering a task as purely verbal or purely spatial is therefore needed.

Caution in interpreting the evidence is needed also because not all tactual performance depends on systems which are fully lateralized in the sense that all fibres cross to the opposite side—as, for instance, discrimination of roughness, texture, and passive tactual discrimination (Gazzaniga and Ledoux 1978).

Further, many tactual tasks do actually involve language as well as non-verbal components. Braille reading is a good instance of this which probably explains the many discrepancies in findings. Some studies have reported advantages in recognizing braille letters by the left hand (Hermelin & O'Connor 1971; Rudel *et al.* 1977). These studies have often been quoted. But there is equally convincing evidence for a right-hand advantage (Fertsch 1947), and for finding neither hand to be superior (Bradshaw *et al.* 1982; Millar 1977a, 1984a), as well as for a superiority when both hands are used together (Foulke 1982). Both hands are used interchangeably for verbal and spatial aspects of texts by fluent braillists (Millar 1987a).

Millar (1977a, 1984a) found that whether the left or the right hand was better at discriminating or recognizing braille letters depended on quite complex interrelations between task demands, reading skill, and habit. This is consistent with other findings that lateral advantages for given inputs change with proficiency. For instance, Kimura showed a left-ear/right-hemisphere advantage for non-speech sounds, including music (Kimura 1964). In contrast to non-musicians, skilled musicians show a right-ear/left-hemisphere advantage for music (e.g. Bever & Chirillo 1974; Gordon 1978).

In practice, findings on hand-advantages in braille can become self-fulfilling. Practitioners who believe that only the right hand should be used for (visual) writing, and braille teachers who are convinced that only the left hand should be used to practise recognizing braille letters do affect performance. Practice effects of this kind are likely to be confined to the skill that is being practised. They are unlikely to affect the overall 'handedness' of an individual which is discussed in the next section.

A reasonable summary of the evidence so far is that the posterior parietal lobes are concerned in the detection of non-verbal spatial inputs by active touch, as well as in vision. This is further evidence that, in humans, the right hemisphere tends to be more important in spatial tasks than the left. At the same time, some caution is needed in order to avoid circularity in interpreting evidence from hand advantages in the recognition of tactual inputs.

IV Gender, laterality, and spatial processing

Hemisphere asymmetry and laterality are sometimes linked to sex differences. In fact, the findings are too confused and inconsistent to add materially to our understanding of spatial development at present. A brief review of studies on sex differences in spatial processing is needed nevertheless. This is partly because evidence for sex differences, specifically in spatial tasks, is often considered to be better established than it is in fact. More important, the studies serve to highlight some components in spatial tasks, as well as important methodological problems.

It is actually very difficult to disentangle evidence from theory and conjecture in this area. The evidence itself involves a number of factors, and it is not at all clear as yet how they are related. It should be noted that the question here is not whether men and women differ. They undoubtedly do. The question is solely whether they differ in spatial processing.

There is, of course, no doubt whatever that sex is determined genetically and that there are genetic and hormonal differences between the sexes. The brains of men and women are bound to differ in some respects, if only because of differences in hormonal functioning and control. There are also a number of less obvious sex-linked characteristics, as well as sex-linked transmission of some diseases or disabilities.

There is little doubt either about the correlation between overt behaviour and hormone levels, for instance, in overt (expressed) aggression. In most societies males and females also differ in cultural roles, expectations, experience and status. Spatial skill relates to choice of activity and perception of sex roles (Krasnoff *et al.* 1989). Social and cultural pressures, as well as differences in physical strength and aggression, may exaggerate and/or produce further differences.

There are undisputed differences in the average height, weight and muscle strength of adult men and women. Further, boys and girls mature at different rates. For instance, ossification of bones occurs around the age of nineteen years in girls, but is not complete until the age of twenty in boys, although maturation is also affected by nutrition. But the precise relation between the respective maturational advantages and delays is not known. It is unlikely, in any case, that these are precisely the same for all systems.

The very fact that there are clear hormonal and genetic differences (e.g. in the transmission of some diseases) has given rise to a number of speculations. The fact that females have two X chromosomes, while males have one X and one Y chromosome, has suggested that males must be cognitively more variable. Other theories use the difference in hormonal influences as a basis for speculations.

Speculative inferences from some known and/or surmised anatomical brain differences often produce useful hypotheses (e.g. Kimura 1992). It is none the less necessary to consider whether the evidence is good enough to support them. The most influential models link sex differences to hemisphere specialization and handedness.

Strictly speaking, the precise relation of genetic and of hormonal sex differences to complex cognitive processes is not known as yet. The same is true of social and cultural factors. Some models assume that cultural factors emphasize existing differences; others suggest that they produce differences in spatial knowledge, for instance, by restricting exploration of the wider environment.

There are certainly credible reports which show poorer attainments by girls than boys in science subjects, mathematics and in geographical knowledge, although there seems to be some reversal of that in recent reports on adolescents in this country. But sex differences in complex tasks are often assumed to be too well established to require specific documentation, although interpretations differ.

The original explanation was that females are generally deficient in analytical reasoning, but are good at perceptual and typing skills. The view that sex differences in cognitive tasks could be attributed solely to differences in the spatial components of the tasks, rather than to general deficiency in analytical reasoning, was due to Sherman (1971).

Sherman's interpretation has been widely accepted and quoted. Her suggestion that differences in spatial training and practice account for such findings has been less popular. Harris (1981) proposed that a recessive gene on the X chromosome of males is responsible for better spatial ability in males. The argument is that females have two X chromosomes, and therefore less chance of having the recessive gene on both these. Some findings are consistent with this view (e.g. Hartlage 1970; Springer & Sealman 1978; Stafford 1961). But some of the correlations conform to the predicted values only when corrections are applied (e.g. Springer & Sealman 1978). Two reviews of relevant studies found little evidence for a direct genetic link (Boles 1980; Guttman 1974).

Gray (1971) invoked endocrine differences in aggressiveness and fearfulness to argue for differences in spatial and verbal abilities. Gray and Buffery (1971) proposed that there are evolutionary advantages in a division of labour between males and females (guarding territory, exploration, dominance patterns). Buffery and Gray (1971), McGee (1979), and Harris (1981) argue strongly that there is a sex-linked dissociation between spatial and verbal skill. Buffery and Gray (1971) suggest that, in humans, spatial sex differences are linked to developmental differences in hemisphere lateralization: women are better on verbal fluency, but not on verbal reasoning or syntactic tasks, and men are better at analytic and reasoning tasks and also better spatially. So far there seems to be little direct evidence for a significant relation between the onset of sexual maturity and spatial ability (e.g. Geary & Gilger 1989).

A much cited review by Maccoby and Jacklin (1974) lists studies conveniently by the age of subjects. Studies of children below the age of 8 years report better performance by girls as often as by boys. More often still, there are no differences at all. It has been suggested that sex differences on spatial tasks are not significant before adolescence, or even before the age of seventeen years (Witkin *et al.* 1967). Fairweather (1976) came to the conclusion that most studies which claim significant sex differences for pre-adolescent children are methodologically flawed.

An important class of theories depends on inference from hand preference to hemisphere specialization and the extent of lateralization. One problem is that findings on sex differences in hand preference do not always agree with findings on ear and visual hemifield advantages. Some studies suggest that hemisphere lateralization is weaker in females than in males (Bryden 1982; Harris 1981; Kimura 1992; Sherman 1971), while Marian Annett (1985) found precisely the opposite on the basis of speed in a peg-moving task and consistency of hand preference. She proposed a 'right-shift' gene, responsible for right-handedness/left-hemisphere (speech) specialization, which is expressed more in women. This allows more room for spatial processing in males.

Another proposal is that testosterone (male hormone) slows down the development of the left hemisphere and allows greater complementary growth of the right hemisphere (Galaburda *et al.* 1987; Geschwind & Levitzky 1968). The more recent account (Galabruder *et al.* 1987) assumes that there are gradations in effects and intervention by random (intrauterine or later) environmental pressures.

The relation between handedness and hemisphere specialization needs to be considered further. The majority of people are right-handed; and the majority of people also show left-hemisphere dominance of speech. Furthermore, handedness probably has a genetic basis, even if it is not the whole story. Social pressures to use the right hand (e.g. for writing) and a possible association between left-handedness and neurological disorder (M. Annett 1985; but see Bishop 1990) need to be taken into account. But only a minority (about 10%) of people consistently prefer the left hand for delicate manipulations (M. Annett 1985). Similarly, for the majority of people, right-hemisphere regions are more specialized for spatial processing, and some (although not necessarily total) genetic predisposition for hemisphere specialization can be assumed (see earlier). Most right-handed people have right-ear/left-hemisphere specialization for language on dichotic listening tasks. Some findings also suggest a direct relation between hand preference and hemisphere specialization, as for instance, observations of hand gestures during speech (e.g. Kimura 1973; Marzi *et al.* 1988). The notion that hemisphere specialization and handedness have the same origin thus seems reasonable. But it is not a necessary implication, and the relation between hand preference and hemisphere function is far from invariable.

The majority of left-handers show left-hemisphere specialization for language in the same way as right-handers on tests other than hand prefer-ence. Thus, in dichotic listening tasks, many left-handers show a right-ear advantage for words, in the same way as right-handers do, although the percentage of left-handers who show the right-ear advantage is somewhat lower than that of right-handers. It is sometimes suggested that ear advan-tages are a better indication of speech lateralization than handedness. But even dichotic listening tasks do not all correlate very highly with each other (Colburn 1978; Jancke *et al.* 1992).

The somewhat confusing findings suggest that direct inferences about sex differences in hemisphere functions, based solely on hand preference, are in some danger of circularity. This is probably true also for any other single (e.g. ear or visual hemifield advantage) measure of laterality. None of the measures seem to be very highly correlated.

The theory proposed by Marian Annett (1985) is elegantly economical. One gene is responsible for handedness and hemisphere specialization, and also for sex differences in hemisphere specialization. Her theory assumes a phylogenetic 'shift' to the right-hand/left-hemisphere, to allow for the special development of language skills. The proposal by Marian Annett (1985) that one gene is responsible for the 'right shift' which produces specialization has much to recommend it. But the further assumption that the gene is more strongly expressed in women than in men runs into the same difficulties as other views which depend on the assumption that findings on sex differences in the degree of lateralization, and specifically in spatial coding can be regarded as firmly established.

According to the account, handedness is a continuous variable, and the sexes differ in degree of lateralization. Women are more strongly right-handed than men, and are better at speech processing. Men are less lateralized, and spatial functions for them are therefore better represented.

Marian Annett (1985) bases her argument on several lines of evidence, including findings which suggest that girls are linguistically more pre-cocious than boys. Her own data suggest that most people show mixed laterality to some extent, in that their hand (and foot or eye) preference is not consistent over all tasks. The theory assumes that mixed handedness is associated with less specialization of the left hemisphere for speech, and that this constitutes an advantage for spatial processing.

In contrast to reports that men are more consistently lateralized than women (e.g. Harris 1981; Kimura 1992; Witelson 1976), Annett suggests that men and boys show more mixed hand preferences and that is assumed to be related to better spatial processing and worse language (output) skills. It is certainly the case that proportionately many more boys than girls are retarded in reading, have speech problems, and suffer from autism. There may well be a common linguistic (speech output) basis for these. Also, more left-handers are found among retarded than among good readers. The difference is small but significant, provided the population samples are large enough. The evidence is thus compatible with her 'right-shift' theory.

The interested reader is referred to the very clear and careful account of the evidence by Marian Annett (1985). At the same time, other interpretations are possible. Annett fully documents the inconsistency in the reports on sex differences in lateralization from unilateral cerebral lesions (e.g. McGlone 1980; De Renzi *et al.* 1980) and the evidence which suggests that males and females are equally impaired on verbal tasks by left-hemisphere lesions (Inglis & Lawson 1982). Moreover, girls mature earlier than boys. That is sufficient to account for earlier linguistic fluency reported for girls (Kimura 1963; McCarthy 1954). Indeed, some studies report right-ear (left-hemisphere) advantages in verbal dichotic listening tasks for men rather than for women (e.g. Lake & Bryden 1976), which seems to imply that men's left hemispheres are more, not less, lateralized for speech.

Boys tend to be more vulnerable to birth traumata (Eme 1979). That might account for the fact that more boys than girls show reading and other language-based difficulties. One suggestion is that the left hemisphere is more susceptible to hypoxia in prenatal or perinatal traumata, although that may not be the full story (Bakan 1978). The larger incidence of left-hemisphere language disorders in men (Kimura 1992) could have a similar origin, if later vascular or other incidents impair normally functioning systems that are potentially more vulnerable.

Recent evidence also suggests that impairment in language functions (speech output, phonological coding and/or segmentation) may not be the sole problem in reading retardation. At least some retarded readers have additional vergence (eye-coordination) problems which interfere with the spatial aspects of reading (Stein *et al.* 1987).

There is no doubt about the preponderance of boys among retarded readers, even in very small samples. The fact that studies on retarded readers often deal with very small samples is not therefore sufficient to explain why left-handedness or mixed laterality is not a significant factor in the majority of these studies. Significant differences would be expected if there were a direct link between sex, laterality, and hemisphere specialization.

There are some difficulties in inferring a sex difference in hemisphere lateralization from hand preference and skill. Positive test results could arise, not from lack of left-hemisphere (speech) specialization in males, but from a differential involvement of gross muscle and/or less lateralized motor control (motor and/or cerebellar) systems (e.g. Kimura & Vander-wolf 1970; Kimura 1992). There is also the problem that the pattern of ear advantages is not directly related to handedness (e.g. Kimura 1967). This suggests that even consistent right-hand preference does not necessarily imply more complete hemisphere lateralization. Moreover, the fact that some researchers consider that males are better or more consistently lateralized while others, on the contrary, consider that lateralization is better established in females cannot be ignored.

A finding which has been cited as evidence for poor spatial skills by females is that females with Turner's syndrome show poor spatial orientation (e.g. Spreen *et al.* 1984). The Turner syndrome is due to having only one X (female) chromosome, and such people are permanently sexually immature females. But, since they lack the second (X or Y) chromosome which normally determines sex, these findings cannot be assumed to imply that spatial skill is carried by the Y chromosome, or that normal females have poor spatial skill.

Direct behavioural evidence for verbal superiority by women and spatial superiority by men is thus crucial. But clear evidence is much less easy to come by than is usually assumed. Findings are often inconsistent. For instance, Kimura's (1967) study has been cited as evidence that girls have a right-ear/left-hemisphere advantage for verbal inputs (Harris 1981). In fact, Kimura's (1967) data show that for only one (lower socioeconomic status) subgroup of five-year-old boys did the right-ear advantage for verbal inputs not reach significance level, and even that was in the right direction. The boys in all her other age groups showed a right-ear advantage as significantly as the girls. Moreover, the five-year-old boys in her middleclass samples also showed the right-ear advantage as significantly as the five-year-old girls. Even the inference that the right-ear (left-hemisphere) advantage occurs earlier for girls than boys cannot safely be made from such data. Another report (Knox & Kimura 1970) finds a left-ear advantage for non-verbal sounds, suggesting right-hemisphere involvement. Boys and girls in all age groups showed this, but boys showed a small, but significant advantage when left- and right-ear scores were assessed together. A further experiment showed left-ear advantages in both sexes for non-verbal sounds, except for seven-year-old girls and eight-year old boys. The samples at each age were relatively small. By contrast, the evidence that non-verbal sounds show a left-ear advantage and verbal sounds show a right-ear advantage, is a quite stable finding across experiments. Sex differences in ear advantage, on the other hand, seem to vary across studies and samples. It may be that this was because the subjects were quite young. But, since some reports suggest that boys have greater right-ear advantage for verbal materials, thus suggesting better lateralization for language in the left hemisphere (Lake & Bryden 1976), contrary to findings that girls are better, it is rather doubtful that dichotic listening tasks can be said to show consistent sex differences.

Our main question turns on spatial processing. Studies on adults are of particular interest, because findings on sex differences in children are equivocal and results before puberty may not be decisive. But, here too, the evidence is surprisingly unsatisfactory, despite the almost universal assumption that the evidence is uncontroversial. Reviews tend to cite each other's opinions in support, but the actual data seem to come mainly from the same rather small number of studies. Better spatial performance by men has been reported in more studies, but other studies have found no differences and not all spatial tasks have shown sex differences (see later).

Conversely, not all tasks which are cited as support for a male advantage in spatial skills are specifically spatial in nature. For instance, a study which tested people with right- or left-hemisphere lesions on an aesthetic preference task (Lansdell 1962) is often quoted as evidence for a spatial difference. The men were considered to make superior choices in indicating their preference for certain line patterns. It is far from clear that such preference actually tests spatial skill. The numbers were very low (single figures) in any case.

Studies which found a steeper loss on composite 'performance' scales by men than by women with unilateral cerebral lesions (Inglis & Lawson 1982) are sometimes quoted as evidence that women use verbal strategies while men use non-verbal strategies. However, there was no independent test for verbal versus spatial processing and no evidence that the extents of the lesions were precisely the same.

Another frequently cited result is a report (Harris *et al.* 1975) that a significant number of college students, most of them women, failed the 'conservation of horizontality' test. The test consists of outline drawings of tilted jugs. To succeed, the subject must choose the jug that has a horizontal line for the imaginary water level, rather than an oblique line that is parallel to the tilted jug. Piaget (Piaget & Inhelder 1956) used failure on the paradigm as evidence that young children are incapable of logic. They can therefore neither understand the logic of conservation (i.e. the fact that an irrelevant change is irrelevant) nor logically coordinate (Euclidean) geometric planes. However, failure can be due to a variety of other factors, such as difficulties with oblique directions, ignorance of the physical principle that tilting the container is irrelevant to the level of the liquid it contains, or failure to apply the principle, even if it is known. In the Harris *et al.* (1975) study, the sex differences actually depended on ambiguities in the instructions. The difference was statistically significant in only two of the five experiments. Males chose the correct item significantly more consistently than females in the first two experiments, where the instructions were ambiguous about the point in time (start or end) at which the imaginary tilting of the container was to be imagined. In the remaining three experiments, instructions were made less ambiguous. In these three studies, sex differences in correct choices were not statistically significant. Harris and his colleagues (1975) argue, nevertheless, that the paradigm tests visuospatial ability and shows, what he takes to be the usual result, superiority in specifically visuospatial tasks by males.

A recent study (Kimura 1992) reports that men learn routes faster than women, but that women remember landmarks better afterwards. It is not clear why this is considered to be a difference specifically in spatial processing. It might stem from a speed/accuracy trade-off or a difference in confidence or in predicting how well one would do in memory tests. In the absence of validating tests, all interpretations must be speculative. If the difference is due to a lack in spatial cognition specifically, that difference should be found invariably. That is not the case.

Spatial tasks for which better results for men have been quoted most often are Witkin's (Witkin & Ash 1948) 'rod and frame test' (RFT), 'body-adjustment tests' (BAT), and the 'embedded figures test' (EFT). Reports for male superiority on the RFT test are the most consistent in the Maccoby and Jacklin (1974) list. The subject has to adjust a tilted luminous rod to the upright or to his body midline in an otherwise dark room. Witkin *et al*. (1967) found larger errors on the RFT by females at the age of about seventeen years. A finding by Sandstroem (1953) suggests that women may become disoriented more easily in locating luminous points in the dark, but they apparently improved with practice, while the men who failed did not. It is thus possible that the sex difference depends on a greater need for stimulus familiarity, rather than on the specifically spatial aspect of the task.

By contrast with the RFT, the actual data reported by Witkin and Ash (1948) show no sex difference for the 'body adjustment test' (BAT), in spite of the fact that this test also demands reference to a coordinate frame. The subject is in the dark as in the RFT. Instead of tilting the frame, the subject is tilted, and has to adjust the luminous rod to the vertical axis of his tilted body. The test is actually more difficult for most people, but people also improve on it. The fact that people can improve on the BAT is the rather curious reason given by the authors for not continuing to use it. Results on the BAT are not often quoted. Moreover, Witkin and Ash (1948) state quite specifically that there were sampling errors in their selection of subjects (also for the RFT and EFT). They used this to account for some failures in predictions from their differentiation theory, but do not consider sampling errors in explaining the variations in their findings of sex differences. The significant male advantage on the RFT is generally quoted; the lack of sex difference on the BAT rarely, if ever, and few, if any, reports refer to the sampling errors which Witkin and Ash (1948) invoked.

Wapner (1968) also did not find a main effect of sex in judgements of the vertical by boys and girls between the ages of seven and seventeen years.

There were small but statistically significant higher-order interactions among all the factors, including age, sex, the direction of errors, and starting position of the rod. Thus adults made larger errors, in the opposite direction to younger children, and were less influenced by the starting position of the rod, while girls changed to that pattern at a later age than boys. The results were held to support the theory that younger children differentiate less between body and external vertical directions than adults. However, higher-order interactions are notoriously problematical to interpret.

It should be noted that Witkin and colleagues (1962) consider their tasks to be tests of 'cognitive differentiation', rather than as tests of spatial skill. Lack of cognitive differentiation, according to their theory, describes subjects who are (*inter alia*) unable to disregard background stimuli. However, the RFT and BAT tests involve indicating locations in the dark. That demands the use of the body as a spatial reference. In that sense, namely as testing the use of self-referent (coordinate) frames for spatial coding, the RFT and BAT must both be considered spatial tests. The fact that one, but not the other produced statistically significant main effects of sex on performance is thus rather puzzling if the assumption is that males are better on spatial tasks.

A task on which the Witkin study (Witkin *et al.* 1967) found more errors by females is the 'embedded figures test' (EFT). In that task, subjects have to detect simple shapes within complex configurations with which they share contours. It has been widely quoted as a spatial task that shows clear sex differences (e.g. Harris 1981; Kimura 1991). A recent study with American undergraduates (Casey & Brabeck 1989) also found women to be worse. However, the main effect was qualified by a significant interaction which showed that women who read mathematical sciences were as accurate as the men. Some familial sinistrality seems to have been implicated also, although the men and women were right-handed on the same criteria. However, studies on Eskimos have found no sex difference on the EFT (Berry 1966; McArthur 1967). A recent project on adolescent boys and girls in Jamaica, conducted by one of my students, also failed to find a sex difference on this task; if anything, the girls were better (K. Stewart 1991, unpublished undergraduate project, Oxford University).

The 'embedded figures test' is a shape detection test, rather than a test which demands the use of coordinates for reference. It requires analysis of constituents in complex configurations. That is true also of the so-called 'Koh's Block' test, and the similar (Block design) tasks which are part of the non-verbal form of the well-known Wechsler (WAIS) intelligence test. In such tests, subjects have to copy complex designs by fitting together constituent shapes. Unlike the RFT and BAT tests, which demand body-centred reference, the EFT and the block tasks depend on relations between constituents within a (small-scale) configuration. The few studies in the Maccoby and Jacklin (1964) list which use that type of test report null results as often as better performance by men.

An often quoted study by McGlone and Davidson (1973) found an overall better performance by males on a figure rotation task (the shortened, spatial part of a larger test) and on a Block design task. McGlone and Davidson divided male and female subjects by handedness, and also by right- versus left-ear advantage in dichotic listening. Their detailed data show that the male advantage in the rotation task was mainly due to the significantly poorer performance by the (rather few) left-handed females with a left-ear advantage. On the Block design test, right-handed females with right-ear advantage actually scored more highly than right-handed men with right-ear advantage. The relevant latter statistic was not computed, and has not been mentioned in the literature.

The study raises an important methodological problem. The fact that the authors divided subjects by hand preference as well as ear advantage is a highly commendable (and rather rare) procedure. But it has the disadvantage that attempts to match on handedness as well as ear advantage necessarily reduce subjects in each category to quite small numbers, because the incidence of decisive left-handedness, especially when paired additionally with a left-ear advantage for verbal inputs, is much lower than that of right-handness and right-ear advantage for verbal inputs. Computation becomes more problematic when the number of subjects in each cell is small. More important, it is desirable to match numbers in each cell as far as possible when testing for factors that are varied experimentally. But this produces subject samples that are not necessarily representative of the general population. When testing for experimentally varied factors, representative samples are not crucial. However, when testing for what is clearly a subject variable (gender), it is important to ensure that the groups in question are representative of the total normal range. Otherwise, the size and composition of the samples is dictated by whatever subjects with the least common characteristics happen to be available. Findings due to sampling errors are likely in these conditions, as indeed Witkin and Ash (1948) found.

Shape rotation is often considered to be a test of mental visuospatial imagery. A male advantage on such tasks is widely accepted and has been reasserted quite recently by Kimura (1992) who cites a rotation study from her own laboratory with patients who had brain damage in either the right or left hemisphere. As the author expected, the women were worse. But, contrary to the assumption that men rely more on right-hemisphere processing in spatial tasks than women, right-hemisphere damage depressed performance by men and women equally. The reported graphed data actually suggest that women were significantly worse on only one of the rotation tasks. This involved matching photographs of mirror images of rotated block figures. By contrast, for a similar task which used instead (mirror-image) rotated drawings of gloves, the graphed data show no difference between men and women with left-hemisphere damage. If anything, right-hemisphere damage impaired the women more. It is not clear whether the numbers were large enough for statistical significance in the latter case. But the difference on the glove task was clearly in the opposite direction to the expectation that women rely less on the right hemisphere, as indeed Kimura (1992) is careful to point out. But it is interesting that the graphed data show that men and women with intact right hemispheres did not differ on the glove task at all. Formally, both tasks depended on the same form of mental rotation. If spatial rotation does discriminate men and women significantly, why did the sex difference not show on that task?

A recent study on a conventional mental rotation test (Kail & Perk 1990) showed no sex difference in overall accuracy or speed between men and women. Some higher-order interactions differed marginally between the younger boys and girls. But they were not in any intelligible or consistent direction. Another sex difference was that the reduction in speed over trials was steeper for females. Precisely what this meant is doubtful. But the findings clearly do not replicate previous reports of decisive differences in efficiency. Furthermore, sex differences have not been reported in some well-known studies on mental rotation (e.g. Shepard & Cooper 1982). They used speed of detecting identical, but rotated, nonsense shapes from impossible pairs, and mental unfolding of paper cubes, and a variety of other tasks to test for spatial imagery. It seems likely that, if sex differences are consistently robust findings, they would have been reported and discussed.

Further to sex differences in Piaget-type conservation tasks, more recent findings also suggest that small differences in instruction eliminate these. Subjects had to understand (from two-dimensional pictures) that water levels remain invariant although the containers are tilted (Liben & Golbeck 1984). When the relevant rule was made obvious, the sex difference disappeared (Liben & Golbeck 1984), suggesting that the difference was due to lack of knowledge of physical laws, rather than to a specifically spatial inadequacy. Lack of geographical knowledge or lack of interest may also explain differences which are sometimes reported for spatial knowledge tests. It is not clear, in any case, how far the Piaget water-level task taps spatial skill (see earlier). The authors rightly suggest that evidence is needed on tasks that specifically depend on reference to coordinate frames before generalizations about sex differences in spatial skill can be made with any confidence.

Small-scale, two-dimensional maze problems are relatively clear examples of tasks that demand spatial memory. In order to find a way out of a finger maze as quickly as possible without entering blind alleys, locations and routes have to be coded and remembered. It is interesting, in that connection, that sex differences on T-mazes in rats do occur, but only in conditions of novelty and stress (e.g. Roderiguez *et al.* 1992). This suggests that, when sex differences are found, they may relate to emotional and/or stress components of task situations (possibly more related to hormonal factors) rather than to specifically spatial/cognitive demands. But recent studies on humans with tactual finger mazes (including the Porteus test) have, in any case, failed to replicate the sex differences which such tests are reported to have produced in the past (e.g. Alvis *et al.* 1989).

Some sensorimotor tasks show sex differences (Kimura 1992), and there certainly are sex differences in most sporting activities. Spatial skill and hand–eye coordination are involved in many of these. But it is not clear that it is the spatial component of javelin-throwing, snooker, high jumps, cricket or tennis which makes the difference. If there is indeed an obvious, specifically spatial difference between the sexes, it is also puzzling that many books on visuospatial processing completely fail to mention sex differences even in the index (e.g. Olson & Bialystok 1983; Paillard 1991; Pick & Acredolo 1983; Stiles-Davis *et al.* 1988). It is unlikely that omissions are simply due to an oversight.

There is a tendency for the same, relatively few, positive reports to be cited repeatedly. More important, positive findings occur mostly in association with other factors and the number of subjects is often quite small (e.g. Cohen & Levy 1986). Not all tasks that can confidently be classed as 'spatial' (i.e. require reference to coordinates) show the requisite sex difference. Conversely, sex differences are reported for tasks that can hardly be considered as purely spatial.

It is possible to attribute the rather confused and confusing findings on sex differences in spatial processing to methodological short-comings. Few of the studies match their male and female populations on baseline tests, or even use the same number of subjects, or ascertain laterality, or do so by more than one test. Recent findings from studies that do use combinations of laterality tests have found rather low correlations between different types of test. That seems to apply even to ear advantages in dichotic listening tasks.

Lack of controls and baselines, inadequate task analyses, the use of single rather than multiple measures of laterality, small samples and the tendency to report findings in terms of received wisdom rather than by critical appraisal are probably mainly to blame for the discrepancies in findings.

Perhaps the most important methodological problem with all the studies reported so far is that few, if any, have used subject samples that are representative of the population on tests that crucially and univocally involve the use of spatial coordinates. When testing experimental factors against control conditions, representative samples of subjects are not always essential. But sex is a difference between people and not a difference between experimental factors. Findings with representative population samples on spatial tasks that clearly involve coordinate reference are therefore necessary. Without such evidence, confident assertions are rather misleading.

In summary, in view of the rather confident general assumption that better spatial skill by males is well attested, it is extremely surprising that clear evidence for a sex difference in spatial tasks is so difficult to find.

The most that can be said with any confidence is that, when sex differences have been reported, they are more often in favour of men, and rarely of women. But that has to be qualified. Even findings with any one task are by no means consistent. There have been as many null results as positive findings. There is some indication also that data which contradict the usual assumption, either because there is no difference or because differences are in the opposite direction, are less often reported or emphasized. That is possibly because null findings are less interesting or expected, or because they go against received assumptions.

It is actually to be expected that genetic and hormonal, social and emotional sex differences should affect performance on any task. Moreover, methodological inadequacies do not constitute evidence to the contrary. But the fact is that we have no adequate notion how to interpret the differences that are found. What evidence we have suggests quite strongly that sex differences in processing complex spatial (and verbal) information are not as clear-cut, or obvious, or as easily unravelled as has been assumed.

The hope that sex differences might provide a royal road to a functional analysis of the link between brain and behaviour (Kimura 1992) has not been fulfilled so far. Nevertheless, the studies have proved extremely useful, in that they are progressively leading to the recognition that we need much more finely grained analyses of task components, if the links between brain and behaviour are to be understood fully.

It is, of course, possible that there are sex differences in spatial performance, but that they are less obvious than was thought previously, because the variation between individuals is so large that the overlap of the two distributions swamps average differences. However, the evidence which has been reviewed here makes it more likely that positive findings are due to a combination of factors, rather than that they depend on a single variable that can confidently be labelled 'spatial'. It is necessary to be rather cautious about repeating the confident claims that are sometimes made on the subject.

V   Brain development, plasticity, and visual deprivation

Two interrelated questions are of particular interest in looking at neuro-psychological evidence on spatial development. One is that of the 'plasticity' of the newborn or young brain. The other is whether developmental processes proceed in sudden 'spurts', or can be described in terms of progressive maturation.

'Plasticity' refers to the extent to which various regions of the brain are pre-empted for certain functions genetically, from birth or before birth, and to the question how far external stimulation and events can alter that. The notion of sudden jumps in development applies particularly to 'critical periods' during which essential stimulation has to be received without which brain structures that are already in place may deteriorate. Conversely, there is the question whether there are periods after which sensory deprivation no longer has major effects on brain structures.

Looked at from the point of view of early brain injury, there is evidence of some, although not necessarily complete, plasticity. Injury to the left hemisphere during development and its effects on language has received more attention than right-hemisphere injury and its effects on spatial development. As noted earlier, the fact that left-hemisphere regions are specialized for language in most people, as well as some evidence that a relevant (planum temporale) region in the left hemisphere is enlarged in fetal, neonatal and infant brains (Spreen *et al.* 1984; Witelson & Pallic 1973), suggests that there is a genetic predisposition for the left hemisphere to be specialized for processing language, although the right hemisphere is not completely 'speechless'.

However, the predisposition does not seem to be unalterable. Children whose left-hemisphere injury occurs before the age of four years apparently learn to speak fairly normally. Adults with similar injuries become aphasic. It implies that the right hemisphere takes over the language functions, if injury to the left hemisphere occurs early enough. It is possible that the 'take-over' is not complete. It has been suggested that even very early left-hemisphere insults may lead to residual language deficits later, but that they are rather subtle specific (syntactic) defects which do not show up on all tests.

It seems likely that the potential of the right hemisphere for spatial processing is not absolute either, and that reorganization can occur with early injury (Gazzaniga 1988). It is not yet clear whether early right-hemisphere injury produces a 'take-over' of spatial learning by the left hemisphere. But there is evidence that early brain damage does affect the final distribution of nerve fibre systems (Gazzaniga 1988).

From the intricate architecture of the neocortex and of subcortical systems which are involved in spatial performance by human adults, one may surmise that the disruptions involve the interrelations between these, depending on the site of the injury.

Looking at questions of plasticity and critical periods from the maturational angle, it seems clear that the brains of newborns are undeveloped in many respects, although the basic architectures for sensory and brain functions are in place, and function at some level.

The myelination of nerve fibres is an instance. The myelin sheath can be thought of as a sort of insulating sheath around nerve fibres. Myelination in the brain is not complete until the second year of life. Not all regions myelinate at the same time. But function can precede myelination.

Newborns can see. But visual acuity, accommodation of the eyes, and especially binocular vision are quite poor in the neonate. It has been suggested that their visual perception is mediated mainly by subcortical centres (Van Sluyters et al. 1990). Nevertheless, behavioural studies with habituation and 'preference' methods have shown that the relevant systems for discriminating shape, orientation, the directions of moving objects and depth perception are largely in place at birth, although the systems undergo considerable further development (Van Sluyters et al. 1990).

It is not possible to do justice to the evidence on these matters in a short review. But it is quite clear that it is not possible to answer either the question of plasticity or the question about sensitive periods in the 'either/ or' form in which they were originally raised. Both growth spurts and regular development occur. Visual acuity, for instance, develops in a relatively slow, steady fashion from birth (Dobson & Teller 1978). Stereoscopic depth perception and binocular rivalry seem to have a much more sudden onset at about three and a half months postnatally, and approach adult levels in relatively few weeks after that (Van Sluyters et al. 1990).

Some of the anatomical evidence on human brain development depends on post-mortem examinations. Neuropsychological information has come from retrospective studies of children who are known to have sustained damage in early infancy. An important part of our knowledge is due to physiological and behavioural studies of young animals, particularly cats and monkeys. However, neurophysiological evidence has also been obtained by a number of non-invasive techniques, such as electroencephalograms (EEG) which record electrical activities of the brain from the scalp. Neuronal activity can be evoked by stimulating the relevant sensory system and recording the difference in electric potential from the scalp, as, for instance, the visually evoked potential (VEP) from the primary visual cortex and, more recently, also from the somatosensory cortex (SEP) of infants and young children. Further progress has been made with computer-aided tomography (CAT) scans, and positron emission tomography (PET) scans. Modern magnetic resonance imaging (MRI) techniques which produce clear pictures of brain structures will, no doubt, be able to improve our knowledge of the architecture of developing brains considerably in future.

The fact that the primary visual cortex contains cells that fire selectively to the perception of specific orientations of edges has already been mentioned. It is also clear that the cells of neonatal animals continue to become more selective only in normal stimulus conditions. Neuronal activity is, in fact, essential for further development to occur (Shatz 1992).

An aspect of vision which is of particular interest for information about three-dimensional space is stereoscopic depth perception. The two eyes of newborn humans function together only erratically. Stereoscopic depth perception becomes established about the time that accurate reaching becomes possible. Early deprivation of sight in one eye, in primates as well as in kittens, is accompanied by clear changes in the visual cortex as well as in subcortical visual areas, and is associated with severely reduced visual capacities. Squinting (strabismus) produces a double image. Vision in the 'lazy' thus tends to get suppressed. Unless the squint is corrected, vision in the suppressed eye deteriorates, and the eye may become blind.

Sensitive periods during which adequate sensory stimulation is critical vary in time and duration between species (Adams *et al*. 1990). For kittens several weeks of monocular deprivation starting in the fourth week to the fourth month of life (possibly even later) make it almost impossible for any cells in the visual cortex to be excited by stimulating the deprived eye, although the non-deprived eye retains some influence over these cells. For both cats and monkeys the sensitive period is shorter for visual areas in the cortex. Children with cataract (corneal opacities) in one eye during the first two years of life, were found not to recover full vision in that eye, even after surgical removal of the cataract. By contrast, children who only acquired cataract at about the age of nine years had normal vision in that eye after removal of the cataract (see Adams *et al*. 1990).

It is not possible as yet to be precise about the time or duration of sensitive periods in human visual perception. The evidence we have so far is nevertheless important in understanding previous work, such as the review by von Senden (1932) of the recovery of sight by blind people who had undergone cataract operations. The fact that in many cases these people had difficulty in 'learning' to see after the operation may be attributed to early visual deprivation. The work of Riesen (1947) on chimpanzees who were deprived of vision from birth also showed very severe impairment of visual acuity and lack of visual recognition of objects (Chow *et al*. 1957). The difficulties seem to be due mainly to the total deprivation of light stimulation. Stimulation by ambient light, even if it is not sufficient to permit shape perception, may be sufficient to maintain the structures that are present already. The precise changes which occur, and the reasons for these, are still relatively obscure. However, it is known that stimulation from the periphery is needed early in life to maintain normal structures.

There are also changes in the adult brain with continued visual deprivation. But these seem to be largely reversible if sight is restored. Scholtz *et al.* (1981) found a slight reduction in neurones and a marked reduction in the average diameter and reduced function of neurones in the subcortical (lateral geniculate body) visual areas of visually severely impaired older people, compared to normals. They also found changes in the amount of myelin in the primary visual (striate area) cortex. All the subjects had full vision until they were well over fifty years of age, and none had been totally blind even after that. Novikova (1973) studied electrical activity (electro-encephalograms) from the visual cortex of people with episodes of blindness. Changes, particularly the absence of the component known as the alpha rhythm, were detected months after blinding. The alpha rhythm reappeared soon after successful operations in people whose sight could be restored by cataract removal. The functional significance of this finding is not obvious, because the alpha rhythm from primary visual areas in the sighted is largest in the dark, and disappears with looking at the environment in the light. However, comparison with early deprivation and recovery suggest that young brains may be more flexible and subject to sensitive periods, so that absence of sensory stimulation has more lasting effects. Alternatively, or conjointly, (synaptic) reconnections may be more possible.

We know rather little as yet about the anatomical and physiological changes in the visual cortex of humans who are totally blind from birth. From work on kittens and monkeys and chimpanzees, it seems clear that there are changes and that they are probably irreversible if visual deprivation continues beyond sensitive periods. However, there may also be benign changes.

Cortical changes which follow blinding are usually regarded as deleterious, because of reductions in the cell population and decreased sensitivity or specialization of cells in the primary visual areas (Adams *et al.* 1990). However, it cannot be assumed that all cortical changes that follow visual deprivation are necessarily evidence of dysfunction. There may be some degree of take-over by other systems, or new connections with other sensory systems may be formed in visual association areas (Hyvärinen & Poranen 1978; Hyvärinen *et al.* 1981).

The possibility that there may be compensatory activity comes from studies of monkeys whose eye-lids were sutured soon after birth, so that they had no shape perception, although they could sense light through the eye-lids, and whose eyes were opened at the age of twelve months. It was found that their visual association areas contained cells that fired when the monkeys were tested for visually directed reaching. That was not the case with control animals who had not been visually deprived in early life (Hyvärinen *et al.* 1981).

The deprived animals had some light perception through the eye-lids. The work may, therefore, have more implications for children with some, if diffuse, light perception than for the congenitally totally blind. There is also work which indicates that visually deprived mice have an increased growth of whiskers. This seems to suggest that, in mice, visual deprivation may lead to an increase in tactual sensitivity. However, I do not know whether these findings have been confirmed.

In humans, the question of compensation of sensory systems by each other is complicated by the fact that maturation differs in different cortical regions. For touch, there is evidence that the mediating somatosensory regions of the parietal cortex depend on slower, more continuous development than the visual cortex. Some indices show continuous maturation in the parietal cortex from birth until later childhood. Components of the evoked potential were recorded from the scalp of normal infants from somatosensory areas of the brain. One of the components of the somatosensory evoked potential, which signals the arrival of an afferent stimulus, was found to change from the newborn to the adult pattern over a period of about eight years, and it showed a remarkable continuity over these years (Desmedt *et al.* 1976).

Myelination in the visual system is more advanced and proceeds faster than myelination of the motor areas, while myelination of the corpus callosum, which mediates information between the two hemispheres, begins at only three weeks after birth (Volpe 1977, cited by Sergent 1988). As mentioned earlier, function can precede myelination. But it is possible that differences in the timing of maturational factors in different regions affect the degree and type of reconnections that may be established in conditions of deprivation. But that is still largely speculative at present.

The notion that there is automatic compensation by other sensory systems, for instance, by touch or hearing for visual deprivation, is not well supported by behavioural evidence. Thus, blind children are superior at discriminating braille patterns by touch, but they are not better than the sighted with unfamiliar tactual patterns (Foulke & Warm 1967). Similarly, the blind are often credited with more acute hearing and sound localization. But what evidence we have so far suggests that compensation comes by a more circuitous route. The advantages seem to depend on increased attention to the inputs from the remaining sensory channels, better strategies for coping with information from these channels, and greater experience with that information. If reorganization of brain structures is consistent with that, it seems likely that, instead of a direct 'take-over' of the deprived primary sensory area by another sensory system, compensation may come about through reconnections in the association areas. However, such speculation awaits evidence from relevant anatomical and neurophysiological studies.

The prefrontal system, which is concerned with the spatial organization and processing of sensory information, is especially relevant to attention and short-term memory for that information (Squire 1987). It has been suggested (Diamond 1991) that immaturity of that system may explain some of the spatial 'errors' by young infants which Piaget noted.

Diamond (1991) argued that difficulties in delayed responses, as well as the 'A-not-B' error, of human infants (see earlier) are due to the immaturity in infants of the dorsolateral prefrontal cortex and its reciprocal network of connections with the parietal cortex and other cortical and subcortical areas.

It will be remembered that in the 'A-not-B' paradigm, an infant has to retrieve a toy from a location 'A' many times; the toy is then switched to a different 'B' location. Infants below the age of about eight to nine months typically try to retrieve the toy from the A, not from the B location (hence the name), even when delays last only a few seconds, although they can remember simple locations for much longer than that. The 'A-not-B', and the delayed response paradigms, both demand memory for a spatial location as well as inhibition of previous responses. Diamond (1991) refers to an earlier suggestion by Harris (1973) that interference from previous responses (proactive interference) to a location is an important ingredient in such errors. The fact that the prefrontal system is immature initially is consistent with behavioural evidence of relatively poor attention and memory in young infants.

A similar argument may apply to the regions in the parietal cortex which are the main foci for the convergence of inputs from different sensory areas, and are important in spatial processing (see earlier). Most of these association areas seem to mature later than the primary sensory regions which they surround.

It is sometimes assumed that intersensory functions can only occur after full development of the association areas of the cortex. But the behavioural evidence (see Chapters 2 & 3) suggests that some form of intersensory matching occurs much earlier. The basis of such matching is not yet clear. The fact that there are multimodal and bimodal neurones (cells that fire to stimuli in more than one modality) in a number of areas (Duhamel *et al.* 1991) is likely to be relevant, although it is not yet clear precisely how they function. There is little doubt from the behavioural evidence, however, that intersensory matching can proceed on more than one basis (see earlier).

The association areas of the cortex, and particularly the convergence of inputs in single neurones in the postparietal regions (see earlier), are clear neurophysiological substrates of intersensory processing. Multimodal cells are not so much 'amodal', or indifferent to modality, as capable of firing to inputs from more than one modality. It seems likely that excitation of such cells is important in crossmodal processing. But it may be assumed that identifying inputs across modalities can take place on the basis of a number of systems. More roundabout (e.g. verbal) routes are certainly possible. Young infants probably use simpler, less differentiated aspects of the stimulation, such as intensity, abruptness of onset, and simultaneity.

The emerging neuropsychological picture is of highly specialized cortical regions for different modalities, and of further specialization within these, so that in one region of the visual system cells fire selectively in response to specific different orientations of contours, another region is concerned with colour inputs, and in yet another (prestriate) region cells fire selectively in response to differences in visual motion. At the same time, there are also multimodal cells, and there is ample evidence for communication and interaction between systems that can apparently function separately (Fessard 1961; Zeki 1992).

Areas of the neocortex are not, of course, the only ones that must be considered. It is not clear as yet, for instance, how differences in the speed of maturational processes between different cortical and subcortical regions should be interpreted (for review, see Van Sluyters et al. 1977). It may be that, in conditions of sensory deprivation during sensitive periods, these connections are particularly important in possible reorganization. We do not know either as yet how multimodal cells react in that case. It is possible that they are specially important, if stimulation from the remaining sensory modalities is increased.

A preliminary conclusion about postnatal development of the human brain is thus that there are sensitive periods during which stimulation from sensory systems is particularly important. However, the various maturational processes do not proceed at the same pace in all cortical regions. Similarly, there is evidence for plasticity in development, in the sense that neuronal change and reorganization result from sensory deprivation. But that reorganization is not necessarily only detrimental.

In the present state of our knowledge, direct inference from the various indices of brain development to behaviour, and vice versa, must necessarily be highly speculative. One-to-one correspondence between developments in specific brain regions and behaviour is likely only for behaviours that depend solely on a very specific connection.

The role of stereoscopic (depth) perception in spatial vision is a pertinent example. The maturation and proper functioning of the oculomotor system is clearly important in depth perception (as well as in the acuity of the non-dominant eye). But stereoscopic inputs are not the only visuospatial cues for perceiving the world as three-dimensional. For vision, motion parallax, the occlusion of one object by another, texture gradients, and correlations between size and distance are further cues to three-dimensionality. In normal conditions these overlap. In normal conditions, they also coincide further in space and time with cues from hearing and body movement.

Although it is doubtful that there is direct sensory compensation of one sensory system for another, some form of—not necessarily deleterious—neuronal reorganization probably does take place, and may be less easily reversed if it takes place during sensitive periods in development.

VI   Convergent inputs and spatial systems

It is of considerable interest that the areas of the posterior parietal lobes of the primate brain, which are crucial for spatial perception and understanding, are also the parts of the cerebral cortex in which sensory inputs from most modalities converge in single neurones (Stein 1991).

The posterior parietal cortex lies at the junction of visual and somato-sensory cortices, and the evidence shows that there is convergence between vision and somatic sensations in that area (e.g. Robinson *et al.* 1978; Leinonen *et al.* 1979).

In primates, at least four distinct areas have been defined on the basis of their interconnections with other cortical and subcortical regions. Convergence between visual and somatosensory stimulation in single bimodal neurones has been demonstrated (Duhamel *et al.* 1991), as has the existence of numerous areas which can be defined by their connections to other cortical and subcortical regions of the brain.

The importance of the parietal cortex for the integration of movement and visual information for visual guidance and updating of movements has been stressed repeatedly (Paillard 1991; Stein 1991). Stein (1991) argued that the posterior parietal cortex brings together proprioceptive, auditory, vestibular and limb movement information as well as visual and motivational signals; this creates a network for transforming sensory signals into signals which are suitable for motor control. Berthoz (1991) also stresses that the representation and control of movements depends on multimodal inputs. Visual, vestibular and somatosensory information comes together in the parietal (parieto-insular) cortex which is concerned with the representation of head movements in space (Akbarin *et al.* 1988).

The parietal cortex is not the only area of the brain involved in spatial processing. At least three other areas need to be mentioned. One is the hippocampus, a region in the 'older' subcortical areas of the brain (e.g. Olton & Papas 1979; Olton *et al.* 1979). O'Keefe (1991; O'Keefe & Nadel 1978) suggested that the hippocampus functions as a 'cognitive map'. The evidence on ablations in rats shows that the hippocampus is crucially involved in memory for spatial positions and in computing new arbitrary paths through an environment (Muller *et al.* 1991).

Rolls (1991) argues that, for primates (e.g. macaque monkeys as models for humans), the hippocampus is not crucial in map-like learning nor in the control of visually directed movements, but is involved in the learning of associations and in short-term (episodic) spatial and non-spatial memory. The important point is that the primate hippocamus receives inputs from many areas of the cerebral cortex (neocortex), and also has many reciprocal neuronal connections with it.

Another reciprocal network which is important in some spatial tasks connects the cerebellum and the motor areas of the cortex. The motor area represents limb movements from the head downwards, with disproportionately large areas devoted to the lips and fingers in primates, including humans. The interconnections between these systems are crucial in voluntary movement, movement learning and motor control, and are also connected with areas that are involved in visuospatial processing. It has been suggested that the network which links the cerebral and cerebellar motor subsystems gradually transfers adaptive control in coordinating posture and movement from cerebral to cerebellar subsystems (Burnod & Dufosse 1991).

In humans the frontal cortex is also concerned in spatial skill. The frontal lobes include the prefrontal areas that lie anterior to the premotor areas and are the largest parts of the neocortex in humans. Damage to the prefrontal cortex produces (among other dysfunctions) impairment in spatial memory. The prefrontal cortex has rich networks of interconnections with the rest of the neocortex, including the parietal lobes, as well as with subcortical parts of the brain. Parts also have direct, reciprocal connections with the hippocampus (Levin *et al.* 1991).

In monkeys, (dorsolateral) prefrontal lobe damage is associated with difficulties in delayed response tasks. In such tasks, the animal is briefly shown food placed under one of two identical cups, but is only allowed to retrieve the food after a short delay. The location of the food is varied, so that the animal needs to remember the location at which the food was hidden. It cannot simply execute the same response as before.

In humans, tasks involving limited capacity memory for recent spatial information (spatial working memory) are associated with a large network which involves the prefrontal areas (caudate principal sulcus), cortical–cortical connections including the posterior parietal cortex, and connections also with areas of the limbic cortex, and hippocampal regions (Goldman-Rakic & Friedman 1991).

In view of the involvement of the prefrontal cortex in spatial memory, it is of particular interest that all the modality-specific sensory areas project also to that system (Squire 1987).

The neuropsychological evidence thus suggests that there is multiple representation of functions with partial division of labour (e.g. Kornhuber 1984). Kornhuber (1984) suggests that the specialization and multiplication of representation has clear advantages. For instance, specific brain lesions may produce impairment in a skill which may be compensated by learning, using other cortical areas that were previously not as central to the particular skill that the lesion has disrupted.

However, if the only reason for the multiple subsystems that are concerned in spatial processing were to provide redundancy in case of insults to the brain, it would be extremely odd that they should also differ from each other. A reasonable surmise is that the different areas, which receive slightly different arrays of convergent inputs, also have slightly different, if overlapping, functions.

What is in common to all forms of spatial coding is the use of some reference cue or frame in terms of which a location can be specified. But it is a mistake to think that reference frames are necessarily all of the same kind.

The major division in behavioural studies has been between body-centred (egocentric) reference frames and references that are based on external (allocentric) information. Paillard (1991), Gurfinkel and Levick (1991) and Berthoz (1991) all suggest that the neuropsychological evidence is also consistent with a multiplicity of possible body-centred and external frames for spatial coding.

VII Summary

In summary, the neurophysiological as well as the behavioural evidence clearly suggests that spatial coding involves processing convergent inputs from different modalities. Typically, inputs are multimodal and converge for spatial processing in a number of different areas of the brain.

Current evidence shows that the posterior parietal cortex and the prefrontal (caudate) areas are particularly important. Both are foci for interconnections with other systems, and both are areas in which inputs from different modalities converge. But processing spatial information also depends on a number of other systems, including the hippocampus and cerebellum, prefrontal areas of the cortex, and interconnections between these. The evidence seems to suggest that different types of task may depend on different nodes of interconnections.

The right hemisphere is more specialized for organizing the convergent input modalities and submodalities spatially than the left. Spatial processing has been linked to hormonal and genetic sex differences. But it is difficult to find consistent evidence for differences that can be attributed specifically to spatial coding as such. The link is likely to be more indirect.

There is evidence that regional specialization of the brain is predetermined and that there is also a good deal of plasticity. That is probably more important during early periods before brain structures are fully mature, where some take-over of function seems to take place after early brain insults.

Precisely what effects sensory deprivation has on the convergence of inputs from different modalities in the important posterior parietal areas is not known as yet. Visual deprivation leads to—mainly adverse—changes in the primary visual cortex. But it is possible also that new connections may be formed in the association areas, at least during the periods when cortical architectures are not yet fully established (Kandel & Hawkins 1992).

The evidence reviewed in this chapter is consistent with the notion of interrelated neural networks which is central to recent models of the brain in neuroscience (e.g. Berthoz 1991; Crick 1989; Gurfinkel & Levick 1991; Paillard 1991; Rolls 1991; Stein 1991). The view taken here is that the neuropsychological findings are not well explained by the idea of a number of separate modules that also have some links between them. The emphasis is rather on the interrelation of networks and the consequent convergence of inputs in areas that are preset, to varying extents, for such convergence. Specialization for spatial behaviours is thus seen as resulting from the confluence of inputs from different parts of the networks. The change in emphasis can explain the degrees and types of specialization found, but also takes account of the effects of task conditions that emerged from studies on sex differences. The view suggests that the convergence of sensory inputs in the regions which are important for spatial behaviours is a factor which needs to be taken into account in considering the organization of information in terms of reference frames.

5

Shape coding by vision and touch

This chapter is concerned with coding the shape of objects, rather than with locating them. The reason for dealing with object shape and location separately is that the neuropsychological and behavioural evidence suggests that 'what' objects are and 'where' they are located, is represented somewhat differently, both in vision (e.g. Trevarthen 1968; Weiskrantz 1963, 1986) and in touch (Paillard 1971).

Broadly, to identify the shape of an object we use distinctive features in contours (the composition of several features) and distinctive features within these contours. In that sense, an object can be recognized or picked out from its background by shape, without reference to any other object or frame.

To locate objects 'in space', on the other hand, requires reference to some frame, or coordinate system, or to a form of organization which relates shapes to each other, or to the perceiver.

The literature on object identification does not always make it quite clear whether the identification refers only to the meaning of objects— whether it is a bird or a book—or also to their identification by shape characteristics, presumably because shape is often the first clue to meaning. The interest here is in shape coding by vision and touch. The chapter is not intended as an exhaustive account of shape perception by either vision or touch, and some aspects have already been discussed in the context of crossmodal coding (Chapters 2 & 3).

I want to make two main points in this chapter. One is to pull out the differences in shape information from touch compared to vision which seem to me to be important. The second is to suggest that the distinction between identifying a shape and coding its location is not absolute; because in some cases identification depends on orientation. Both points seem to me to explain some of the apparent controversies in the literature on haptic coding.

The point that I want to make about shape is to suggest specifically that there is a major difference between touch and vision which is often neglected. I shall argue that, in touch, the complementary information from other sources which is needed to identify a shape differs with the size and type of object (Millar 1989a,b). This has important consequences for a theoretical description of haptic coding and for apparent discrepancies in findings. It also has practical implications.

The stress here is on differences rather than on similarities between vision and touch. This is not to deny the importance of the fact that the same information can be derived from both. The point is that questions about how the modalities function can be asked at several levels of enquiry. There are legitimate descriptions that apply across differences. The front of a house and a six-millimetre dot pattern can both be described as having the same (e.g. rectangular) shape. For some questions that is more important than differences in size, depth and materials. For the purpose of looking at effects of informational conditions, the differences are important. In any case, descriptions in terms of abstract shape characteristics tap a different level of question than descriptions in terms of informational differences. Both are valid and indeed necessary. An eventual full description or explanation demands answers at a number of different levels (Marr 1982).

Shape recognition by touch will be discussed at greater length than visual recognition. This is partly because far less has been written about touch than vision. But the main reason for devoting more space to touch is to highlight the fact that, in touch, to recognize objects across differences in size, depth, and composition requires convergence of quite different complementary information. Generalizing across differences in the size, depth, and composition (e.g. linear versus punctiform) of a previously unknown configuration is much easier (more directly available) in vision than in touch.

In the sections that follow, I shall first briefly report the evidence for the distinction between shape identification and location which shows that the distinction obtains in both vision and touch. Findings on shape coding in vision and then in touch are considered next. The difference in information given by touch with different sizes and dimensions of tactual shapes are related to the role of tactual acuity, the type, amplitude and presence of complementary, active movements, and to the presence or absence of spatial reference cues. The sections on orientation which follow suggest that, for shape, the 'where/what' distinction is not complete. Shape identification by vision and by touch can involve spatial coding in some contexts. Shapes can be distinguished even if they differ only in the relative position of distinctive features within each. A picture of a geometric form can be discriminated from a picture in which exactly the same distinctive features are organized in a different spatial order, even if they are both unfamiliar and neither can be named.

Shape orientation thus straddles the distinction between identification and location to some extent. However, this depends on the presence of reference information. It will be argued that evidence on the recognition of haptic shapes and on shape-orientation in touch and vision shows that apparently contradictory findings actually relate lawfully to the information that is available in different contexts.

I   Where and what in vision and touch

The distinction between 'where' something is and 'what' it is, came initially from work on visuomotor behaviour in the hamster (Schneider 1967). But the hypothesis of two visual systems has also been supported by work on primates and man (e.g. Humphrey & Weiskrantz 1967; Trevarthen 1968; Weiskrantz 1963, 1986).

The neuropsychological evidence suggests that processing 'where' a shape or object is located is subserved by visual inputs from the striate cortex (in the occipital lobe) through to the post-parietal association cortex (Anderson 1987). Processing 'what' objects are, that is to say, recognizing their identity, is subserved by a network of inputs from the visual striate areas to the temporal association areas where object features are analysed (Anderson 1987).

Clinical patients with visuospatial disorders show a dissociation between 'where' and 'what'. Patients may fail on spatial problems but nevertheless recognize objects and faces. On the other hand, prosopagnosia is a disorder in which patients fail to recognize faces or other classes of objects, but have no difficulty in locating the items spatially (e.g. Ratcliff 1991).

The phenomenon known as 'blindsight' shows a dissociation between visual recognition of an object and locating it. The patients usually suffer from field defects; that is to say, they are unable to recognize objects which are placed in the blind part of their visual field. Nevertheless, such patients may reach to the correct location of an object which they do not recognize, if they are asked to guess 'where' the object may be (Weiskrantz 1963, 1986). Such behaviour can occur after the complete destruction of the striate cortex, which normally deals with visual inputs, or the destruction of input paths to it from the thalamus.

The usual explanation has been that the ability to locate objects which subjects cannot recognize visually is due to subcortical mechanisms. However, recent evidence (Cowey 1992) suggests that, when the striate (primary visual area) cortex is damaged or absent, a more complicated thalamocortical pathway may be involved. The suggestion is that innervation is carried from optic axons to the lateral geniculate (subcortical visual) body and from there to the remaining visual cortical areas and that innervation from thalamocortical centres to the cortex may be involved. Such evidence suggests importantly how the multiplicity of connections between subsystems in vision function when some of the information is blocked by injury or insult to another route.

Different routes for the identification of an object and its location also seem to occur in touch (Paillard 1971, 1991). Paillard and his colleagues presented a tactile analogue to the phenomenon of blindsight (Paillard *et al.* 1983). This concerned a patient with an obstruction of the artery that nourishes the left posterior parietal cortex, who exhibited specific tactile deficits which extended from the finger tip to below the elbow of her right arm. The patient was unable to report that she had been touched on that site. Nevertheless, she was able to point with the other hand to the correct location of the touch on the right arm which she could not feel. She did feel moving stimuli on the right arm, however, and was able to judge the direction of the movement.

Understanding what an object is and locating it and the direction in which it is moving thus seem to be processed along somewhat different routes also in the haptic modality, although we know far less about this at any level than about functions connected with vision. The example from Paillard (1971) suggests that coding locations differs from shape coding also in touch.

II   Shape, size, and depth in vision

There are obvious similarities in recognizing three-dimensional shapes by vision and by touch. People can apply the same descriptive term to a shape and recognize the same object by its shape in vision and touch. The same geometric and adjectives of round and square, oblong or cuboid apply. There is also a sense in which the 'edginess' of corners and the smoothness of spheres can be seen as well as felt.

The findings considered earlier (Chapters 2, 3, & 4) show that visual perception of three-dimensional objects is serviced by the interaction and convergence of information from a number of different sources. Nevertheless perception in the absence of vision is not precisely the same as when vision is present.

There is evidence that even neonates perceive visual shapes as three-dimensional from the outset (e.g. Gibson & Spelke 1983). As we saw earlier, the relevant information for three-dimensional shapes is available, even if not all systems are totally mature at birth.

In principle, depth information for infants as well as adults comes from a number of different sources. Movement parallax refers to the fact that slightly different aspects of an object are seen when the head and/or eyes move, and that information is available to some extent from the start.

Binocular depth perception is another instance of the fact that convergent information from slightly different sources produces more information than inputs from either source alone. Many cells in the visual association area of the brain cannot be activated by stimulation from one eye alone; their activity is significantly modified by concurrent patterns in the other which is not being stimulated directly (DeValois & DeValois

1988, p. 114). The fact that inputs from the two eyes join on to one cell in the cortex provides slightly different views of objects (stereopsis), and this is important in depth perception (DeValois & DeValois 1988). Reliable eye convergence is not fully established until the age of about five months. It seems likely that depth perception is greatly improved once the eyes move convergently.

There are also a number of other potential depth cues in vision. Occlusion of one object by another that is in front is one of them. Difference in texture or shading is another. Moreover, there is an inverse relation between size and distance in vision, of which the convergence of parallel lines at distance is an instance. However, phenomenologically, the diminution of size with distance only obtains at relatively far distances. Object size is perceived as constant within near space. Objects do not seem to get smaller as they recede.

The visual acuity of the newborn is too poor to perceive much shape detail beyond a distance of nine to twelve inches. However, differences in size, and the fact that one object may partially obscure another, can be gathered with a little experience of moving the head to see one stationary object behind another. It is sometimes suggested that young infants perceive two objects as one object if the objects share a contour (Bower 1974). Nevertheless, visual perception of shapes and depth is present very early on.

The implicit assumption that only descriptions of functioning at the most general level deserve the name of explanations has led to the tacit, but illegitimate corollary that whatever is true of visual perception must also be true of tactual perception. That is not so. The point will be explored further in the next section.

III Complementary information and shape, size, and depth in touch

The difference between touch and vision that I want to emphasize has not been sufficiently recognized in the literature so far. It is that perception by touch depends on complementary information from tactual acuity, active movement, and spatial cues that are not the same for shapes of all kinds.

Seminal studies by Davidson (1972) and Berlá and Butterfield (1977) showed that shape perception depends on systematic exploration. Moreover, haptic perception of shape properties depends on the type of exploratory activity that is deployed (Appelle et al. 1980; Millar 1987b). Some researchers have therefore concentrated on describing exploratory activities when people try to identify haptic objects (e.g. Lederman & Klatzky 1990).

I think that we need to go even further. The point stressed here is that the range and type of information needed for shape recognition differ among different sizes and types of object. That needs to be made explicit, especially because the differences involve the availability of reference cues. The point is that the description of processes in tactual recognition differs for different types and sizes of shape, in a way in which that is not true of visual shapes. In vision, differences in size and depth are not a major problem. By contrast, studies of tactual recognition show up many apparent contradictions if we assume that precisely the same description applies in the case of three-dimensional objects that can be handled, raised dot patterns and flat objects that are felt passively from being placed on the skin.

The recognition of that difference between vision and touch is crucial, particularly for resolving needless controversies about shape perception by the two modalities.

In touch, as in vision, shape perception depends on the nature and kind of complementary information. But in touch that complementary information differs for different types of tactual patterns with the size of object, continuity of stimulation, the means of exploration, and with task demands and prior knowledge.

As in vision, the discrimination of three-dimensional shapes by touch depends on convergent information from other sources. For instance, monkeys can discriminate round from straight objects blind, by grasping them in the hand. Sakata and Iwamura (1978) found that this depends on a combination of inputs from the skin and joints. These converge into single neurones in parietal cortex (posterior part of the hand area of S1 at the boundary of 2 and 5, in the lateral part of the anterior bank of the intraparietal sulcus). To determine this, Sakata and Iwamura (1978) used single-unit recording. Microelectrodes are implanted, and the activities of single neurones can be recorded while the animal is awake and active. The findings showed that the units from which they recorded depended on a combination of submodalities, namely, the stimulation from (bent) finger joints and the skin.

Evidence from grasping objects without vision is consonant with Gibson's (1966) notion, also put forward by Revesz (1950), that cutaneous (tactual) and articular motion (active movement) vary concomitantly to produce haptic information.

However, shape perception by touch cannot be generalized across differences in size and depth to the same extent that this is possible in vision. In vision, the shape of an object within the field of vision is easily recognized as the same shape even if its size (larger or smaller) differs. In touch, generalizing shape across size is certainly possible, but it is much less easy. The reason is that the complementary information for recognizing the shape of an object often differs markedly with its size, its composition (punctiform or continuous), with the type of task (active or passive), and with the type of exploration (cued or uncued) which is needed.

Traditionally, the majority of studies on touch perception have concentrated on psychophysical measurements of touch thresholds to ascertain or compare acuity in touch with other modalities. But it has rarely been pointed out that acuity measures are more important for some types of shapes than for other.

There seems to be little doubt that tactual acuity, or the power of resolution by the skin, is poorer than visual acuity (Craig & Sherrick 1982). The main measure of tactual acuity has been the two-point threshold. The measure depends on how far apart two points on the skin must be before they can be felt as separate points when touched. Touch receptors are scattered all over the skin. But they are far more concentrated in some parts of the body than in others.

The finger tip and lips are probably the most sensitive. The two-point threshold for the finger tip of human adults is significantly lower (therefore more sensitive) than other regions of the finger, and these in turn are significantly lower than the threshold tested on the palm of the hand (Vallbo & Johansson 1978). The spatial resolution in psychophysical two-point threshold tests is closely related to the density of tactile sensory units in the glabrous skin, and thresholds also probably relate to the size of receptive fields in the cortex.

In the nature of the case, the two-point threshold measure is relevant mainly to perception of shapes which depend on simultaneous passive stimulation of an area of skin. It is thus presumably involved in the perception of flat and outline forms pressed on to the skin, and should also have a function in what (in analogy with eye movements) may be called 'fixation times' during active tactual exploration. At the same time, psychophysical evidence on tactual acuity is not the only factor that we need to consider in understanding tactual shape recognition.

The relative importance of tactual acuity differs for different types of shape recognition. In some cases, it is probably less important than has sometimes been thought. It is much less relevant, for instance, to the recognition of very large shapes that need to be explored by large active movements of the arm and hand. In principle, these can be coded in relation to the body-centred coordinates in a way that simply is not possible when exploring six-millimetre dot patterns.

I am suggesting that we need to distinguish at least six types of tactual shapes if we look at the type of complementary information that is needed for these to be recognized as shapes (Millar 1989a).

Tactual shape perception will therefore be discussed under six different headings, depending on the information which is needed for recognition. The main distinctions here concern vibrotactile stimulation which is delivered to the skin; shapes placed on the skin and felt passively; manipulable, small three-dimensional objects; very large three-dimensional objects; continuous raised outline shapes, and very small raised dot patterns. For a number of reasons, the amount of available evidence on touch perception and recognition differs considerably for these different types of shape. Space devoted to each will vary accordingly.

The main differences in information between the six types of shape concern the relevance of tactual acuity, whether, and if so what type of exploratory movements are needed for recognition, and the possibility of using reference cues by which the patterns can be organized spatially.

The recognition of shapes from vibrotactile stimulation

The recognition of vibrotactile patterns depends on passive, but dynamic (intermittent, successive) stimulation of the skin. Vibrators are arranged in a rectangular matrix and applied to the skin. Such systems have been used extensively in protheses designed to substitute information to the skin for that supplied by vision.

Vibrotactile stimulation is delivered to the skin via arrays of rounded pin-like vibrators. It has been used for research and for practical purposes in devices intended to aid communication, particularly for the blind and deaf (Sherrick 1991). Perception of vibrotactile stimulation has been investigated extensively, and excellent reviews are available (Sherrick 1991; Sherrick & Craig 1982). Only a brief account is given here of its main characteristics and the information which is available to the subject.

Three points are worth noting. Acuity is particularly important in vibrotactile pattern recognition. By contrast, complementary information from active hand or arm movement is irrelevant, because the subject receives the stimulation passively. The third aspect worth noting is that vibrators are arranged in a rectangular matrix. Large arrays are strapped to the body, or the matrix is small enough for the ball of the finger to cover it. In either case, the array matrix forms a (rectangular) frame which could, in principle, be used as a coordinate reference frame to code the stimulus elements spatially.

The devices vary. People have used relatively large arrays of vibrators, strapped to various sites on the body, or limbs, or on the back, as in telesensory devices (Bach-y-Rita 1972). Alternatively, the ball of the finger rests on a small matrix of vibrators, as in the *optacon* (literally the optical to tactile converter; Bliss 1978; Sherrick 1991).

There has been a good deal of experimentation with the size and relative density of vibrotactile arrays. Acuity in vibrotactile stimulation depends on the time interval which is needed between the pulses of two vibrators for these to be detected as separate impulses, as well as on the distance between vibrators (density) in an array. The density, timing and intensity of pulses are thus major factors in the discrimination of vibrotactile stimulation.

The optacon has proved the most useful of the devices for blind people (Sherrick 1991). The ball of the finger rests passively on a small (5 × 20, or 6 × 24) array of 'benders' which can deliver vibrotactile stimulation at a frequency of 230 Hz. The optacon has a hand-held camera with electronic sensing devices which is used to scan print. The patterns of print letters are picked up by the electronic eyes of the scanning device, and translated into pulses which are delivered to the pad of the finger via the array of vibrators. To the untutored, the letter 'S', for instance, feels like a small pulse delivered to the top right, followed by a pulse located at the bottom left on the pad of the finger resting on the array.

Although the finger rests passively on the matrix of vibrators, the impulses are dynamic. Stimulus change is, of course, needed for perception by touch, as it is for other modalities. Without change, sensation is lost. However, vibrators provide stimulus change in any case because the pulses are successive. In terms of stimulus change the information is similar to the information which active movement over the same patterns would provide. But there are also differences which will be discussed later.

The vibrators in the optacon form a rectangular array. The longer sides are roughly parallel to the sides of the finger resting on it. The optacon therefore has available complementary coordinate reference information. In principle, the top and sides of the finger-tip could be used as a frame to determine the location of successive pulses from the vibrators which translate print letters into pulses on the ball of the finger and to organize these locations in terms of shape.

Whether subjects actually use the rectangular array of vibrotactile stimulators as a reference frame in the optacon has not as yet been studied as such. The main investigations so far have addressed question of pattern discrimination and identification (e.g. Craig 1976, 1977, 1982, 1989). An important method is the use of 'masking' stimuli. In masking, an irrelevant pattern precedes or follows the target at various intervals.

One question which has been studied is how fast that interval needs to be for the target to become degraded or unrecognizable. Craig (1989) showed that targets are easier to discriminate than to identify. This is important because it raises questions about what additional information is needed for identification to take place. Craig and Sherrick (1982) suggest that localizing elements within an array is easier than identification. It is not known as yet whether this is due at least partly to the fact that the array has an invariant (stationary) layout which acts as a spatial frame. If so, it seems possible that this may explain why attempts to use vibrotactile stimulation to augment auditory information for people with hearing loss suggest that speech perception is best augmented by vibrotactile information when the signals are translated into spatial form.

Parameters relating to thresholds are important also in the design of vibrator arrays for touch reception keyboards as interfaces with computers for blind users (Schiff & Foulke 1982). Several problems arise in the design of touch reception keyboards, because these are designed to display more than one letter or word by means of vibrators. They therefore require scanning, that is to say, they require active movement of the finger(s) across the text. In reading with the optacon, single letters are perceived by means of changing vibrations under the ball of the immobile finger. Average reading speeds of about 30 to 60 words per minute (wpm) have been reported for practised subjects, although some individuals show impressively high reading rates (Craig 1977).

However, keyboards with similar vibrators seem to combine passive reception of (right-to-left) vibrations with left-to-right active scanning. An interesting question is what parameters govern the combination of passive touch and active movement. It is possible that the passive movement of vibrators under the ball of the finger interferes with the information gained by scanning actively from left to right across the keyboard (Millar 1988b).

The optacon necessarily confines the reader to letter-by-letter processing of texts. It has nevertheless proved extremely useful.

Flat and outline forms placed on the skin and in the hand

Perception of flat or outline shapes placed on the skin depends on passive stimulation of an extended area of skin. The perception of objects that are grasped passively in the hand depends on a combination of tactile and finger joint stimulation.

Much less attention has been paid by researchers to passive perception of complex shapes (Sherrick & Craig 1982), except for questions of acuity in terms of two-point thresholds. Acuity measured in terms of two-point thresholds is, however, important in the perception of flat and continuous outline shapes placed on the skin.

Perception of these shapes depends on passive stimulation. But the stimulation is not merely passively received, it is also static and unvarying, unlike dynamic stimulation from vibrotactile devices. Unvarying, static stimulation prevents it being felt after a time. Adaptation to the stimulation so that it can no longer be felt is therefore a problem when there is no complementary information from active finger or limb movement which changes the stimulation.

Gibson's (1962) seminal study on active touch stressed the contribution of movement in object recognition. Gibson distinguished between active and passive touch, suggesting that passive touch depends on the excitation of the skin receptors and underlying tissues. By contrast, in active touch there is concomitant excitation of receptors in the joint and tendons and the whole skeletomuscular system.

When a form is placed on the skin, there is also relatively little reference information as such, unless people relate other felt body parts to it. Thus prominent features of a felt shape may be related to body-centred cues. But, if the object or feature is small, coding by body-centred references can only provide rather crude localization. The adequacy of such reference must depend on the size of the object, the presence of the distinctive features, and where on the body the object is placed.

For shapes placed in the hand, the thumb or fingers may be used as anchor points or complementary reference for distinctive features (Appelle et al. 1980). It has been suggested that the thumb is not used as a spatial anchor in the detection of reversed orientation of tactual forms by children (Roemer et al. 1986). However, the reason may be that the study used active tactual exploration. Since the hands move during active manipulation, the location of the thumbs would be less invariant as an anchor than body-centred (based on the trunk midline) coordinates. For passive touch, features of an object placed in the hand may well be referred to the relative location of the thumb. But we do not have sufficient evidence on that so far.

The evidence on which Gibson (1962) based his conclusion that active touch is superior to passive touch came from a study with small 'cookie-cutters' which were either pressed into the subject's hand, or the subject was allowed to trace around the forms. Identification by active touch was far superior.

Nevertheless, shapes can also be recognized from passive stimulation of the hand. Krauthammer (1968) also used 'cookie-cutters' as stimuli, and showed that human adults have no trouble in recognizing these shapes placed into their hand, and can match them quite accurately with visual shapes (Krauthammer 1968). Moreover, Schwartz et al. (1975) showed that, when shapes were moved over the passive finger so that the contour was felt at the same time, the performance produced was as accurate as with active exploration. Reference information from the passive finger should be able to be used in the passive condition here.

Another factor in assessing active versus passive perception is that the person who is actively intending to explore a shape has advance information about how and from where to move, which is usually not available to him or her when the stimulation is passive. Such advance information is likely to be important for recognition in haptic conditions (see below). Richardson et al. (1981) showed that active exploration of raised finger mazes was less accurate when the subjects did not know which way to move compared with a passive condition in which this information was known to the subjects. Passive (guided) movements are also likely to differ from the perception of static impresses on the skin.

The developmental path of passive tactile perception is not yet clear. It is likely that an account will have to differ to some extent according to the body site and the contribution of complementary information. Evidence that infants who are only four weeks of age discriminate objects placed in the mouth (Gibson & Spelke 1983) involved active mouthing. The evidence suggests that the discrimination may be based on texture (hard/soft or edgy/smooth) differences.

Objects placed in the hand are clutched tightly even by newborns. But such clutching is evidently triggered automatically (Twitchell 1965). Objects drop out of the infants' hands without apparent notice by them. Not until the age of about four months do infants move an object which they grasp by hand into their field of vision. Before that age, objects felt passively thus seem to be ignored initially. Nevertheless, the infant reacts to differences in pressure, temperature and stretch as well as pain.

The fact that monkeys discriminate three-dimensional shapes grasped in the hand, and the way in which cutaneous and finger joint information contribute to this (Sakata & Iwamura 1978), has already been mentioned. Presumably, information from (bent) finger joints will converge with information from the skin in the human primate as in the monkey (e.g. Sakata & Iwamura 1978).

In general, shape recognition by passive touch, whether the shape is pressed on to the skin or grasped passively by the hand, is less accurate than recognition by active haptic exploration (Berlá & Butterfield 1977). The fact that this also depends on the amount of prior information in the two types of situation has already been mentioned. For instance, if the hand area or the (stationary) thumb in passive touch is used as an invariant cue to which a distinctive feature of a shape can be referred, spatial location becomes possible. It is likely that adults will infer that as a possible strategy more quickly than young children. But there is no reason, in principle, why young children could not use that information also.

Small three-dimensional shapes actively manipulated by both hands

The objects to which I refer here are small three-dimensional shapes that can be manipulated by both hands, or held in one hand and manipulated by the other. Perception depends jointly on touch and movement information from active exploration by the fingers and palms of one hand and passive tactile information from the other hand. Unlike young monkeys, human infants, as noted above, pay little attention to objects placed into their hands before the age of about four months, when they start to bring them into view. It should, however, be noted that this does not apply to all forms of touch. The mouth is different. Gross shape differences between objects placed in the mouth do seem to be noticed even by very young infants (e.g. Meltzoff & Borton 1979).

Such perception by the mouth probably involves tongue and mouth movement as well as cutaneous information. If so, it should allow the infant to discriminate the size and depth (within the limit of the mouth) as well as between straight and round objects. The evidence on the specific information that is available is scanty so far. Nevertheless, it suffices to suggest that shape perception by touch, albeit relatively crude or lacking in discrimination at first, is probably present from birth, as is visual shape perception.

The seminal studies of Davidson (1972) and Berlá and Butterfield (1977) on active hand movements showed that these provide important evidence that exploratory movements have to be deployed systematically if shape coding is to be achieved. Davidson (1972) showed that even in order to recognize relatively small shapes, exploration has to be systematic.

This suggests at least some prior knowledge about where to start and stop. A similar implication follows from a study by Berlá and Butterfield (1977). Thus, some form of pre-cuing, either about an anchor point or about which direction to move in and where to start and stop, is needed in addition to the movements made in exploring the pattern.

The findings actually imply that the person has to know something about the forms before she starts exploring them. Without such knowledge and with no cues that could be used for spatial reference, recognition tends to be poor (Millar 1971, 1972a, 1974, 1978a). Recent studies on the recognition of objects (e.g. Lederman & Klatzky 1990) further show the importance of systematic exploration and advance knowledge in identifying objects by touch.

Identification of small three-dimensional objects that are explored actively by both hands and moved or shaken so that they cannot be referred to a stationary body part is less likely to depend on spatial coding because there is no stationary body cue by which a given feature could be located. However, object-centred spatial coding may still be possible, depending on the differences between features of the shape. Prominent features may be used as anchor points in relation to the hand that grasps the object. However, when the aim is to identify the object as a particular commodity, people move the object around, shaking it and subjecting it to pressure and the like. In this case, identification seems to depend more on information from pressure, temperature and texture (e.g. Lederman & Klatsky 1990). In such object identification tasks, spatial coding and orientation is probably less important than identification through information about hardness, temperature and shear pattern.

Large three-dimensional objects that cannot be grasped in the hand

For large three-dimensional shapes that cannot be grasped in the hand, the relative role of active movements in spatial coding of features is different again. Tactual acuity is less important. Touch and pressure, heat and cold are important in assessing the material. But for shape coding, they must be less useful. By contrast, movements and body-centred reference are presumably essential.

The famous mid-nineteenth-century physiologist Weber (1834, 1836) gave a classic, almost lyrical description of how we perceive a very large three-dimensional object by touch. Shut your eyes, and imagine touching a large vase or vessel. According to Weber, we build up a picture of its size and shape by moving our hands over it.

Active large hand and arm movements are clearly crucial for form perception in this case, while tactual acuity is not the major problem in this situation. The two-point threshold tells us very little about the processes which underlie perceiving by touch the face of a friend or the fine shape of a Chinese vase. Clearly, tactual information about the temperature, resistance to pressure (hardness), as well as about surface (rough/smooth) texture is involved in the identification of an object. But for really large new objects, coordinated two-handed movements will be needed to explore and understand their shape. For the shape of large objects, therefore, information from the joints and stretch muscles is crucial, and probably more important than purely passive tactual information.

Recognition of very large objects has rarely been studied empirically since Weber's description. The reason may simply be that large objects are less convenient for experimental investigations. As a task, exploring large three-dimensional objects has as much, or more, in common with tasks using larger-scale spatial configuration than with the recognition of small objects. This is both because movement information is important in both tasks and because body-centred coordinates, including gravitational information, can in principle be used for spatial reference.

The conditions which make movement information useful in recognition tasks with larger spatial configurations will be discussed in more detail in a later chapter. Perception depends on large active arm movements, movements of the hands and fingers, and information from pressure and touch, as well as from the fact that the arms and hands move conjointly.

Small continuous raised outlines

Raised-outline configurations have been used as symbols or characters in tactile maps and reading systems. Provided that configurations are large enough, raised lines are typically explored by active movements, usually with the forefinger of the preferred hand. Most of the forms are never-theless too small to code them by reference to body-centred (e.g. gravitational-vertical and transverse plane) spatial coordinates.

Shape coding depends on using features internal to the form as reference or anchor points, provided that the contours contain one or more distinctive features. But systematic exploration is evidently important (Davidson 1972; Berlá & Butterfield 1977).

Robin and Pêcheux (1976) also suggested that systematic exploration by visually handicapped children determined their successful recognition of two-dimensional stick shapes, and the reproduction of three-dimensional shapes made out of small cubes. However, the data are difficult to assess because the refusal rate was high and the experimenters only reported overall percentages for the whole group, although the group differed widely in age and many of the children actually had a good deal of sight.

Berlá and Butterfield (1977) were concerned with getting blind students to recognize raised outlines of countries on geographical maps. When they were taught how to explore systematically, by using anchor points to which exploratory movements could be related, recognition became easy (Berlá & Murr 1975). The results as well as Davidson's (1972) findings clearly suggest that pre-cuing or prior knowledge is needed (Berlá & Butterfield 1977).

When it comes to much smaller (one centimetre or less) outline shapes, there is a problem with clutter. Simple small shapes are used as symbols in tactile maps. The problem is that large shapes would make the layout too unwieldy and slow for practical purposes, while too many shapes or complex shapes make the layout unintelligible. Work on map symbols has come up with a variety of simple shapes (points, lines, curves, squares and circles), used either singly or in combination, which can be differentiated further by varying texture (rough/smooth stippling). These can be embossed on plasticized paper (Armstrong 1978; Gill 1973; James & Gill 1974; James 1982). Training is needed for their use, but quite adequate results have been achieved (Armstrong 1978).

Very small complex contours are difficult to recognize. This is not entirely the same question as acuity in terms of two-point thresholds. Points that are only millimetres apart can easily be discriminated by the moving finger. The added difficulty is that the embossing procedures tend to produce thicker lines than print, so that it is necessary to separate contours further if they are not to be felt as variations in texture rather than as differences in shape, and so produce clutter rather than clear information.

It is probably for that reason that simply translating visual print letters into raised outlines has not been a very successful solution for reading by touch. Even the outlines of capital letters are too complex not to feel cluttered. On the other hand, if they were enlarged sufficiently to be felt easily, this would produce enormously bulky and unwieldy texts.

One solution, originally devised in the mid-nineteenth century by a Dr Moon of Brighton, was to emboss simplified derivations of upper-case letters. The Moon system has undergone considerable change since its original inception. Moon is still in use, although much less so than braille, because the characters are mainly just over half a centimetre in height and width, and texts made up of them suffer from being very bulky, and they are consequently also rather slow to read.

Moon characters are relatively easy to learn (Tobin & Hill 1984, 1989). Perception depends typically on exploring each pattern with one finger and so involves active touch and movement. The forms are relatively uncluttered, but they are too small for reference to body-centred coordinates. However, Moon characters consist of curves, straight lines, dots and lines in different orientations and configurations. Like print, they therefore differ from each other on more than one dimension, although they are simpler than print shapes. The fact that they do have distinctive features means that these can be coded with reference to each other, so that discrimination and shape coding should be possible in principle.

Moreover, because Moon derives from upper-case print letters, at least for people who have prior knowledge of print, that should provide some pre-cuing which, as was mentioned earlier, allows informed and systematic exploration. The other potential advantage of knowing the origin of the forms is that it limits the number of alternative interpretations any one of the characters may have. It is well known that limiting the set of possible candidates for any item reduces the time needed to identify that item.

It is not clear as yet whether the relatively fast learning of Moon characters is due to better legibility, ease of shape coding, or to prior knowledge of the print from which many of the characters are derived, or all three. The Moon system has so far been tested mainly with people who had some prior knowledge of print. The question is of some practical interest, because it has been suggested that the system could be used to teach learning-disabled blind children for whom braille is thought to be too difficult. The main problem with Moon, compared to braille, is the size of individual letters. Reading continuous prose is slower, and books are heavy and bulky.

Very small raised-dot patterns (braille)

For perceiving very small raised-dot patterns, the important parameters are different again. These are important, because braille, which is still the most important written medium for the blind, consists of such patterns.

Braille patterns derive from a tiny (6 mm × 2 mm) six raised-dot matrix.

The presence or absence of any dot from the 2×3 matrix denotes a different character. The characters therefore vary only along a single dimension and consequently lack distinctive features. The patterns have an invariant upright orientation, but there is no concomitant external frame by which the orientation could be coded automatically. The patterns are also too small to be specified accurately by body-centred reference. Perception of each pattern typically depends on exploration by one finger. Without prior knowledge there is nothing to guide systematic exploration.

Poor tactile acuity is generally invoked to explain difficulties in learning braille. But there is good reason to believe that the lack of redundancy of the braille system, and the absence of an automatic reference frame, are at least as important. Unlike print letters, which differ on many features, braille patterns may differ by a single dot. The lack of distinctive features is particularly problematical in the absence of reliable reference anchors.

When they are perceived by vision, braille patterns certainly make simple, recognizable outline shapes. It was generally assumed originally that braille letters are coded as global shapes, in the way visual print letters appear to be coded as outline shapes (Apkarian-Stielau & Loomis 1975; Foulke 1982; Nolan & Kederis 1969).

Apkarian-Stielau & Loomis (1975) suggested that tactual perception is similar to perception of shape in 'blurred' vision. The evidence came from findings which showed that visual recognition was reduced to tactual levels of efficiency when visual information was degraded (e.g. Loomis 1981). Loomis (1990) proposed a two-stage process for both tactile and visual character recognition. The first stage depends on (low-pass) spatial filtering which is 'compressed' by stimulus intensity. For the second stage, it is assumed that the transformed stimulus is compared to an internal 'template' representation of the letter. However, in an important recent study, Loomis (1993) showed that lateral masking effects differ between vision and touch, and suggested that the hypothesis of functional similarity between tactual and visual pattern perception needs to be revised.

It is important to note that some studies use visual exemplars in pre-test training. The difference between this and purely tactual (blind) conditions is extremely important. In visual conditions, background cues are present. It means that the subject knows the configuration of the shape and its distinctive features, and how these are specified in relation to the static background. That information remains available after the light is turned off or the hand is screened.

It is, of course, of interest to know that reducing visual legibility reduces perceptual accuracy and/or speed to tactile level. However, it is not possible to infer the basis of coding in recognition by touch or by vision solely from measures of efficiency. For instance, it has been found that, even with reduced visual legibility, global outline information can still be recognized

(Broadbent & Broadbent 1980). By contrast, there is considerable evidence that braille dot patterns are not initially coded as global shapes by touch (Millar 1977a,b, 1978a,b, 1983, 1984b, 1985a).

It is not an accident that Louis Braille used dot patterns as a basis for reading. In fact, Loomis (1981) showed that, for touch, dot patterns are easier to recognize than print letters. The reason is that very small print letters feel too cluttered. On the other hand, as mentioned above, if large outline shapes were used, it would take far too long to read a line, let alone a whole text.

In fact, although acuity is a problem in braille learning, it is not the main one. The small braille patterns are quite easy to discriminate by touch. That is so even for beginners (Katz 1925; Millar 1977a, 1978a, 1983, 1985a). The discrimination can rely on differences in dot density and on difference in the size of gaps between dots. The basis of that discrimination seems to be a kind of texture (density) difference. The difficulty comes in recognizing them as shapes.

Findings from studies which use a variety of different methods converge in their implications for the question. Millar (1977a) found that even sighted children who did not know braille were able to discriminate braille letters very accurately by touch alone. Nevertheless, they had no idea at all of the shape of these letters when asked to draw them. The finding suggested that their discrimination was not based on the global shapes of the letters.

Millar (1977b) used enlarged braille letters as well as letters in normal format. It was argued that, if braille characters are coded as global shapes, it should be easy to generalize these to enlarged forms, as it is in vision. Contrary to that hypothesis, braille readers took longer to match enlarged letters. Indeed, poorer readers needed training before they could recognize enlarged forms of letters, although they could name these accurately in the normal format. Limits on tactual acuity could not have been the cause of the failure to generalize, because enlarged forms should actually have been easier to discriminate. Similarly, matching by physical features was quite accurate and faster than matching by name (Millar 1977b). The difficulty in generalizing to enlarged forms could therefore not be explained by lack of discriminability.

Three other studies (Millar 1985a) tested directly whether braille letters are coded in terms of their outline shape as had been suggested (Nolan & Kederis 1969). The studies compared continuous raised outlines of braille letters with letters in their normal dot-pattern format. The argument was that, if braille letters are coded as outline shapes, matching these to the dot patterns should be faster, or at least as accurate and fast as matching dot-format letters only. The reverse was found for both normal and retarded readers, and for proficient as well as beginning readers (Millar 1985a).

Matching the dot patterns was faster than matching outline shapes, whether these preceded the test letter as cues or followed a dot-pattern cue.

Symmetry of form is another salient aspect of visual shapes which even young children find easy. Walk (1965) found that students learned symmetric nonsense shapes more easily than asymmetric shapes in vision, but showed that was not so for touch. Millar (1978a, experiment 2) asked whether this is also the case for the recognition of tactual pattern by blind children. Millar (1978a) used a larger (3 × 3) raised-dot matrix to produce symmetric and asymmetric patterns of nine and of five dots. It was argued that if children coded the dot patterns by shape, matching symmetric and asymmetric patterns should be easy, regardless of the number of dots. Again the reverse was found. The symmetry or asymmetry of patterns proved to be a relatively poor cue for same/different matching. By contrast, similarity and difference in dot numerosity were recognized easily.

As suggested earlier, the type and size of haptic shapes makes a considerable difference to the contribution of scanning movements in detecting and recognizing shapes. This is also important in trying to understand the effects of shape symmetry on haptic recognition. Locher and Simmons (1978) used flat plastic nonsense shapes which differed in complexity (Attneave & Arnould 1956), and which were large enough (15 × 19 cm) to need scanning. Shapes were either asymmetric, or symmetric around the vertical axis (straight ahead in the horizontal plane). However, without pre-cuing, the symmetry of even these shapes was more difficult to detect than asymmetry. But, when the task was to recognize stimuli that had previously been learned, recognition was faster for symmetrical shapes (Martinez 1971).

Words are even less likely than letters to be coded as global shapes in braille. Millar (1984b) had children indicate which of three braille words was the 'odd one out', on the basis of word sound, or meaning, or shape, or dot numerosity. They found it easier to base their choice on sound or meaning than on shape. Dot numerosity, on the other hand, was quite a good cue. Braille letters are exceedingly small. But tactile acuity is not the only, or even necessarily the most important difficulty in braille learning.

Millar (1977a, 1978a, 1983, 1984b, 1985a) suggested that, initially, braille recognition is based on felt 'texture' differences rather than on the global shape of braille characters or words. Texture differences depend on the density or numerosity of dots in a character.

It has been suggested that texture discrimination is not involved, on the grounds that shape coding by touch has been found for three-dimensional objects. However, there is no doubt whatsoever that shape can be coded by touch. What is questionable is that global shape is the initial basis of coding small raised-dot patterns.

The findings which were reviewed above show considerable, and convergent, evidence that braille patterns are difficult to code as global shapes (Millar 1977a,b, 1978a, 1983, 1984a, 1985a, 1987b). Thus, it was difficult for beginners to generalize braille patterns to enlarged formats. Matching the outline of braille shapes was no faster, and outlines were less well recognized than the dot patterns. Moreover, symmetry around the vertical axis which is easily recognized even by young children in visual conditions was less useful as a recognition cue than differences in dot density. Patterns were discriminated relatively easily as same or different, even by beginners, but pattern recognition and identification was often difficult. Finally, braille words were matched more easily by their semantic or phonological similarity, than by their shape.

Knowing the basis on which dot patterns are coded is important, both for an adequate theory of haptic perception and for the practical purpose of learning braille. Evidence that too great a reliance on texture coding in the early stages may even be detrimental came from a study (Millar 1983) which used an interference paradigm (Peterson & Peterson 1959) to assess the basis on which a severely retarded reader matched letters, as compared to her braille-reading peers. The children had to judge whether successive letters were the same or different. A short interval between the successive letters was filled with one of three repetitive tasks. One was verbal. The child had to repeat the irrelevant word 'the the'. It would interfere with matching if the child had covertly named the standard letter. Another task was spatial. The child had repeatedly to feel around two different small shapes. The third task tested whether the letter had been coded by texture by having her feel two different textures repeatedly during the delay. Having to feel anything during delays interfered with matching, but, for the retarded reader unlike the others, texture differences interfered significantly more with accuracy of matching than the other interpolations.

Findings which showed that dot-density cues are easy (Millar 1977a,b, 1978a, 1983, 1984b, 1985a) were used to test whether it would be possible to import redundancy into dot pattern systems, by varying shape and texture cues concomitantly.

Millar (1986a) used an adaptation of the Garner (1974) paradigm for visual cues. In vision, hue and brightness are highly correlated dimensions, and people find it difficult to judge one without being influenced by the other. If the two dimensions vary concomitantly with each other, judgements become easier; if they are opposed to one another unpredictably, judgements are more difficult. By contrast, judgements of shape and brightness interfere relatively little with each other.

Millar (1986a) asked whether the tactile shape and texture of raised-dot patterns are correlated dimensions. The results were quite clear. Adding irrelevant, but easy, density cues improved the discrimination of size and form; whereas making irrelevant dot-density cues orthogonal to them interfered with size and shape judgements. Facilitation and interference could be reversed by reversing the relative dimensional difficulty, but interference occurred also when the dimensions were equal in difficulty. The effects were shown by blind and by blindfolded sighted children. The findings show that texture cues can be used to make shape discrimination easier.

Poor tactile acuity can certainly not be considered as an absolute limitation in braille. Braille patterns which the beginner finds almost impossible to identify are easily recognized by fluent readers. Fluent braillists achieve reading rates that are not far behind average rates for print (e.g. Millar 1987b), even if they are not as fast as the fastest print readers.

It is, of course, clear that some form of spatial coding is needed for letter identification. The very fact that braille letters can differ in the location of a single dot makes that imperative, as well as very difficult. That is clear also from the important studies of letter recognition by Nolan and Kederis (1969). Errors occurred predominantly because some (lower) locations were missed and because letters were confused if they had the same number of dots and differed only in the location of the dots.

The fact that familiarity or prior knowledge is important was shown by Foulke and Warm (1967). They found that ease of dot-pattern discrimination is not due to sensory compensation in conditions of blindness. Blind children who had learned braille were certainly superior on matching braille letters to blindfolded sighted children who did not know braille. But they did not differ on other raised-dot patterns that were as unfamiliar to the blind as to the sighted.

There are several reasons why braille patterns are not easily coded as global shapes. Tactual acuity is only one, and probably not the most important reason. The fact that the characters are very small also means that they cannot be coded spatially by reference to the subject's body. But the fact that all characters derive from a six-dot matrix, and so vary only along a single dimension, is important also. The presence or absence of any dot denotes a different character. Braille thus lacks the distinctive features of print letters. This is important because it means that there are few or no features that could act as anchor points which could guide exploration, or in relation to which other internal aspects of the pattern can be organized spatially or as global configurations.

In fact, to code braille dot patterns in terms of continuous outlines of the pattern would not even be useful. To do so would confuse letters that differ not in the lines that the dots make, but in the number of dots that make up that line. The size of gaps between letters is relevant to the meaning of a letter.

Unlike optacon patterns, braille characters are not embedded in an invariant external surround and therefore have no frame which specifies the major vertical and horizontal directions. It is therefore not possible to use the alternative strategy of locating the dots in a character in relation to external spatial coordinates.

With experience and consequent pre-cuing, hand and finger movements do become more systematic. The fact that braille is difficult to code in terms of global outlines does not, of course, mean that shape coding is impossible. I found, for instance (Millar 1984a), that subjects can be taught to use word shape as a basis for finding a word. It was less efficient than using dot numerosity as a distinguishing mark. But it can be done, and experienced braillists are better at it than beginners (Millar 1984b, 1987b).

Indeed when it comes to reading continuous texts, the necessary information is different again. Hand movements and the relation of such movements to body-centred references become increasingly important. The normal path of movements from left to right describes an arc. The reader has to learn to keep the hand movement on the line of text. Beginners tend to lose the line. Fluent readers never do so under normal conditions of reading.

In reading continuous texts, there are even more requirements to keep track of the spatial position of words or sentences. It is necessary to find the next line of text without losing the previous location and to know where to regress to a previous sentence which the reader remembers, but which no longer makes sense in the present context (Millar 1987a, 1988b).

Spatial coding of the whole page in relation to lines and the location of meaningful contexts becomes necessary in reading for meaning (Millar 1987b). But configurational coding of individual letters as global shapes is less useful in reading for meaning. It is, however, used when the task is proof-reading rather than text comprehension (Millar 1987b).

Change in information pick-up with practice

It is worth asking precisely how recognition improves with familiarity. We tend to think of information as 'given' by an unchanging form 'out there' which totally determines what is perceived by touch; experience merely improves the accuracy and speed of detecting it.

It is therefore of considerable interest that, with experience, there is an actual change in the information which is picked up (Millar 1987b). The evidence for this comes from normal text reading by fluent braillists and less proficient readers. It should be stressed that this is not merely a question of an improvement in accuracy and speed with familiarity. More startlingly, the evidence shows that the information perceived by the proficient reader differs from that perceived by the novice (Millar 1987a).

The original suggestion that fluent braille readers scan 'dynamic patterns' came from Grunewald (1966), and to some extent also from Kusajima (1974), who commented on the smooth lateral scanning movements that are typical of text reading by proficient braillists. However, there was no experimental evidence to show what form of coding fluent readers actually use, whether this differs with proficiency, or in what way 'dynamic patterns' might differ from what is normally thought of as shape coding. Millar (1987b) suggested that in fluent reading fast scanning from left-to-right produces lateral shear patterns on the ball of the reading finger. These would provide lateral dot-gap density information rather than vertically oriented information about global shapes.

The hypothesis that fluent reading was based on dot-gap density information was tested against the alternative that rapid reading results from fast coding of letter shapes (e.g. Foulke 1982). An apparatus was devised which allowed braille texts to be read normally while the hands and the text were videotaped from below transparent surfaces, together with voice output and 1/100 second cumulative timing (Millar 1988c). Accurate time measures for letters, words, sentences, and the whole text could therefore be taken, as well as records of any errors or regressions.

A design which varied the reading task and levels of braille proficiency was used to decide between the alternative hypotheses. Reading for meaning and letter search (quasi-proof-reading) tasks were used. In all conditions the texts were oriented so that reading was in the unfamiliar near-to-far, rather than left-to-right direction. In one condition, the reading finger was held in the usual vertical orientation. This meant that the finger orientation in reading was familiar, but that the normal shear patterns on the ball finger would be disrupted. In the other condition, the hand had to be held at right angles to the normal orientation. The finger and hand orientation would be unfamiliar and slightly less comfortable, but the lateral shear (felt resistance) patterns on the ball of the finger would be the same as in normal reading.

The hypothesis that fluent reading for meaning depends on coding lateral dot-gap density patterns predicts that reading speed and accuracy differ for the two types of finger position and that these differ further with reading proficiency and the task. Fluent reading for meaning would be disrupted by vertical finger orientation because, although the position is familiar, it disrupts lateral shear patterns. The lateral inversion of the reading finger would be unfamiliar, but, because it preserves the lateral shear pattern information, reading for meaning would be less disrupted. Finger position would not affect slow readers or letter search, because it is assumed that slow readers are not coding dynamic patterns and that letter search needs to focus on single letters.

The alternative hypothesis was that braille reading depends on coding letters as global shapes. This predicts that reading proficiency should have a major effect, as before. But reading skill should not vary with the type of task. The hypothesis assumes that fluent readers are faster because they are faster at recognizing letter shapes.

The experimental findings (Millar 1987b) clearly supported the first hypothesis in the case of fast, fluent readers. Reading for meaning by fluent readers was severely disrupted by vertical but not by lateral finger orientation. By contrast, letter search was not differentially disrupted by finger orientation at all. For slow readers, neither task nor finger orientation produced significant differences in accuracy or speed.

The same results were found with a different method (Millar 1987b, experiment 2). Texts and finger positions were oriented normally, but some texts contained a few, randomly scattered degraded dots. These would disrupt expected dot-gap density patterns when scanning the text for meaning by lateral movements. By contrast, even degraded dots could be felt in search for a single letter pattern by small up/down and circular movements. Fluent reading for meaning was disrupted differentially, as predicted by the hypothesis that this depends on lateral scanning of dot-gap density patterns. Search for single letters typically elicited small vertical movements, rather than the lateral scan that was typical of reading for meaning. As predicted, the effect of degraded dots was significantly less for the letter search task.

We are beginning to know something about complementary information in the development of braille reading. Braille is almost always started by learning letters and their sounds. Initially, active finger movements are actually confusing rather than helpful. This is because unsystematic movements ('rubbing') over a pattern loses track of dot positions.

Training and experience are needed to use active hand movements systematically for braille, particularly for reading connected prose. Typically, beginning readers have difficulties in keeping to a line, and tend to trail downwards. The relation between finger position and body posture, and lateral hand movements and body posture, are particularly important for learning to keep to the line and for other spatial aspects (e.g. transition between lines, regressions to previous parts) of text reading (Millar 1987b). Fluent readers seem to use the complementary touch, kinaesthetic and movement information automatically.

Reading braille texts is, of course, an extremely complex process, which demands a large number of procedural skills and knowledge. As a written language, its acquisition could not be discussed adequately without doubling the content and size of this book, and this will not be attempted. The main point here has been to look at the complementary haptic information needed to discriminate and identify very small raised-dot patterns, because these are important in tactual recognition.

Taken together, the findings suggest that how we perceive small raised-dot patterns through touch changes both with experience and also with task demands, although 'objectively' the stimuli are precisely the same. It is also possible to chart, at least in a preliminary way, a path from the discrimination of new patterns to the stage at which the patterns are recognized without difficulty.

Initially, raised-dot pattern discrimination seems to be based on relatively easy dot-density (texture) differences. There seems to be no initial appreciation of the pattern as a global outline form. The stage at which the patterns are recognized effortlessly seems to depend on coding lateral dot-gap density patterns, resulting from smooth lateral movements across the text.

The overall shape of patterns can be recognized before this, if such recognition is demanded. Even so, shape does not seem to be the basis for recognizing the meaning or the sound of braille words. It is not yet clear at what point smooth lateral movements replace the small, slow, up/down regressions over single patterns. It seems likely that the transition depends on the ability to locate dots and gaps in patterns spatially, and that this in turn depends largely on deliberate practice of hand movements in relation to the transverse body plane.

IV   Orientation of shapes in vision

Shape orientation spans the topic of 'what' and 'where' to some extent. It is clear that shape recognition and spatial coding need to be distinguished. Nevertheless, the orientation as well as the shape of an object can specify its identity. The orientation of shapes can be determined either in relation to the perceiver, or to other shapes or contours.

In shape recognition the 'what' and 'where' distinction is therefore somewhat blurred. In some conditions, the orientation of a shape is critical to recognizing its identity (Ghent 1960; Rock 1973, 1984). Consider a square and a diamond. They are recognized as different shapes, or even as different types of objects. Nevertheless, their shape may be identical, in terms of features and contours, so that the difference in orientation is the only clue to the identity of either. By contrast, in many other situations, the orientation of the object or shape has to be disregarded for it to be identified.

Orientation can thus act as the only valid clue to the identity of an object, and it can also be the only misleading cue about the identity of an object. That ambiguity is a factor in shape coding.

In 'real life' (i.e. outside the laboratory) three-dimensional objects and shapes usually differ from each other on a variety of contour and internal features, while their orientation often has to be discounted. Shape features are thus more often clues to object identity, than are differences in orientation alone.

The hypothesis that performance by young children depends more on the familiarity, redundancy and consistency in the information that is available to them explains why orientation has less effect on recognition by young infants and children than shape (contour) features (e.g. Gibson 1969; Rice 1930), although they can discriminate orientation in suitable conditions.

As always, the findings do not imply an initial 'inability' to code orientation, as was originally supposed. McGurk (1972) showed that six- and nine-month-old babies discriminate the orientation of simple figures (stick with a top). He habituated the babies to the upright orientation of the figure. Looking-time decreased significantly over four familiarization trials and recovered significantly on the fifth trial, when the figure was oriented differently. It takes longer (more trials) to familiarize younger babies sufficiently for them to show habituation. Habituation procedures are more problematic with still younger infants. But when they are successful, even younger infants can be shown to discriminate orientation as well as form.

Some orientations are easier to code than others. There is a definite order of difficulty, other things being equal. The vertical upright, and also the straight-ahead projection, are easier than horizontal orientations, and both are considerably easier than obliques. The difference between vertical and horizontal lines is recognized more easily than differences between oblique orientations. The order of difficulty in coding particular orientations seems to be related inversely to the type and amount of information we need to have (e.g. Pufall & Shaw 1973).

The importance of the vertical direction for spatial coding was well captured by Howard and Templeton (1966, p. 175), 'Gravity is the most constant, pervasive, and significant of all the features of man's environment to which he orients himself. Under normal conditions it is virtually constant, both in strength and direction, and affects practically every aspect of man's overt behaviour . . . A man has a mid-body axis which is normally kept in line with the direction of gravity.'

We have a good deal of redundant information about the gravitational direction from (proprioceptive and vestibular) sources within our bodies, as well as from visual perception, according to any theory on how the mechanism are to be described (e.g. Gibson 1979; Marr 1982; Rock 1973, 1984). We therefore have concomitant, and normally redundant, information from internal as well as external sources about the vertical orientation.

In a gravitational environment, objects, backgrounds and people are normally vertically-oriented. Ghent and her colleagues (e.g. Ghent 1960; Ghent & Bernstein 1961) found that young children use the 'upright' orientation more than older children to recognize meaningful and non-sense shapes. But the importance of the vertical upright direction is not, of course, confined to children.

Vertical directions are the most accurately judged, both with and without vision. The visual straight-ahead direction is also functionally extremely important and seems to depend on the point at which binocular perception by the eyes gives a single fused picture. Asymmetry or imbalance in stimulation displaces the direction judged to be straight ahead (e.g. Howard & Templeton 1966).

Horizontal judgements are relatively accurate but more so in the light than in the dark, probably because there is less information from pro-prioceptive sources about the across-the-body midaxis than about the vertical midaxis (Howard & Templeton 1966). However, there is also some redundancy between vision and proprioception (e.g. from the midriff) for the horizontal direction. In terms of the amount and consistency of infor-mation we have for these directions, it is therefore perfectly intelligible that horizontal as well as vertical orientations are used as major references for determining the location of shape features.

It is important to note that the 'ease' or 'difficulty' of directions is not so much a question of perception, as of coding in memory. It is usually possible to discriminate even 'difficult' directions from each other, when both are present simultaneously. Differences in performance are found more often in the accuracy and/or speed of recognition or recall of success-ive stimuli. In other words, the amount and redundancy of information about a direction from internal and external sources are important factors for coding it in memory.

An example is the fact that up–down or near–far (straight ahead) distinctions are much easier to remember than left–right distinctions. That is so for adults (Corballis & Beale 1976; Carreiras & Gärling 1990; Maki & Ghent Braine 1985; Maki et al. 1977, 1979) as well as for children (e.g. Cox 1986; Fisher 1979; Fisher & Braine 1982; Gibson 1969; Huttenlocher 1967; Piaget & Inhelder 1956).

The up–down distinction is quite clear for vertical directions. We seldom stand on our heads; when we do, the inversion is fairly obvious. Similarly, gravitational forces determine the top of objects, and it is often difficult to invert them without upsetting their balance. Lateral inversions have much less obvious external markers, particularly if objects are symmetrical about the horizontal axis. But left–right or mirror-image confusions occur in recognition tests with successive rather than with simultaneous presenta-tion (e.g. Over & Over 1967a).

Right–left confusions occur particularly with shapes that can only be differentiated by orientation. Examples of these would be rather impover-ished, identical stick figures or outlines, for which the sole difference is the orientation of one constituent or feature, when the shape is 'rotated'. Other typical examples are lower-case letters such as b and d, p and q. Difficulties with right–left orientations also occur more with figures that are symmetrical about the midaxis (e.g. Mach 1897). Such errors are also often considered to be 'mirror-image confusion' and to be due solely to the symmetrical nature of the stimuli. However, 180-degree rotations of figures that are symmetric about the vertical midaxis are much less often confused with each other (e.g. Rock 1973, 1982). Symmetry cannot be the only factor, therefore, although it is probably a contributing one.

Again, the difference in difficulty is perfectly intelligible in terms of informational cues. The symmetry of features on either side of a central axis means that the two sides of the figure are identical, that is to say, they have no distinguishing features. Given that we have less decisive (redundant and/or familiar) information about horizontal than about vertical orientations (see earlier), lack of distinguishing features between the right and left ends of a horizontal direction would be a more serious additional difficulty for coding right–left than it would be for coding up–down directions.

The evidence thus suggests that speed and accuracy of coding left and right in memory depends on the adequacy of information available for distinguishing between them. Redundancy of differentiating cues would be needed less with familiarity. The consistent left–right scanning that fluent print readers have learned also makes left–right confusions less likely.

Obliques are more difficult to code than either vertical or horizontal directions. That applies to adults as well as to children (e.g. Corballis & Beale 1976, 1981; Gibson 1969; Over & Over 1967a; Rock 1973, 1984; Rudel & Teuber 1963). Confusion of 'mirror-image obliques' was initially considered a peculiarly developmental problem, which young children (and the octopus) could not solve at all. Bryant (1973) suggested that obliques are difficult for young children, because obliques do not normally parallel background features. He showed that successive discrimination of oblique lines improved significantly when the display contained a constant reference that paralleled one of the obliques.

The finding highlights the fact that spatial coding requires reference information. Bryant (1973) was probably right to suggest that, for coding successive obliques, an invariant compatible reference with one of them is more important than whether successive obliques mirror each other. However, asymmetry between the slopes of successive oblique lines can also be used as a differentiating cue. Corballis and Zalik (1977) found that children discriminate obliques better if the lines differ in slope. Interestingly enough, Bryant's data suggest that coding improved rather than changed with age. Seven-year-olds made fewer errors than pre-schoolers. But they were all more accurate when an invariant cue matched one of the obliques. The fact that age did not interact with reference conditions suggests that coding improves rather than changes with age and redundant (compatible) background information.

The fact that difficulties with right–left, 'mirror-image', and oblique directions were originally supposed to be characteristic only of young children (Over & Over 1967a; Rudel & Teuber 1963; Huttenlocher 1967) is mainly due to insensitivities in measurement. Adults are usually quite accurate in judging right and left sides, whereas young children are much less so. But when time measures (reaction time, or tachistoscopic exposure) are used for adults, the order of difficulty of directions is the same for them as for children (e.g. Corballis & Beale 1976).

The point is of interest for understanding the general developmental picture. The fact that the order of difficulty of coding vertical, horizontal and oblique directions is the same for adults and children strongly suggests that the order is due to the amount of consistent, unambiguous or redundant information that is available for coding them, and does not depend on developmental factors.

The contribution of developmental factors, on the other hand, is revealed by effects on accuracy as well as on speed. It suggests that there are larger effects on young and inexperienced subjects, with the result that the more difficult problems may depress performance to chance levels. Information thus needs to be made more consistent and redundant for young children than is necessary for older children or adults.

Oblique lines do present a more difficult memory problem. Pufall and Shaw (1973) suggested that this is because obliques require more complex description in terms of Euclidean coordinates. For obliques, it is necessary to specify the degree of deviation from both vertical and horizontal axes. For verticals and horizontals, only one such specification needs to be calculated.

On the other hand, it is also the case that our environment abounds far more in actual vertical and horizontal than in oblique contours (Gregory 1966), and the visual system is specialized for detecting the orientation of contours (see earlier). Furthermore, it has direct connections with vestibular information about head position and proprioceptive inputs from eye muscles. Visual reference to gravitationally oriented background features is thus easily available from all these sources. Questions of spatial coding in visual conditions are discussed in more detail in later chapters on spatial coding.

In considering developmental findings, I take it as a reasonable working hypothesis that ambiguity or uncertainty about any information affects performance adversely, and does so in inverse relation to age and experience.

V   Orientation of shapes in touch

The studies on shape orientation in vision show a clear order of difficulty
for different orientations. Vertical directions are easier to remember than
horizontal directions, because body-centred as well as external information
about the upright normally coincide and are unidirectional. There is also
some coincidence of information about the horizontal direction, but there
is less invariant information about the right and left ends than about the
top and bottom of verticals. Obliques are the most difficult to code because
two coordinate axes are needed to specify the directions of the slopes (see
earlier). It was argued that the order of difficulty relates closely to the
amount and reliability of reference information that is required to code
each orientation.

For touch, I would expect the same order of difficulty in the coding of
directions if and when reference information is available and reliable.
However, background cues are less obvious in touch, and complementary
movement inputs differ with the type and size of objects. Orientational
effects in touch are thus likely to depend far more on the size and type of
object and the specific task conditions.

An interesting study by Appelle and Countryman (1986) shows that this
is indeed the case. They use wooden dowels, mounted on axles in the
horizontal plane. The oblique effect was shown to depend on prior knowledge about references. With unimanual exploration in which the second
hand could not act as a reference anchor, and when there had been no
prior sight of the rod, and no prior information about the orientation to be
produced, performance with oblique directions did not differ from that
with vertical or horizontal directions. The results of Lechelt and Verenka
(1980), by contrast, show the oblique effect in touch. It is of interest that
the subjects in their study had seen the stimuli and surrounds prior to test
runs.

Questions about orientation are of particular interest for braille pattern
recognition. The orientation of braille patterns is invariant. In vision,
braille patterns are seen as vertically oriented, simple outline shapes
(Millar 1977a). With prior sight or knowledge of the shapes, changing the
vertical to an oblique orientation would make recognition more difficult.

By contrast, without prior vision or knowledge of the orientation of the
patterns, the difficulty lies in locating the dots in the first place. The
reasons for this have already been mentioned in the discussion of shape
coding of small raised patterns (see earlier): spatial reference is difficult;
there is no concomitant external reference frame which could specify dot
locations automatically; the patterns are too small to code relative to a
body-centred frame; they lack redundancy, and consequently lack anchor

points for shape-centred spatial coding; and, without prior knowledge, exploratory movements are unsystematic and cannot be used for coding. The confusions occur not because these are oblique directions, but because shapes can differ solely in a 2-millimetre displacement of one dot.

Also, the fact that, in braille, the presence and absence of any dot in the 2×3 matrix specifies a different character means that many characters are, and look like, mirror images of each other. It is, consequently, often assumed that this is the reason for difficulties in recognizing braille patterns. However, in totally blind conditions, that is not so.

Millar (1985a) found that for congenitally blind beginning readers the main reason for confusing 'mirror-image' patterns came from uncertainty about the position of a single dot which differed by only 2 mm from the comparable location in the other shape. Similarly, when totally congenitally blind readers were asked to draw the outline shape of braille letters, the most common sources of confusion were the spatial position of dots and the alignment to the major axes, rather than mirror-image reversals. Confusion between patterns thus depends more on the presence or absence of dots, than on their location within a pattern.

The findings suggest that whether or not orientation affects shape recognition by touch depends crucially on the possibility of using reference information. When such information is available, the oblique effect occurs in touch as well as in vision. When there are no adequate reference cues, the oblique effect is not found.

The point is that reference information is much more difficult to obtain in blind conditions. It has already been mentioned that braille, unlike optacon shapes, does not have an external coordinate frame, and patterns are not easily related to coordinates based on the body midline.

With experience, however, adequate reference information can be established even for the tiny raised-dot patterns of braille in totally blind conditions. There are three main sources for this. The frame of the stationary finger tip can be used to specify the location of dots in a single character. To do so, it is necessary for the child to have established an invariant orientation of her finger tip, and a light touch. The latter is necessary because the impression on an immobilized piece of skin fades quickly (as visual impressions do when the eye is immobilized). To establish the orientation of the finger in the first place pre-cuing may be necessary. It could also be derived from systematic vertical (median plane) finger scans of the vertically oriented matrix, although that is less possible for characters that occupy only the top half of the matrix. Finally, familiarity with the characters and knowledge of the finger positions relative to the body midaxis permit systematic scanning.

For fluent reading, it is essential to have established lateral scanning movements, orthogonal to the vertical edge of the text and maintaining a constant distance from the horizontal base and top edges of the paper. These are initially established by reference to body-centred coordinates. But the scanning movements of beginning readers veer downwards towards the end of lines in reading from left to right, so that beginners tend to lose lines of text.

Orientation of the finger to the text becomes crucial for fluent braille reading by readers who have established accurate lateral scanning movements and use the relation between the position of the two hands for spatial reference (Millar 1987b, 1989a).

VI   Summary

Evidence that object identification and location of shapes are differently represented was reviewed briefly. It was also suggested that for shapes the distinction between recognizing a shape and recognizing its orientation is not absolute.

It was argued that differences as well as similarities in shape coding by vision and touch have to be considered, but that they belong to different levels of enquiry and description. In the present context, the questions mainly concern differences in perceptual conditions.

The visual system provides redundant reference information for coding shape, size and depth from birth, although discrimination improves in all of these, particularly in depth cues. Haptic shape discrimination (by mouth) is also early. But while in vision shape is recognized as invariant across size that is much more difficult in touch.

It was argued that shape coding by touch differs with object type, size and depth, because the complementary information that is needed for recognition differs in three main respects: in limitations due to tactual acuity; whether and what type of information is available from active exploratory movement; the presence/absence of reliable reference cues either within patterns, or usable external or body-centred information for spatial coding and the extent of prior knowledge or pre-cuing.

Haptic coding was therefore discussed under six headings for shapes that differ in the complementary information that is available for coding: Vibrotactile patterns, shapes placed on the skin, manipulable objects, large three-dimensional objects, raised line patterns, and small raised dot patterns.

Findings on shape orientation in vision and touch were found to depend on the availability of reference information. The order of difficulty in recognizing vertical, horizontal and oblique directions, as well as right–left confusions and difficulties in coding obliques by young children, could be attributed to the amount and redundancy of reference information that distinguishes these from vertical directions. That explanation does not require an additional, specifically developmental factor.

Similarly, the presence or absence of the oblique effect in touch was accounted for by the presence or absence of reference cues in the experimental conditions. Actual differences in the complementary information, including reference cues, also explained apparent discrepancies in findings on haptic shape coding.

It was argued that, in addition to similarities between visual and haptic perception, models of coding by touch need to take into account that informational conditions, and consequent complementary inputs about tactual acuity, type of exploratory movement, and the presence and type of reference cues, differ with the size, depth, of type of objects, and with prior information in important respects.

6
Spatial coding: studies in small-scale space

The term spatial coding is used here for coding in terms of some form of reference. Thus, the location, distance and direction of the position of an object has to be specified (whether or not explicitly) with respect either to oneself, or to external anchor points or coordinates, or to both. Such specification is by no means always complete, or accurate. This chapter reviews studies which suggest how coding relates to the information that is available to subjects.

Historically, a good deal of research on spatial coding has used small-scale spatial displays. In some ways these may be thought of as 'table-top' experiments, because subjects are typically seated at a table or work-top in front of the spatial display which is the basis of the task. The reasons for that are partly practical. It is easier and quicker to set up and manipulate materials and conditions in small-scale space. Also, young infants are not yet independently mobile and tend to go to sleep when lying down. But by far the most important reason, whether or not this is explicitly recognized, is that small-scale displays such as drawings, maps and models can symbolize large-scale geographical space. Small-scale spatial layouts are thus an obvious medium for testing spatial coding.

The present chapter therefore deals with memory for locations, distances and directions in small-scale space. The use of small-scale displays as representations will be discussed in later chapters. Differences in information gained from small-scale and large-scale tasks are considered briefly first.

Mental rotation and reorganization tests of spatial representation are considered next in the context of developmental theories. Infants, school-age children, and results for blind conditions are discussed in that order. It is argued that the information which is available from the task and from longer-term experience influences modes of coding by individuals.

Representation in terms of maps and models, pictures and drawings will be considered more specifically later in relation to the topic of imagery. In the present chapter, small-scale spatial tasks are considered as tests of spatial memory and coding, in the context of hypotheses about development.

It is recognized increasingly that the informational conditions in small-scale displays are not entirely the same as conditions in large-scale or environmental space (e.g. Acredolo 1981; Slator 1982). The distinction is not absolute, particularly in visual conditions. But there are differences as well as similarities which have effects on what can be concluded from the findings.

It is necessary first to look briefly at the informational conditions of small-scale studies, before discussing the questions and findings of studies which have used small-scale displays.

Given that spatial coding means coding relative to some reference cue or frame, the first thing to consider is what information is available in small-scale space which enables such coding to take place.

The distinction between self-referent frames and external frames is important. Self-referent frames are centred on the person's body. External frames are based on information from the environment. In vision, small-scale displays can, in principle, be coded by reference to either, or to both frames.

In viewing a display from a sitting position, body-centred frames are useful, because the body is more or less stationary in that position. The body midline, head and eye positions can, therefore, provide invariant proprioceptive information about the body orientation and its relation to the limbs, and both can be related to the head and eye position.

Several different body planes (Howard & Templeton 1966) could, in principle, serve as reference frames. The most important single reference is the body midaxis (midline) or gravitational vertical axis. The transverse, horizontal plane crosses the body midline at a 90-degree angle to it. In conjunction, these can constitute body-centred coordinates. Body parts can be located with reference to each other and to this axis. Further, an external location which is viewed from a fixed position can also be referred to the body-centred frame. Moreover, people can also code the location of an object that is seen in the environment in relation to their head (e.g. Howard *et al.* 1990), hand or to other body parts.

In vision, external frames are consistently available in addition. Looked at from above, for instance, a small-scale display and its surround can be seen 'at a glance' from a single view point (Acredolo 1981). Object locations within the display can be related to each other, but can also be viewed in relation to the surrounding external frame. Moreover, eye and head movements are possible, even when the person is sitting in one position and the body is stationary. That enables the viewer to glance back and forth between objects and the surround by a few rapid head and/or eye movements.

With small-scale displays, other external frames are also provided by the room and surrounding walls. The display and the location of objects in it can be referred to that frame or to fixed external cues, since the stationary person can look beyond the table-top array and code locations by reference to the larger surrounding frame. In fact, some small-scale studies have failed to exclude these external cues when attempting to control currently available information. Clearly, interpretation of results must depend on whether or not such external cues were available to subjects.

The fact that external cues can be used in conjunction with body-centred information is important. Coordinated reference frames can be very powerful in coding spatial information, although the conjunction is not always recognized explicitly. In many studies that exclude sight, subjects initially view the target location, and only the subsequent testing is performed completely without sight (e.g. Cohen 1961; Marteniuk 1978; Paillard 1971; Polit & Bizzi 1978). For some questions that is, of course, the correct procedure. But it should not be confused with total exclusion of sight. It is possible, for instance, in these conditions to locate the target position initially in terms both of an external frame, and also as relative to current proprioceptive from eye and/or head position. The latter can be maintained after light has been excluded. Current (proprioceptive) reference cues are thus available. Such current information is relevant, if sight is excluded in order to test for memory for spatial locations. The whole point of excluding visual information is that doing so eliminates external cues which could otherwise be used as current guiding or reference frames.

Hearing is another important source of external information for spatial coding, even for small-scale displays. Within personal space, reliable sound cues produce good spatial performance in early blind subjects (Wanet & Veraart 1985). However, although testing-rooms are not necessarily completely noise-proof, ambient noise from the outside cannot usually be used to locate positions accurately on very small-scale displays. Noise from manipulating the displays itself is usually minimized for the same reason that vision is excluded.

In completely blindfolded conditions, when sitting so that the body is stationary, and there are no deliberately added auditory cues, there is usually little, if any, reliable information about external frames for coding small-scale displays. Body-centred frames, by contrast, are reliable, and self-referent coding can be used (e.g. Stelmach & Larish 1980). Such coding is not confined to the position of limbs relative to each other or to other body parts. Body-centred frames can also be used to code object locations, for instance, by coding the hand position which is touching an object by reference to the body midline.

When subjects are stationary in blindfolded conditions, information is necessarily restricted to 'personal' space, that is to say, to spatial locations that are within reach of the two arms without moving bodily to another place. Such conditions are thus of particular interest in studying both short- and long-term effects of modes of perception on coding.

I   Spatial reference in infancy

There is no doubt that children get better with age at spatial tasks, as in most other respects. The interesting question is what conditions produce this improvement. It was argued previously that spatial coding means coding with regard to reference cues or frames. A number of developmental psychologists have assumed that spatial development consists in the substitution of more advanced or complex frames of reference, for simpler or more primitive ones. Evidence on these views will be considered first.

Piaget's (Piaget & Inhelder 1948) theory assumes that infants are 'egocentric' (see earlier) spatially as in every other respect. Spatial development consists of the substitution with age of Euclidean (geometric) frames for egocentric coding.

It should be noted that in Piaget's theory the term 'egocentrism' is used in a much wider sense than is implied by the notion of body-centred reference systems. It implies that the baby has to progressively dissociate his body and his actions from the outside world and the objects in it (e.g. Werner 1948; Wapner & Werner 1957; Piaget 1954). According to Piaget, the use of external cues for search develops with the development of the object concept (see earlier) in the first two years of life.

The view that there is a qualitative developmental change from egocentric coding to coding by external reference frames is also sometimes expressed by developmental psychologists who do not subscribe to Piagetian theory (e.g. Acredolo 1977; Pufall & Shaw 1973). But they use the term in the stricter sense of body-centred coding. The infant locates objects in relation to his own body, instead of using cues in the external environment for reference. The theoretical description assumes a sequential acquisition of types of spatial knowledge (e.g. Acredolo 1977) and does not ascribe development to a change in logical/cognitive mental structures, as Piaget's theory does.

The experimental evidence, therefore, has to be looked at with two questions in mind. One is whether developmental stages are structures in the child's mind which, *inter alia*, explain performance, or whether they are merely a convenient classification device for the researcher.

I suggested earlier (Chapter 2) that describing performance formally in terms of the implied logic is not the same as a description in terms of psychological processes. Nevertheless, it is pertinent to ask whether developmental 'stages' are labels for somewhat arbitrary classifications that conveniently reduce otherwise unmanageable data or whether they label distinct qualitative changes in the child. Evidence for a substitution with age of one form of reference frame for another would constitute support for the latter position.

The second question is about the type of empirical findings which are acceptable as evidence for describing performance levels in terms of 'stages' rather than in terms of continuous development. That question is easier. Mathematically, at any rate, abrupt change can be formalized in terms of step-functions. These differ in graphic distribution and the equations which produce them from continuous mathematical functions, such as binomial curves, ogives (S-shaped functions), and more complex asymmetrical distributions of data. It is possible in principle, therefore, to look at the actual distributions of data in relation to age to see whether they conform to step-functions or to continuous distributions. However, this alone does not solve the first question. For instance, Harlow (1949) showed long ago that step-functions can be produced by amalgams of continuous data. The question at the time was whether rats and children learn mazes through sudden insight or by slow 'trial and error' procedures in which errors are progressively eliminated by negative experiences. Nevertheless, the assumption of developmental stages implies, as a first requirement, that the distribution of data should satisfy step-functions.

Looking first at the question of the substitution of reference frames, it becomes clear that the findings on object search by very young infants do not unequivocally support that assumption. The 'A-not-B' error in Piaget's theory is usually taken as evidence for 'egocentric' coding by infants (Chapter 2). This is the finding that infants below the age of nine to ten months search at the original place of hiding, rather than searching at the location to which the object has been moved subsequently. It is assumed that, if they had used external cues to guide their search, they would have looked for it at the new location. There are other possible explanations for this finding (see earlier).

On the other hand, Acredolo's (1978) longitudinal study found that, in the same informational conditions, younger infants showed more egocentric coding than older infants. Acredolo (1978) trained infants to look for the appearance of a person at one of two windows, on the right- and left-hand side, respectively, of an otherwise totally featureless room. One window was marked with a simple landmark sign. The infants were then moved (by 180 degrees) to the opposite side of the room. Six-month-olds now looked in anticipation at the wrong window, suggesting that they depended on body-centred information, which they did not update to compensate for the rotation. Eleven-month-olds looked at the correct side. They must therefore have used the 'landmark' to code the location, rather than specifying it by reference to their own body position without updating that. However, it is possible to explain this finding also by assuming that the younger subjects simply needed more salient landmarks than older infants in order to use them. That is not necessarily evidence for egocentrism. It could merely mean that coding by bodily cues is a fall-back position when there is some doubt about external information, a condition not unknown to adults.

Bremner (1978), for instance, found that distinctive external cues also obviated the 'A-not-B' error in nine-month-olds. The two hiding places, marked by visually very distinctive covers, were located to the left and right of the infant on the table at which the infant was seated. The infants were trained to retrieve a toy from 'A', as usual, and were then moved to the opposite side of the table. In these conditions they retrieved the toy from the correct (original) side. The same conditions, but using differentiated background as the visual cue, and visually identical covers for the hiding places, had produced 'egocentric' coding in an earlier study. Distinctive covers hiding a coveted toy are likely to be more salient external cues for infants than different coloured backgrounds. Bjork and Cummings (1984; Cummings & Bjork 1983) also found that specific task conditions elicit the 'A-not-B' error. They showed that infants do not necessarily return to the original place when more than one hiding place is used. This indicated that memory rather than the stage of concept development was involved. The findings suggest that infants search at what seems to them the most likely place of hiding, in all the circumstances.

It seems reasonable to suppose that independent locomotion provides infants with more evidence that external cues are useful in search tasks (Bai & Bertenthal 1992), if only because movements and changes in the external visual information correlate reliably (see Chapter 2).

Active, self-produced movement is consequently sometimes considered as essential for the change from egocentric coding to coding by external cues. Acredolo (1988a) cites a number of studies in support of the view that infants with experience of self-produced movements show less egocentric coding. Thus Bertenthal *et al.* (1984) found that infants who could crawl, and also infants who could not crawl but had experience of moving in a 'baby-walker', were better at compensating for changes of their own position to the right or left than infants without such experience. The Bremner (1978) findings also suggest that success on the A–B task was best in the condition which involved moving the infant as well as the use of differentiated covers. However, the infants did not actually move by themselves. They were carried to the opposite side of the table. One may surmise therefore that the change in visual information which movement entailed, rather than self-produced movements alone, was the important factor.

Moreover, correlations between self-produced movements and visual information also occur much earlier in visually directed reaching, for instance. The onset of independent locomotion, which happens roughly around the first birthday (plus or minus a few months), may therefore be a further reason for greater attention to external cues. But that is not necessarily evidence for an abrupt change in the use of reference frames.

Butterworth *et al.* (1982) showed that the 'A-not-B' error occurs when there is no external visual frame by which infants can monitor the movement of the object. Meuwissen and McKenzie (1987) used a circular room with a 'landmark', and trained infants aged eight months to look at a particular, fixed location, for a rewarding sight. In these conditions, the infants used the external visual cue or landmark to anticipate the reward. The experimenters point out that infants use both vision and movement. Information from these sources therefore needs to coincide rather than be discrepant. As we saw earlier (Chapter 3), even five- to six-month-old infants are sensitive to external visual movement in maintaining posture in the newly achieved skill of sitting up (Butterworth & Hicks 1977; Bertenthal & Bai 1989). Rieser (1979) tested six-month-olds to look at one of four identical windows, placed symmetrically around their line of sight. They were then turned around. At the sound of the bell which was their training cue, they looked at the window that had the same relation to their body as in training. But when the windows were distinctively patterned, the infants searched at the appropriately patterned window after being turned around. McKenzie *et al.* (1984) used a testing room from which landmarks were deliberately not excluded, and also took care to show the landmark information in front of the infants, that is to say, in their direct line of vision, and moved them only within their line of sight. These infants also coded by external cues, as was shown by their looking in anticipation at the correct window after moving.

The importance of the specific task conditions cannot be overstated. The rotation paradigm is often used to assess spatial strategies. In principle, search errors which occur after either the subject or the object is displaced by 180 degrees can certainly show whether the subject coded the location of the object by body-centred or by external reference. But not all rotation errors are due to the use of body-centred reference. Precisely the same error occurs if the person codes the position of an object by an environmental cue, and fails to update the relation when necessary.

Acredolo (1981) rightly pointed out that environmental cues were available in a number of studies which focused on rotation of small-scale models. This means that so-called 'egocentric' errors could have been due to the use of a fixed external cue to locate the object, rather than to body-centred coding of locations.

Nevertheless, it is possible to pull out some of the conditions which elicit coding by body-centred rather than by external cues. The most convincing evidence for body-centred coding comes from experimental set-ups which specifically exclude external cues. In such set-ups round spaces are created with uniformly covered walls, and without extraneous pictures, furniture or place markings. Subjects also tend to neglect specially provided external landmarks if the visual information they provide is rather marginal. Thus, landmarks are more effective if they contain an element of change that attracts attention, belong to a relevant figure rather than the background, are placed centrally instead of peripherally, and are central to the task rather than irrelevant or incidental, and when they do not conflict with body-centred information.

The fact that younger infants need more salient and reliable external cues, and that they tolerate discrepancies between vision and movement less than older infants, does require explanation. But the explanation is unlikely to involve only a single factor. The period from birth to two years sees faster development than any other period in life in physical, physiological and psychological functions. For instance, myelination (the formation of insulating sheaths around the axons of nerve fibres) is more advanced in the primary visual and motor areas of the brain than in the parietal and frontal lobes and other 'association' areas during that time (Chapter 4). Also, the striate visual cortex develops particularly fast after the age of six months.

Similarly, the behavioural evidence on the development of reaching, sitting, standing and walking (Chapter 3) suggests that motor output (executive) functions come progressively more under visual control or guidance (e.g. Bertenthal & Bai 1989).

There are thus some differential improvements that are consonant with the notion of developmental discontinuity. But the notion of discrete jumps is an exaggeration for descriptive convenience. Thus function precedes myelination, although the function is probably less efficient than when myelination is complete. Precursors of reaching for something are shown even by neonates. Further, 'stage' descriptions seem to be more appropriate for motor output skills than for input processing. The evidence on input coding in crossmodal conditions (Chapters 2 & 3) suggests that inputs from vision, touch and proprioception (haptics) are complementary and converge at all ages. It is clear that there are also general improvements in cognitive functioning, including memory (Diamond 1985). All these factors have to be taken into account in explanations of development.

In interpreting the data on infants it is salutary to remember that even adults use body-centred information in conditions of uncertainty. Any one can testify to that who has ever looked out of the window of a stationary train to wonder whether his own train, or the one next to it is moving. To make sure that it is the other train, not ours, that is moving, we stop looking, and attend to our bodily sensations.

The question whether infant development is best described in terms of continuity or discontinuities is thus misleading. It tacitly implies that spatial performance depends on a single mechanism, and ignores the fact that spatial tasks involve a number of different factors. At the least, inputs from a number of different sources and output (executive motor) factors as well as input processing must be considered. It is becoming clear that not all of these necessarily follow the same developmental path.

The findings suggest strongly that the use of external visual information is not a sudden achievement during the first two years of life, as would be expected if spatial development proceeds by stages in which one coding system is substituted for another. Quite young infants make use of external cues, as well as of body-centred cues. Better use of information with development, rather than a substitution of reference frames, therefore seems to characterize development during the infant period, while the salience of visual cues, the amount of memorizing required by the task, and the discrepancies in information between vision and movement sources seem to be responsible for apparent 'shifts' in coding systems.

II   Development: substitution or improved processing of reference information?

The notion that spatial development during childhood consists of the progressive substitution of Euclidean concepts for egocentric modes of thinking is still often accepted, even by critics of Piaget's theory of cognitive development. Moreover many of the studies on egocentric coding were originally designed to examine Piaget's theory. To look at the evidence, therefore, the terms and concepts used by that theory have to be examined first.

The important development during childhood, according to Piaget, is the substitution of egocentric representation, first by topological concepts, and finally by Euclidean metric concepts (Piaget & Inhelder 1948).

As was stressed earlier, because it is not always made explicit in experimental studies, the Piagetian notion of 'egocentrism' is a good deal wider than the notion of spatial coding in terms of body-centred reference frames, which is how the term is mainly used (e.g. Howard & Templeton 1966). Experiments testing Piaget's notion of 'egocentricity' are considered first. Later sections centre on experiments which look specifically at coding by reference to body-centred information.

The other point which was raised earlier (Chapter 2) and needs to be considered briefly concerns Piaget's notion that only children after the age of two years are able to think at a symbolic level. Younger infants merely achieve 'action schemata', which then become 'internalized' at the age of about two years. These internalized 'intuitive' representations are initially 'egocentric' and tied to what has been experienced. They have to go through stages similar to those of the earlier action schemata, but now at the level of symbolic but pre-logical intuitions. As suggested earlier

(Chapter 2), infants cannot be considered incapable of any form of representation (see also Harris 1983; Sophian 1985). At the very least, infants respond systematically, even if not always correctly, in looking for objects. That is evidence of memory for the original event. It implies some form of coding or representation (e.g. Sophian 1985).

There are clearly some distinctions between spatial behaviour and spatial thinking or problem-solving. To assume that some form of image or representation is involved in perception (e.g. Marr 1982) seems superfluous, at least phenomenologically. But when tests involve memory, some assumption that events are represented in memory needs to be made. Unfortunately, the term 'mental representation', has become something of a 'buzz' word with too many meanings. I shall, therefore say that I am using the term as operationally defined, and synonymous with coding in memory.

To test whether and how people code spatially it is necessary to demonstrate that they use reference cues to determine a location, and to assess what form of reference they are using. Such tests necessarily involve memory for a previous experience. The tests for older subjects are made more demanding; more of the information has to be remembered, updated, coordinated, or merely imagined. Consequently, the task conditions provide increasingly less, or no, current perceptual supporting cues, and impose more 'mental work' load. There is therefore no absolute distinction between testing spatial coding in infants, children and adults and good reason to suppose that representation is involved in both.

I do not mean to imply that coding is necessarily the same in all respects in all forms of mental representation (see also DeLoache 1989). For instance, older children and adults are more likely to be aware of what is required of them, and what they can do about it, and whether they know how they ought to proceed. Moreover, young children are worse than older ones also at using egocentric strategies (Rieser & Heiman 1982). But such findings can be explained without assuming stages of development.

As would be expected from his theoretical stance (Chapter 2), Piaget (Piaget & Inhelder 1948) used the formal description of performance as its psychological explanation. Children tend to code qualities such as similarity, succession (order), continuity, proximity or segregation, inclusion (inside/outside), closure (closed/open), regularity, and other relations that obtain principally within figures. Piaget therefore describes their initial spatial representation by topology, the geometry of continuous surfaces that can be bent, stretched or compressed.

According to Piaget it is the experience of manipulating objects at the same time as seeing them that leads the child to analyse forms and geometrical features. It is this which makes representation in terms of projective geometry possible. Essentially qualitative relations are projected on to extrinsic information. Coding from a fixed viewpoint precedes the coordination of different viewpoints. It is only when locations are coded from more than one viewpoint, and children can coordinate these, that they become capable of Euclidean (metric) geometrical concepts. Adult levels of logical reasoning are necessary before it is possible to use Euclidean geometry and (orthogonal, vertical and horizontal) coordinate axes to represent distance, direction and angular separation.

Laurendeau and Pinard (1970) showed that the predicted sequence of performance can be demonstrated with the type of tasks used by Piaget (Piaget & Inhelder 1948). Interestingly enough, topological coding was demonstrated by using touch. Topological features (e.g. holes which could be poked) on three-dimensional tactual shapes were discriminated and named earlier and more easily than Euclidean (metric) ones. Projective coding was found when subjects had to construct straight lines from small blocks, or to point to congruent locations on two horizontally aligned identical maps, especially when one map was also rotated by 180 degrees (Laurendeau & Pinard 1970; Piaget & Inhelder 1948). Young children do use near visual cues more than distant ones, but they can also respond to distant cues (Newcombe & Huttenlocher 1992; Presson 1980).

It is now clear that this developmental sequence depends crucially on task factors. There is ample evidence, for instance, that even very young infants visually discriminate shapes which differ in geometrical features (see earlier). The question is therefore about the task conditions which produce different forms of performance.

The fact that tactual rather than visual shapes were used to demonstrate topological relations is significant, because shape coding by touch depends crucially on systematic exploration (see earlier). Systematic exploration was found to be more difficult, in any case, for younger than for older children even with visual materials (Vurpillot 1976); this was shown in a series of experiments in which children had to judge whether two pictures of houses were identical or not, when the only differences occurred unpredictably in one of six windows. Older children scanned the windows systematically from left to right in a downward sequence, while the scanning of the houses by younger children was quite chaotic.

The reasons for more systematic scanning with age cannot be ascribed to one simple developmental factor either. Even quite young babies search systematically when looking for a familiar toy in a familiar environment, for instance.

Acredolo (1977) suggested that shifts from one form of coding to another during early and later childhood depend on the presence and salience of landmark cues, and also on familiarity. That is important. It suggests that, although formal descriptions of performance may be cast in terms of differences in spatial coding, the actual factors underlying performance differences do not consist in a change in reference frame, but evidently have to do with the attention-getting characteristics of external cues, and degrees of familiarity.

I also (Millar 1979) found that even pre-school children use current coordinate external frames to code locations in small-scale displays. In this experiment, the display was either square- or diamond-shaped and contained different toys in each of the four corners. The task was a very simple one, but was carried out with blindfolds throughout. The child was encouraged to feel the surrounding square- or diamond-shaped frame. Subjects then had to move the toys from corners of the square- or the diamond-shaped display, to the identical corners on an identical display, which was either placed either by the side, or above the standard. The square frame produced more accurate placements than the diamond shape for sighted children, whereas it made no difference whether the placement movements were in horizontal or in vertical directions. Four-year-olds were much less accurate than five-year-olds. But the pattern of responses, which showed that their location placements were affected by the type of frame or surround, were precisely the same. The results showed very clearly that even very young children use external frames, and that their relatively poor performance cannot be ascribed to the use of a different coding system than shown by older children. Evidence that young children use external reference frames for coding has also been shown by Somerville and Bryant (1985) and Bryant and Somerville (1986).

It needs to be stressed that different findings with different task conditions should not be considered an obstacle to explaining spatial coding. On the contrary, they are an extremely important part of the description and explanation. The rotation paradigm is a particularly good example of this, and will be discussed further both for that reason, and because the paradigm has been used more than any other in studies designed to look at mental spatial representation.

III   Mental rotation and mental spatial reorganization tasks

The main methods of investigating the manner in which people represent spatial information mentally have been tests of mental rotation or reorganization. Typically people view a spatial array and are then asked to imagine the display as rotated, or updated, or they have to infer the relation of unseen locations or directions from current information in the display.

The most famous example of the rotation paradigm for testing mental spatial representation is the 'three mountains' task, invented by Piaget (Piaget & Inhelder 1948) to show that children below the age of ten years cannot use logical coordination of perspectives. The child sat facing one

side of a model of three mountains (from 12 to 30 cm high) pasted on a
(1 m) pasteboard square. The child's task was to imagine what a wooden
doll would see from various different locations at the edge of the square,
and to reproduce these perspectives by arranging three pieces of cardboard, shaped and coloured like the mountains, in the appropriate perspective arrangement. A second test was to move the child to the different
positions, and get her to reproduce the arrangement she saw from these.
Finally, the child again had to imagine the doll's view from different
positions, and to recognize which of ten pictures represented the doll's
view. Groups of children aged 4 to 6, 6 to 8, 8 to 9, and 9 to 12 years took
part. By looking at the details of all the tests, performance was classified
into a number of substages, ranging from the child reproducing only his
own view, to what was called 'a simple coordination' of perspectives by the
age of about 10. It is not entirely clear whether even the oldest children
solved the first rotation problem in these conditions.

In an unpublished experiment with 32 Oxford University undergraduates, I found that only three of these highly intelligent, educated adults
actually performed correctly on an only slightly more complicated version
of the perspective task. A pen was placed, for three seconds only, on the
table in front of them, with the tip pointing straight towards the opposite
side of the table. The subject was then asked to visualize mentally what the
pen would look like to some one who stood at a different (opposite corner)
position of the table, and to draw that view immediately on a nearby
(upright) board. Nearly all subjects kept looking back at the test corner
while drawing, as if to visualize the direction, and also reported that they
had tried to imagine it visually. Most of the responses by these spatially
sophisticated people were 'egocentric' in the sense that they depicted the
subject's own original viewpoint. A few subjects showed the pen in an
altered direction, but failed to realize that the pen would necessarily lie at a
45 degree angle relative to the corner, with the tip pointing down from left
to right. They had no such difficulty when asked subsequently about the
relevant geometric relations.

The task and conditions had been complicated quite deliberately, of
course. The instruction to 'visualize' the pen was intended to (and evidently
did) focus attention on visual information and imagery. It suggested that
the actual recent visual layout should be mentally transformed. To do that
required at least two changes in the direction of surface planes to get the
correct new baseline for drawing the direction of the pen. The point is that,
with the exception of the time constraints, these conditions were essentially
similar to those imposed by Piaget, and led a high proportion of intelligent
young adults to make the same error as young children.

The apparent paradox that visual strategies, rather than body-centred
information here contributed to 'egocentric' coding, is instructive. As we

saw earlier, so-called 'egocentric' errors can result if environmental land-marks are present and are used as 'fixed' cues (Presson 1980; Proscura 1976). Piaget indeed specifically maintained that young children tend to be deceived by perceptual appearances, and considered this as further evidence for intuitive (non-logical) egocentrism.

Humans (and apes) do tend to rely on visual information, and for very good reasons. Vision normally provides reliable, and continuously updated information about the relation between external planes as we move about the environment. It is precisely for that reason that it is easy to fail to realize, or to forget, that attending solely to visual information can be deleterious in some spatial tasks. Many mental rotation tasks are solved more easily by ignoring than by using current visual information. Typically, in these tasks current visual information is static and conflicts with the correct final disposition of distances, angles and directions of constituents of the layout, and with attempts to envisage moving constituents and update their relations (Newcombe & Huttenlocher 1992).

Evidence that the current view of a scene does interfere with imagining the layout from a different perspective was found for children by Walker and Gollin (1977). They used a small dolls' house with distinctive walls, a hand puppet as the supposed observer, and photographs from which the child had to choose the puppet's various viewpoints. Removing the immediate visual input by shielding the child's view from distracting cues reduced specifically 'egocentric' errors significantly. Other types of errors were not affected by removing the immediate visual input. There is a good deal of further evidence that egocentric responses depend on task conditions (e.g. Fishbein *et al.* 1972; Pick & Acredolo 1983; Salatas & Flavell 1976; Schacter & Gollin 1979).

A point that needs mentioning is that the form in which instructions are given is another factor which elicits different forms of coding in mental rotation tasks. Huttenlocher and Presson (1979) showed experimentally that the form in which the mental rotation question was asked determined the kind of errors children made. In an earlier (1973) study they had found that a perspective-taking task in which the viewer imagines himself (or some one else) in a different position was more difficult than a similar task in which the subject is supposed to rotate the display to different test positions. The differences were reversed when the question was altered and subjects actually moved to the test positions in the perspective-taking tasks.

Huttenlocher and Presson (1973) originally assumed that, in mental rotation tasks, children, like adults (e.g. Shepard & Feng 1972; Shepard & Metzler 1971), visually imagine spatial layouts and mentally track positions on them. But they also found evidence of a simpler strategy by which children evidently attempted to mentally reconstruct the spatial layout from the final location. Evidence for such coding was also found by Millar (1976) in a rotation task. Young children had to imagine the orientation of a line after rotating its surround or walking around the surround. The pattern of errors suggested that they tried to think of the rotated location from the endpoint.

Shantz and Watson (1971) showed that when an impossible 'perspective' view is included, young children choose that more often than they choose the egocentric view, as representing the view that a doll would have from a different perspective. It suggested that quite young children know that the doll would see a different view, even if they did not quite know precisely what that would be.

A neat mental rotation study by Fishbein *et al.* (1972) also questioned whether young children are unable to imagine that someone else's viewpoint differs from their own. They showed pre-school children a display with doll figures, and asked which side of a doll another doll would see from a given position. The children selected the correct photograph.

The task was clearly simpler than the Piaget task in a number of ways. The question was both more familiar, and presumably made more sense within a child's everyday experience. The question was also less misleading than the Piagetian one. The difference about which the children were asked pertained to different sides of a single object or shape, rather than to differences in the spatial alignment of three objects. The fact that different sides of a person differ in rather more respects than the three mountains in Piaget's paradigm may also have contributed to the conditions which allowed pre-schoolers to solve the mental rotation problem correctly.

We do not know as yet whether all potential sources of error in rotation tasks are of equal weight. However, the fact that complicated rotation problems often involve a change in the baseline between presentation and solution is known to be a source of error also.

Another complication relates to the type of responses that children are asked to produce. As Kosslyn and his colleagues showed (Kosslyn *et al.* 1977), it cannot be assumed that children's drawings are a direct indication of their spatial understanding.

The evidence from studies of spatial development during childhood thus suggests that development cannot be described adequately in terms of a change from using one type of reference frame for another.

Mental rotation (and reorganization) tasks vary in the complexity of information they involve, and in the amount of mental work load that they impose. The developmental data can be explained more simply in terms of the informational conditions to which the child is exposed: the salience (e.g. proximity) of cues, conflict between actual and imagined reference frames, and the amount and complexity of mental work which is involved.

The other famous paradigm which has been much used to assess mental rotation was pioneered by Shepard and his colleagues (e.g. Shepard & Cooper 1982; Shepard & Metzler 1971).

In the prototypical study, sighted adults viewed two drawings of three-dimensional nonsense objects which consisted of a number of small cubes that had apparently been built to project at various angles. Subjects had to judge whether two drawings depicted the same objects, rotated with respect to each other, or different objects. The time it took people to judge the same objects correctly increased linearly with the degree of rotation of the objects relative to each other. A linear increase with the degree of rotation would be expected if a person actually rotated the objects in order to judge whether they were the same. The linear increase in judgement time was therefore interpreted as showing mental rotation of a visual image. A linear increase in response time was also found in a task of mentally unfolding paper cubes and the like (Shepard & Feng 1972), again suggesting that mental manipulation mirrored the time it would have taken to actually manipulate the object. Similar findings have been reported for young children (Marmor & Strauss 1975). The topic of mental imagery which this raises will be considered in a later chapter (Chapter 8). Here it may merely be noted that the degree and number of rotations that would be required to solve a task, if subjects follow instructions literally, may also add to the memory load.

IV Evidence from blind conditions

Only the manifestly false assumption that vision is the only source of spatial information could imply that mental spatial rotation tasks and reorganization or inference tasks are impossible to solve in the absence of visual experience. As would be expected, there is evidence that such tasks *can* be solved by blind people (e.g. Kerr 1983; Landau, Spelke & Gleitman 1984; Leonard & Newman 1967; Millar 1975b, 1976, 1981b, 1990a).

At the same time, there is also considerable evidence that congenitally totally blind children and adults usually have specific difficulties in tasks that require mental reorganization of spatial relations between external locations and directions (Byrne & Salter 1983; Hatwell 1985; Millar 1975b, 1976, 1979, 1981b; O'Connor & Hermelin 1975; Warren 1974, 1977; Worchel 1951).

The findings do not, of course, contradict each other. They appear paradoxical only if the question is about the presence or absence of a supposed 'ability'. At the same time, it is not possible simply to substitute one set of findings for the other. The fact that people without sight can solve spatial problems cannot even be treated as a refutation of philosophical empiricism, because although vision is important, it is not the only sense modality that can provide spatial information. Equally, spatial difficulties neither indicate lack of potential, nor can they be considered irrelevant. It is essential to analyse findings in detail if we are to understand the factors and conditions that drive performance.

Consider the careful series of experiments by Hatwell (1985). It showed that congenitally blind children were seriously retarded on Piagetian spatial tasks, compared to adventitiously blind children and to sighted children. The tasks involved displacement of differently shaped objects on symmetrical and asymmetrical spatial layouts, as well as rotation of a frame with six compartments which contained six different objects. On the rotation task, the congenitally blind eleven-year-olds worked at the level of six-year-old sighted children.

Curiously enough, as Hatwell (1985) points out, the mental rotation of six locations which she used should actually have been very familiar to her blind children, because of their experience in writing braille by hand frames. Writing in that manner consists of indenting the relevant braille dots from the reverse side of the page. In terms of spatial orientation, the indented (written) letter shape is thus the rotated (mirror) image of the raised-dot (read) shape. Not only that, in addition to having (apparently) to mentally rotate mirror images on reversed sides of a page to represent the same letter, braillists would also have to assign different letters to the same mirror images when they appear on the same page. Hatwell explains that this apparent experience in mental rotation evidently did not help, because braille patterns are usually learned initially by numbers. The first (left) three vertical positions of the six (2×3) dot matrix are numbered '1-2-3-'. The second (right) three vertical positions are numbered '4-5-6'. The number formula for a letter (e.g. 1-3-4-5 for 'N') is therefore the same in writing the letter from right to left (indenting from the reverse side), as in reading the same (reversed shape) letter on the other side from left to right.

I have also assumed (Millar 1978c) that mediation by numbering can explain how beginners cope with the fact that the Perkins braille machine, which is currently used for writing by English children, has a horizontal keyboard, although braille letters are oriented vertically. Depressing the appropriate, horizontally aligned keys (e.g. 1-3-4-5 for 'N') simultaneously, produces the vertically oriented (1-3-4-5 'N') character on the page for reading. If braillists actually coded braille characters as global shapes (i.e. as they look visually), they would need to mentally rotate each side of a character by 90 degrees in order to translate between read and written forms. Mediation by numbering obviates the need for constant complicated mental rotations. It may be noted in parenthesis that the initial numbering system evidently drops out as recognition and production of characters becomes more automatic. Coding certainly changes with fluency (Millar 1987b).

Two considerations are relevant to the apparent rotation puzzle. One is the assumption that braille reading necessarily constitutes special practice in training mental rotation, because braille patterns are reversed in writing. That is not so, because the system used in early training obviates the need for mental spatial rotation. The second is that levels of efficiency are not necessarily indications of how the performance was achieved.

Blind children certainly can and do read braille letters in one orientation, and write the same letters in the completely (180 degree) reversed orientation. They thus solve what is formally a rotation problem. The point is that there is more than one way to solve most problems. It is important to discover what these are.

Hatwell (1985) is almost certainly right to suggest that the reason why congenitally totally blind children often have more difficulty with mental spatial reorganization and rotation than the sighted has to do with differences in perceptual information.

Theories (e.g. Revesz 1950) which suggested that the blind rely on haptic coding did not consider mental representation or coding heuristics as identical with the formal logical description of performance levels, as Piaget did. But, more importantly, the Piagetian scheme implies that solutions to (progressively more difficult) Piagetian tasks indicate the developmental nature of mental spatial structures. The fact that the blind children solved the Piagetian tasks in the same order as the sighted, but at later ages, is thus taken to mean that the nature of spatial structuring is the same, but that visual deprivation retards that construction (Hatwell 1985, p. 66). That inference, however, follows only if it is assumed that the formal (logical) description of the performance level is isomorphic with the psychological processes that underlie that performance.

Hatwell's (1985) studies need to be considered carefully. The lag in performance which she reports is important. It will be argued later that sudden 'jumps' in performance levels need to be examined in relation to the (usually complex) task conditions. The question is whether Hatwell's findings necessarily support the widespread view that the blind lag behind the sighted in spatial/cognitive development.

It should be said that Hatwell herself (1985) does not interpret her data as evidence for stages. Her data on the performance of children at different ages do not actually indicate the 'jumps' in accuracy which the assumption of developmental stages implies. Millar (1976, experiment 1) also failed to find sudden discontinuities in accuracy with age, or with blindness when simple tactual recognition (matching to sample) of directions was compared to tactual recognition of the same directions in a difficult Piagetian perspective-taking task. Older children were better than younger ones, as might be expected. But there was no evidence of the interaction between age and tasks which is implied by the assumption that eleven- to twelve-year-olds operate on a different intellectual plane than five- to six-year-olds.

Equality or difference in performance level does not, as such, necessarily allow us to infer whether or not subjects used logical/spatial (geometric) constructs, or some other form of coding. Indeed, the findings mentioned earlier which showed that task factors, such as salience of information, memory load, and familiarity of task and materials influence performance indicate that performance levels alone are not sufficient as evidence for such an interpretation.

Levels of efficiency do have to be considered in relation to the forms of coding which are elicited by task demands and informational conditions. Errors can be described in terms of their formal logical status. But without specific evidence the idea that the formal description entails that the child possesses matching logical (or illogical) internal mental 'structures' cannot be sustained.

The alternative view implies that it is important to distinguish between what is designated as a 'spatial task', the information that is currently available to a person in that task, and the manner in which the person codes the information in memory.

A case in point was the apparent need for complicated mental shape rotations in reading and writing braille, whereas this can be solved by a number system that does not involve shape coding at all (Hatwell 1985).

Further, for the sighted, mental rotation tasks typically provide conflicting current (external) views. Current external references need to be excluded by blindfolding subjects if we want to test for coding in memory. However, that raises the question of what current (short-term) cues are actually available in blind conditions and what, if any, effect they exert on coding.

Short-term as well as long-term informational conditions are relevant. Consider the earlier example of intelligent adults who were deliberately misled into using a visual rather than a geometrical strategy to solve a difficult mental rotation problem. The ease with which they were misled suggests a habitual reliance on visual information. If we look at the long-term experience of the sighted, such reliance is normally perfectly justified. Conversely, in blind conditions, touch and movement normally provide the most reliable information about the relation between directional planes. The blind would be equally justified in relying on that information in memory.

The problem is not, therefore, whether the mode of perceptual experience determines logical constructs. The question is rather whether, and if so how, long-term prior experience, derived respectively from vision or from touch and movement, influences habitual, or preferred, forms of coding.

My (Millar 1976, experiment 2) study was specifically designed to look at modes of coding (representation) rather than at the level of efficiency exhibited by blind and blindfolded sighted children. There was no reason to suppose that they would differ on simple haptic recognition or on Piaget-type tasks that primarily test intellectual skill and memory load, and that was borne out. The blind and sighted were equally good on a matching-to-sample task. They had to choose a matchstick, fastened to a square base, from others that were fastened to the base in different orientations. Similarly, the typical Piagetian instructions to find an orientation which some one else would see or feel from changed baselines produced a lot of errors. These were not noticeably 'egocentric'. Most children knew quite well whether the matchhead was near the subject or near the experimenter who sat opposite.

The hypothesis was that long-term informational conditions would affect the mode of coding, rather than reduce the level of efficiency on all spatial tasks. In vision, directions are most easily coded by reference to the spatial layout. It was therefore expected that sighted children would be predisposed to code in terms of configurations or 'layouts'. In purely haptic conditions, on the other hand, movements are more reliable than external layouts. It was argued, therefore, that long-term haptic experience would predispose congenitally totally blind children to rely more on memory for movements in haptic conditions.

Blindfolded sighted children between the ages of 5 and 12 years were matched on age, sex, socioeconomic background, intelligence and memory span (verbal/digit span) to congenitally totally blind children. Subjects felt a single straight line from one position on a table. The subject then moved to test positions (at 45–90–135–180–225–270–315 degree locations) around the table, and had to draw (on paper that produces raised lines) the line from these positions. In another condition, the subject remained stationary and rotated a square with the (previously felt) line to the same test positions.

Evidence for coding differences was looked for in error patterns rather than overall efficiency. To assess modes of coding, easier forms of rotation (Huttenlocher & Presson 1973) were used. Huttenlocher and Presson (1973) suggested that their children used a 'regenerative' strategy. They tried to mentally reconstruct the layout from the test positions. With such a (not necessarily conscious) visuospatial strategy, there should be no difference in reconstructing the final direction from different test positions. There should, therefore, be no significant drop in accuracy for constructing directions to test positions that involved more rather than fewer movements, such as oblique and distant positions. By contrast, coding in terms of movements should produce lower accuracy specifically for those test positions.

Evidence for movement coding was therefore expected to show increased errors for far compared to near rotations, and for oblique directions. Movements tend to be organized sequentially, by event-to-event
rather than by event-to-position associations (Keele 1968). Also, short-
term haptic memory (see also later) deteriorates relatively rapidly (Laabs
& Simmons 1981; Posner 1967) with delay, unless haptic inputs are familiar
or recoded (Gilson & Baddeley 1969; Millar 1974; Sullivan & Turvey
1974). If subjects use movement coding, therefore, accuracy would de-
crease rapidly with the number of movement shifts in rotations. It was also
assumed that coding movements would make it more difficult to rotate a
straight line to oblique directions. That is because obliques require two
coordinated specifications (e.g. Pufall & Shaw 1973). An oblique needs to
be specified relative to both vertical and horizontal axes, for instance, as
'top-right to bottom-left', or 'bottom-right to top-left'. Such coordinated
reference would be more difficult if directions were coded in terms of a
sequentially organized movement sequence.

The results were consistent with the coding hypotheses. The blind children showed haptic coding, in that they were less accurate at distant than at
near test locations and had particular difficulty with positions that should
have been produced with oblique directions. The patterns of scores by the
blindfolded sighted children did not differ with particular directions or test
locations. It was thus consistent with a 'regenerative' strategy.

It must be stressed again that the difference between blind and blindfolded sighted children was not in overall efficiency, or accuracy of rotation. The difference lay in the form of coding they used, which was evident
from the detailed pattern of results. Thus the configurational–regenerative
strategy by the sighted was not particularly accurate overall. Moreover, the
blind were quite as good on rotating to near orthogonal directions, a very
important finding in its implications for means of training.

Further evidence for movement versus quasi-configurational modes of
coding was also found in a memory task which used forward and backward
recall of positions in a (hand) movement path (Millar 1975b). An open
five-sided maze-like figure, presented in four different orientations, was
traced with a stylus to near (to the start) and far (near the end) stop
locations. Forward recall was tested by retracing the path to the (near or
far) test (without stop) position. The movement sequence to the stop was
thus the same. Backward recall was from the end of the figure. If the
location had been remembered by the movement sequence, the sequence
and the location on it had to be reversed. On the other hand, if the location
was remembered relative to a (reconstructed) configuration of the path,
there was no reason for backward recall to be worse. Blind and blindfolded
sighted between the ages of six and twelve years were matched on age, sex,
intelligence, and also on backward as well as forward verbal (digit) recall.

Age was significant, as usual, and, interestingly enough, interacted with the use of advance information (given in half the trials) about what needed to be recalled. That use of general information was not related to sighted status. But the pattern of error was different for the blind and sighted. Errors by the blind conformed to a sequential movement strategy: forward recall, especially for the near (the start) position, was as accurate as for the sighted. But their errors for backward recall were significantly higher than for forward recall, especially for the near (i.e. now furthest from the end) position. The error pattern by the sighted children (tested blind) was consistent with a (not very accurate) regenerative strategy. Errors were no worse for backward than forward recall, and, if anything, the near (furthest from the end) location was rather more accurate in backward recall. An attempt to reconstruct the layout from the position reached at the end of the movement sequence best accounts for that.

The findings clearly suggest that, in these conditions, the quasiconfigurational (regenerative) coding shown by the sighted in blind conditions was not very accurate. Indeed, such coding is not necessarily more efficient overall. Coding a location in terms of the movements made to reach it does not imply that coding is impossible. Configurational (regenerative) coding, although usually inaccurate, does have specific advantages over sequential movement coding in some conditions. For instance, where the to-be-remembered movement sequence is long, or when the problem involves the coordination of sequences, coding in terms of a spatial layout or configuration can be easier.

A deservedly much-cited study which apparently contradicts these results is that of Marmor and Zaback (1976). The study is usually quoted as if it showed that rotation effects were identical for blind and sighted adults. In fact, Marmor and Zaback (1976) actually reported significant differences for far rotations, similar to Millar's (1976) result.

Marmor and Zaback (1976) used discrimination of rotated objects, rather than recall of mentally rotated locations or directions. Flat V-shaped objects with asymmetric rounded tops, indented on one side, were used. Congenitally blind (some with residual light perception), late blind, and sighted adults judged whether or not the left-hand standard was the same shape as the rotated (by 30 degrees from 0 to 150 degrees) right-hand object. The assumption, based on Shepard & Metzler (1971), was that an increase in response time with increased degrees of object rotation indicates mental rotation of a visual image. The fact that the blind showed an increase with increased degrees of rotation was thus taken to mean that the blind performed mental rotations, and that mental images are abstract. However, the blind actually showed a significantly steeper increase in response latencies and errors with degrees of rotation than the sighted. That does not square with the hypothesis, either in the original or revised form. The additional assumption that prior visual experience produces an overall advantage might have accounted for the overall significantly slower (higher intercept) response times and larger errors by the blind. But that would not explain why they showed a significantly steeper increase with far rotations, nor would these be expected on the hypothesis that the blind and sighted mentally rotated an abstract image. By contrast, the hypothesis that the blind tend to code in terms of movements would predict a steeper increase for far rotations by the blind, and this was found also by Millar (1976). Further, Marmor and Zaback (1976) also found that at least some of the sighted adults reported strategies which were very similar to the 'regenerative' coding observed in sighted children (e.g. Huttenlocher & Presson 1973; Millar 1975b, 1976), which accounted for the fact that the response times of sighted adults showed a much flatter slope and some curvature.

Results which show significant differences in the rate of increase of response times and errors, rather than overall slower or less accurate responding, strongly suggest differences in coding. Moreover, these differences were in precisely the same direction as those found for children by Millar (1975b, 1976). Thus, the detailed findings on coding in these studies, far from being contradictory, are in fact completely consistent.

The same is true for the findings of the widely known and quoted study by Carpenter and Eisenberg (1978). The underlying hypothesis was, as before, that a linear increase in response time with increased object rotation is evidence for mental rotation of an image. Subjects were congenitally blind (although seven out of twelve reported some restricted prior visual experience) and sighted adults, tested in haptic conditions. They had to judge whether a (raised) capital letter (F or P), that is to say, a known form with one straight side and a right-branching top, was in normal or in laterally reversed format. The letter was presented in a clockwise-rotated orientation (in 60-degree steps from 0 through to 300 degrees from the upright). It included the 180-degree (vertically inverted) orientation which had not been included in the previous study. Perhaps not surprisingly, response times tended to be highest for that orientation, probably because a 180-degree inversion of a right branching form is most easily confused with the reversed inverted orientation of that form. However, the important increase of response times with increased rotation was significantly steeper for the blind than for the sighted, and it was also significantly linear only for the blind. Response times by the sighted were actually curvilinear, as Carpenter and Eisenberg (1978) were careful to point out. A curvilinear distribution of responses is clearly not consistent with the hypothesis that the sighted rotated an image (whether visual or not) in that experiment. Carpenter and Eisenberg (1978) also varied the subject's arm and hand position relative to the stimulus orientation in some conditions, and showed that the sighted, but not the blind, seemed to code stimulus orientations relative to the hand. That certainly supports their suggestion that the sighted used some form of spatial coding. However, that interpretation cannot, at the same time, explain the significantly different findings for the blind. Nor can such specific differences be attributed to the overall slower response times by the blind. Any argument that lack of vision simply slows responses is contradicted by the fact that the congenitally blind were actually faster on unrotated letters, but showed linear increases with further rotations. The assumption that the mode of experience has little or no effect on mental representation is not consistent with such findings.

In a study which assumes that the distributions of response data indicate modes of coding, significant differences in the predicted distributions for different groups have to be taken seriously. On that criterion, the blind clearly differed in coding from the sighted. More interestingly, if the original assumptions were correct, the results show that the blind, but not the sighted, used mental rotation of an image. That would be quite difficult to explain. By contrast, the hypothesis that the blind used movement coding more than the sighted (e.g. Millar 1975b, 1976) would have predicted the differentially steeper increase in response time by the blind with far rotations.

It is of considerable interest that the Carpenter and Eisenberg (1978) findings are similar to the findings of Marmor and Zaback (1976), and are also consistent with Millar's (1975b, 1976) results for children.

The findings have been examined in some detail because such details show the conditions on which apparently contradictory findings depend. It is evident that blind children 'can' perform mental rotations, even from studies which have found considerable delays with age (e.g. Hatwell 1978) or higher error rates in some conditions (Worchel 1951). The point of looking at the nature of coding (e.g. Millar 1975b, 1976, 1979, 1981b) rather than at levels of efficiency is to explain how differences in difficulty may arise.

The fact that modes of coding differ does not, of course, imply that shape cannot be coded by touch. Modes of coding are important, not because coding strategies are unalterable, but, on the contrary, precisely because they are alterable if one knows what information is needed for given tasks.

What the findings suggest is that in blind conditions reliable information comes mainly from proprioceptive sources, and spatial coding tends to depend on body-centred reference. When these sources are disrupted, as in tasks that demand rotation or updating, errors are more likely. The simple 'can/cannot' dichotomy confuses the task label with the processes that underlie solving the tasks.

V   Spatial reference, movement coding, and cognitive strategies

Memory for movements is not, of course, peculiar to the blind. Evidence on movement coding in blind conditions comes from a whole body of findings on short-term motor memory by sighted adults (e.g. Laabs & Simmons 1981). Most of the literature on movement is concerned with control systems in the execution of tasks, rather than with movement as a potential system for gathering and remembering information. The enormous and fascinating topic of the organization and control of movements is beyond the brief of the present book. But the findings on short-term memory for movements by adults are pertinent, and are considered next, even if only briefly.

One question about short-term motor memory is whether or not it depends on attentional and cognitive resources. Short-term verbal memory has typically invited such a description (e.g. Atkinson & Shiffrin 1968; Miller 1956). A major test has been to see whether irrelevant, but cognitively demanding, tasks disturb recall. If that applies to motor memory, recall of a movement should be disrupted if the person has to perform another cognitively demanding task simultaneously, or during the short delay before recall is required.

Linear positioning tasks have been most often used in such studies. Subjects are blindfolded. Their task is to trace a line, or move a slide along a horizontal guide to a stop. The movement is then reproduced by the subject (without the stop) after a short delay. During delays the subject either does nothing, or performs a secondary task. The results were variable. Posner (1967) argues that visual and movement (kinaesthetic) codes differ. When vision is present, recall does not change over short delays, except when the delay periods are filled with attention-demanding tasks (e.g. counting backwards in threes). By contrast, recall of blind movements deteriorates with delay (e.g. Adams & Dijkstra 1966; Pepper & Herman 1970) rather than with difficult cognitive tasks (Posner & Konick 1966).

Laabs (1973) distinguished experimentally between kinaesthetic (felt movement) coding and spatial coding in blind conditions. To do so, he varied cues for movement distance (extent) and the end location of the movement, independently. To test for memory of extent, the movement started (and needed to end) at different locations in recall than in the original presentation. To test for recall of the end position, the (same) end location was to be recalled, but the extent of the movement was changed for recall.

Under these conditions, adults are much more accurate in coding the end location than the extent of the movement (Kelso *et al.* 1978, 1982;

Laabs & Simmons 1981; Stelmach *et al.* 1975). The main interpretation is that recall of movement distance is variable and less accurate because it depends mainly on memory of the kinaesthetic (movement) input, and that recall of end locations is accurate because they can be coded by reference to a body-centred spatial frame (Marteniuk 1978; Russell 1976). An example would be to code the end location by reference to a frame centred on the trunk midline. There would be no need to change or update that coding for recall.

The detailed examination of consistent findings from quite diverse studies suggests that prior haptic experience tends to elicit more sequential movement coding, while prior visual experience tends to elicit more coding with respect to some current or remembered spatial reference. The literature on the short-term motor memory of adults also suggests the importance of reliable position information (e.g. Imanaka & Abernethy 1992; Larish *et al.* 1984; Wallace 1977; Wallace *et al.* 1982; Walsh 1981).

The findings raise further questions about the short-term informational conditions which may elicit movement coding and also coding by spatial reference, either relative to a (remembered or reconstituted) external frame, or by reference to a body-centred frame.

In the studies by Marmor and Zaback (1976) and by Carpenter and Eisenberg (1978) subjects were discriminating actual objects that had been placed in different orientations. Blind as well as sighted subjects therefore had reliable body-centred as well as hand-movement information. In principle, they could have coded object orientations in terms of exploratory hand movements, or else spatially by reference to body-centred (e.g. midline) frames, or both. My own (Millar 1975b, 1976) experimental conditions, by contrast, made body-centred coding deliberately difficult, in order to elicit mental updating of the direction or location of the object. The rotation tasks (Millar 1976) involved movement in geographical space, or rotating the square plate which contained the to-be-rotated line. In the memory experiment (Millar 1975b), the actual configuration of the traced path was presented in four different orientations. Coding a direction relative to the body did not, therefore, bear an invariant relation to the orientation or location of the object in either study.

The results thus suggest that conditions which disrupt self-referent spatial coding tend to elicit coding by some (not necessarily accurate) reconstructed external frame, and more movement coding, respectively, by the sighted and blind. The relation between short-term body-centred and movement information thus needed to be explored further.

It may be assumed that body-centred reference frames are crucial for all moving animals. It is necessary for the animal to know (how far that is conscious is a separate question) where its limbs are in relation to each other and to the head and the trunk of the body. Further, body-centred frames can also be used to code the location of external objects which are touched by parts of the body. That also applies to movement directions, in so far as they are specified relative to a reference frame centred on the body (e.g. Howard & Templeton 1966). However, the sighted do not normally need to rely on that system alone.

In blind conditions, body-centred as well as movement information is available, and is more reliable than external cues when the subject remains stationary (Revesz 1950). In Piaget's terminology, body-centred spatial reference and memory for kinaesthetic cues are both 'egocentric'. However, movement coding is 'egocentric' only in that the information depends on what is felt. Body-centred spatial coding, on the other hand, implies that the body midline (or some other body part) is used systematically as a reference frame, so that locations and directions are to be specified in relation to it. To elicit body-centred spatial coding, therefore, the to-be-remembered location must have a relatively invariant relation to the body-centred frame. That also needs to be distinguished experimentally from memory for movements.

It is sometimes argued that cues from positioning movements are irrelevant even in blind conditions, because adults code locations spatially (e.g. Paillard 1971; Polit & Blizzi 1978). However, spatial coding in terms of body-centred information which includes proprioception is important in that case (Diewert & Stelmach 1978; Schmidt 1968; Stelmach 1969).

The role of body-centred information in studies using blind conditions when there has in fact been prior sight, if only briefly, of the target location is more complicated. In such conditions it is possible first to code the location of the target relative to an environmental (external) frame, and also to orient the eyes and/or head and body, and to maintain that orientation sufficiently accurately during delays, so as to point to or reach the target also in darkness. Cues from the positioning movement as such would be less important in that case.

Jeannerod (1991) suggests that a 'proprioceptive map' of limb positions may need calibration by vision. This is based on findings which show that reaching and aiming movements are more accurate with vision than when vision is occluded.

There is a wealth of evidence from studies of the posterior parietal cortex (Jeannerod 1988, 1991) that inputs from vision, touch and movement, including eye movements (proprioception), converge. At the same time, even when vision is excluded, memory for (end) locations is more accurate than memory for kinaesthetic information (Laabs & Simmons 1981; Marteniuk 1978). Moreover, even irrelevant cues from movement extents and directions interfere with target location by adults in blind conditions (Laabs & Simmons 1981; Marteniuk 1978; Wallace 1977).

Ann and Michael Colley (1981) tested recall of the distance and end location of horizontal arm movements by congenitally blind adults, and adults blinded later in life. The congenitally blind showed larger errors and more variance than the late-blind, but both groups were more accurate on recall of the end location than of distance. The findings show that location and distance are also coded differently from each other in the total absence of vision. They also show that long-term visual experience was an advantage for both distance and location coding. One explanation is that all subjects used body-centred reference frames (e.g. Marteniuk 1978; Russell 1976), and that long-term visual experience served to calibrate that reference system. Alternatively, prior visual experience may elicit coding in terms of a more externally based reference frame.

Few studies on children have varied memory for movements and self-referent spatial coding independently. Millar's (1981b) study aimed specifically to separate these. To ensure that body-centred coding could be used reliably, the test locations were invariant (right or left) relative to the subject's body midline. Distinctive toys marked the near and the far locations in the projected vertical plane. To test for self-referent coding, the display was rotated by 180 degrees. The subject was informed of this and was also able to feel the change in the location of the two toys. The subject's task was to indicate the test position relative to the reversed toy figure after rotation. To test for movement coding, the end location and distance of the positioning movement remained invariant relative to the subject's midline in recall. But the kinaesthetic input of the recall movement differed from the positioning movement, because it started from a different location.

The results showed that congenitally totally blind children, aged between six and fourteen years, were as accurate as (closely matched) blindfolded sighted children in control conditions, in which movement inputs were unchanged, and self-referent coding was appropriate. But changing the recall movement disturbed recall, and more so for blind children (Millar 1981b). The finding is consistent with the Colleys' (Colley & Colley 1981) results on adults, and suggests that movement information was used in memory. The blind children also showed a highly significant tendency to use self-referent coding. Thus, the proportion of responses that related the test location to their own midline after rotations was well above chance level for the congenitally blind even up to the age of fourteen years. Although some of the responses by the sighted were also to the wrong side, the proportion of such responses by the sighted was below chance level even for six-year-olds. Thus, although rotations produced larger errors by all subjects, the type of error which showed self-referent coding related specifically to prior visual experience, and not to age.

These findings are important because they distinguish specifically between self-referent spatial coding and memory for movement in children, and support the hypothesis that movement information is coded in short-term memory. The results also suggest that long-term haptic experience tends to elicit self-referent coding more than prior visual experience.

Mental rotation and reorganization problems tend to impose a considerably greater memory and 'mental work' load than more straightforward problems. The question whether modes of long-term information also influence coding in simple tasks that involve no mental rotation and have a minimal mental work load was tested in the experiment, described earlier (Millar 1979) which varied the shape of the background frame, and the direction of hand movements in a simple shift task. The background was either an easy square shape, or a more difficult diamond shape, and toys had to be moved from one of these to identical locations on a similar shape. The hand movements in moving the toys were either in vertical directions and could be coded relative to the body midline, or they were horizontal shifts which produced a change in the relation of the object–hand position relative to the child's body midline. As reported earlier, even quite young sighted children, although they were blindfolded, used the external frame as a reference. They placed objects significantly more accurately when the surround was square, while the direction of the movement made very little difference. Congenitally totally blind children were more accurate with vertical than with horizontal movement shifts, but their accuracy was not affected by the background shape.

Again, the contrast between congenitally totally blind and blindfolded sighted children was not in efficiency or in the total number of errors they made in all conditions. The difference related specifically to whether movement information or the external frame or surround had greater effects on performance. Blind children were actually better than the younger sighted when vertical placement movements were required. Their errors showed self-referent and movement coding, rather than coding by external shape cues, although they had felt the shapes prior to performing the task. This was not because of any developmental lag. The congenitally totally blind actually did better than young blindfolded sighted children in the conditions to which self-referent and movement coding were appropriate. Interestingly enough also, blind children who had some early or residual visual experience coded by the external background shape like the sighted, although they were less accurate up to a later age.

Three things are noteworthy. First, even minimal visual experience seems to have some effect in drawing the child's attention to the usefulness of external cues. There is a good deal of other evidence which suggests that even minimal visual experience influences spatial performance (e.g. Warren 1974). The effect is on the propensity to use external cues for spatial reference.

Practically and methodologically, this is important. The practical implications will be discussed more fully later. But they clearly mean that the informational needs of totally congenitally blind children and of children with prior or residual vision differ. Methodologically, the findings suggest that scores which are averaged across blind children with different amounts (none or some) of visual experience may be misleading.

The importance of specific movement conditions also explains an apparently discrepant result in the literature. Hermelin and O'Connor (1975) reported that blind children judged distances better than locations, although most other evidence suggests that blind, blindfolded sighted children, blind and blindfolded sighted adults code locations more accurately than distance (Colley & Colley 1981; Laabs & Simmons 1981; Marteniuk 1978; Millar 1981b). The reason can be found in the relation of arm movements to the important body midaxis, on which self-referent frames are often based. Most studies on motor memory have used horizontal (across the midline) positioning movements. Hermelin & O'Connor (1975), by contrast, used a vertically (gravitationally) upright stand, so that movements were in a vertical direction, and were therefore aligned with the subject's upright body position. Distances could, therefore, have been coded spatially by reference to the body-centred frame. By contrast, the test locations were above the children's heads and, as the authors suggest, the blind children would have less experience or confidence with these.

Taken together, the studies imply that movement coding occurs mainly when spatial coding by external spatial layouts and by self-referent frames is made difficult, or unreliable (e.g. Colley & Colley 1981; Laabs 1973; Millar 1975b, 1976, 1979, 1981b; Russell 1976; Wallace 1977). Moreover, when spatial coding is possible, either because external reference cues are available (e.g. Millar 1979; Polit & Bizzi 1978; Paillard 1971), or because locations can be coded reliably in terms of body-centred reference frames (Laabs 1973; Marteniuk 1978; Millar 1981b), movement cues seem to have relatively little effect.

To explore the question of short-term motor memory by children for location and distance information, I used the Brown (1958) and Peterson (Peterson & Peterson 1959) interference design to test memory for small positioning (four and nine inch) movements. The question, as in studies on adults (e.g. Laabs & Simmons 1981), was whether memory for a fixed end location depended more on cognitive demands than memory for the extents of the movements. The end location was always aligned to the subject's body midaxis, but started from either the right or left at variable (four or nine inch) distances. For the variable end positions, subjects were given fixed blocks of one or other length that ended at variable positions, and never in alignment to the body midaxis. Blindfolded sighted children with mean ages of seven and nine years in comparable schools in the intake areas for blind children were matched on age, and on backward and on forward digit span to blind children. In addition a group of older (aged between eleven and thirteen years) blind children were tested. In one condition, the delay period was unfilled. Subjects simply waited for ten seconds until they got the recall signal. In the other condition, subjects had to count backwards during delays.

The results (Fig. 4) for the blindfolded sighted showed significantly better recall for position than for lengths, and more accurate recall in unfilled than filled delay conditions for both position and length. The blind children were also significantly better on recall in unfilled than in filled delays. But in their case that applied only to position recall. It should be noted that their accuracy on that was quite as good as that of the sighted. However, the blind differed from the sighted on the recall of lengths in that this was not affected by attentional (cognitive) demands during delays; and, moreover, length recall improved significantly with age. The older two groups were quite as accurate on length as on position recall. The findings again suggest differences in coding rather than in efficiency.

The fact that attentional demands during delays disturb both length and position recall suggests that sighted subjects may have used some form of

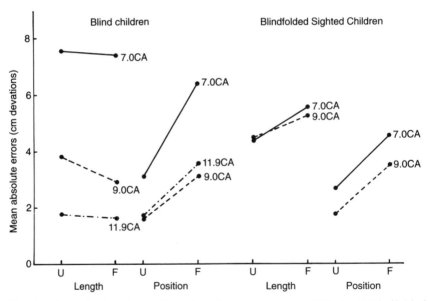

Fig. 4 Mean absolute (regardless of sign) errors by matched blind and blindfolded sighted children with mean chronological ages (CA) of 7.0 and 9.0 years, and an older (mean CA of 11.0 years) group of blind children in a linear positioning task, testing for recall of movement extent (length) and end location (position) after unfilled delays (U) and delays filled with a difficult cognitive (F) task.

spatial reference even when body-centred information was disrupted in length judgements. Comparable findings are reported in studies with sighted adults (e.g. Walsh *et al.* 1981). The results for the blind suggested that, with age and/or experience, reliance on movement information in memory may become as good as coding spatial position in relation to the body midline.

Evidence that the probability of an event (Keele & Boies 1973), or the amount of practice or repetition are factors in whether spatial coding is disrupted by attentional demands also came from earlier (Millar 1974, 1977c) studies. The study that is of particular interest here compared recall of a repeated (4 cm) horizontal positioning movement with a (9 cm) movement that was presented only once. Subjects were 16 four-year-old and 16 eight-year-old sighted children. As usual, there were highly significant effects of age, and also of delay. A circular movement that had to be executed during delay intervals affected both the repeated and the new input, compared to unfilled delays. By contrast, a difficult verbal distracter (four-year-olds had to produce names in a given category; eight-year-olds had to count backwards) disturbed only the repeated movement.

The implication that memory for spatial position is necessarily superior to memory for movements thus needed to be examined further. Some of the literature seems to imply that kinaesthetic cues are always simply peripheral after-effects from sensations, and have little or no functional significance. It has also been suggested that kinaesthetic cues are automatic effects of the movement (large/small) context. Nevertheless, there is little doubt that the movement context does have effects (e.g. Laabs & Simmons 1981), and that movements seem to produce relatively minor effects when spatial coding is possible. Marteniuk (1978) suggested that movement cues may be more important for younger than for older (sighted) children. The relation of memory for kinaesthetic cues to self-referent coding with age and absence of vision thus needed to be looked at further.

A study was therefore designed which varied reference and movement cues, but kept movement distance constant by using the same movement (ten cm) extent for presentation in all conditions (Millar 1985b). Movement directions were also of interest. The subject traced the standard to three locations, in vertical (median sagittal plane), horizontal (mid-transverse plane) and oblique (mid-transverse plane) directions, respectively. Recall movements were freehand. To show whether kinaesthetic cues were coded, the movement to recall locations was either the same, or started from the opposite side. To test for body-centred coding, difficult mental rotations were avoided. Instead, the subject either sat 'facing' the display, or sideways. When facing the display, all movements started at the body midaxis. When the subject sat sideways, the movements and directions were out of line with the body midaxis.

The results for blind children supported the hypothesis that movement cues are used mostly in conditions in which self-reference is difficult. But the age results were the reverse of the predicted prevalence of movement coding by younger children. The younger (seven to nine-and-a-half year olds) ones showed self-referent coding. Their errors were largest when the locations and directions were out of line with their body-midline, while changed movement cues had relatively little effect. The older children (aged from just below ten years to twelve years), by contrast, were affected by changed movements rather than by body orientation. Their errors were due to undershooting locations when the recall movement had to start from the opposite side. Accurate memory for the location would have needed a much longer movement. The finding showed that the older subjects remembered the positioning movement, rather than the spatial location.

The older blind were certainly more accurate than the younger blind, both in control conditions and in keeping to the movement path in freehand recall. Since they had been matched on intelligence tests, their mental age (cognitive skill) level was also higher. The fact that they relied on the repeated movement rather than on body-centred coding in these conditions thus suggested that the influence of the repeated movement was not simply a peripheral effect.

Further evidence for movement coding came from testing blindfolded sighted children in the same conditions (Millar 1985b). They were of the same age as the younger blind children, but they were considerably more accurate. On tests they performed like the older blind. The difference in body orientation had relatively little effect. But the changed positioning movement produced the large undershooting scores which showed movement coding.

These reversals of the usual relation between movement and location cues with repeated movements are of particular interest. The kinaesthetic effect clearly arose from deliberately keeping the positioning movement identical in all conditions, so that it received continual repetitions. Since the better performers showed the effect more, it can hardly be explained in terms of persistent peripheral sensations. An explanation in terms of 'automatic' context effects is also doubtful in these conditions. It is possible that repeated trials acted as feedback about the movement extent. But however it arose and whether or not subjects were aware of it, the fact that the information was clearly taken into account differentially more by the 'better' performers indicates that it had functional significance.

The relation between cognitive strategies and movement coding has seldom been tested directly (Imanaka & Abernethy 1992). The Millar (1985b) study explored the question with blindfolded sighted children. The children were tested under three forms of coding instruction, in addition to the control condition which simply asked for recall of the end location of movements. The set-up was the same as for blind children (Millar 1985b, experiment 1). In one condition subjects were instructed to pay attention to the 'feel' of their own movements, and to use these 'feels' in order to remember target locations during testing. In another condition, the emphasis was put on self-referent coding. Subjects were encouraged to feel their body-midline and to relate the end location of their hand to it, and were told to remember the target locations in that way. The third form of instruction encouraged coding the end locations relative to an external frame. The children felt around the (square) surround of the display, and were told to think about it later and to relate target locations to the imagined surround during testing.

The findings suggested that cognitive or strategic factors can be involved in memory for movements. They are not solely confined to spatial coding. Thus the main movement effect was replicated, although less steeply. But there was no doubt that movement and self-referent instructions had different effects, in the near (to the subject) and distant sections of the display, on movement bias in vertical, horizontal and oblique movement directions. Instruction to code by the (remembered) external surround eliminated bias differences in movement directions in both display sections. The findings have theoretical and practical implications which belong to later discussions (Chapters 9 & 10).

Something more needs to be said also about horizontal arm movements. In the Millar (1985b) study, the horizontal (mid-transverse plane) movements were the least accurate, and most easily perturbed, of the directions. That was so for the older blind, and also for blindfolded sighted children, except under instructions to use the external display for reference. The horizontal movement also produced the largest deviations from the movement path in freehand recall. The younger blind were much more inaccurate in pathkeeping than the older blind in all directions. But for the older blind and for blindfolded sighted children, lateral movements showed more bias, and veered more, than movements in the vertical direction. It is often assumed that the directions of arm movements in personal space are coded automatically, and that deviations can be ignored. Arm movements that are pivoted on the elbow describe a semicircular motion. That would produce angular deviation from a strictly horizontal path in any case. However, the deviation which such a movement would produce at the short (10 cm) distance could not account for the actual size of the error that was found (Millar 1985b). Moreover, the notion that deviations are necessarily automatic could not explain the finding that deviations were influenced by coding instructions, and that differences between horizontal and vertical directions disappeared with instructions to code locations relative to the remembered external surround.

The practical implications of findings on instructions to use particular forms of coding will be discussed further in a later chapter (Chapter 9).

VI   Conclusions

Taken together, the findings show that the spatial reference information which is available in sighted and in blind conditions can predict to a very large extent how young sighted and congenitally totally blind children will code location and movement cues.

The findings on infants and young children show little support for the notion that spatial development consists of a change from egocentric to allocentric coding. Coding in spatial tasks was examined by looking at memory for locations and directions, and for the extent or distance of movements. The findings showed that children, as well as adults, can use more than one form of coding. Coding can be in terms of external cues, frames or configurations, but it can also be in terms of body-centred frames, or people can rely on memory for movement information. The information that subjects have both from the current task and from longer-term knowledge can account for the extent to which different forms of coding are elicited.

Two conditions seem to elicit body-centred references. One is the absence of invariant current external cues by which a given location may be coded in relation to external planes. The blind and sighted did not differ when body-centred frames provided adequate reference to determine a location.

A reliable means of spatial coding in haptic conditions is to use body-centred kinaesthetic and proprioceptive information convergently. Kinaesthetic information from the body, or a body part, can act as a location anchor for starting or stopping a movement. Alternatively, the body or body part can act as a coordinate reference frame to determine the location of a felt object (Howard & Templeton 1966; Millar 1985c).

When body-centred reference is difficult (e.g. after moving) or inappropriate to the task, it is possible to code movements in terms of kinaesthetic sequences which can be remembered. Such coding seems to be better for recognition of distance, and for sequential changes in direction, than it is for remembering configurations or spatial locations (Laabs & Simmons 1981; Millar 1981b, 1985b).

It is sometimes assumed that blind positioning movements are typical examples of arid laboratory experiments, with no relevance to 'real life'. The lengthy discussion of actual and possible factors in hand movements may therefore seem to be unduly academic. However, the details of conditions which influence deviations from horizontal movements are of particular interest for practical as well as theoretical reasons.

To give only one instance, beginning braillists are very prone to deviate from lines of text in reading from left to right. It is important to know the factors that influence such veering, in order to provide the conditions that prevent it.

Movement sequences can, of course, also be coded as configurations. In order to do that, some additional information is usually needed. It is easiest if there is some additional cue or frame that can be used for reference, for instance to locate the start, turns, or end of the movement sequences. By using convergent and complementary information from touch and kinaesthetic sources, sequential movement information can thus be coded in terms of movement configurations. Evidence on this will be discussed in a later chapter (Chapter 8).

The evidence reviewed in this chapter supports the assumption that spatial development is best explained by considering what information children have at their disposal, both from task conditions and from longer-term experience.

The fact that the information which is reliably available in long-term prior experience influences modes of coding explains coding in blind conditions. The main developmental difference is that younger children need more salient and prominent cues and more familiarity with the task and procedures. It will be argued that this applies both to retrieving relevant information from longer-term memory and to maintaining new inputs in short-term memory (Chapters 8 & 10).

7

Information and understanding large-scale space

In looking at the information available in large-scale space, it seems that locomotion presents few problems for the sighted. We certainly do not normally have to give children who can walk special lessons for them to be able to cross a room, walk in a straight line to a distant cue, or avoid obstacles.

Provided there has been previous sight of the target, adults are also extremely accurate in judging distances in walking to it without sight (Rieser *et al*. 1990). Not surprisingly, the variability of errors increases with the distance of the target (e.g. Thomson 1983). Rieser and his colleagues reasonably interpret the accuracy in walking without vision to previously seen targets as evidence for the close calibration of efferent and pro-prioceptive information about locomotion with visually perceived distance. They suggest that the basis for this calibration is the developmental history of experiencing simultaneously the visual and efferent/proprioceptive (see earlier) changes that accompany locomotion.

The main reason for the ease of moving about in geographical space is the fact that vision provides constant and continuous updating cues from external sources. For the sighted, vision provides a constant optic flow (Adams *et al*. 1977; Lee 1980), which changes reliably with locomotion and gait.

Also, the viewer perceives the relation between different external planes, so that they are seen as lawfully coordinated. Further, since the person's body as well as other objects in geocentric space are oriented gravitationally, there is an important correspondence between self-referent and external frames. What is at the top in the external environment is also at the top when referred to the body-centred system, even during locomotion. In standing upright, body-centred gravitational information corresponds to information about external vertical orientations.

Such correspondence seems to be an important factor in the ease of coding particular directions (see earlier). It is probably for that reason more than any other that vertical directions are the easiest to code in the large-scale gravitational environment. Horizontal directions come next. For these, self-referent (transverse) and external horizontal frames also coincide. But the correspondence is less complete.

East–west poles are completely specified by coordinates centred on the external environment. But externally specified right and left sides correspond to right–left sides on body-centred coordinate frames only so long as the body maintains the same front–back (sagittal plane) direction relative to the external east–west relations. When a person turns around (180 degree body turn), left–right relations are reversed. For sighted adults, that hardly matters, because visual information about the external environment provides constant updating cues in that case also. In normal conditions, changing visual information from external sources is lawfully coordinated with changes in locomotion.

Given the apparent ease with which people move about the environment, it is perhaps not surprising that the study of spatial skills in large-scale environments is relatively recent. The current interest has been fuelled by the general growing importance of environmental issues, and more particularly by Gibson's (1979) ecological theory, but also by advances in explaining the skill with which other primates move rapidly and accurately in complex environments (Trevarthen 1968).

Coding information from large-scale environments is increasingly being tested by judgements in geographical space. But the majority of studies which address the question of how people represent geographical space have used small-scale displays to test for that. One consequence of testing orientation in large-scale space by small-scale displays or maps is that the information in the two types of display differs not merely in size, but in kind. Map information is symbolic in form. This will be discussed in more detail in Chapter 8.

An important point about information in large-scale space is that, even in sighted conditions, many environments, especially urban environments, actually provide rather limited information for locomotion (Acredolo 1981; Slator 1982). There is no overview of the kind that is possible when looking at a small-scale display from above. Although external updating cues are constantly present, large-scale built-up environments limit the view of the goal of travel to intermediate stages. It is not possible to look through doors or around corners. That means that neither the ultimate goal of locomotion nor the original starting point are in view if the route contains bends and turns. Looking back to intermediate starting points and forward to intermediate goals may still be possible. But the information is typically received in a sequential fashion, compared to the single view which is possible in small-scale space (Slator 1982).

These limits on information which obtain in large-scale environments even in vision are not always recognized explicitly in theoretical accounts of spatial development (Slator 1982).

I Developmental theories and evidence

One of the best known theories which is specifically concerned with the development of spatial coding in large-scale, or geographical space is that of Siegel and White (1975). Siegel and White (1975) assumed that development is hierarchical, and proceeds from particular and concrete to more general and abstract knowledge. In learning about a geographical space, the child, or indeed the adult, first remembers particular 'landmarks', then organizes these landmarks sequentially into 'routes'. With further experience landmarks and routes are first coordinated partially, and finally are fully coordinated into map-like overviews or configurations of the whole terrain. The sequence of stages is assumed to be invariant.

In the account proposed by Siegel and White (1975), the person starts with knowledge of isolated facts, progresses to organizing these to some extent in a linear fashion, and finally reaches a survey map type of organization which is assumed to be the most complete and complex form of organization. Theirs is an information-processing account. The differences in performance between adults and children are explained by differences in information-processing capacity. It is also assumed that there is an invariant developmental sequence in the type of spatial coding exhibited by children (Siegel 1981; Siegel & White 1975).

There is a limit to the number of discrete items of information which people can remember in the short term (Miller 1956), and there is also good evidence that memory spans improve with age (e.g. Chi 1976, 1977; Conrad 1971; Dempster 1981; Millar 1975b,c). The relevant tests typically demand the immediate repetition of a number of separate items, usually digits or words, in the same order in which they have just been presented. Below the age of about three or four years, young children can repeat barely two items, and this typically increases to five items at the age of seven, and to seven or slightly more (Miller 1956) in adulthood. The findings imply that younger children can hold fewer items in short-term memory than older children or adults, and this has consequential effects on tasks which impose a memory load.

Siegel and White (1975) used the notion of an increase in processing capacity with age (e.g. Pascual-Leone 1970) to explain why children are likely to lag behind adults in achieving the successive stages of representation which they assume. Young children tend to code in terms of concrete items such as 'landmarks' for longer, and their inability to hold a sufficient number of items in mind limits their ability to organize successive landmarks fully into routes. Young children are also less flexible in their manner of coding. The theory assumes that increased processing capacity is needed for the final integration of route information into map form. The integration is partial at first. But with experience, metric relations are understood and partially coordinated. Finally, fully coordinated map-like representations are possible. The theory thus seems to accept the notion that young children are incapable of representing external space in terms of Euclidean coordinates. But it substitutes the notion of limited processing capacity for Piaget's assumption of pre-logical thinking as the explanation.

The notion of increased processing capacity with age is a powerful one. The main evidence comes from studies on tests of immediate memory or apprehension 'span' with alphanumerical materials. As mentioned earlier, these tests require the immediate repetition of unrelated serial items and there is little doubt that the number of items which can be reproduced in strictly serial order increases linearly with age (Chi 1976, 1977). However, the evidence suggests strongly that performance on span tests depends on the combination of a number of different factors. The type of material (digits or words), verbal facility (Conrad 1971), the speed of naming the items (Millar 1975b,c, 1978b), familiarity with the material and with the task, and the mode of inputs and of response tests (Henry & Millar 1991, 1993; Hitch & Halliday 1983; Millar 1975b) are important, if not exhaustive, ingredients. Span tests tap some important aspects of temporary memory.

The relevance of temporary memory to spatial development will be discussed more extensively in Chapter 8 on non-verbal representation, and in the final theoretical chapter. To anticipate briefly, I agree very much with Siegel (1981) and Acredolo (1988b) that memory span and familiarity are important in explaining spatial development. I assume further that the increase in span with age is due to a number of factors, including modes of coding and their organization. Moreover, my explanation does not assume that there is a necessary developmental sequence of spatial organization. The question in this section is therefore whether forms of coding differ developmentally, rather than with the kind of informational conditions that often happen to be associated with age.

The idea that landmark information is more important for younger than for older children has been put forward by a number of researchers (e.g. Acredolo 1976; Hart & Moore 1973). Acredolo (1976) found that young children were better at remembering the place in a hallway where a set of keys had been dropped, when there was a landmark present near the site. In a further study, Acredolo (1977) showed that three- and four-year-old children who had been taught to find a trinket that was hidden in a cup which was situated to their left or right, made egocentric mistakes after they had been moved to the opposite side of the wall of the testing room. But these errors disappeared when the left and right sides of the walls of the room, or else their own starting points, were marked distinctively.

It seems to me that such findings can be interpreted completely in terms of differences in the amount, salience, and redundancy of information that young children need. It is not necessary to assume that there is an invariant and qualitatively different developmental sequence in coding. The findings that are discussed in this section suggest strongly that younger children need more salient information and more redundancy than older subjects. That is not necessarily evidence for a developmental change in spatial coding. Evidence that older children and adults are also less likely to rely on external cues if these are ambiguous, difficult or uncertain was reviewed earlier.

An interpretation of that kind is more consistent with the findings of another study by Acredolo (1976). Pre-schoolers were taken to a table in a testing room. They were then blindfolded and moved around the room. During this time the table was silently moved from its original position to the opposite wall. The blindfold was then removed, and the children were told to return to the place in the room where the walk had started. Many of the younger children went to the table, although it was now situated in a new location. Ten-year-olds, on the other hand, were not fooled. They went to the original location. They were evidently able to do that because they had coded their starting location in relation to external cues or landmarks in the room (e.g. window, door, etc.). The table must also be considered an external or landmark cue. The difference was that the older children had noticed more, or paid more attention to, features of the room which were not immediately at hand. The younger children ignored cues that were further away. The age difference here thus seems to lie, not in the frame of reference that is used for coding, but in what information is more likely to catch young children's attention, and how easily they can be fooled.

Siegel's theory that there is a sequence of knowledge, beginning with knowledge of landmarks, then route organization, and finally configurationally-organized cognitive maps, explicitly rejects the Piagetian notion that young children are incapable of representing space in terms of Euclidean relations (Siegel 1981). Siegel (1981) suggests that methods of testing, and especially the use of small-scale layouts, may be responsible for the initial underestimation of young children's use of external cues.

Tests using small-scale layouts have actually provided evidence that even infants (e.g. Bremner 1978) and very young children do use external cues (e.g. Huttenlocher & Presson 1973, 1979; Millar 1979, 1981b). On the assumption that young children have limited processing capacity (for whatever reason), the multiplicity of views in large-scale space is likely to constitute a greater mental load if an integrated representation is demanded.

The theory (Siegel 1981; Siegel & White 1975) seems to assume an invariant sequence of spatial coding with a developmental basis as well as a basis in experience. In addition to the notion of increased processing capacity, Siegel and his colleagues (e.g. Siegel and Schadler 1977) invoke

Werner's (1948) differentiation theory of development. Werner put forward what he called an 'orthogenetic' principle. It asserts that genetic development proceeds from the global and undifferentiated to the particular and differentiated. The principle is assumed to be genetic, and to apply to all development, including the cognitive development of children. In common with Piaget, if for different reasons, it is therefore assumed that at first children have difficulties in differentiating themselves from the environment and are therefore egocentric. They progressively attain first that differentiation, then differentiate external objects from each other. Finally, they are able to differentiate still smaller features of the environment.

It is not made entirely clear how the developmental aspects of the Siegel theory relate to the informational account. Knowledge of landmarks, ordering these as series, route organization, metric interrelations and conversion into configurations are assumed to be four-component processes which operate in a cumulative hierarchical fashion (e.g. Cousins *et al.* 1983). It makes good sense that prominent features are noticed before less salient ones. But there is little evidence for a general developmental progression from general to specific, any more than for a maturational trend from specific to general (e.g. Rosch 1973). Some additional mechanism would have to be assumed to explain how increased differentiation, as such, necessarily makes processing cumulative and hierarchical.

By contrast, a great deal of evidence supports the suggestion by Siegel and his colleagues that familiarity with materials and task demands are important factors in young children's performance (Siegel 1981; Siegel & Shadler 1977).

Siegel and his colleagues (Herman 1980; Herman & Siegel 1978; Siegel *et al.* 1979a) used miniature model towns with roads, rails and buildings. In one study (Herman & Siegel 1978), five-, seven- and ten-year-olds walked through the space and then reconstructed the layout from memory. The procedure was repeated three times and, although older children did better than younger ones, all children improved with repetition. Siegel (1981) commented that performance by the youngest group was better when the miniature layout was close to surrounding walls than when the layout was placed in the middle of a large hall. The finding that young children take external cues into account more when these are relatively close at hand suggests that they are more likely to ignore information which is further away from the objects of their immediate attention. It should be noted, incidentally, that paying more attention to near than to far objects is not itself sufficient evidence that the children used a topological rather than a Euclidean system for coding as Piaget assumed. The description applies to the performance. But these findings as well as more recent studies (Allen & Kirasic 1988) provide further evidence that even very young children use external cues for coding, even if they do so more when the cues are near enough to be salient. The findings are thus entirely consistent with the results of small-scale displays in blindfold conditions (e.g. Millar 1979).

One problem with miniature replicas which are laid out on the floor is that they permit overviews over the whole layout. They therefore do not actually mimic the conditions that prevail in large-scale environments which do not normally permit overviews (Siegel 1981; Slator 1982). That applies also to potentially ingenious methods of testing in which subjects first see a space which contains a layout of objects. The space is then screened and subjects have to point (using a sighting tube) to various objects from three different vantage points. Triangulation of angular deviations from these points gives a very accurate measure of location errors and the relative configuration these suggest. Siegel (1981) reported a study by Kirasic, Siegel, Allen, Curtis, and Furlong which used such a method with adult students who were still relatively unfamiliar with the campus layout that they were supposed to judge. Hardwyk *et al.* (1976) used a large-size space to test how people represent routes. But the simulation was limited by the fact that the entire bounded space was initially visible from a single vantage point. That situation does not usually obtain in following a route in large-scale space (Siegel 1981).

Siegel and Schadler (1977) tested five- to six-year-olds on memory of their classroom. The children had either had experience of the room for eight months, or for only about one and a half months. They had to construct a miniature model of the classroom by placing small replicas of the furniture at the correct locations in a scale model.

Length of experience again had a very clear effect on accuracy (Siegel & Schadler 1977). Landmarks were also shown to be important, in the sense that 'cued' recall was better. In cued recall, the places of a few of the items were already fixed. However, the findings varied somewhat with the measure that was used to assess accuracy. Cued recall was better for relative placements of items with respect to each other. It also produced high scores for a global measure which counted the relation between subordinate clusters of items. But the prediction that children with less experience would benefit more from landmark cues was only supported in the absolute placement scores. The authors use Werner's differentiation theory to explain these results. However, the study showed no age effects and no independent evidence of better differentiation with age. These (Siegel & Schadler 1977) findings are thus evidence for the importance of contextual cues and experience, but they do not provide strong support for a theory of an invariant developmental sequence in which the basis of coding changes with age (e.g. Sophian 1985; Sophian & Wellman 1987).

Cousins *et al.* (1983) make the important distinction between tests that assess way-finding or route-finding, and tests which assess route knowledge by small-scale displays. The latter tests demand more than knowledge of the route. They require in addition the translation of knowledge from large-scale, three-dimensional space to small-scale, and often two-dimensional, space. The experimenters found that even quite young children are accurate on way-finding in a familiar environment. The relation between age levels and accuracy depended on whether tests demanded landmark knowledge, the ordering of route information, or coordination of disparate parts information. But the sequence which is predicted by the original model (Siegel & White 1975) is not always found even when knowledge of large-scale environments is tested by small-scale models.

An important study by Hazen *et al.* (1978) is a case in point. They used large-scale displays of four or six connected rooms, respectively, for preschoolers and five- and six-year-olds. The subjects were taken through the rooms via a U-shaped, and also via a zigzag path. Once the children had learned the routes and landmarks along them, they were tested on reversing the route and on making inferences about parts of the rooms through which they had not travelled directly. Interestingly enough, younger children needed more trials to learn. On tests, even three-year-olds were nearly a hundred per cent correct on travelling the routes in reverse. They were slightly less good than five-year-olds in predicting the sequence of landmarks, and relatively poor on the inference tests, compared to six-year-olds. In way-finding tests there is evidence for the priority of landmark over route knowledge (e.g. Anooshian *et al.* 1981, 1984) which the Siegel and White (1975) hypothesis predicts. But there is no evidence that this is an invariant developmental sequence.

Pick and Lockman (1981) did find that accuracy was lower on inference compared to route reversal tasks. That is consistent with the theoretically predicted sequence, provided that it is assumed that the inferences depended on the mental construction of a coordinated layout (Pick & Lockman 1981). However, the authors report that there was no consistent correlation between the inference results and results from reconstructing the layouts with small-scale replicas. This suggests that inferences did not necessarily depend on a coordinated picture of the situation. Also, it was found that the scores of the younger children were influenced significantly by the size of the display, and the complexity of the Z-shaped compared to the U-shaped route, as well as by the type of task (Hazen *et al.* 1978). These results show it is necessary to take into account factors other than just the components predicted by the hypothesized sequence.

Allen *et al.* (1978) used a potentially powerful multidimensional scaling procedure to simulate the multiplicity of viewpoints of large-scale space. Subjects were shown a simulated walk (in slides), and subsequently had to assess the distances between various landmarks from photographs. There was again good evidence that familiarity improves accuracy. Repeated viewing of the walk increased the accuracy of distance judgements.

Moreover, distance judgements were more accurate in environments with large numbers of landmarks than when there were fewer landmarks. However, the only developmental difference which was reported with this method concerned the selection of useful landmarks (Allen *et al.* 1979). Ten-year-olds judged more accurately when using pictures that adults had selected as containing useful landmarks, than when judging from pictures that had been selected by their peers. Younger children were equally inaccurate on both. Although this is consistent with the notion that knowledge of landmarks is needed to judge distances along routes accurately, it does not provide clear evidence of a developmental trend for the priority of landmark over route knowledge. For one thing, the youngest children in this study were ten-year-olds, while the notion that landmarks are more important for younger children is usually applied to pre-schoolers. According to Pick (1981) this type of finding is a problem for any account that predicts invariant sequences as due to strictly developmental factors.

It should also be noted that the findings show that adults were better than children at selecting useful information for a given task. This introduces the yet further factor of 'metacognitive' knowledge. Metacognition, or monitoring how one does something or thinks about something, can be distinguished from simply knowing how to proceed, or knowing solely that something is the case (e.g. Brown 1975; Flavell 1988).

It has been suggested that metacognition itself depends on a stage-like process, which is absent before the age of three or four years (e.g. Flavell 1988). It is also possible that the child's growing awareness and monitoring of external and internal events depends on the interaction of a number of conditions, rather than on a single mechanism which is either present or absent. In either case, knowing what to do, how to do it, when to do it, and which procedures help one best to remember or to solve a problem are likely to be involved. All of these improve with age and experience.

Active movement is another factor which is often assumed to be age-dependent and to contribute to the hypothesized priority of route over configurational representation. Historically, the view that young children rely more on active movement than older children or adults stems partly from the motor theories of the Russian school (e.g. Shemyakin 1962; Zaporozhets 1965). These assume that movement-based information is primary. Another source is the influential Piagetian notion that pre-logical representations are internalizations of earlier action schemata (Chapter 2). Vygotzky's (1962) action-based account of cognitive development and Bruner's (Bruner *et al.* 1966) proposal that coding changes with age from movement to iconic and finally to verbal representation made similar assumptions.

The empirical evidence is equivocal. To a large extent this is because the notion of self-produced active movement is interpreted and tested differently by different developmentalists. For instance, findings on the role of self-produced movements in the development of placing-responses by kittens, and accurate visually-directed reaching by primates, reviewed earlier (Chapter 3), are sometimes cited as evidence for the primacy of movement in spatial development.

It has also been suggested that active locomotion is necessary for onto-genetic development, because voluntary movement produced better recall by four- to six-year-olds than being passively transported (Foreman *et al.* 1990). The detailed findings, however, suggest that it is the correlation of two sources of changing information, rather than the primacy of one over the other, which confers the advantage. Similarly, in object search by very young infants, active movement seems to be important principally because it produces attention-getting changes in the visual environment, and be-cause these changes in movement and external cues relate systematically to each other (Chapter 3). The findings thus actually show the importance of the systematic correlation between movement and visual information, rather than the predominance of either at a given age.

Another frequently cited body of work is the review by Shemyakin (1962) of the Russian literature. The review assumes that activity is neces-sary for the acquisition of spatial knowledge, and that this applies to both route knowledge and to survey-type knowledge. But the evidence here is quite different, because it is based mainly on children's drawings of familiar environments. Younger children evidently produced drawings showing the route more often than map-like drawings. However, both types of draw-ings occurred at all ages, and both became more detailed and sophisticated with age. In any case, it is not possible to consider drawings as direct reflections of mental representations (Kosslyn *et al.* 1977). Young sighted children recognize two-dimensional drawings as representations long be-fore they are able to produce them (Maccobee & Bee 1965).

Advantages for young children from actively moving through an en-vironment were found by Cohen and Weatherford (1980). However, the relevant association between grade level and activity was qualified by a higher-order interaction which suggested that the association depended on the type of route being tested. The association between activity and age or grade thus seems to be indirect rather than direct. Herman (1980) found that five- to six-year-olds benefited from moving through an environment and at the same time having their attention directed to relations between external landmarks. The fact that older children, whose performance was better, also benefited from the combination of activity and guided atten-tion implied that active movement, as such, did not explain the age differ-ence in performance. Herman (1980) suggested instead that the older children learned faster and remembered better.

The growing evidence that findings on age differences can differ quite radically with apparently small differences in context and information accords better with theories which explain development by various factors, such as growing familiarity with tasks and materials, faster processing and better memory (e.g. Pick 1988), than with developmental assumptions about specific qualitative changes in spatial coding with age. Nevertheless, age effects in spatial performance are still often ascribed to an invariant developmental sequence, which starts with landmark knowledge, and progresses to partial route organization, while the final stage of coding is in terms of configurations or survey maps. It is assumed that this form of representation is superior and that achieving it is delayed because young children are assumed to have specific difficulties in coordinating information.

In fact, the usual assumption that map-like organization is necessarily superior to route or sequential organization is unwarranted. Route and survey-map knowledge differ in kind and are optimal for different tasks (Thorndyke and Hayes-Roth 1982). Thorndyke and Hayes-Roth (1982) proposed that procedural knowledge of a route is gained typically from active navigation; survey knowledge is typically gained from encoding global spatial relations from map-like overviews of the layout. They compared adults who only had information about an environment from having walked through it with adults whose information derived entirely from being trained to memorize a small-scale floor-map of that environment. The subjects were tested on estimating the route distances and Euclidean (straight line) distances between various locations, and the direction of a location from different actual standpoints in the buildings, and also relative to a fixed coordinate (map) system. Their results suggested that different kinds of knowledge are optimal for different tasks. Thus subjects with navigation experience were better on orientation tasks; subjects with map experience were more accurate on locations. Route distances were estimated more accurately than Euclidean distance by subjects with experience in navigation, while the two forms of estimates did not differ for subjects who only had map experience. Subjects' exposure to route versus map information was unfortunately confounded with length (months versus days) of their experience. But evidence that, for children as well, forms of spatial coding depend to a significant extent on the form of the input as well as on the form of output test was found in an ingenious series of studies by Slator (1982).

She argued that large- and small-scale space differs mainly in the manner in which information is available at input and test. For the person who walks through large-scale urban spaces, information about the total environment is necessarily piece-meal and successive. But tests of spatial knowledge acquired in this way typically require map-like output. There is thus a discrepancy between the form of input information and the form in which output is tested.

Slator (1982) invented a simple but effective means of testing route and map-like information with the same layouts at input and test. She simulated the manner in which route information is obtained in large-scale space by using a moving round or ragged 'window', which successively exposed limited portions of a route and its associated landmarks. Survey-map information was simulated by exposing the whole route and associated landmarks simultaneously in a square frame. The square surround thus also provided the orthogonal coordinate reference frame which is typical of map formats.

The children were tested in four balanced conditions of input and test. In the route input condition, they pushed a toy car along a 'road' which had replicas of buildings along the sides. A screen was moved along with the moving toy car in route conditions, so that it operated like a moving window. The screen revealed a limited view of successive portions of the road and associated buildings. In map input conditions, the whole layout of routes and associated buildings or landmarks was visible simultaneously in map-like form with a square frame surround. The total exposure time was the same for route and map input conditions. In tests, the children were given the same route or map conditions without the buildings. Their task in both route and map tests was to replace the buildings accurately. In route tests, the child pushed the car along the same road, and replaced the landmarks as sequential portions of the road were revealed by the moving window. In map tests, the whole road without buildings was simultaneously visible in the frame, and the child had to replace the buildings at the correct locations.

The series of experiments showed quite clearly that, for simultaneous map presentation at input, map tests produced the best results. Far from being less accurate, map conditions produced more accurate placements than route conditions by young as well as by older children. That was not simply due to the 'single' viewpoint predicated of small-scale space. Five- to six-year-olds, as well as eight- to nine-year-olds, used the external map surround as a reference frame. They produced more accurate placements when the layout was surrounded by a distinctive square frame, than when that frame was replaced by an irregular, ragged surround which provided no coordinated orthogonal axes.

Sequential route presentations and tests produced lower accuracy in subjects of all ages. This related to the relative lack of reference information in sequential conditions. When the amount of reference information was varied, all children did better in conditions with more, compared to fewer cues at input and/or test. The spatial characteristics of the input and output conditions were thus shown to determine the accuracy of locating items and of remembering their relative position to each other.

An important finding was that items in route presentations were remembered in serial form. Younger as well as older subjects replaced the items in the order in which they had been experienced. That was not the case, or occurred significantly less often, with map inputs, although subjects had also physically moved the toy car along the map road in that condition. In other words, the manner in which the input had been experienced was found to affect the manner in which it had been coded. Quite young children learn layouts better from maps (Uttal & Wellman 1989).

By contrast, the only factor which related specifically to age, consistently across experiments, was the effect of repetition. In Slator's study older children improved significantly more quickly than younger children with repeated trials of the same conditions. In other words, younger children required more replications of the same condition to benefit repetition to the same extent as older children.

Slator's (1982) findings are quite consistent with previous and, indeed, with subsequent findings on spatial coding. First, only familiarity and task replication relate consistently to age differences across experiments. These factors were important in all the studies that varied them specifically, whatever the spatial display or method of study (e.g. Acredolo 1977; Cousins *et al.* 1983; Hazen *et al.* 1978; Herman & Siegel 1978; Siegel & Schadler 1977; Slator 1982). An exception is the report by Anooshian and Young (1981) that reports of familiarity with the neighbourhood did not correlate with performance. However, they used a sophisticated judgement technique which, though excellent in principle, may have been equally unfamiliar. That could have equalized other forms of familiarity.

The term 'familiarity' is itself a 'portmanteau' word that needs to be unpacked. Familiarity can refer to the degree of long-term acquaintance with classes of materials, or with specific items, or with the task and context, or with the procedures demanded by the task. Even familiarity with the people who are administering the tests can be a factor. These probably do not all relate in the same way to levels of performance in a given task. But the relation between the various factors is not as yet known.

Similarly, the finding that young children need more repetitions in learning than older children is also unlikely to refer to a single developmental condition, or to have the same importance for all tasks or skills. Familiarity and repetition have long been known to have effects on learning. It is necessary to emphasize these two general factors yet again, precisely because we do not as yet know what they cover, or how precisely each of the subsidiary aspects operates in relation to age. In our current state of knowledge, evidence that younger children depend more on familiarity and need larger amounts of repetition is not an explanation. It is a basis for further questions.

There is, of course, no doubt that landmarks are crucial in finding one's way, particularly in a novel environment. Nevertheless, landmarks have different functions in different tasks and contexts. They may act simply to elicit attention to environmental information, or may constitute anchor and/or guiding cues, or mark turning points for locomotion, or act as pointers to a particular direction. It is therefore doubtful that the need for more landmarks distinguishes spatial coding specifically by younger compared to older children or adults, once differences in the effects of familiarity and repetition have been taken into account.

Thus findings which show that young children need more landmarks are balanced by finding that young children also need more spatial reference information. The need for more landmarks thus seems to require much the same explanation as the general need for more informational redundancy in conditions of greater uncertainty or lack of knowledge.

The situation is somewhat different if a sequence of landmarks is the only information that people have for finding their way. Short-term memory for items in serial order is indeed less efficient in younger children (e.g. Dempster 1981). When the task demands memory for serial items beyond a child's immediate memory span, age-related effects would be expected for that reason. The underlying mechanism, even for that, is unlikely to be a single developing process (Henry & Millar 1991, 1993).

Slator's (1982) experimental design did not involve supraspan sequences of landmarks. That explains why age did not relate specifically to poorer performance with sequential (route) than simultaneous (map-like) conditions. The important point is that serial inputs lead to more accurate placements when the test demands serial outputs. That is not age-dependent. It was found for children at all ages, although the overall accuracy was, of course, higher for older children. The findings by Slator thus suggest that for children, as for adults in the study by Thorndyke and Hayes-Roth (1982), route and map information lead to different forms of encoding.

Accumulating evidence that route and survey map knowledge are optimal for different types of task runs counter to the traditional assumption that map-like organization is necessarily superior, and therefore characterizes adult mental spatial representation.

The findings also show that, for children of all ages, spatial coding is similarly influenced by differences in information and by the manner in which that information is presented and tested in route and map tasks. This evidence further undermines the notion that route and map organization form an invariant developmental sequence.

The predicted sequence of route and configurational knowledge (Siegel 1981) certainly occurs. But it occurs only when the input information is from routes and output is demanded in terms of knowledge which is more easily obtained from maps or other global overviews.

That is intelligible. Tasks in which input and output organization differ demand more mental work than tasks in which these are compatible. Compatible forms of knowledge do not require reorganization. Spatial coding is thus likely to be more difficult if configurational organization has to be derived from sequential inputs, if only for that reason. The reverse would also be expected, unless the map condition provides route information at the same time. That was the case in some of Slator's (1982) studies.

Map reading in order to find one's way in the environment often requires skill, as geography teachers know well. Some loss of efficiency in accuracy and/or speed can be expected at all developmental levels when the knowledge being tested differs in form from initial information. Other factors, for instance, familiarity, may produce perfect performance (ceiling effects) on the one hand, or chance responding (floor effects) on the other. The evidence suggests that there is some loss of efficiency whenever subjects have to translate from one type of input to another: from sequential inputs to dealing with map information, and from map information to sequential procedures. But there is no evidence that loss of efficiency due to having to translate between configurational and route knowledge is specifically related to age.

It is also useful to look at the distinction between route and configurational knowledge in terms of the distinction between declarative knowledge (knowing what is the case) and procedural knowledge (knowing what to do and how to do it). That distinction applies also in other areas of psychology (e.g. Berry & Broadbent 1984; Broadbent et al. 1986). For instance, it is perfectly possible for a person to speak a language correctly without being able to describe the syntactic rules that govern it. Conversely, knowing the principles on which the stock exchange is run does not necessarily imply knowing how to operate these in practice, or how to 'play the market'.

'Knowing that' and 'knowing how' are probably not stored in precisely the same form, nor are they always closely associated in memory in adults (e.g. Berry & Broadbent 1984) or children (Brown 1975). To derive route knowledge from maps is analogous to changing from declarative to procedural knowledge.

It is, of course, perfectly possible to derive configurational representations from procedural knowledge. It is equally possible to derive procedural knowledge from map-like representations. The question is how this takes place and what informational conditions are needed for the mental reorganization of spatial information.

One factor which is known to facilitate change from route to map organization is an overlap between different sections of routes. Moar and Carleton (1982) got adults to learn two routes which shared a common block. Travel along the routes was simulated by sequential slides which always had some overlap in features. In these conditions, subjects used a combined 'network' schema for the two routes from the outset. Judging relative locations between the two routes was as accurate as judging locations within either route.

Moar and Carleton's (1982) findings showed that, although people combined route information when routes shared a common section, backward recall was nevertheless worse than recall in the order in which landmarks had been experienced. This is further evidence that the order in input information influences the form of encoding by adults. This is entirely consistent with results on young children (Slator 1982), and on children whose main long-term experience comes from sequential movement inputs rather than from vision (e.g. Millar 1975b).

The finding that route information was encoded serially, but that information from two routes was nevertheless integrated, provided they had a section in common, implies that the form of encoding was affected by all the available information. Such processing calls on cognitive skill.

The evidence thus suggests that factors in addition to the currently available information have to be considered if we are to understand how people derive fully integrated knowledge from sequential information.

The fact that familiarity and repetition are salient factors is evident from almost all studies. But it is not so clear precisely how these operate. I think it likely that familiarity and repetition function most effectively when different forms of information overlap or have aspects in common. Repetition could enhance the recognition by people that two landmarks, or two sequences, are the same. That recognition would facilitate the relevant inferences. On that hypothesis, familiarity and repetition would act on temporary memory. Retrieval of familiar cues would take less time. Identities between landmarks and/or routes would therefore be more obvious.

Similarly, a repeated (blind) movement sequence that always ended at the same landmark would make that landmark progressively more familiar. The landmark would thus provide information for the configurational inference that the route is circular. The point is important and will be taken up again later.

Further factors which influence coding of spatial information are suggested by some surprising illusions and distortions which have been reported when people are asked to judge distances and directions in different contexts. These will be considered next.

II   Bias in judging distance: the influence of events, time, and value

An amusing finding by Sadalla *et al.* (1979) was that people who walked along a path that was marked at intervals with easy (high-frequency) names judged that path to be much longer than an identical path that was marked with more difficult (low-frequency) names.

The result is surprising on two counts. One is the very clear influence of language, or at any rate of word familiarity, on distance judgements. Hemisphere differences as well as behavioural evidence suggest that spatial and verbal skills belong to different areas of knowledge. Large distortions of a spatial judgement from purely lexical (word or item) knowledge thus seem somewhat unexpected (McNamara & LeSueur 1989). The relation between verbal and spatial processing will be considered further in Section IV.

The other surprise is that familiar rather than unfamiliar names led to overestimation. Intuitively, it seems more reasonable that difficulties rather than ease or familiarity might lead to overestimating a distance.

There are other areas in which such surprises occur. Any one who has ever got stuck in an elevator can testify that the period of time in which nothing seemed to happen seemed much shorter at the time than it turned out to be in reality. Contrary to what one would expect from boredom, empty time is judged to be shorter than time that is filled with many events. In analogy, routes marked with high-frequency (easy) names may be overestimated because they seem less filled with events, although the 'event' filler in this case probably relates to easier and/or faster retrieval of high-frequency (familiar) labels from memory, rather than to the number of experienced events.

The fact that time and distance should be closely connected is not surprising. Other things being equal, long distances take longer than short ones. But overestimation of distance can also be associated with increased difficulty, and with an increase in the number of events encountered during travel. For instance, there is good evidence that people overestimate the length of routes which have many turns or bends, or many intersections, when compared to routes that have fewer turns or fewer intersections (Byrne 1979).

A relatively early study by Lynch (1960) showed that routes in the centre of a city were thought to be longer than routes outside it. Lee (1970) found that students in Dundee overestimated outward journeys from the centre of the city, compared to walking into the centre. The opposite illusion was found in Columbus, Ohio (Briggs 1973; Golledge & Zannaras 1973). The fact that the outward journey from Dundee is steep, while Columbus, Ohio is flat, may be one reason for the difference. The greater attraction of the city of Dundee for students who live outside may be another (Canter 1977).

Canter (1977) suggested that apparently contradictory illusions of distance can be explained by taking social and individual as well as environmental factors into account. He cited evidence which suggests that distance judgements by adults and by children are influenced by the attractiveness of the goal of travel, and the value attached to the goal, as well as by the frequency, mode and speed of travel, and the amount of information it conveyed. Canter (1977, p. 101) was probably right to suggest that 'distance estimation may only be understood in the broad context of a person's use of places'. That clearly applies also to young children whose goals and use of space may differ from those of adults. But there is no clear evidence that distance judgements diverge specifically on the basis of age.

The sight of physical barriers along routes also has predictable consequences on distance estimates by seven-year-olds, eleven-year-olds, and young adults (Cohen & Weatherford 1980). The effects of the context in which judgements are made influence judgements quite intelligibly. In practice, barriers are likely to take longer to negotiate, and thus have some of the same effects as a longer distance.

There are also consistent biases in judging distances which depend on 'context' only in a much narrower sense. The context here is the range of lengths within which a judgement takes place. Children as well as adults are influenced by the range of available stimuli. The well-known 'tendency to the mean' is one of these consistent biases.

It has long been known that people tend to 'overcorrect' small movements and underestimate large ones (e.g. Woodworth 1989). Fitts (1958) quotes a laboratory experiment by Wheeler (1949) which showed that the amplitude of other responses in a series determines the direction of bias. Large responses are underestimated; small amplitudes are judged to be larger than they are. Very similar biases are found in estimates of distances in large-scale space: short distances are overestimated; long distances are judged to be smaller than they are (e.g. Byrne 1979; Newcombe & Liben 1982).

The question is why distortions in distance judgements should occur at all. Here the very fact that there are a considerable number of quite disparate factors which can influence distance estimates (e.g. Canter 1977) is instructive. It suggests some lability in the underlying process. Moreover, this is not confined to large-scale judgements. As we saw earlier (Chapter 6), when location and distance information are experimentally distinguished, short-term memory tends to be less accurate for sequential movements than for information which is specified in terms of a spatial frame.

It seems probable, therefore, that distortions in distance estimates occur mainly in the absence of a definitive spatial frame by means of which start and end locations and the intervening space can be specified. It makes sense that, in the absence of defining spatial frames, judgements should be maximally liable to distortion by powerful if irrelevant factors.

More important still are the factors which normally correlate with the distance experienced in moving through space. The duration, speed, and force of movements and fatigue with time are likely to influence distance-estimates, particularly in the absence of a specific determining spatial frame for the distance travelled.

Systematic errors (e.g. Poulton 1979), such as central tendencies (reverting to the average) and the tendency to overcorrect, also become intelligible as a result of uncertainty about reference frames. In conditions of uncertainty about the spatial frame by which a distance can be specified, people seem to make (not necessarily conscious) attempts to establish some norm or standard in relation to which they can achieve consistent estimates. Consistent errors in such conditions can then be seen as the result of establishing inaccurate standards, based on some average of recently experienced ranges of stimulus inputs.

III   Bias in judging directions

Systematic biases are also found in representations of directions. Perhaps the most common error is a bias towards representing all types of angular joints as right angles. Adults as well as children frequently draw road junctions and intersections as right angles, regardless of the actual angle at which the roads meet (e.g. Byrne 1979; Moar & Bower 1983; Tversky 1981).

The fact that adults show this type of error is of particular interest in understanding possible developmental differences, because the assimilation of obliques (acute and obtuse angles) to the nearest right angle has been considered as peculiar to children, and indicative of their understanding of spatial relations (Piaget & Inhelder 1956). Young children certainly show such errors in their drawings, and even when copying (Howard & Templeton 1966). They affix chimneys at right angles to sloping roofs, draw water levels at right angles in tilted jugs, and stick wires at right angles on to oblique lines (Ibbotson & Bryant 1976). On Piaget's theory (Piaget & Inhelder 1956), such errors occur because young children code topological relations and are incapable of using Euclidean coordinates (see earlier). However, that explanation will not do because young children do code Euclidean relations in simple and familiar contexts, especially if recognition, rather than recall tests are used (e.g. Fishbein *et al.* 1972).

Kosslyn (1987) suggested the interesting idea of a fundamental dichotomy between organizing information in terms of semantic categories which is carried out by the left hemisphere, and right-hemisphere organization which is in terms of spatial coordinates. I should like to amend that picture somewhat because, as it stands, it does not account for the fact that the error in question here does not occur in perception, only in memory.

The error of representing obliques as rectangular directions typically occurs more with tests of construction or reconstruction. This suggests strongly that the error depends critically on retrieval from memory, not on perception. The fact that adults make the same error as young children thus does not require a different explanation. It can be considered in terms of common memory processes, but one which makes greater demands on young children.

Consider that right angles are typical joints in the orthogonal frames of our gravitationally oriented environment. An easy way to remember all other angles is thus in terms of the (right-angled) prototype, qualified by deviations. The deviations, as additions, would be less easily accessible in memory than the prototype, and consequently more vulnerable to forgetting or being ignored. It therefore makes sense that even adults are prone to using prototypical joints when representing unfamiliar layouts, and that young children make the same errors more often and also in apparently less demanding tasks.

The notion that we often think in terms of prototypical examples was used by Rosch (e.g. 1973, 1976; Rosch & Mervis 1975) to explain semantic classifications of 'natural kinds' by children and adults. Her model involves the (Wittgenstein 1958) idea that classification depends on family resemblances rather than on categories that are separated by strict and invariant criteria. Some examples of the family resemblance are more central or typical of the category because they have more of the common features. A sparrow is recognized more quickly as a bird than a duck, and the term 'red' is learned faster for saturated (pillar box) reds than for red patches tinged with blue or yellow.

Euclidean geometric concepts are, of course, defined by strictly necessary and sufficient criteria. Such logical description does not leave room for marginal cases or overlaps between categories. The notion of 'family resemblances' does not apply to these. But it is useful for classifying 'natural kinds' precisely because such classifications do overlap, and can contain marginal instances. A plank balanced over tree trunks may not be classed as furniture until it is used as a table. By contrast, the definition of, for instance, a right angle, in Euclidean theory does not depend on how it is used.

It is useful, I think, to consider a good deal of spatial coding as analogous to coding in terms of prototypical examples. The analogy does not have to imply that the spatial concepts which are instantiated in this way are pre-logical. On the contrary, it is clear from the evidence discussed so far that even infants and young children do implicitly respond to Euclidean characteristics of the environment when they have the information to do so.

Euclidean definitions do, of course, apply to the real, gravitationally oriented environment, and to the organism's means of experiencing the environment. In that sense, Euclidean relations between vertical and horizontal directions are experienced as 'natural kinds'. The frequency of normal spatial experience and the logic of Euclidean description tend to coincide. But few right angles in the real environment live up to the strict logical definition which is needed for geometrical calculation. 'Fuzzy logic' (see Chapter 3) rather than standard logic is more likely to apply.

The suggestion that people—infants and adults—use Euclidean relations in a prototypical fashion does not imply that they are necessarily aware of doing so. Nor does it imply that they are employing all relevant logical definitions and their implications, even implicitly, at the time. It only needs to be assumed that people are equipped to acquire at least implicit procedural knowledge of major directions under normal conditions of experience.

I reviewed evidence on differences in recognizing orientation earlier (Chapter 5). The same considerations about vertical, horizontal and oblique directions also apply, or apply even more strongly to representations of large-scale spatial directions. But there is also good evidence that the conceptual context can bias the choice of reference and spatial organization (Hirtle & Mascolo 1986; Tversky 1981; Tversky & Schiano 1989).

This account can explain why adults as well as children tend to represent turns as right angles, and under what conditions the error occurs. It also explains how a child, who does not know the name of any angle, remembers and represents these most easily as right angles. It implies a form of classification that does not depend on language or verbal labels, but nevertheless shows 'prototypical' processing. Simple shapes are used as tokens or symbols for more complex ones.

The error of using right angles to represent all angular changes in direction can thus be understood as the outcome of symbolic activity. It is the use of an exemplar to symbolize something, despite the fact that the symbolization may be inaccurate, and is therefore classed as an 'error' in the context of a given task. The explanation will be considered further in Chapter 8.

IV   Language and spatial knowledge

The fact that distance judgements by adults were biased by the familiarity of names along a route may seem surprising in view of the specialization of language and spatial processing considered earlier (Chapter 4).

Clearly, language is not a necessary prerequisite for spatial competence. After all, even animals (Bresard 1988) and preverbal infants orient themselves correctly in space, unless adults give them conflicting cues to test their knowledge or ability (Chapter 2). Moreover, the neuropsychological evidence (Chapter 4) showed ample evidence for specialization, not only of the two cerebral hemispheres, respectively, for verbal and spatial processing, but also quite specific functional subdivisions within regions. Why then should normal adults be affected by the semantic familiarity of labels they encounter along a route?

Fodor (1983) argued for the virtual independence of specific knowledge systems. The idea is that mental activity depends on components from a number of separate 'modules' or processing systems which function independently of each other. The analogy with 'expert systems' in the sphere of computer software organization suggests that a complete area of knowledge or expertise may be captured on a single disc, slotted into the computer memory, and retrieved for use in current workings, when this becomes expedient.

The more general notion that the mind and brain are organized in a modular fashion, has been fuelled by evidence that neurological damage can be associated with very selective impairments (e.g. Coltheart *et al.* 1987; Zeki 1992). Thus, selective impairments are not merely found between large domains, such as language and spatial skills, but in quite restricted areas within the domain of language processing (Coltheart *et al.* 1987) or visual perception (Zeki 1992). The implication seems to be that different regions of the brain are highly specialized in function. It has been suggested that modular organization has important advantages in economy of effort and efficiency, particularly for very complex systems such as the brain (e.g. Marr 1982). It could have been dictated by evolutionary pressures for that reason.

At the same time, the extreme notion that there are specific, spatially distinct brain regions, which correspond to specific mental or representational modules, in a more or less one-to-one fashion, considerably overstates the case (Ellis 1987; Gazzaniga 1988). Taken to its logical conclusion, it implies that there should be little interference between different 'modules' of knowledge-systems. That clearly does not account for evidence of interference from one system with another.

Interference between verbal and non-verbal information is also found in other areas, as for instance in the well-known 'stroop' effect (MacLeod 1991). Thus, it is more difficult to recognize the word 'green' when it is written in red letters, or 'small' written in large letters. The theoretical controversies in accounting for stroop effects are beyond the scope of this book. But it is clear that learned associations between perceptual features and verbal labels have powerful effects on processing.

The older Whorfian hypothesis that language completely structures perception and thinking (Whorf 1956) has to be dismissed. The evidence simply does not support the implication that the perceptual system discriminates more shades of green if (and because) a language contains names for each. That is so even for the more sophisticated version which assumes that a language system is required for solving problems and for memory (rather than perception) of events and locations. Some cases of brain damage can produce virtual dissociations between language and spatial processing (see earlier).

A more sophisticated version of the linguistic hypothesis is that spatial concepts have structural descriptions that depend on the number of features and dimensions that have to be indicated as present or absent. Distinctions between deictic terms such as 'I/you', 'come/go', 'this/that', 'here/there', 'right/left' are more difficult to learn, because their linguistic features are complex (e.g. Bierwish 1967; Clark 1971; Clark & Clark 1977; Clark & Garnica 1974; Klein 1983; Talmy 1983). The meaning or reference of deictic terms changes with the speaker and/or her location. A somewhat similar position is taken by Olson and Bialystok (1983), except that the complexity is assumed to lie in the abstract structural description of objects. The model sounds as if it implied that Euclidean concepts are part of the innate mental furniture. However, the authors also suggest that the order of structural description depends on the invariance of perceptual information, and cite evidence that terms for vertical directions and canonical orientations are acquired early.

As noted earlier, we rarely stand on our heads and, if we do, the fact is generally very plain to us from inside as well as from outside sources. Turning to the right or left, by contrast, is signalled most obviously by changes in the external surround, although these correspond lawfully with our movements in geographical space. But turning to the right or left may also be confusing if there are no obvious cues to distinguish the view when it is symmetrical about the midaxis.

It is sometimes suggested that young children confuse directions because they cannot yet name these consistently, rather than because of genuine spatial errors. Young children are sometimes considered to have difficulties with deictic expressions and in giving adequate instructions about what route some else is to follow, not because their spatial knowledge is deficient, but because the expressions demand complex verbal actions. It has been suggested that even eight-year-olds apparently have difficulties in using the terms 'right' and 'left' correctly, although they can indicate the directions correctly by pointing.

However, it is simpler to assume that the terms 'left' and 'right' cannot be applied consistently because the directions are not, in fact, invariant over the positions of the speakers and listener. It is not necessary to assume that difficulties must either be spatial or that they occur only when names have to be applied to left–right directions. The one depends on the other, and on the degree of association between perceptual features and the labels that name them.

Many adults claim to have difficulties with left–right distinctions, and usually refer to difficulties in executing verbal commands. Any one who has tried to follow instructions to 'place your right leg over your left leg and your left elbow against your right knee, and your right hand on the floor behind your right shoulder' will know the difficulty. Terms that have ambiguous references are likely to be more difficult to learn and to apply. Following the verbal instruction would, in that case, add to the difficulty created by the ambiguity of spatial reference.

Dissociations between verbal and spatial descriptions can also be documented. Adults are also notoriously poor at giving verbal directions to someone else, even when they know the route perfectly well. Before interpreting such difficulties as purely spatial or purely verbal, it is useful to consider the complexity of the task with which the person is confronted. One would like a 'job analysis' of the skills that are needed to specify directions verbally. For instance, by definition, deictic terms label locations or directions that could mean the opposite, depending on the origin or anchor point by which they are specified. As we saw earlier, such directions are more difficult, for adults as well as for children, than unambiguously specified locations. It seems reasonable that it is more difficult to learn labels for ambiguously specified than for unambiguous directions.

In addition, in order to give directions about the route other people need to follow in order to get to a destination, people have first to construe their implicit, procedural knowledge to fit with the current positions of speaker and hearer. Failure to adjust communications to the listener's needs is by no means confined to children. A very nice project by two Oxford undergraduates showed that sighted adults who habitually escort blind people usually give them advance information about obstacles on the path, but they often fail to inform them about overhead obstacles.

Another difficulty in giving verbal directions is that procedures that one may only know implicitly how to execute have to be translated into explicit declarative statements. To do so, people need to retrieve appropriate verbal symbols and linguistic structures and to convey landmark and directional information in a form some one else can understand and follow. Looked at like that, it is not actually surprising that understanding and uttering verbal descriptions of route information is more difficult than simply indicating a direction in more compatible form, for instance by pointing.

Verbal commentaries do not necessarily convey the same information to every one. A bright blind adolescent of my acquaintance who was an ardent football fan and had listened to commentaries on football games regularly in the family circle for years believed that there was only one goal post in the middle of the field, into which both sides kicked the ball to score.

At the same time, because a child cannot experience a given visual quality directly, her use of words for it is not necessarily empty of meaning.

Blind children are often considered to produce 'verbalisms' (speech without meaning) of this kind. Experimental evidence from a study that was designed to test this showed quite clearly that this is not necessarily the case (Millar 1983). Like the child to whom I referred in the introduction, subjects were congenitally totally blind children. Sighted cohorts were matched to them on age, sex, digit span, and vocabulary. The task was quite simple. Subjects merely had to judge whether or not a noun and adjective word pair was a sensible combination. Half the pairs were inappropriate combinations (e.g. tall dwarf, soft iron, black snow) interspersed randomly with appropriate pairs (e.g. round ball, hard wood, red rose). The word pairs were in four modality blocks, using auditory, tactual, spatial and visual adjectives in, respectively, appropriate and inappropriate combinations. The experimenter spoke the word pairs at equal rates, and responses were timed. Subjects had to press the relevant response bar as soon as they made their decision. Errors were negligible for both groups. Blind children were actually slightly faster on auditory, tactual and spatial word pairs than the sighted. The critical adjectives were colour words. Clearly, totally congenitally blind children could not ever have experienced colour. They can, and do, of course, learn appropriate colour–noun combinations, and the older group made no more mistakes on such word pairs in this experiment than the sighted. More importantly, however, they also judged the inappropriate pairs correctly. These they could not have learned by rote. Their semantic judgements were thus quite as good as those of children who clearly did experience colour directly. There was however a difference in time. The blind did take significantly longer to judge the inappropriate colour pairs. The basis of their judgements may thus have been a different strategy. Nevertheless, colour words were not meaningless for them, but belonged to an appropriate semantic domain. The blind did not differ from the sighted at all on the spatial pairs. This is consistent with experiments by Landau (1983) who also found that blind children use spatial terms perfectly meaningfully. Direct haptic experience is, of course, relevant to this. But the findings on colour words show also that direct experience of a sensory quality is not necessary for correct semantic judgements (Millar 1983).

We do not as yet know precisely how such semantic judgements are built up. The meaning of a word may be derived from analogy with other forms of experience and knowledge. The neuropsychological evidence on spatial coding that was discussed earlier suggested that when all functions are intact, there is interaction as well as specialization between different forms of input (Chapter 4). Indeed, it is probably more correct to say that specialization depends on the convergence of multitudinous inputs which interact in various ways within the whole of the central nervous system, including verbal and spatial functions of the two hemispheres (see Chapter 4).

One method of studying the relation between verbal and spatial aspects of tasks has been to ask under what conditions different sources of information interfere with, rather than improve performance. The stroop effect (MacLeod 1991), like the results on processing dual inputs from different modalities or submodalities (Chapter 3), suggest facilitation from the relation between highly correlated verbal labels and spatial codes, and interference with each other when the correlation is disrupted or made ambiguous. Relatively independent spatial and verbal codes, by contrast, should not produce more errors and/or slower processing.

Results from further studies support these predictions, the relation between verbal and spatial coding could be regarded in much the same way as the relation between the modalities and submodalities, that is to say, as complementary analyses which converge and partly overlap under normal conditions. It should also be possible to use biases in coding as a measure of the strength of association between the two forms of coding in children and in patients with relevant forms of neurological insult.

V   Information and orientation in large-scale space without vision

The bulk of research on spatial development and spatial skills in large-scale space is concerned with its mental representation or cognitive mapping. That is also the main topic of the book. The studies that I am mainly considering look at representation of large-scale layouts, either in terms of small-scale tests, or by tests of in orientation or way-finding in large-scale space. However, before we look at representation of large-scale space in the absence of sight, we have to ask what long-term information is actually available to congenitally blind subjects.

There is no doubt that knowledge derived from longer-term visual experience, prior to blinding, affects both posture and locomotion in large-scale space (e.g. Hollyfield & Foulke 1983). However, as many will know from party games, it is actually very difficult to exclude all sight. Most bandages leave chinks at nose-level through which the floor space can be seen quite clearly. By elevating the head a little so as to look down it is possible to walk 'blindfolded' to the correct location. That is less possible with the eyes shut. But some light filters through the eye-lids, nevertheless. Even if it is not enough to discriminate shapes, changes from very bright light to darkness can be recognized. There is thus some potential for detecting gross obstacles or obstructions.

The majority of people who are legally blind or visually handicapped to a degree that requires education for the blind have some residual vision. Moreover, a good deal of residual vision is potentially useful, and children can be trained to make the most of it (Chapman et al. 1989). Even merely being able to identify the source of bright light across the room could, in principle, act as an anchor cue for guiding locomotion, or serve as the basis for learning what and where the window is.

Another potentially confounding condition which has been considered in interpreting findings on small-scale spatial coding is brief prior vision of a target, even when there is subsequent complete exclusion of light. The short-term, prior vision of the target is especially useful if it was correlated with body posture (e.g. head or eye position). For instance, the target location can be indicated quite reliably if the body posture is maintained after sight has been excluded (e.g. Polit & Bizzi 1978). Thus, it has long been known that infants can remember which of two identical boxes conceals the sweet they wanted, if they maintain the same bodily orientation to it during concealment or after a delay is introduced before they are allowed to touch or retrieve it (Hunter 1912). The initial body posture also affects walking without vision, if only briefly.

Reference information in large-scale built-up or enclosed environments is limited even in fully sighted conditions, if only because people cannot see round corners. That has often been described as having a multiplicity of views, compared to the single viewpoint that is possible in small-scale space (Acredolo 1981; Ittelson 1973; Slator 1982).

There are nevertheless at least three advantages from visual information. First, there is a coincidence of information about external and body-centred directions which characterizes visual perception during locomotion. This is important for the current updating of movements within the visually limited large-scale route. Another is that the continuous updating of external cues during walking provides some continuity of information. Even when turning a corner, it is possible to look back and forwards, so that intermediate starting points and goals can be considered in relation to each other. Limiting visual perception to near objects has effects on locomotion (Strelow & Brabyn 1981). Further, vision provides a knowledge base for coding the relation between external surfaces and planes reliably. In principle, that knowledge can be used to compensate for the limits in current information.

Now consider information about large-scale space in conditions in which sight is completely excluded. The concern here is with current information available for actual orientation in the external geographical environment, and moving around in it. The main advantage of vision for simply moving around and orienting oneself in large-scale space is undoubtedly the fact that, in vision, 'optical flow' information is continually and reliably available (e.g. Lee 1980). When there has been prior sight of the target, walking without vision is quite accurate for about 5 m; after that accuracy becomes poor (Thomson 1983). The initial question is about information in an unfamiliar environment in the total absence of sight.

The nearest analogy for sighted people is probably that of orienting oneself in thick fog, when there are no recognizable landmarks, or wearing blacked-out goggles that really exclude all light.

In the total absence of external guiding cues, there is a well-known tendency for people to veer to one side, often to the right, so that they come to walk in circles. It is not entirely clear what factors produce that. Cratty (1967, 1971) investigated veering in blind children and adolescents, and found that individuals were quite consistent in veering to one side rather than the other. They were unaware that they were not walking in a straight line. Veering related neither to intelligence test scores, nor to levels of anxiety in walking.

Interestingly enough, veering was not necessarily the same in all environments, although it is by no means clear that veering depends solely on perceptual cues (e.g. slope of ground).

The initial facing position does, however, contribute to some extent. Apparently, even a brief training period reduces the amount of veering. It is not clear whether such training generalizes to all environments. It thus seems again that no simple statement is possible about whether and in what direction people veer, unless the precise informational conditions are detailed.

In long-term blind conditions, attention to sounds is, of course, an important substitute for visual cues to distance and direction. It is the main alternative modality which provides information about the external environment in large-scale space. It is therefore particularly important for locomotion when vision is excluded. The direction of an external source in hearing is computed by the time difference between the sound waves reaching the left and right ear, respectively. Major cues for the direction from which a sound comes are time- and intensity-differences between the arrival of sound waves (pressure in the canals) at the two ears. Because temporal and amplitude cues for different sound frequencies are also available for natural (complex) sounds, their direction is detected relatively easily. Detection can be enhanced by lateral head movements, while vertical head movements provide further information about the elevation of the sound source.

Localization by sound of what is straight ahead can be extremely accurate. So long as there is a stable external cue, blindfolded adults have relatively little difficulty in moving towards it in a reasonably straight line. Brabyn and Strelow (1977) found that accuracy of walking towards a source of sound at a distance of 11 to 12 metres was comparable to accuracy in walking towards a light mounted on a pole (at 11.6 m), when vision was degraded to diffuse light in conditions in which subjects wore face masks with glass that permitted only diffused light vision.

In the course of pre-tests for a study (as yet unpublished) on attending to sounds in walking, I found that congenitally totally blind school-age children had no difficulty in walking straight to the source of a continuously emitted sound, at a distance of nine feet. That was in an unfamiliar classroom. Subjects were also reasonably accurate in arriving at the source of sound when asked to respond after a short (five to ten second) delay. Subjects heard the sound briefly from the starting position. It was then turned off before they started to move towards it.

I also noticed that the more competent subjects tended to adjust their body posture to face in the direction of the sound before it was turned off. The position of the head and feet seems to be particularly important for walking in a straight line once the sound is turned off.

Differences in intensity of a continuous sound from a stationary source can be used to estimate distance from that location. In principle, such differences in intensity may also be used as a reference to guide movements in different directions, at least for a short distance. However, it seems likely that some learning or experience is needed to use sound locations as reference rather than as guiding cues.

I used a nine foot square experimental room to test this. Subjects wore a light backpack that carried a lightweight metal pole which extended above the crown of the head. The top of the pole was connected to three spools of thin but strong thread, mounted on a triangle of strands that were located outside the experimental space. The spools paid out and retracted the thread, as the subject walked around the experimental space. Potentiometers on the stands, connected to the spools, registered the pay-out and retraction by means of a three-channel recorder which recorded the movement information in analogue form on tape (Uher 4000 Report-L). The design of the apparatus was initially based on a measuring device by Strelow and Brabyn (1976). However, it had to be adapted so that it could be transported to the schools in which testing took place. The experimental 'room' and recording devices were all portable. Analysis took place subsequently in the laboratory, by (computerized) transformation of the analogue output from the recording device into digital form. The output form that traced the actual path taken by a subject with great accuracy.

A study was conducted with the apparatus on the use of an extraneous, fixed, but discontinuous sound with congenitally totally blind children. The presence of the sound did not produce significantly greater accuracy in walking to a destination at a distance of nine feet, when that was in a different (opposite or orthogonal) direction to the source of the sound. Indeed, for some of the youngest children, the sound proved confusing. They tended to turn and walk towards the source of sound, rather than in the opposite or orthogonal direction. The precise conditions in which children learn to use fixed sounds as references for other directions, rather than as guiding cues, requires further study.

However, people can use self-produced echo-location as a guiding cue.

Echo-location can be produced by hand-clapping, tapping with the foot or cane, or by means of prosthetic devices which throw out sound waves that return from walls or solid obstacles. There are now a number of such devices, which are used to judge the presence of obstacles and distances and directions from targets (e.g. Bower 1989; Kay 1974; Strelow & Brabyn 1982).

Hearing is thus an important source of complementary reference information, although localization by hearing tends to be less accurate than by sight. In a manner of speaking, you can hear sounds around corners, in a way that is impossible for sight. But it is rarely precise. Fixed distant sounds can give a 'preview' of a distant goal. But the meaning of fixed reference sounds has to be understood, and they are more likely to be recognized in familiar than in strange environments.

In the wider geographical environment there is no preview of the ultimate goal of longer routes or routes that deviate from a straight path, nor perception of the initial starting point. That applies to vision as well as to hearing. But intermediate goals in vision normally allow some anticipation of what will be encountered (Hollyfield & Foulke 1983). However, unless sound sources or haptic cues are deliberately stationed at the start and relevant turns, or can be recognized in familiar environments, intermediate references are less available in hearing. It has already been mentioned that with vision you can look back at intermediate starting points and forward to intermediate goals.

The most striking, and probably the most important, difference between vision and hearing as sources of external reference is that vision provides information about the relation of external surfaces to each other. Sounds alone do not provide information about the relation between external planes. In visual conditions, it is obvious, for instance, that vertical and horizontal planes are at right angles to each other. The viewer may be totally ignorant of the names or notations for orthogonal directions. But the fact that the location of an object remains invariant if it is specified in relation to external coordinate planes is, *ipso facto*, a significant aspect of a subject's experience.

Gibson (1966, 1979) was clearly right to insist on the importance of the invariance of perceived relations, even if one cannot accept the existential assumptions for the description which he seems to make. Change and invariance are, after all, necessary for experience to occur at all, in whatever way experience is tested.

The argument here is that both the reliability of information and the extent to which the outcome of given procedures can be predicted affect mental representations of the environment.

The absence of information about the relation between large-scale (distant) external planes in walking without vision is, therefore, perhaps even more important than the paucity of reliable external cues by which movements can be updated. The fact that sounds alone do not provide concomitant information about the relation between different external planes makes such information a less reliable basis for coding in terms of coordinate external reference frames than visual conditions. In blind conditions knowledge about the relation between external planes as well as current updating cues need to be supplemented by other means.

One form of information that is clearly available and reliable in blind conditions is proprioceptive and body-centred information. It can be used even for locomotion, provided that spatial coding in terms of body-centred frames is updated by other means. For instance, when we turn round or retrace our steps, adequate spatial coding is still possible even without external spatial frame information, by the use of updating rules (e.g. upon a 180 degree turn, left–right relations are reversed).

Another possible strategy is to use memory for the movement sequences for blind locomotion in large-scale geographical space. To do so successfully, however, it is necessary to maintain the same body position for head, trunk and feet, and to compensate adequately for the degree of turning.

Moving around totally without vision in the larger environment makes more demands on memory and cognitive skill. It means looking for guiding cues, paying attention and interpreting them in a way that can be taken for granted in vision. Except in highly familiar environments, remembering prior instructions about landmarks and turns, making inferences about distances and directions from one's own movements, remembering to update these, and building up some notion of the relation between different directions in order to make correct inferences, are only some of the tasks that are involved.

VI   Some sources of discrepancies in coding large-scale space

In the course of a study some years ago, I demonstrated a tactual compass to an extremely intelligent blind eleven-year-old, whom I shall call Sally.

Sally had no difficulty at all in learning compass directions. She also learned the rule that west–east relations, and the consequent left–right body directions, are reversed when walking back from north to the south starting point, and she demonstrated the rule correctly when asked to turn back from a given point.

On leaving the room in which we had worked, Sally turned in precisely the same direction into the corridor as she had done on coming into the room. She should, of course, have turned in the opposite direction into the corridor on the way back. The route between her classroom and the testing room was not one Sally used very often. Nevertheless, it was rather surprising that she did not apply the reversal rule that she had just learned when going back to her classroom.

Now consider Kelli, the little two-and-half year old blind toddler, whose correct spatial inferences were described by Landau *et al.* (1981). Kelli had been taught to walk between four landmarks in a diamond-shaped space. She succeeded at better than chance level on the inference tests which consisted in walking from any one of these landmarks to another along a new route, leaving out the intermediate landmark.

How did it come about that these two children differed so radically? Why did an intelligent older girl have difficulty in reorganizing spatial directions mentally, while little Kelli did not?

It should be noted that Sally's behaviour is, in fact, the most common finding, not only for congenitally blind children (Casey 1978; Hatwell 1985; Millar 1975b, 1976, 1979, 1981b; O'Connor & Hermelin 1975), but also for adults who are totally blind from birth (e.g. Byrne & Salter 1983; Dodds *et al.* 1982; Herman *et al.* 1983).

It is instructive to look as closely as possible at the detailed circumstances and conditions in which these two children were tested. Such details are neglected when questions are posed in 'can/cannot' form, but they are essential to understanding the underlying processes.

The value of the study by Landau *et al.* (1981) is not in question. We are extremely indebted to them for important further evidence that neither full vision nor life-long periods of reinforced associative learning are necessary pre-requisites for spatial competence. The issue is simply whether their evidence necessitates the assumption of an innate Euclidean knowledge system, as they imply.

In my view, that claim cannot be sustained (Liben 1988; Millar 1988a). The important point is that Kelli's inferred paths were not straight lines. Landau *et al.* (1981) provide meticulous profiles of the paths Kelli took to the test locations. They were curved. As the authors themselves report, Kelli started out in the wrong direction and corrected her movements. Such corrections are normally found only when there are updating cues (Millar 1988a). Something must have occurred for the child to change direction half-way through, after starting out in the wrong direction. As far as the theoretical claim is concerned, a curved path between two points is certainly not a basic tenet of Euclidean geometry. The evidence is not compatible with the assumption of an innately operating Euclidean system.

The hypothesis of an innate Euclidean knowledge system would also make it difficult to explain why Sally did not use that system, especially as she had just had an opportunity to re-learn the relevant spatial relations. Sally was well above average in intelligence. She had no history of any brain damage which might account for spatial difficulties. Nevertheless, her spatial errors in relatively unfamiliar environments were too frequent for these to be simply accidental. I met Sally again when she was an attractive, intellectually and verbally highly accomplished seventeen-year-old. She no longer turned in the wrong direction when going back to her classroom. But she was still uncertain in orienting herself in the wider environment.

The conditions under which Kelli orientated herself correctly are therefore of great interest. Some of these must depend on conjecture. It is not possible to reconstruct completely from the reports what factors contributed to Kelli's undoubted competence. Nevertheless, there are some useful pointers (Liben 1988; Millar 1988a), and these need to be considered in some detail.

One potentially important fact is that in the original study Kelli was tested many times on the same spatial layout. There must therefore have been at least growing familiarity with the situation, with the general environment in which the tests took place, with the landmarks, and also with the task demands.

Repeated testing also has some influence on how task instructions are understood. To carry out the tasks, Kelli must have been told what she was to do. Given repeatedly, the very instructions—namely to walk to one of the four test locations—would have conveyed that it was at least possible to get to any of these four landmarks from any of the others. That is a very crucial piece of information. Whether or not Kelli inferred from the instructions that the display must be a bounded figure with four salient corners, she must have understood from the repeated requests that the same landmarks can be reached from all other starting points.

The reports show further that, on trials on which she failed, Kelli was carried to the correct target location. Kelli, therefore, had no opportunity to walk the new path initially. Nevertheless, being picked up and carried, instead of arriving independently at a familiar landmark, would feel different even to a very young child. The difference would also be salient, because being picked up and carried occurred only when Kelli failed to reach the goal independently. There was therefore some knowledge of results, a well-known ingredient in learning.

Two other conditions are known to influence the direction of locomotion without vision. Body posture at the start of locomotion, and especially the position of the feet, makes an important difference to the direction in which the person starts out. We do not know whether, or how, this was established or corrected. The other condition is the tendency to veer from straight paths when walking without vision (e.g. Cratty 1971). The reported data do not take such veering into account. What may be conjectured, however, is that the constant sympathetic attention which the adults must have provided during testing, to Kelli's movements, to the directions in which she moved, and the locations she reached, could not have been entirely without effect. These details do not amount to a training programme. But it cannot be assumed that repeated testing and re-testing, by sympathetic and approving adults, conveys nothing even to a young child.

A more important finding which must be considered, comes from tests which were conducted some three years later (Landau *et al.* 1984). The authors again provide meticulous evidence. This time, it showed clearly that Kelli now walked in straight lines to the inferred locations. The paths to test positions were no longer curved. Something had clearly therefore been learned in the meantime by that bright little pre-schooler (Liben 1988; Millar 1988a). That achievement itself is, of course, extremely impressive.

It is not known whether her parents encouraged Sally to explore independently as an infant, or whether they knew how to convey spatial information to her. When Sally came to school, shortly before I first met and tested her, she was verbally extremely competent, but poor at such apparently simple tasks as using scissors to cut a tactually marked straight line. Like most children in schools for the blind, Sally received some mobility training. So did the other children whom I tested. However, the frequency and quality of such training in schools for the blind depend crucially on extra resources, and these are usually scant. There can be no doubt at all about the dedication of teachers in schools for the blind (some of which are now alas closed), in trying give the children as much spatial experience as possible. This includes well-prepared outings to places in the immediate and wider environment. Nevertheless, in the normal school situation it is almost impossible that an individual blind child can get exclusive attention from highly knowledgeable adults, let alone attention which focuses specifically on a spatial inference task in the same experimental space.

The fact that Kelli had achieved straight-line paths to inferred locations by the age of five or six years is remarkable by any standards. In some ways, it is actually more important than the earlier finding. It is not evidence for the operation of an innate knowledge system. But it is evidence that the potential for learning spatial (including Euclidean) relations is not subject to a maturational cognitive delay until late childhood or adolescence in the blind. The finding adds to the results (e.g. Leonard & Newman 1967) which have shown that visual experience is not necessary for spatial learning and for making spatial inferences.

However, it is not irrelevant that Kelli was later found to have perception of light at a distance of some three or four feet. At the time of their first tests, Landau and her colleagues (1981) were not aware that Kelli had residual light perception. When the authors reported the fact later, they suggested that Kelli had not, in fact, used her residual vision originally to guide her to the test locations. The possibility cannot, of course, be ruled out completely. But the authors are probably right. The very fact that Kelli did not originally move in straight lines to the test locations suggests that she had not used her residual vision at the time. We do not know how, after starting out in the wrong direction, Kelli was able to correct her path. It is possible that she missed intervening locations by veering from the straight path to an incorrect location, so that the chance of arriving at correct locations was increased. Alternatively, there must have been some form of updating cue. Neither Euclidean inference nor visual guidance would produce curved paths. The fact that Kelli in later years walked straight to the inferred locations does show that she now knew enough about the spatial layout to make correct inferences, although it is not quite clear why errors still occurred.

Nevertheless, the fact that Kelli had some light perception is important, whether or not she used it for orientation in the original tests. By contrast, Sally's blindness was congenital and total. It was due to a congenital (bilateral glaucoma) condition which allowed no useful sight even before the age of five months, when the operation that totally blinded Sally (both eyes enucleated) was carried out. Her locomotion (a nodding gait as if testing out the ground before her) was typical of the type of posture and movement often found in congenital total blindness.

Although residual vision of the kind that Kelli evidently possessed, may be quite minimal, and can vary with time and circumstances, it does mean that Kelli and Sally did differ in degree of blindness. Kelli differed also from the congenitally totally young blind children in my studies.

Evidence that even very minimal residual light perception, without the perception of shape, or of hand movements, as well as prior vision before the age of two years, relate to spatial coding has already been discussed (e.g. Millar 1979). The difference was not one of efficiency but of the type of strategy mainly used.

It is sometimes argued that sensory deprivation produces a general lowering in the level of stimulation and knowledge, and a general 'developmental lag'. That may be a contributing factor in some cases. But it does not account for findings on children who are functioning extremely well verbally and in general cognitive performance, but show specific differences in spatial coding without any evidence of brain damage.

The findings considered in this section suggest that total lack of visual experience can have quite specific effects on spatial coding, without any lack of competence in other areas of cognitive functioning (e.g. Casey 1978; Byrne & Salter 1983; Herman et al. 1983; Hollyfield & Foulke 1983; Millar 1979; Rieser et al. 1986; Warren 1974).

A study I conducted some time ago with a 'large-scale' (four foot square) experimental space, is a case in point. Some of the results have been reported before (Millar 1981a, 1990b). The details of interest here concern representations of the space by two age groups of children who were either congenitally totally blind, adventitiously blind (blinded after the age of two years), or had some useful light (no shape) perception. All came from the same two schools for the blind and were tested on the same intelligence tests, and on forward and backward digit spans. The average age of the younger blind children was about seven years; the average age of the older blind was about ten years (above eleven years for subjects with light perception). Within the age groups, the children could be considered equally cognitively competent. Because it was not possible to match all the blind subjects precisely on age, the age-gap comparison was with two younger groups of normally-sighted children, aged six and eight years, respectively, from a primary school in the same intake area, who were tested blindfolded.

The experimental space was initially enclosed by a guiding rope, suspended from the four corners at midriff level. The level at which the rope was suspended was convenient as a guide during the acquisition phase. The four corner posts had platforms, on each of which there was a distinctive toy as a landmark. Subjects walked around the four sides, without vision, in a clockwise direction. They were encouraged to feel and to name the toys they encountered at the corners in the acquisition trials. The walk was repeated until the child was able to recite the names of the toys in the correct sequence on at least two occasions. The guiding rope was removed only after that. The child was tested, after the rope had been removed, on going from the start to the next position; then on inferred paths between toys. For these the child was guided to one of the corners, and was then asked to go to the next but one corner toy. Finally, the children were asked to draw the space where they had walked, and to indicate the position of the toys on it.

As reported earlier, young congenitally totally blind children could not cope with inferred directions and tended to veer from the straight path. Young adventitiously blind children who had some previous visual experience were significantly better, although not as good as younger blindfolded sighted children. But above the age of ten to twelve years, the blind were quite good even at inferred directions, and indeed differed very little from the older blindfolded sighted children.

The results for representing the space by drawing showed the apparent jump in efficiency even more clearly. Drawing on plastic paper with a rubber underlay produces raised lines (see Chapter 8), so that the children could easily feel what they had produced. The drawings were scored on several counts. Scores were given for producing a line or lines (rather than a scribble) to represent the walk, for placing the toys in the correct sequence, for placing toys at equal distances (or in relation to the start location), for representing the walk by a closed figure, and for representing it as a square (Figures 5 & 6). The gap in scores between younger and older

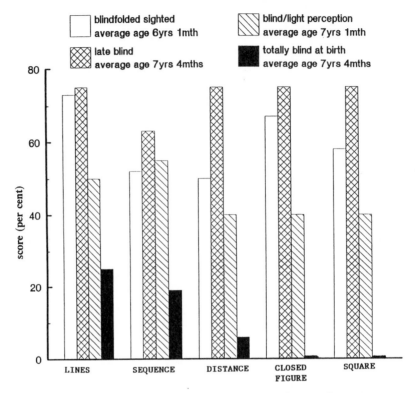

Fig. 5 Scores for representations of a square route (see text) by the younger groups of blindfolded sighted, late blind, blind with light perception and congenitally totally blind children. Percentage points scored on: LINES (one or more lines, not scribbles); SEQUENCE (toys as landmarks placed in the correct sequence from the starting point); EQUAL DISTANCE (indicating equal distances between the landmarks); CLOSED FIGURE (representing the route by a closed rather than open figure); SQUARE (representing the route by a square figure).

subjects was significantly greater for the congenitally totally blind. Perhaps more important, the age gap for the congenitally blind was not the same for all types of score.

The differences between the younger groups depended on what was being tested. Most late blind children and some children with light perception, as well as blindfolded sighted children who were a year younger than the blind groups, produced closed figures. The congenitally totally blind did not. The late blind, that is to say, children who had vision for two to five years, were actually better than the younger sighted, but above the age of ten to twelve, the differences between groups disappeared. The older blind performed at ceiling level before their younger sighted cohorts. It is

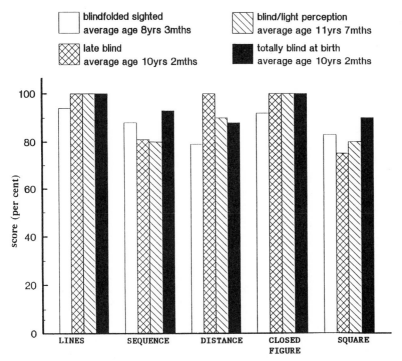

Fig. 6 Scores for representations of a square route (see text) by the older groups of blindfolded sighted, late blind, blind with light perception and congenitally totally blind children. Percentage points scored on: LINES (one or more lines, not scribbles); SEQUENCE (landmarks in the correct sequence from the starting point); EQUAL DISTANCE (indicating equal distances between the landmarks); CLOSED FIGURE (representing the route by a closed rather than open figure); SQUARE (representing the route as a square figure).

of interest that such discontinuities with age are mainly found with small-scale displays, especially if these are used to symbolize large-scale spatial knowledge (see Chapter 8).

Thus, the discontinuities in skill with age, were similar to those reported by Hatwell (1985), and they were also found mainly with small-scale displays. The series of studies by Gomulicki (1961) are particularly relevant in looking at the factors in such discontinuities. He reported that young blind children were much worse than sighted controls on a variety of small-scale haptic tasks, but they later caught up in speed and accuracy.

His data suggest that the age at which this happened differed with the complexity of the task. In doing up buttons, hooks, and shoe-laces and also in matching three-dimensional shapes, blind children reached ceiling level performance by the age of eleven to twelve years. To learn small-scale stylus (haptic) and large-scale (life-size) mazes, poorer performance occurred until the age of thirteen to fifteen or more.

Gomulicki (1961) implicated the mode of learning as well as task complexity. He found that performance differed with teaching methods that provided 'a picture of the maze pattern as a whole' (p. 43), in contrast to presenting segments in a particular sequence. Gomulicki (1961) found evidence that blind children need to be more intelligent than the sighted to reach comparable levels of performance. Correlations between efficiency of performance and intelligence levels were higher for blind than for sighted children.

The relative difficulty of tasks and the number of different factors they involve thus needs to be considered also in understanding Sally's and Kelli's performances. Kelli's task sounds more difficult because she had to make an inference. Kelli had to apply her knowledge of how to get from location A to B, and from B to C, to reaching A from C. But the inference could draw on information that was implied in the instructions, and in repeated procedures with the same layout, namely, that the required destination could be reached from any of the others. Sally's task sounds easier, in that she only had to return to her classroom. However, the route was relatively unfamiliar to her, and no one had told her that it might help if she applied her recently acquired knowledge of compass directions. Sally had learned a new rule, and had exhibited the correct reversal procedure in the original environment. But to apply this correctly in a relatively unfamiliar environment would constitute an additional load on memory. Without any specific incentive or instruction to do so, it would be easy to fall back on the more habitual, sequential mode of organization, which explains her performance. In order to turn in the correct direction, on the basis of the recently acquired knowledge, she would have had to retrieve the recently acquired information about compass relations on a small-scale layout, and translate these into a set of procedures in large-scale space.

Knowing how to reach a location does not automatically enable even the sighted to map the relevant space correctly. Conversely, blind as well as sighted children learn Euclidean geometry at school. But neither they, nor adults, necessarily apply these propositions automatically to orientating themselves in geographic space. Knowledge of rules or propositions which say 'that' something is the case needs to be distinguished from the development of knowing 'how' to proceed or to implement procedures (Brown 1975). There is evidence that the connection between the declarative knowledge that something is the case, and procedural knowledge, or knowing how to do something, is indirect even for adults (Berry & Broadbent 1984; Broadbent et al. 1986). The question of using maps, whether actual or cognitive, to orient oneself in large-scale space will be discussed in more detail later (Chapter 8).

It is thus clear that, to understand how vision affects spatial coding, more than one factor has to be considered. Familiarity with the task and the environment, the number of repetitions in acquisition and testing, the repetition of tests over time, and implicit forms of feedback from repeated trials to reach the goals are only some of these.

The fact that errors occur more in relatively unfamiliar surroundings is important. It suggests that the person has to attend to constituents of the situation in a way that is not needed when task conditions are familiar. Lack of familiarity with task conditions or constituents thus imposes a greater mental work load and more demanding memory requirements (Hollyfield & Foulke 1983). Furthermore, it is the combination of favourable conditions for learning, as well as prior or minimal vision, which seems to be particularly propitious for learning without vision.

The case of the famous deaf and blind Helen Keller (Keller 1905) exemplifies this. It is often forgotten that Helen Keller was not, in fact, congenitally blind or deaf. She had normal vision and hearing for the first 19 months of her life. Such early experience, during a period of fast maturation and learning, is extremely important. We clearly do not need to learn to see or hear. But seeing and hearing provide initial experiences of the environment to which the developing infant adjusts, and which form the bases of her or his knowledge. It is also relevant that, after years in which her teaching was entirely neglected, Helen Keller had a teacher who devoted herself exclusively and permanently to understanding what information Helen actually needed and how best to convey it.

We do not have sufficiently detailed knowledge as yet as to how minimal visual experience facilitates orientation and coding relative to external spatial frames in large-scale space. However, even being able to distinguish bright light from total darkness conveys at least that there is something 'out there'. The advantage of seeing a light patch may consist solely in eliciting the child's attention to external cues. But its correlation with her movements and with other cues that emanate from external sources is likely to increase his or her confidence that such cues can be used reliably.

A potential advantage of even minimal vision is the fact that any light source, or brighter external patch that can be discerned when walking, is likely to coincide in space and time with auditory cues which emanate from the same or from a nearby source. Such coincidence is likely to reinforce reliance on external information and provide more incentive to explore the external environment.

Questions about the function of various forms of minimal visual cues, and how they may combine with other information, require a great deal more study. But there is little doubt that even very restricted visual experience, either from prior or from residual vision, is related to spatial performance. The evidence from studies with small-scale layouts has shown that the difficulties in mental spatial reorganization tasks experienced by the blind can largely be accounted for by the tendency to code in terms of the haptic information. When moving about in large-scale space, locations cannot be specified strictly in terms of body-centred coordinates. But coding in terms of movement sequences is possible.

However, in trying to understand the differences that occur, it should be noted that it is not the efficiency, but the patterns of spatial performance that indicate strategies, which provide our information. People who have had prior visual experience are more similar to the sighted in their patterns of performance (Byrne & Salter 1983; Dodds et al. 1982; Herman et al. 1983; Millar 1977c, 1979; Rieser et al. 1980).

The fact was exemplified by the study (Chapter 6) with congenitally totally blind children in a 'perspective' task that involved moving in relatively unfamiliar large-scale space (Millar 1976, condition 1). This was a task in which subjects had to judge the direction of a line, after walking to positions at the surrounding oblong table.

The blindfolded sighted children were not particularly accurate in that task. Specifically, they were no better than the blind children in mentally rotating to near-orthogonal positions; they were only better in respect to far positions and diagonals. It was the pattern of errors which suggested that the blind attempted to track their own successive movements, whereas the patterns of their blindfolded sighted cohorts showed that they had used the relation of the line to the table surround as the main means of coding.

Byrne and Salter (1983) obtained comparable findings for adults in large-scale space. Byrne and Salter (1983) use the terms 'vector' versus 'network' maps to describe the difference in coding found, respectively, for blind and sighted adults. They tested congenitally totally blind adults, aged between 22 and 62 years, and sighted adults, matched on age and sex. The task was to estimate directions and distances between named locations. The space was an environment that was familiar to both the blind and sighted from everyday experience. Blind and sighted subjects did not differ in their estimation of distances. But the blind adults were severely impaired in estimating direction, especially if the estimates had to be made from locations other than the home base.

The difference is similar whether the distinction is between route versus survey-map representation, or between coding in terms of sequential movement versus configurational coding. Rieser et al. (1980) distinguished instead between inferred Euclidean (straight line) distance estimates that demanded knowledge of the spatial layout, and functional (walking) distance estimates, between pairs of locations. Congenitally blind adults were impaired on Euclidean judgements, but judged functional distance as accurately as sighted adults.

The interpretation that blind subjects tend to use sequential haptic coding explains difficulties in judgements that require updating directions relative to external coordinates. Distance judgements demand such specification less, and should therefore not differ greatly between blind and sighted people.

The evidence on adults as well as on children, and for large-scale as well as small-scale spaces, is thus quite consistent. Forms of coding do differ with long-term informational conditions. The findings suggest strongly that, in the total absence of vision, information about large-scale space tends to elicit sequential coding. It is clearly a sensible procedure when external information is unreliable. Described in terms of 'memory for movements', 'route knowledge', or as 'vector map representation', it is often considered to be a less adequate strategy than survey or configurational organizations of routes. That is not necessarily so (e.g. Wilton 1977).

In some tasks, sequential modes of coding do make solutions more difficult. However, such difficulties can, of course, be overcome. It does need more effort, cognitive skill and familiarity with the situation. Coding in terms of sequential inputs make it more difficult to specify or reorganize directions than when coding in terms of coordinate reference frames is possible. By contrast, distances and locations present few difficulties, if they can be coded in terms of movements or by self-reference. The fact that sequential coding makes it more difficult to reorganize directions does not, of course, imply that spatial or configurational coding is impossible. On the contrary, it will be argued later that configurations can be derived perfectly well from movement sequences.

For small-scale displays, findings showed forms of coding which, although perfectly efficient in principle, do make some tasks more cumbersome. It was argued that lack of vision favours coding by movement sequences and self-reference, because that information is more reliable in blind conditions than information about external frames. The point to be noted here is that the commonly reported performance by congenitally totally blind people is perfectly intelligible in informational terms, and in the light of the evidence which has been considered here on how informational conditions influence modes of coding. Moreover, this evidence strongly suggests that the deficit in information in congenital total blindness is quite specific.

The findings from a well-known, fairly early study (Leonard & Newman 1967) are consistent with the above analysis. Leonard and Newman (1967) tested six intelligent (Grammar School) blind adolescents to show that visual experience is not necessary for spatial thinking. Five were congenitally blind, although some had light perception. They had been deliberately trained in the use of tactual maps, over a period of time prior to tests on two 'detour' problems. Subjects encountered a road block on a path in the school grounds. They had to go around two blocks of buildings to get back on to the path. The detours could be followed only by using a tactual map of the layout. One boy failed to solve the first problem, but all six solved the second problem with relatively few (self-corrected) mistakes. It is implied (rather than stated) that these included one or more congenitally totally blind subjects. Data on (control) subjects whose residual vision was somewhat better showed that the control subjects took significantly less time to solve the problems.

Usually, the Leonard and Newman (1967) study is quoted solely as evidence that visual experience is not a necessary condition for solving inferential spatial problem. But the study tells us far more than that. Thus, the detailed findings show that the children who had residual vision were better at solving the map and detour problems. More important perhaps, the report also makes clear that crucial information had been made available to all subjects. Subjects had been taught quite explicitly in previous weeks how to use (small-scale) maps as references to large-scale routes, and how the small-scale indices relate to large-scale routes. They had also been instructed to use that map information to solve the new detours.

In other words, Leonard and Newman (1967) demonstrated importantly that information about the use of maps for reference to large-scale routes can be made available without recourse to visual experience. The authors clearly did not assume that such knowledge was innately available without training. They did assume, correctly, that the information and its use can, and should, be conveyed by means other than vision.

What is needed urgently in studies of this kind are detailed analyses of task conditions, and of what information is available to the child from touch or vision. That includes also the incidental information that is implicit in the instructions that the child receives.

In the total absence of visual experience, even when hearing is not impaired, systematic assistance in obtaining crucial information about external spatial relations, and familiarity with the environment and tasks, are probably even more important.

VII Summary

The evidence on spatial development in large-scale environments was found to support what may broadly be termed information-theory explanations, such as those of Siegel (1981) and Pick (1988), which emphasize the role of familiarity, salience of perceptual cues and their utilization, and improvements in coding for short-term and longer-term memory.

The notion that there is a specifically developmental progression from reliance on landmarks to coding in terms of routes, and finally to forming cognitive maps was not supported. The findings suggested rather that the progression could be explained completely by differences in information between conditions, and the means of coding that these elicit.

There is evidence that distortions and biases occur when knowledge of large-scale environments is tested by map drawing. The errors suggest that people may be using coordinate reference frames as 'fuzzy' categories. The analogy with semantic categorization suggests that deviations from the major directional categories tend to be ignored in output. Other forms of distortion arise from the fact that large-scale environments usually have personal significance for people. That evidently influences coding large-scale environments to a much larger extent than is likely when simply testing formal geometric layouts.

Verbal labels can interfere with spatial judgements; at the same time, people often have difficulties in describing a route verbally. It was argued that linguistic and spatial coding should be regarded as complementary and converging analyses and symbol systems, rather than as belonging either to a completely unitary or to two quite separate systems.

The information about large-scale spaces that is available with and without vision was discussed, both in terms of effects on moving around the environment and in terms of effects on coding strategies. Sounds, including echo-location, were compared to sights as useful guiding cues for loco-motion, especially in familiar environments. Coding heuristics are in-fluenced by the available information in the short as well as the long term. Total absence of visual experience tends to elicit heuristics that have variously been characterized as sequential, route or vector forms of coding, because information in that form is obtained more reliably in totally blind conditions than information about external configurations and relations between external planes. Sequential strategies are not necessarily less efficient, nor do they preclude map-like coding, but they do produce more difficulties (require more cognitive skill) in some tasks. Differences in coding strategy rather than in the possibility of spatial competence are implicated.

The final section looked in some detail at the conditions that can explain the competence of a very young blind child, who had minimal sight and a great deal of assisted spatial experience, compared to the difficulties in mental spatial reorganization tasks commonly found for blind adults and children and here exemplified by the performance of an intelligent con-genitally totally blind girl, whose mobility experience was no more than ordinary. The two examples illustrate further the need for analyses of the conditions that influence means of coding, rather than for assertions or denials of competence.

8

Non-verbal representation: images, drawings, maps, and memory

> I see meaning as a blue-grey tip of a kind of scoop, which has a bit of yellow
> above it (probably as part of the handle), and which is just digging into a dark
> mass of what appears to be plastic material (Titchener 1909, p. 19).

The American psychologist, Titchener, who wrote this at the beginning of
the twentieth century, must have infuriated his Würzburg school opponents,
who argued that thought is imageless. Titchener took his introspection to
be empirical evidence that we think in images. According to him, the
'conscious attitude', which was all that Watt, the English member of the
opposing German (Würzburg) school, discerned introspectively, was also
an image, albeit a kinaesthetic rather than a visual one. But the Würzburg
school held that their introspections showed thought to be abstract.

The demise of introspection as a reliable empirical method of psychological enquiry owed much to the fruitlessness of that debate. The subjec-
tive nature of the method led behaviourists in the early part of this century,
to dispense with mental notions, like images or thought, altogether. Stimuli and responses could be measured, and therefore provided an objective
scientific method. The relation between these measures was the goal of
psychological enquiry. Everything else belonged to an inaccessible black
box. The fact that human behaviour was not always predictable from the
immediate stimulus conditions was explained by secondary, covert response systems. Speech, as a 'second signal system' (Luria 1961) or
as learned, covert verbal labelling (Kendler & Kendler 1962), mediated
human problem-solving and development.

The nature of representation in memory became of interest again in the
middle of the century, when more sophisticated and repeatable experimental methods had been invented to investigate human memory. These made
it possible to begin to study the nature of covert processing. For instance,
Conrad (1964) showed that short-term memory for lists of verbal items is
based on sounds. The method is to show people lists of items (letters,
words or pictures) that have names which sound the same (e.g. cat, hat,
mat, rat), or lists with names that are phonologically dissimilar. Recall of
lists of items that have phonologically confusable names is poorer; subjects
must therefore have used sounds to remember the items (Conrad 1964).

That can also be shown for children to whom items are presented visually (Conrad 1971) or by touch, provided that the children can name the items easily (Millar 1975b,c).

In the early 1960s, the main theoretical concern was still with verbal materials. Thus, long-term memory was investigated in terms of semantic organization (e.g. Atkinson & Shiffrin 1968). Modality-specific or sensory aspects of the information were supposed to be available only initially (Atkinson & Shiffrin 1968) for a very brief (milliseconds) period (Sperling 1963).

I   The return of visual imagery

Images returned to respectability in the second half of this century. That was partly due to increasing evidence on hemisphere specialization (see Chapter 4), but also to behavioural findings on memory for pictures and other non-verbal materials with adults (Paivio 1971) and young children (Reese 1970; Rowher 1970). The results suggested increasingly that memory could not be described solely in terms of inner speech and verbal concepts.

Luria (1968) studied a man with a fabulous memory for digits. He could recite all the numbers in a 13×3 matrix he had seen, as if reading them off mentally from a visual image of the matrix.

A variety of empirical methods were devised to show that imagery is used. One was to rate words and sentences for imageability. Those rated high in imageability were remembered better (Paivio 1971). Pictures of objects are easier to recall than names, whether by adults (Paivio 1971), by young children (e.g. Reese 1970; Rowher 1970), or by deaf children (Reese & Parkington 1973). Millar (1972c) found that instructions to form images enhanced recognition of nonsense shapes even by four-year-old children.

The most frequently quoted experimental findings came from the studies on mental rotation and paper-folding by Shepard and his colleagues mentioned in Chapter 6 (e.g. Shepard & Cooper 1982; Shepard & Feng 1972; Shepard & Metzler 1971). The fact that the time needed to decide whether or not rotated objects were identical increased with the degree of rotation is precisely what would be expected if people mentally imagine rotating the shapes (Shepard & Cooper 1982). Furthermore, the empirical findings agreed with subjects' introspections in all paradigms with non-verbal stimuli.

Paivio (1971) put forward the theory that information is stored in terms of visual imagery as well as verbally, and the second round of the imagery controversy took off. Opponents of the imagery view argued that memory and thought depend on abstract propositions (e.g. Clarke *et al.* 1973; Kintsch 1977; Pylyshyn 1973, 1981). The main problem about the controversy for and against the notion of imagery, is the failure to distinguish between, on the one hand, arguments about the type of theory at which psychology ought to aim and, on the other, purely methodological questions about empirical findings. A great many arguments against the notion of imagery are of the latter kind.

There is little doubt that many findings from studies on imagery can be explained by factors other than imagery. For instance, improved learning and memory could be due to the concreteness, rather than to the imageability, of words and phrases. The fact that concrete words are more frequent, call up more associations, and are better organized could thus explain improved recall. Differences in modality-specific interference could occur because of the greater similarity between interfering stimuli and materials in the main tasks, rather than because of their visual character. The fact that the gist of statements tends to be remembered better than the literal wording was taken as evidence that memory is stored in terms of propositions rather than images (Kintsch 1977). Increased response times are influenced by factors other than increased rotation, and increased latencies with increased rotation could be due to an increase in the complexity of algorithms needed to solve the problem, rather than to rotation of images (e.g. Pylyshyn 1973, 1981).

However, these are empirical matters. The fact that alternative interpretations of the data are possible raises questions about the adequacy of methods to demonstrate the use of imagery. But it does not establish the opposite interpretation. The question as to what heuristics subjects actually use is an empirical issue. For instance, people who are totally blind from birth can solve mental rotation tasks (see earlier). Consequently, vision is not necessary to solve such problems. But that alone does not tell us anything about the basis of their solutions. It cannot establish that the form of coding was 'abstract', let alone that it is so always. Visual imagery is not the only form of coding people can use. The nature of imagery is not necessarily the same for congenitally blind as for sighted people (Arditi *et al.* 1988). Schlaegel (1953), for instance, found that intelligent blind adolescents report imagery in modalities other than vision.

Similarly, the fact that people can mentally see through and around imagined objects that in perception would be opaque (e.g. Neisser & Kerr 1973) has been considered evidence that imagery is abstract. However, an abstract image is something of a contradiction in terms. What such reports do show is that visual imagery is not identical with visual perception.

Imagery, even if it is so vivid as to almost resemble hallucination (eidetic imagery), is a memory phenomenon. People make mistakes in recognition that would be impossible if they were 'reading off' from a photograph (e.g.

Haber & Haber 1964). Even the very vivid 'eidetic' images which some people report thus depend on memory, and are not simply due to a persistence of actual perceptual stimulation.

Kosslyn (1980, 1981) postulated that memory systems include a visual memory buffer. It works on analogue, rather than digital conversions, functions as if it were a coordinate space, and makes computer simulation perfectly possible. That has probably helped to confer greater respectability once again on the notion of images. Visual images could be conceptualized as transitory data structures in a short-term memory buffer that uses an analogue, rather than a digital system.

Pylyshyn (1981) countered that the alleged spatial character of images is best accounted for as tacit knowledge about spatial relations. Images are like toothaches. People report them, but they have no explanatory power. However, the latter objection to the notion of imagery is actually on quite different grounds. It is not about the methodology of empirical studies of imagery. It is about the metalinguistic level at which theoretical models should aim.

The distinction between arguments about levels of description and about empirical methods is briefly considered next.

II The imagery controversy: a category error

As is often the case with apparently endless controversies, they are endless because the arguments blur meanings of terms which are quite legitimate, but belong to different universes or levels of discourse (Millar 1982b). It is a category error to compare 'images', as reported empirical phenomena, with 'propositions', which are formal constituents in a metalanguage.

In ordinary language, the term 'imagery' names an empirical phenomenon, an experience that people report. It is legitimate to ask whether imagery, as a reported experience, can be demonstrated in overt behaviour, and whether, how or under what conditions that affects performance. These are wholly empirical questions; they are matters of experimental ingenuity in devising experimental procedures. The answers cannot be asserted or denied *a priori*.

By contrast, the term 'proposition' normally labels the formal (abstract) relations between the components of a statement. Propositional functions, in that sense, are necessarily 'abstract' because they are formal descriptions in a metalanguage. They are not experiences nor dimensions abstracted from experience. It is legitimate to ask whether the description of memory as the storage of propositional functions is more or less useful for explaining existing evidence or has more or less predictive power than, for instance, description in terms of mathematical functions. It is wholly inappropriate to ask whether such 'propositions' could be experienced.

Unfortunately, the terms have also been used in the converse contexts. Thus, it has been questioned whether or not the concept of imagery has any explanatory force. But that is not an empirical question, and cannot be decided by empirical test. That question demands an answer in terms of the choice of metalanguage which ought to be used to describe behaviour. Such choices demand decisions about the level of generality at which the model is aimed, its adequacy in accounting for a given range of empirical data, and its predictive power.

Similarly, the term 'proposition' is sometimes used to label the empirical fact that people remember the gist of a message better than the mode of input. That is an empirical matter. It is perfectly appropriate to ask whether the people can remember the mode of input as well as its propositional content. That is subject to empirical test. As it happens, we remember the meaning of what was said more than its precise form, but the form and mode of inputs can also be remembered. But, in that context, the term 'proposition' is used as a label for an empirical finding, namely, recognition —accuracy for semantic versus lexical content or tone of voice. The term is not here a second-order explanation of the findings.

The question whether we think in images or in propositions is thus ambiguous. The empirical and theoretical meanings of the terms are some-times used (adversarially) in the wrong contexts. But the distinction be-tween empirically demonstrable, or potentially demonstrable, phenomena and the metalanguage which is used to describe them in theoretical models is important. Questions require quite different types of answer in the two contexts.

For Pylyshyn (1981), the main point was clearly the relative explanatory power of abstract descriptions versus description in analogy with experienced events. His argument is about the choice of metalanguage at which a theory should aim. Pylyshyn (1981) escapes the main confusion by using the term 'tacit knowledge' as an alternative to the notion of an analogue spatial translation memory buffer. The argument is thus about explanations, rather than about empirical phenomena, although this formulation shifts the problem to equally thorny questions about consciousness. Questions about what type of explanatory model we should use will be taken up later. Here, it may simply be noted that, for Pylyshyn (1981), images are like toothaches. They occur. They are not explanations.

The trouble is that reported images are not quite like toothaches. Few doubt the reality of toothaches; even fewer worry about their ontological status. A toothache stands for nothing but itself. An image often stands for other things. In other words, images function as symbols. That does not make them abstract any more than a word is abstract because it functions as a symbol.

Interestingly enough, Titchener (1909), the arch exponent of the imagery view of thinking, actually regarded images as symbols. That is extremely interesting. He prefaced the account of his image of 'meaning' by the remark that, in his consciousness, concepts are usually represented by impressionist pictures. He goes on to explain that the particular icon of a scoop, which represented 'meaning' for him, probably arose from his having to 'dig out' the meaning of particularly abstruse Latin or Greek passages in his youth.

Titchener was evidently conscious of having images—as conscious, probably, as Pylyshyn was of his toothache. But he considered that images *represent* concepts, not that they are identical with concepts. His thesis therefore makes precisely the same assumptions as Pylyshyn, namely that concepts are tacit knowledge. But he assumed further that images can represent or act as symbols for tacit knowledge.

Looked at in these terms, Titchener's view that we think in images is perfectly compatible with the apparently opposite view that thought is 'imageless'. Processes of retrieval from memory and from (metaphorical) 'knowledge stores' are tacit; they are not necessarily open to conscious inspection.

However, 'tacit knowledge' also characterizes a much wider notion of 'representation'. Marr (1982) defines that notion of representation as a formal set of symbols with rules for putting them together. For instance, the representation of shape is a 'formal scheme for describing some aspect of shape, together with rules that specify how the scheme is applied to a particular shape' (Marr 1982). That is not, of course, an account of perceptual experience. It is a (general) instruction for how it might be simulated in computers or at the level of algorithms. Whether or not Marr's notion of 'representation' applies to perception, that is to say, whether we need to assume that perception is mediated by representation, is not the question here. The interesting distinction is between 'representation' as applied to the whole of a rule or knowledge system, and 'representation' as applied to the symbols within such systems.

The term 'symbol', of course, also means 'representing' something other than itself. The two uses of the term 'representation' function at different levels. Marr (1982) emphasized rightly that different levels of description should not be mixed.

The interesting point is that images in Titchener's sense are symbols. He uses the term to mean that images are representations of concepts. They are not identical with concepts. In that sense, they function as words do, as indeed Paivio (1971) implies. They are neither identical with the concepts they represent, nor with the propositions that formally describe a knowledge system.

Most of us recognize feelings like the 'Bewusstseinslagen' (conscious attitudes) of the Würzburg school: the 'tip of the tongue' feeling of being sure (often incorrectly) of knowing a name we cannot recall; images which look like dream pictures, and tunes that we cannot get 'out of our heads'.

Images of that kind seem to relate to modes of input. It may be asked in what respect they do so and whether such images are like toothaches and merely haunt us. These are empirical questions. They have to do with how images can be demonstrated empirically.

The notion of images is confusing precisely because images are experienced rather like toothaches, but can function as symbols that represent tacit knowledge, although they are not identical with tacit knowledge, nor a description of it.

In fact words function similarly. They can be used covertly. However, words are known to be learned, and the relation to memory is therefore more obvious. Images are usually assumed to be unlearned, and to arise spontaneously from perception. I shall argue that imagery can also be learned. But words have the additional advantage that they can be uttered. That is important.

The assumption that output factors mediate short-term memory is, of course, fully accepted in the domain of language. Evidence that covert speech is a major means of maintaining items in memory in the short term will be reviewed briefly, before looking at the link between input and output coding in other modalities.

I shall argue that images can function as symbols for tacit knowledge. They are not descriptions, less still explanations of tacit knowledge. But they can and do act as symbols or means of coding in short-term memory. That is not a noticeable characteristic of toothaches.

The next section therefore looks briefly at the relation between input and output factors in verbal coding, and then considers input and output factors in other modalities.

III Modality-specific input coding and output organization

It seems to me that the main reason why it has been difficult to demonstrate imagery empirically is that we have not stressed sufficiently the important link between input coding and output plans. The close link between heard and spoken speech, by contrast, is obvious, and occurs early. I shall look briefly at such effects in verbal memory because we know far more about it than about other modes of coding.

There is ample evidence that short-term memory for discrete verbal items is maintained by rehearsal or covert speech (e.g. Atkinson & Shiffrin 1968; Baddeley 1986, 1990; Conrad 1964). We say telephone numbers to ourselves in order not to forget them between looking them up and using them. When people have to mouth an irrelevant syllable ('blah, blah, blah

. . .') while trying to remember items, their recall for the items presented during that time is poor (Baddeley 1986, 1990). Tapping during delays, or executing other irrelevant activities that do not use the speech system, do not have that effect, whether the verbal memory items were heard or presented visually (Baddeley 1986) or by touch (Millar 1990a). Articulatory suppression (mouthing an irrelevant syllable) occupies the speech output system; memory for longer words is poorer, because such words take longer to say, and consequently take longer for output plans to be formulated so that they can be said in recall tests.

Baddeley's working memory model (Baddeley & Hitch 1974; Baddeley 1986) assumes an 'articulatory loop' to account for subvocal rehearsal. The loop is specialized for speech-based material and accounts for the temporary storage of verbal material in memory. Indeed, the importance of output factors in verbal memory is stressed in other theoretical accounts (Broadbent 1984; Monsell 1987). Broadbent (1984) and Monsell (1987) propose that output processes and output plans are mainly responsible for the effects which, in Baddley's model, are attributed to an articulatory loop.

The powerful method pioneered by Conrad (1964, 1971), which shows that people tend to remember by name sounds, has also sometimes been interpreted as depending on output factors. There is now ample evidence that lists of items are recalled less well if they consist of items with phonologically similar, rather than dissimilar, names, even though the lists are presented visually. Broadbent (1984) and Monsell (1987) suggested that some of the effects of presenting phonemically confusable items occur at the output level.

Facility in covert naming of items relates to the increase in short-term memory span with age, regardless of the mode of presentation (Conrad 1971; Millar 1975b,c, 1978b). Millar (1975b,c) used Conrad's (1971) method with tactual presentation. Children had to remember a series of tactual shapes that were either tactually similar or similar in the sound of their name. The test did not require speech, only pointing. Children who were fast at naming showed larger memory spans, and their recall was significantly disturbed by phonologically similar items (Millar 1975c,d). The reverse was true of slow namers, or children who did not know the name of the items. They remembered few items, and their recall was disturbed by tactual similarity between successive items, not by the name sounds. The crucial variable was naming-speed, rather than age. Nameable shapes produced larger spans, that improved still further when the items were grouped in threes. Nonsense shapes produced short spans, and grouping made recall worse if anything (Millar 1978c). Although the findings suggest some form of phonological (name sound) storage, it is nevertheless possible that the effect depends on response rather than input coding. For instance, motor programmes may be involved in translating from visual or tactual inputs to coding by name (Allport 1979).

The influence of sound on input coding has been more difficult to show, even in verbal memory. Short-term memory for sounds has sometimes been attributed to a literal persistence of sensory stimulation after the off-set of the heard stimulus, in some 'raw' or uncoded form. For instance, the well-known 'recency effect' in which the last item of a list is recalled best (e.g. Waugh & Norman 1965) is reduced when the lists are seen rather than heard. The auditory effect has been termed 'echoic' memory in analogy with a kind of sound box. However, other findings suggest some form of temporary auditory or 'buffer' memory in which the items are not completely uncoded, or depend solely on output factors. One instance is that presenting an 'O' after an auditory memory set, in fact affects the last item only, while making people say the 'O' affects the whole series (Crowder 1974). Besner (1987) proposed two forms of phonological memory, only one of which depends on the speech output system, while the other does not. Vallar & Baddeley (1982) found that speech output is not always necessary for rehearsal. Baddeley (1986) assumed that auditory inputs are first stored phonologically. Unattended speech has 'privileged access' to the articulatory (rehearsal) loop. Input coding of sounds is thus assumed, although they have to be maintained in temporary memory by the articulatory rehearsal loop if they are not to fade or drop out of memory.

Coding of input sounds also needs to be assumed to explain how memory span increases with age (Henry & Millar 1991). Speech rate by children increases with age as does rehearsal (e.g. Hulme & Tordoff 1989). But it is not sufficient to explain increases in memory span that occur before children are good enough at naming covertly to use covert naming and rehearsal. We (Henry & Millar 1991) tested the hypothesis that speech rate is the sole factor in the development of children's auditory memory span by equating the speech rate for given words, and then used these to test memory span. The memory span for auditory inputs increased with age and familiarity, despite the fact that speech rate for the relevant words had been equated between age groups. The rate of covert verbal rehearsal is therefore not the only factor in larger spans. Auditory input coding must be assumed.

Any one who has tried, and failed, to sing correctly the tune they can hear distinctly 'in their head', will probably be surprised that it has been so difficult to demonstrate temporary memory for sounds, which does not depend on output.

Visual input coding has been even less easy to demonstrate, partly because visual imagery studies have often used verbal materials (e.g. Holyoak 1974). Speech-based coding is likely to win out with verbal materials (Salamé & Baddeley 1982), even when they are presented visually, and their content is highly imageable.

However, visual input coding does occur. Posner (1973) showed that adults match letters faster if they are visually identical than if they have the same name but differ perceptually. Segal and Fusella (1970) found that giving instructions to image pictures reduces the detection of visual stimuli selectively; imagined sounds impair the detection of auditory stimuli.

Conrad (1972) was the first to show that deaf children who cannot name pictured objects easily are likely to code them in terms of visual characteristics. Short-term memory in the profoundly deaf is more disrupted by visual similarity between letter strings than by their similarity in sound.

The fact that very young children tend not to recode visual pictures into rehearsable names (e.g. Bruner *et al.* 1966; Conrad 1971) also suggests that they rely on visual coding. Millar (1972c) tested this directly by instructing four-year-olds to visually rehearse ('try to see it in your head') nonsense shapes during short delays. The instruction improved recognition significantly, although the children were unable to name the stimuli.

A number of people have used a dual-task paradigm (Brown 1958; Peterson & Peterson 1959). As described earlier, the method looks at the nature of coding in short-term memory by using a secondary task during the delay interval between presentation and recall, or concurrently with the main task. Filling delay intervals with stimuli in different modalities produces modality-specific interference. Visual digits, to which subjects have to respond during recall intervals, interfere more with memory of highly imaginable phrases; heard digits, by contrast, interfere more with recall of abstract phrases (Atwood 1971). One problem is how to equate the relative difficulty of the main and secondary tasks (Logie 1986). However, even when that is controlled, monitoring random visual matrix patterns interferes with a visual imagery mnemonic task (Logie 1986).

Studies of visual imagery have not always distinguished tasks that demand spatial (where) coding from tasks that require object (what) identification (Logie & Baddeley 1990). Logie (1986) found effects of visual distractors in conditions where no spatial responses were required. The vividness of visual imagery by adventitiously blinded people seems to relate to the time lag between blinding and such reports (Hollins 1989). There is now evidence for the involvement of the visual cortex when people try to form visual images (Goldenberg *et al.* 1990).

At the same time, visuospatial tasks seem to be particularly vulnerable to disruption by visual information. Brooks (1967, 1968) found that irrelevant visual tasks disrupted memory for spatial relations, but that irrelevant auditory tasks interfered more with verbal memory. It takes longer to scan images of distant than of near locations (Shepard & Cooper 1982), and scanning speed relates to the size of imaged objects (Kosslyn *et al.* 1978).

The fact that spatial coding is disrupted by secondary tasks which are difficult cognitively (e.g. Johnson 1982) is sometimes considered to be evidence that the nature of spatial coding is abstract. However, the disruption may merely mean that inputs were being organized in terms of reference cues (Millar 1981a; Millar & Ittyerah 1991). Organizing inputs in any form may take mental effort, whatever the form of the organization. It does not follow that the mode of representation is the same in all cases.

Baddeley (1990) included a 'visuospatial scratch-pad' in his model of working memory, as a further adjunct to central decision-making processes, in addition to the articulatory loop. The notion of a 'visuospatial scratch-pad' (Logie & Baddeley 1990) was proposed to account for the storage of visuospatial information temporarily as imagery. However, it does not seem to have an output connection similar to that of the articulatory loop, although some link to movements is implied. Gopher (1984) showed that memory for visual codes speeded training of a movement skill. Smyth and Scholey (1992) did not find a relation between spatial span and movement speed, but they tested spatial span by serial recall. Also, speed of movement may not be the main link between spatial coding and movement information. The main question seems to be whether visual distractor tasks reduce memory for visual items because they interfere with the visual, or with spatial aspects of the main task (e.g. Logie *et al.* 1990).

It may be noted that visuospatial coding can be demonstrated in behaviour whenever visual inputs are linked with output systems. Thus, speech-gestures other than articulation are also coded in temporary memory. Locke (1970) showed that deaf children who know sign language code information covertly in terms of visuomotor signs.

Similarly, it is of interest that dual-task paradigms which test visuospatial coding often require movement output. For instance, tracking, pointing, or other gestures are used as secondary tasks. These tasks require the organization of movements in terms of visual reference cues. These constituent aspects of the secondary task are rarely considered sufficiently in deciding on what factors mediate visuospatial imagery. The point will be discussed further in relation to the effects of imagined movements.

Imagery in modalities other than vision is much less often reported. Indeed, the term 'imagery' is often used synonymously with visual imagery. It is likely that individuals differ in the extent to which they can deliberately 'bring to mind' perceptual characteristics of different modalities. Verbal reports certainly differ considerably in the vividness and details that are remembered by people with eidetic imagery compared to reports by people who deny experiencing visual imagery at all. Nevertheless, imagery in modalities other than vision has been reported and demonstrated experimentally.

Schlaegel (1953) found that blind adolescents reported images of sound, feel, smell, temperature, and the like. Blind children are trained to attend to perceptual cues in as many modalities as possible (e.g. Cratty 1971). The question is how these forms of coding sustain temporary memory.

Tactual coding was demonstrated experimentally in the studies mentioned earlier on coding by sound (Millar 1975b,c, 1977b, 1978b). Patterns that were tactually identical were matched faster than patterns that were identical in name and outline shape, but differed in feel (Millar 1977b). Recall by children who could not yet name the tactual patterns, or who were slow to name them on pre-test, was disturbed by tactual similarity between serial items, but not by phonological similarity. That was in complete contrast to fast namers. Their memory was disturbed by phonological (see earlier), rather than by tactual similarity: nameable braille letters that were presented in groups of three increased recall significantly; by contrast, grouping tactual nonsense shapes which could not be named had almost the opposite effect on the same children (Millar 1975b, 1978b).

Moreover, input coding is not precisely the same for all modalities. Visual and tactual input coding differ, for instance, in the conditions which enhance recognition. Thus, visual recognition of difficult nonsense shapes by young sighted children can be improved by instructing them to imagine them visually (Millar 1972b). A further (unpublished) study showed that instructing the same children to mentally imagine feeling tactual shapes failed completely to improve their recognition.

The interesting fact is that memory spans are much smaller when people code in terms of input characteristics alone. Children who coded in terms of 'feels', as shown by tactual similarity effects, achieved recall spans of only two to three items (Millar 1975b,c). Similarly, small recall spans are found for tactual nonsense shapes, and grouping had adverse effects on these (Millar 1978b). Millar (1975b,c, 1978b, 1989b) suggested that the small tactual spans shown by young children for tactually presented items were due to their coding tactual 'feels', and these are difficult to rehearse or 'output', even introspectively. Hitch and his colleagues (e.g. Hitch & Halliday 1983; Hitch et al. 1989) came to a similar conclusion with regard to visually presented materials; young children rely on visual input coding rather than recoding into verbal form.

It is noticeable that two conditions can be identified when memory spans for tactual items are reduced to two or three: lack of familiarity and coding passive 'feels'. The two are related, in that lack of familiarity means that there is little link between input and output conditions. However, the difficulty of remembering tactual items that cannot be named is in contrast to memory for haptic inputs which depend on movements (Chapter 6).

An instance is the effect of repetition on movement coding (Millar 1977c, 1985b, 1986b). There is a considerable body of work which points to an important role for movement coding in short-term memory for non-verbal materials (Chapter 6). The tasks are spatial in character in that they demand memory for distance or location. However, the inputs and tests are hand-and arm-movements. The evidence that kinaesthetic and location coding can be distinguished was reviewed earlier. Movement coding is elicited particularly in the absence of vision, when information about reference anchors is less easily available, or made less reliable (Laabs 1973; Laabs & Simmons 1981; Marteniuk 1978; Millar 1975d, 1976, 1979, 1981b, 1985b; Wallace 1977).

Typically, memory for movement extent is much poorer than memory for the end location of the movement. The fact that position memory tends to be more accurate has been attributed to spatial coding. But, as shown earlier, when the same movement length is executed repeatedly, it significantly influences position recall, albeit adversely in that context (Millar 1985b).

The finding suggests that movement repetition, even without externally administered feedback, results in better (covert) organization which is reflected in effects on recall. The point is that, when there is a reliable output system, the information can be rehearsed covertly and can therefore be maintained in short-term memory.

Complex skills are likely to depend on tacit knowledge. In spatial tasks, this may be tacit knowledge of the terrain, or of the location of landmarks, or specific points of reference. Tacit knowledge of that kind can be retrieved. More importantly, it can be translated into overt performance.

Overt output of spatial knowledge is not at all mysterious. People can describe the route to be taken, or what landmarks need to be passed, verbally. Alternatively they can draw a map. Both are forms of representation of tacit knowledge. But they differ in form, that is to say, in the form of symbols which represent the knowledge.

The view here is that movement outputs can also be used symbolically. This is less startling when we consider actual representations by drawing. I applied the term 'representation' to images in order to emphasize that they can function as symbols (Millar 1985c). I now propose to look at representational drawing as an instance of a symbol system. The point is not always sufficiently acknowledged (but see Liben & Downs 1989 for a similar view). Evidence on the development of drawing in the sighted child and drawing by the blind can give important clues about the emergence of non-verbal symbol systems.

The fact that symbols in representative drawings are not entirely arbitrary has led to an unreasonably sharp distinction between drawing and learning a language that has arbitrary symbols. Unlike verbal symbols, which are rarely onomatopoeic, the two-dimensional symbols of drawings are intended to resemble what they represent. Moreover, there are constraints from lack of knowledge of procedures, or lack of skill. Nevertheless, drawing is a non-verbal symbol system. The resemblance to what is depicted is the conventional view of drawing. The point here is that two-dimensional shapes function to represent (symbolize) three-dimensional objects and environments.

Drawings are examples of representations. They are themselves concrete objects. But they function symbolically in that they represent something other than themselves. It is therefore of interest to look more closely at the beginnings of drawing by young children and by children without sight to gain some insight into the emergence of a symbol system.

The findings on drawing as an emerging symbol system have been set out previously (Millar 1975e, 1986b, 1990b, 1991). I am taking the topic up again here because some of the findings on drawing, particularly by congenitally totally blind children (Millar 1975e; 1985b), first suggested one aspect of what has become the theory that I am proposing.

What I am suggesting is that overt forms of representation can be an alternative (albeit not the only) basis for covert non-verbal, non-visual coding and imagery.

The beginnings of actual representation in drawing are considered next, first as a developmental question, and then in conditions in which vision is totally excluded.

IV Representation by drawing: the emergence of non-verbal symbol systems in vision

It is commonly assumed that drawing is a typically visual activity. The view that vision is essential to it is shared by blind children when asked to draw for the first time (Millar 1975e).

Gibson (1971) argued that drawings, as pictures, are explained by point-for-point mapping of the optical array. Picture recognition is immediate, and requires no intervening image or representation, because the same cues obtain for both. The specifications for perception are relevant to producing illusory depth and ambiguous geometric figures. But that is not a sufficient explanation for drawings.

The current fashion in art is against 'trompe-l'oeil' productions, which fool the eye into immediate recognition. The intention, except when it is for the purely decorative, is to represent abstract ideas. Like Titchener's image of 'meaning', the symbols are idiosyncratic, and shapes are not combined according to known rules. That is, no doubt, why they can be irritating, or else interesting, if the search for clues turns out to be worthwhile.

The trompe-l'oeil ideal of representation, needless to say, is achieved by few adults, except trained artists, and even not always by them. Curiously enough, studies of drawing by young children have nevertheless centred largely on their failure to portray depth and perspective 'correctly'. The question seems to be why they cannot immediately reproduce what is obvious in perception. In that sense, the role of vision in drawing seems to be implicit, or at any rate unquestioned, in a good deal of developmental work. One of our questions is precisely what the role of vision may be.

Some explanations have focused explicitly on vision as the central developmental factor. The simple explanation that drawing 'errors' are due to immature visual perception (Rice 1930) can be dismissed. Young children can recognize shapes and visual scenes which they cannot produce by drawing (e.g. Maccoby & Bee 1965). Instead, theoretical explanations have assumed better visual analysis with age (Maccoby & Bee 1965), or the development of 'visual concepts' (Arnheim 1969) which involve thinking as well as vision. Goodnow (1977, p. 154; 1978) argues that her own studies show that children's graphic work is 'visible thinking', but she also emphasizes the fact that drawing involves solving problems.

A purely 'cognitive' view is implied in Piaget's theory (Piaget & Inhelder 1956). Young children's drawings are assumed to exhibit their immature, pre-Euclidean spatial concepts. Piaget and his colleagues used children's drawings as evidence that they do not understand perspective, or viewpoints which differ from their own, and cannot use Euclidean coordinates. Piaget also took over the suggestion by Luquet (1927) that the young child draws what he knows, rather than what he sees. That concept is married, a little uneasily, to the assumption of 'egocentric' and, later, topological forms of representation.

There is no doubt that children's drawings do differ from those of even rather incompetent adults. Houses are transparent and show the people in them; tables are drawn with four legs, even if the child's view occludes two of them. Cups have handles, although they are drawn from positions in which the handle is invisible. Chimneys sit at right angles on sloping roofs; paths do not converge; human figures lack tummies and their arms sprout from their heads; dogs are drawn upright with faces like humans. Only the full front view is depicted. Profile drawings typically start with sideways-pointing feet, rather like figures in early Egyptian reliefs.

What has particularly intrigued developmentalists is that drawings are highly stereotyped and that 'errors' of various kinds typically appear at given ages, and seem to occur universally. That appeared to vindicate the notion of developmental stages which successively and universally approach adult, that is to say 'realistic', representation. Willats (1977) has suggested that the stages depend on learning different pictorial devices for handling external spatial relationships.

An alternative theory focuses on movement as the limiting factor, and proposes analogies with language acquisition. Difficulties in executing and/or planning movements are certainly involved in very young children's productions (Goodnow & Levine 1973). A well known example is the fact that children below the age of about seven years, on average, fail to copy diamond shapes correctly. They generally manage the first two diagonal (up and down) strokes. But the further angular return is too difficult, and they tend to use circular movements to complete the figure. Triangles can already be copied at the age of five (Gesell 1940), and squares by the age of four.

Goodnow and Levine (1973) proposed an analogy between movement sequencing and Chomsky's (1965) innate language (syntax) acquisition device. They suggest that there is an innate movement 'grammar', with progressive acquisition rules for sequencing movements. The fact that children's drawings tend to be stereotyped for relatively long periods before being elaborated further is attributed largely to limits on the ability to sequence movements.

In a later version (Goodnow 1977), Goodnow's analogy with language acquisition is with semantic rather than syntactic development. The reason for stereotyped productions is the child's limited drawing vocabulary, although problems of movement sequencing are limiting factors also. Van Sommers (1984) demonstrated that there were effects from the following factors: starting locations; maintaining contact with the paper; anchoring lines; limitations imposed by the direction in which a stroke is executed; and forward planning, which is needed to draw hierarchically-organized forms. Van Sommers (1984) proposes a much more elaborate analogy with language, but assumes that constituent signifiers are not arbitrary but 'iconic'.

The evidence is, on the whole, against explanations of drawing in terms of simple maturational stages. Young children recognize highly complex scenes from photographs, pictures and drawings, long before they can draw anything like them. It is thus highly unlikely that their drawings are accurate reflections of cognitive stages (Kosslyn et al. 1977).

A number of important studies have also shown that drawing 'errors' can be reduced by changing the viewing conditions, altering the context, or asking the child to aim at getting other children to understand what they want to convey (e.g. Cox 1986; Freeman & Cox 1985).

The theoretical interpretations of these findings assume that young children understand spatial relations perfectly well. The peculiarities of depiction are due to other factors. Freeman (1980) pin-pointed short-term memory limitations. Young children draw people without tummies, because middle items tend to be forgotten. The arms thus have to be attached to the wrong points. The need to keep several things in mind at once may also determine the progression to using paired lines for arms and legs, from the initial circle with many radial lines (Goodnow 1977). Freeman and Cox (1985) and Cox (1986) suggest that young children prefer to represent canonical views of objects. Stereotyped productions and impossible views of the handles of cups are due to preference for the canonical view.

There is an apparent contradiction between the finding that children know more than they can draw, and evidence that young children's drawings correlate with intelligence test scores (e.g. Harris 1963). Indeed, drawing the human figure has been used as an intelligence test; that is to say, it is a relatively reliable means of predicting future cognitive performance (Harris 1963).

The contradiction is resolved if drawing is regarded as a problem-solving task (Goodnow 1977), or rather as a task which presents children with a series of problems which they have to solve (Millar 1990b). Solving problems is precisely how cognitive skills are tested or assessed. The view implies that cognitive skill is involved. But that also is not sufficient as an explanation.

The main, although not the only, problem the child has to solve in representative drawing is how to translate from three to two dimensions (Millar 1975e, 1990b). The child sees a three-dimensional world and three-dimensional objects. To represent these on the flat page requires adequate symbols to represent parts of objects, as well as procedures which fit these together, and devices that locate these in the two-dimensional space (Millar 1975e). Goodnow (1977) suggests that young children have a limited drawing vocabulary. Willats (1977) proposes that young children learn pictorial devices in progressive stages. I think that both are involved. The child has to find some solution for representing three-dimensional objects in two dimensions, and solves that by using simple shapes that he or she can produce (see later). He also progressively learns more pictorial devices which allow him to solve some of the problems.

Above all, drawing is not a unitary skill (Millar 1990b; Van Sommers 1984). The different theories that have been considered above are not actually alternatives. Rather, they emphasize different factors, all of which are involved, although to varying extents and in different conditions. Analogies with language certainly capture some aspects. But symbols in drawing, unlike words, are not arbitrary. There is a tacit understanding that productions ought to resemble perceptions. This has an important bearing on the problems children have to solve in their drawings.

Drawing by congenitally totally blind children is of special interest, because most theories assume a role for normal visual information, either explicitly, or implicitly, as a matter of course. But the nature and emergence of drawing as a non-verbal, and non-arbitrary, symbol system, and the factors that are involved in that emergence become more obvious when considering drawing without visual information of any kind, even from memory.

V Drawing without visual information: representation and movement

Young blind children rarely, if ever, scribble spontaneously. Sighted infants do so almost as soon as they can deliberately make marks on paper.
Producing visible marks seems to be the incentive. They give up if their
pens or pencils do not make a mark (Brittain 1979). Raised marks (scribbles,
lines, curves) that are easily felt can be produced with a biro on plasticized
paper by using a (stiff) rubber underlay. I showed a young blind child how
to produce raised marks in that way. It made him want to go on producing
marks and, incidentally, started my interest in drawing by blind children
(Millar 1975e).

The most exciting finding in the initial study, was that children whom I
knew for certain to be congenitally totally blind, and, moreover, never to
have drawn before, produced much the same sort of stereotyped body
scheme as the sighted, when asked to draw a person (Millar 1975e).

Kennedy (1982) has argued for some time that blind people understand
pictures in much the same way as the sighted and can also use sophisticated
metaphorical simulations in drawing (e.g. Kennedy & Gabias 1985). This
strongly suggests a great deal of cognitive involvement. My own interest is
in probing the relation between input and output (including cognitive)
factors in the emerging systems.

I discovered some interesting pointers when I compared blind children
who had never seen or drawn before with the sighted children who had
experience of vision and of drawing, but were matched to the blind on all
other possible counts (Millar 1975e).

Blind children aged about ten and upward produced much the same
figure scheme as their sighted cohorts: circles for the head, vertical lines or
circles for the body, and two pairs of lines, attached (more or less) to the
middle and bottom, respectively, of the 'body' line or circle, as arms and
legs.

It is difficult to think of a more powerful incentive to immediately
regarding this as evidence for an innately specified drawing system. That
would be a mistake—as well as a question stopper. It does show that such
schemes are not necessarily learned by imitation. Nor can they be considered as learned, culturally determined conventions. The blind cannot
have seen pictures by others.

However, blind children are, of course, familiar with their own bodies
through touch and movement. They are also familiar with three-dimensional
replicas of objects from lessons in modelling with plasticine and clay. But
my subjects had never drawn in two dimensions before.

Further studies suggested how such representations without vision come
about. The evidence has been described before (Millar 1986b, 1990b,

1991). Here I want to consider only how it fits into the theory that I am proposing.

No head is a circle, either in touch or vision. There are several reasons why the blind and sighted use precisely that symbol for the head, nevertheless. It solves two major problems. The first is to represent three-dimensional features in two dimensions. The second is the implicit demand that whatever representation is chosen must resemble the object physically. Arbitrary symbols are not enough. Unlike language, in which words are rarely onomatopoeic, drawings are expected to be physically 'like' the object they are supposed to symbolize.

Both the blind and sighted solved the first problem by using flat shapes for three-dimensional ones. The further problem of resemblance can be solved most easily by using a circle, because it is the two-dimensional shape which has a very simple general feature in common with heads as they are felt as well as they are seen. The same reasons apply to the use of lines for the limbs.

The differences between the blind and sighted were also instructive. One difference was the relatively trivial one, that drawings by the older blind-folded sighted were somewhat more elaborate than those by the blind. For instance, they tended to use two parallel lines for a single limb and oblongs, often with buttons, for the body. A more important difference was the placement of the figure on the page. The sighted placed the figure in the conventional 'upright' position. The lower horizontal edge of the page serves as 'ground' at this age. The blind, by contrast, placed their figures on the page regardless of orientation. They did not as yet devise a means for indicating the relation of the figure to the external environment. When asked, they simply said that the floor or ground was 'underneath' the drawing pad. This suggested that they did not as yet have an adequate two-dimensional translation for that.

Perhaps the most important difference was that the younger blind, with few exceptions, produced only scribbles. There was thus a considerable gap in competence between the older and younger blind. That gap did not occur at all between the older and younger sighted children, although they were tested wearing blindfolds. The younger blind produced scribbles that were either undifferentiated, dense blots, or separate scribbles for each body part. A few used relative orientation of lines to mark different body parts—long horizontal lines for legs and arms, and small vertical ones as tokens for other body parts, or a horizontal line with two orthogonal vertical ones for the head and legs, respectively. Only the brightest of the younger blind asked what she 'should do for the head', and solved that problem, after thinking about it for some time, by using a circle. All the younger sighted children used two-dimensional shapes, and none 'scribbled'.

These differences actually relate lawfully to some of the processes on which drawing depends. In discussing the drawings of young sighted children, it became clear that at least one of the problems is how to translate from three to two dimensions. The older blind and the sighted children of all ages initially solve that problem by using two-dimensional shapes as symbols for three-dimensional objects.

The running commentary that all children had been asked to give while drawing showed that the younger blind children were not using shape as a means of representation at all. Further studies which tested this confirmed the hypothesis. This has been reported earlier (Millar 1985c, 1986b, 1990b). Briefly, getting the children to assemble a figure from cardboard cut-outs produced much the same results as the drawings. Children who had used shapes as symbols for the body parts in their drawings selected similar shapes in the assembly task. Those who had used scribbles assembled cardboard cut-outs, regardless of their shape. The younger blind were not simply handicapped by lack of skill in drawing movements. They had not yet thought of two-dimensional shapes as possible symbols at all.

The use of shapes as symbols for body parts is actually a major step in the development of drawing. That is so also for the sighted. But it occurs very much earlier. Its relatively late spontaneous use by young blind children can be explained most simply by the advantage in information that vision provides.

Perhaps the most important advantage for the translation between two and three dimensions is that contours of three-dimensional shapes in canonical orientations are seen as the same as contours of the 'same' two-dimensional shape. Moreover, the size of the shape differs with distance, but the contour remains constant. The similarity in contour between three- and two-dimensional shapes, and between large and small shapes, makes it much easier to make inferences from one to the other. Such identity of contour is by no means perceived so directly from touch and movement (see earlier).

The 'point-to-point' optical mappings (Gibson 1971), which make the similarity of three- and two-dimensional shape more obvious in vision, account for differences between blind and sighted drawings. It explains how young sighted children come to use two-dimensional shapes as symbols for three-dimensional spaces much earlier than the blind. The similarity in gross outline is more obvious, feedback from their own productions is easier, and they do have the opportunity to see two-dimensional drawings.

There is no problem in teaching blind children that aligning their figures with the side of the page can be used to represent the upright position in two dimensions. All that is needed is to alert them to the fact that the small-scale vertical direction can be used to symbolize the upright in three-dimensional space. But it does need to be pointed out in a way that is unnecessary for the sighted.

Information about the invariance of up–down directions in the midaxis and transverse projection plane is available from haptic, as well as from visual information. But recognition of the invariance is less obvious and less direct without visual information. It is thus intelligible that it should take more time, and/or more cognitive skill, to use such information not merely directly, but symbolically as a representation of something other than itself.

The similarities and differences between blind and sighted children in producing representations by drawing for the first time thus show that blind children discover, invent, or infer the same type of symbolic representation as the sighted. It also suggests that they do so by a slightly different route; in blind conditions the crucial information is haptic. It depends on active movement rather than vision. Information from movement output thus plays an important, and probably crucial, role in tactual recognition.

An unexpected, but telling, further result also suggested that output factors are crucial in haptic shape coding. Blind children were better at producing drawings of the human figure than in recognizing by touch (Millar 1986b, 1989a, 1991).

The reverse lag between drawing and recognition by blind children, is startling, but instructive (Millar 1985b, 1986b, 1990b, 1991). In fact, with hindsight, it ought to have been predicted from results on haptic shape recognition which show the importance of pre-cuing and prior knowledge for systematic exploration and recognition (Chapter 5). Pring (1988) showed an analogous reverse generation effect when testing blind and sighted children on name versus picture-recognition.

The reverse lag in picture-recognition versus production, as well as Pring's (1988) findings, is completely consistent with the view that tactual recognition depends on prior cuing (Millar 1989a, 1990b), and that production plans can act as retrieval cues for recognition. When subjects are told the names of all the objects first, this narrows the range of possible shapes and allows them to generate output plans more quickly than from unsystematic exploration.

The idea is that output plans have to be thought of as involving feedback from moving, and also from 'feedforward', that is to say, information from the initial intention to move, and comparison with the end product. It includes the notion that motor outflow produces a form of 'forward' feed (corollary discharge) and is involved in motor plans, as put forward by Jones (1974). But I also assume that such movement plans involve cognitive skill. The evidence for that assumption will be discussed in Section VII.

I want to stress that coding inputs in terms of sequential movements, or output plans, does not make sequential organization 'fragmented' or chaotic. On the contrary, I am arguing that such coding can provide the basis for shape organization and recognition. Furthermore, I am suggesting that movement plans can also form an extremely useful basis for a non-verbal imagery and symbol system (Millar 1985c).

Visual conditions do, of course, provide visual feedback from the shapes produced on the page which can be compared immediately with the three-dimensional object. In sighted conditions there is, in addition, coincident feedback and corollary discharge from movements. Sighted children thus have more informational redundancy from diverse sources in visual conditions. In principle, young sighted children thus have a firmer knowledge base from which to derive analogies between three-dimensional and flat shapes. It requires less cognitive skill to see simple flat shapes as representing more complex three-dimensional ones in vision than in touch. That would also explain the age gap found for blind children. It takes more cognitive work for the blind than for the sighted child.

Nevertheless, the ingredients for covert non-verbal representation of shape are available to the blind in terms of memory for movements and/or movement plans. It may take more cognitive sophistication for them to think of these as symbols that not only represent, but also fulfil the requisite, if implicit, demand for similarity with the object of representation. But they clearly also have a potentially viable means of representation.

Solutions based on purely haptic inputs are more difficult. That is not because solutions are impossible, but because the absence of vision means that there is less corroborative or correlated feedback. It therefore requires more mental work. In visual conditions, visual feedback is immediate, and is correlated in time with movement outputs. Feedback is potentially available also in haptic conditions. But with unfamiliar inputs, this has to be in terms of haptic consequences in the external environment that have to be sought subsequent to the movements.

When inputs are familiar, or recognition has already been cued by prior naming (e.g. Heller 1989), the exploratory movements themselves provide confirmation. In conditions of considerable practice, feedforward (corollary discharge) as well as feedback is available. That is precisely why there is often an apparently inexplicable gap in performance between younger and older blind children.

I am arguing that movements and movement plans are an extremely important basis for haptic shape recognition. The evidence from previous chapters shows that movement information can be coded. For blind children and adults that has particular advantages because reference information is less salient and reliable. Neither these findings, nor the finding on drawings, mean that shape cannot be coded.

On the contrary, the empirical evidence suggested that movements were used to represent three-dimensional configurations, and producing representations was easier than recognizing them. The drawing data thus suggest how movement imagery may emerge as a useful non-verbal symbol system.

VI   Actual and cognitive maps in touch and vision

The term 'cognitive map' was introduced by Tolman (1948) to describe spatial coding in the rats he used in his experiments. Rats remembered locations in a maze, whether they had run through it or swum through it. It may thus seem curious that modes of input or output should affect humans. If rats have internal 'cognitive maps' of the environment, humans must surely have even better and more abstract ones?

In fact, the tacit equation of 'more abstract' with 'better' or more akin to human thinking does not work. For humans it is not irrelevant, for instance, whether information is gained from maps or from walking through an environment (e.g. Slator 1982; Thorndyke & Hayes-Roth 1982), or whether restricted modes of input provide information mainly from body-centred sources.

However, Tolman's (1948) important point was to dispute the older learning theory view that the rats only learn responses to specific stimuli, and that these are then generalized. In fact, the specific cues, from swimming or running through the maze, were irrelevant. Thus rats seem to pick up and use information in an organized fashion; that is to say, they go beyond the specific inputs that are currently given from a single source. That is, of course, typical also of humans.

Cognitive mapping is a useful metaphor also because it suggests an illuminating analogy with actual map use. Spatial coding depends on the organization of converging inputs that provide reference cues. If the map metaphor is taken seriously, it implies that this information is represented, or symbolized, in memory. That is precisely what humans are good at. The interesting thing is that rats do it too.

The analogy with mapping is important, because actual maps use yet another non-verbal symbol system. Like drawings of objects and spatial scenes, maps use two-dimensional lines and shapes as symbols for three-dimensional environments. But the symbols differ from drawings, because they are used to emphasize 'where' rather than 'what' aspects of the environment.

Drawings of objects and scenes do not have to be point-to-point transcriptions of light and shade. The aim is to elicit recognition. Cartoons exaggerate typical features. The organization of lines needs to resemble the shape of the object or scene sufficiently for identification. It is not identical with it. Maps use shapes and lines to indicate locations and distances and directions between these and are organized in terms of Euclidean co-ordinates. The aim is to guide locomotion or wayfinding. They are organized in terms of vertical and horizontal coordinate reference frames. The relations to the reference frames may be accurately proportional to the geographical relations, or may approximate these only rather loosely.

The essential difference between mapping and drawing objects and scenes is not the level of abstraction. Both use abstractions of essential features, and symbols to represent what is needed from the actual three-dimensional world. The difference lies in what features are of interest, and are therefore 'abstracted' and symbolized.

On that analysis, imagery or covert coding of features that identify objects is not necessarily less abstract than the covert mapping of features that indicate locations and directions. In both cases, processing depends on using representations or symbols (e.g. Shepard & Hurvitz 1984). Symbolic processing involves cognitive processing almost by definition. But the nature of the symbols is also influenced by modes of input and output. There is no contradiction between these factors.

The fact that mapping is essentially a form of symbolic processing has to be emphasized. This is rarely made explicit, but it is important, because the meaning of the symbols has to be understood by the user.

Map symbols are not necessarily transparent because they bear some resemblance to the aspect that is signified. An arrow that points towards the route to be taken is perceptually more similar to a pointing gesture, or a movement direction, than a word is to its referent. It is, nevertheless, a symbol which may not necessarily be immediately obvious.

The use of maps for testing spatial coding or representation is, of course, implicit in most of the studies that were reviewed in Chapter 7. Small-scale, usually two-dimensional, spatial layouts are used by preference. In some studies, the layouts are the only basis of the task. In others, experience in a large-scale space is tested by means of a small-scale layout. In so far as small-scale layouts are intended to represent large-scale space, they function essentially as maps.

Some researchers seem to have used drawing maps from memory as direct indications of mental representations (mental 'cartography') of an environment (Canter 1977; Lynch 1960). However, drawing is a complex skill which involves knowledge of procedures as well as knowledge of the object that is to be represented. It cannot be assumed that map drawing directly externalizes people's covert spatial knowledge (Kosslyn *et al.* 1977). Moreover, maps exemplify yet another, slightly different symbol system than drawings of figures and objects. It is thus of particular interest to know how young children, and blind children without visual experience, come to acquire that symbols system.

Typically, maps are small, schematic layouts in two dimensions, specifically intended as guides to locations and routes in unfamiliar environments. Like drawings, maps are concrete objects that represent three-dimensional information in two-dimensional space. Neither drawings nor maps are replicas of objects. The difference in representation is that drawings aim to convey the identity ('what') of objects or spaces. The resemblance depends on the use of features and configurations that help to identify these. Maps represent locations and the directions and distances ('where') between them by organizing the symbols by reference to specified vertical and horizontal coordinates (Carreiras & Gärling 1990; Gärling et al. 1982, 1986).

The question of 'translating' between the symbols and the aspects of the three-dimensional environment that they represent thus arises in a somewhat different form for maps. Some map symbols can be quite arbitrary. Their significance has to be learned. But symbols correspond to those special features of the environment (landmarks and directions of potential movement) that they are intended to represent. It is worth asking how young children and blind children come to these translations between two and three dimensions.

Studies that have focused specifically on map use by young children, are still relatively recent. It was felt, presumably, that, since adults often have considerable difficulty with map-reading, very young children would be incapable of reading maps. However, the findings (e.g. Acredolo 1988b; Bluestein & Acredolo 1979; Herman et al. 1987) show that quite young children understand how maps work. They seem to have no difficulty in accepting that a square on a flat sheet of paper may stand for an actual room, and that locations on the square should be taken as corresponding to analogous locations in the room. Nevertheless, younger children are less efficient, particularly with complex displays, and make more mistakes.

The fact that very young children can 'read' maps may seem surprising. Moreover, as we saw earlier, blind children can also understand maps (Leonard & Newman 1967), and can construct maps from partial information (Herman et al. 1983b) although earlier sight and residual vision as well as full visual experience are usually found to confer an advantage. Landau (1986) showed that at the age of four years and eight months, Kelli, the blind child she had studied before (see Chapter 7), was able to use a small-scale display of a room to find an object in that room. Landau (1986) proposed therefore that map use is an innate ability.

However, that theory fails to account for far too many findings. Mapping, like drawing, depends on more than one process. It involves knowledge from a variety of domains and a number of different subsidiary skills (Liben 1991). Not all mapping tasks call on all of these equally.

Consider Leonard and Newman's important (1967) study. They familiarized their intelligent blind adolescents with a map of a portion of their school grounds over a longish period of time, well in advance of testing them on inferring detours in large-scale geographical space. That would not have been needed if map use, as such, were innate.

What we can assume is that humans are predisposed to use symbols. It follows from the potential ability to represent events that are not present. That demands some form of overt or covert token or code. Indeed, pretend play, and the tendency to use token objects to stand for something else, occurs before the age of two years (Millar 1968). Children invent symbols when necessary, as we saw when discussing figure drawing by blind children who had never drawn before.

But the form of symbol is not innately given, either for words or for non-verbal symbols, although the latter often depend on some perceptual resemblance between the symbol and the referent.

A second point that is so obvious that it is often forgotten is that people of all ages pick up a good deal more information from contexts and task conditions than instructors specifically intend. Such information, or a child's interpretation of it, does not necessarily require a long period of learning (see later). It is nevertheless often crucial for task performance. The task conditions for Kelli are a case in point.

Kelli was seated in a room and was given a small square layout. She was told that the layout represented the room in which she was sitting, and she was encouraged to explore it. There were two blocks on the layout. She was told that one block represented her own chair and position in the room; and that the other block represented the object she was to find in the room, and that it was placed in the same location that the object occupied in the actual room. The locations tested were either the straight ahead, or locations to the right or left, or behind the block which marked Kelli's chair.

To find the object, Kelli thus had to code the location of the small block which represented the object, in relation to the position of the block which represented her own position. She also had to use that relation to direct her locomotion in real space, from her seat to the object. Her performances were above chance level; she made fewer errors in retrieving the toy from the straight ahead position, than from the mid-position behind her chair, or from either side of it.

Landau (1986) was quite justified in suggesting that Kelli's above-chance performance indicates organized spatial coding, that is to say coding relative to a reference frame. Nevertheless, the findings are not evidence for an innate Euclidean map. Kelli's performance was far from error-free. More importantly, the errors differed for different orthogonal directions. A Euclidean geometrical (objective) representation should not produce different errors for different orthogonal directions. By contrast, the error pattern is precisely what would be expected if Kelli coded the directions relative to her own position, and transposed these (albeit not perfectly) to large-scale space.

Coding in terms of egocentric reference, and transposing that to large-scale space, is remarkable enough for a blind four- to five-year old. We are indebted to Landau (1986) for the findings.

It is no denigration of Kelli's achievements, or of Landau's interesting results, to look further at the details of the conditions under which Kelli performed. On the contrary, these details are extremely important, both for our theoretical understanding, and for practical purposes.

We may assume that Kelli had a good deal of previous spatial knowledge, because she was familiar with the specific situation. Familiarity and prior knowledge is known to be important (see earlier). Thus, the room in which Kelli was tested was familiar to her from the earlier studies on spatial inferences in which she took part (Landau *et al.* 1981, 1984). Moreover, Kelli did, of course, have a good deal of previous experience of a large-scale space which formed a four-sided configuration. She also had experience of locating objects in that space, from walking to adjacent and to inferred locations. In the map tests, Kelli was tested repeatedly with the object in the same locations. She thus also had feedback from correct (finding) trials.

Landau (1986) describes Kelli as totally blind, and does not refer to the earlier (1984) report that she had light perception. Presumably, Kelli lost any residual sight at some point prior to the map test. Distinctive sounds had been excluded, as before. However, Landau reports that the experimenter stood behind Kelli's chair, and occasionally corrected Kelli's movements verbally, if she seemed in danger of missing the target accidentally. It is not possible to say whether Kelli used the sounds as additional directional information. It cannot be entirely excluded, although it is unlikely that it was sufficient information for her task.

More important for understanding something about the spontaneity of mapping shown by Kelli are the task conditions. It is often forgotten that the very instructions that are necessary to get the child to understand the task can unintentionally convey crucial new information.

As a part of the (necessary) task instructions, Kelli was told that the small layout in front of her represented the room in which she was sitting. Kelli would also know from the information about the significance of the blocks which represented her chair and the object, respectively, that they were located in the analogous positions on the layout as in the large room. Kelli thus did not have to invent a two-dimensional representation of three-dimensional space. The information was implicit in the instructions. The fact that she was (rightly) encouraged to explore the small layout and position of the blocks also implied two other pieces of information. First, it allowed her to relate the position of the object to the surrounding frame, as well as to her own position, through actual movements. Second, it implied that going from one to the other by hand movements could be used as a guide to the locomotion she would have to undertake to find the objects in real space. The task instructions also gave some indication that exploring by hand movements was relevant to subsequent locomotion to find the object. Such indications would make it easier to draw analogies between hand and body movements.

The above analysis suggests that Kelli was able to use the analogy between small- and large-scale movement directions to organize these in terms of spatial, although not necessary Euclidean, configuration.

Such analogies are crucial if, as the findings on drawing suggest, movement information and movement plans are important in representing configurations. In my drawing studies, the proposal that the use of hand movements and movement plans are important for haptic shape coding accounted for the fact that the younger blind did not initially use shapes to represent body parts, and for the reverse lag between production and recognition by the blind.

There is further evidence that the process of producing movements and haptic feedback from these can play a major role in overt and also in covert representations. The explanation that knowledge of common configurations is gained through movements, or action plans intended to produce three-dimensional configurations, can also account for the age gap in mapping, which I found between normal congenitally totally blind young and older children compared to their blindfolded sighted cohorts.

In the study in which I used a roped-off square as the experimental space, with different toys marking the four corners, as described in Chapter 7, congenitally totally blind, adventitiously blind, and blindfolded sighted children were tested on walking to sequential and inferred locations, and were also asked to draw the experimental space. The drawing pad with plasticized paper which shows raised lines was again used. Almost all the blind children had taken part in the figure-drawing study about ten to fourteen months previously. It may be remembered that the map drawings were scored in terms of several criteria, one of which was whether the route was represented by a closed figure. Reproducing the correct sequence of the toys on the configuration was another. Further scores were given for the extent to which the closed configuration approached a square shape in terms of parallel lines, right angles and equal distances (Figures 5 and 6, Chapter 7).

The point of interest in relation to map drawing is that the discontinuities in scores with age which related to the amount of long-term visual experience of the children were most obvious for closed figures. Young totally congenitally blind children did not score at all, compared to younger sighted children, most (although not all) of whom did, although they wore blindfolds throughout the acquisition and testing periods. Typically, the younger blind children represented the route as a long line, with little scribbles at various intervals, for location of the toys. All of them clearly had the notion that walking to a location could be represented as a line that 'goes on', as it were. But the younger blind did not depict the walk as a closed figure, let alone as a square. Most of even the young blind children were perfectly well aware that they had turned several times during their walk (Millar 1986b, 1990b). Most of them were also aware that the toys were located at the turns. It turned out that the main problem for the younger blind was that they did not initially connect their movements in walking around the square with hand and arm movements. Thus the younger blind did not include turns in their maps, because they did not connect hand movements with locomotion. They knew that they had turned. But they did not know that they could represent such body movements by making the same type of movement with their hand, and mark the paper accordingly. An instance was an eight-year-old totally blind child. She drew a continuous straight line, as did the others, but said that she had turned in her walk. She was simply told to 'show that on the paper'. That was quite sufficient information for her to draw a very reasonable (although not perfect) square with toys marking the corners.

In other words, the child inferred from my request to 'show the turn' that she could use her drawing movements to represent body movements, including turns. Once she understood that, she was able to represent the configuration of the walk, without any further special tuition. That is important. Traditionally, we tend to think of learning as a long drawn-out process of reinforced tuition and repetition. Some skills do need that. But not all learning is of that kind. Information can be picked up in 'one trial', even by rats.

We can now specify some of the ingredients for the development of mapping. The importance of familiarity with the large-scale space to be represented, for both sighted and blind children, has been sufficiently documented in earlier chapters, and need not be laboured further. But it is important to recognize that a major difference between Kelli and my young blind children was Kelli's considerable prior experience with a relatively circumscribed external spatial layout.

Kelli's prior experience suggests how an important aspect of spatial knowledge may be gained in the absence of vision. Further, unlike Kelli, the younger blind children in my study did not know the particular experimental space they were to map, except from repeated clockwise walks during the learning phase of the experiment. It was clearly not enough to enable them to recognize that the square walk which they experienced was a closed configuration.

The very request to represent a three-dimensional space by drawing gives the untutored blind child important extra information. At the very least, the request conveys that she can do it, that it requires no vision, and that space can be represented by making marks on paper. Drawing certainly also presents the further problem of how to represent something. But that engenders a search for suitable symbols and procedures.

The fact that quite young children understand easily that something can stand for, or symbolize, something else is important, but not perhaps as surprising as it sounds. Implicitly, the notion is familiar enough to young children, whether they are blind or sighted. The encoding and decoding of sounds that stand for something other than themselves occur from a very early age.

The use of non-verbal symbols is obvious from the very first attempts at playing (Millar 1968). Children are encouraged to play with dolls, to produce small replicas of objects in plasticine, and the like. That was certainly the case for the young blind children in the schools in which I tested, and, I take it, must have been the case for Kelli also.

The main further advantage that Kelli had was that the instructions implied that to explore the small-scale display would help with moving to the target in the large-scale room. It thus implicitly pointed to the important relationship of her exploratory hand movements to the means of finding objects in large-scale space. She did not have to show the space as a configuration. In the study with normal (untutored) young blind children that was just described, the instruction to draw did not specify which features of the event were intended to be emphasized and implied nothing about the procedures that might be used to represent these features. The children did know from previous experience of drawing that they could make marks on paper. Further, the task instructions implied that marks on paper could represent their movements in walking. But it did not imply what form their movements should take, or imply a link between body movements and hand movements. The children had to think of (invent) the analogy between directions and locations in three-dimensional, body-movement space, and hand movements in two dimensions.

The reason for suggesting that the analogy between large- and small-scale movements is a further, crucial step in mapping by blind children is that it further explains the gap in performance by normal young blind compared to sighted children, and how that gap may be closed.

Take spontaneous scribbling. Sighted children find out quite early that they can make marks on paper, and so go on doing it (Brittain 1979), at least until the novelty wears off, or they discover that it can be made to look like something new.

Unassisted discovery of haptic feedback is likely to occur much later when there is no concomitant visual feedback. But it takes only a simple demonstration of how to make marks on plastic paper that provides haptic (raised line) feedback for the blind child to want to go on making marks. Blind children initially ask for additional plastic paper to be able to go on 'drawing'.

Similarly, the child's discovery that hand movements can represent body movements in large-scale space, and vice versa, provides a further step in 'mapping'. But, the less current or prior information children have for making or deriving such analogies, the more cognitively skilled or older they need to be to think of them spontaneously.

The apparent discrepancies in findings on mapping by young blind children can thus be explained by quite specific differences in information conditions.

Spatial representation and mapping is not a unitary skill. The fact that spatial configurations may be represented by movements at least initially suggests how the development of actual spatial representation without vision may take place.

The further step is from overt to covert use of symbols to represent knowledge. Young children, particularly, find it more difficult to use speech and pointing gestures covertly than overtly (e.g. Luria 1961; Vygotzky 1962). The question of covert movement coding is considered next.

Millar (1986b) argued that new haptic inputs are recognized, and movements are rehearsable, precisely because movement organization is geared to performance output.

VII   Movement output, mental practice, and temporary memory

The notion that movement imagery can be learned, and that it has its basis in output plans (Millar 1985b, 1986b, 1990b, 1991) was partly based on the finding that congenitally blind children are better at representing spatial configurations by drawing movements (and feedback from these) than at recognizing the same figures from raised-line displays. Perhaps more important was the fact that recall by quite young children could be influenced by coding instructions. Instructions to remember the positioning movement produced a different pattern of performance than instructions to remember the end position of the movement relative to their body or to an external surround (Millar 1985b).

The fact that non-verbal movements can be attended to, monitored, and become more organized with repeated outputs of the same kind supports the argument that covert movements can play an important role in the mental representation of non-verbal materials.

More recently, we (Millar & Ittyerah 1991) have shown that merely imagining irrelevant movements during delay periods has significant effects on recall. Movement imagery can therefore be demonstrated experimentally.

The implication is that imagery can be learned. That may sound odd initially. Most people assume that images arise spontaneously from perception. Output factors (see earlier) are rarely considered in connection with spatial imagery, mainly because spatial imagery is usually identified with effects of visual perception, and other modalities are rarely considered.

In fact, an analysis of how sighted, as well as blind, children actually produce representations shows that modes of output and feedback from these are involved as well. I am proposing that a good deal of what we consider mental representation or imagery is acquired in a similar manner, and depends at least in part on covert movement output. The findings on coding movement information have been considered at some length in Chapters 6 and 7.

The phenomenon of 'mental practice' takes these findings an important step further. It has been shown that adults can improve their motor performance by 'practising' mentally. Instructions to imagine the movements are found to have similar effects to those in carrying them out (Annett 1985; Finke 1979; Johnson 1982; Ryan & Simmons 1981; Sackett 1934). We have found that children can also show mental practice of movements (Millar & Ittyerah 1991).

Interpretations of mental practice have varied. Richardson (1967) and Ullich (1967) considered that improvements in motor tasks, with covert practice, depend on incipient movements, as detected by electromyographic recording. Ryan and Simmons (1981) and Sackett (1934) suggested instead that mental practice effects depend on the cognitive demands of the task, because they found that mental practice improved maze learning rather than performance on a stabilometer. Johnson (1982) used a linear positioning task. He suggested mediation by visuospatial imagery, and rejected the neuromuscular explanation.

I do not believe that these explanations are necessarily mutually exclusive. Indeed, I want to argue quite strongly against 'either/or' views of spatial coding which assume that representations must be either purely cognitive and abstract if they are not solely a question of peripheral effects. Cognitive skill is needed even for symbol systems that are derived from perceptual information. Mental practice can take different forms in different task conditions. The phenomenon of mental practice is of particular interest, in any case. It is thus worth looking at the studies in some detail.

Johnson (1982) used a paradigm which assumes that mental practice effects are demonstrated, when imagining an event has the same effect on behaviour as if that event had actually occurred (Finke 1979). In linear positioning tasks, subjects have to remember a movement distance after a delay. If irrelevant (larger or smaller) lengths are interpolated during the delay, these bias recall of the target (to-be-remembered) distance (Johnson 1982; Laabs & Simmons 1981). Johnson (1982) showed that biasing errors occurred as often when subjects had merely imagined the irrelevant interpolated movement, as when they had actually performed it.

The demonstration that merely imagining an event can have the same effect as executing it is clearly important for understanding mental representation and imagery.

The finding raised two main questions for us (Millar & Ittyerah 1991). The first was whether mental practice effects depend crucially on visuospatial coding, or can also be mediated by movement imagery. The second was whether such effects can also be shown by young children. A previous result had shown that young children, at the age of seven to eight years, can change their coding heuristics in response to instructions (Millar 1985b). Children of that age should thus be able to cope with the relevant instructions. In order to answer the two questions, we (Millar & Ittyerah 1991) replicated Johnson's (1982) study with some modifications.

Like Johnson, we used recall of a linear positioning movement. But, because our subjects were below the age of eight years, we used only one target (recall) movement and two biasing movements. One was half the length of the target (to-be-remembered) movement. The other was double the length of the target movement. Half the children were tested first on merely imagining the interpolated movements and after that in conditions in which they actually carried out the interpolated movements. For the other half of the children, the order of testing was reversed.

The main difference in conditions was that in Johnson's (1982) study subjects could see the apparatus and the room. Only their hand movements in carrying out the tasks were shielded from their view. Subjects thus had plenty of visuospatial information, by reference to which they could specify the start and end of the movement spatially. Our children (Millar & Ittyerah 1991), by contrast, were blindfolded throughout. They thus had no external reference cues available. Furthermore, we wanted to elicit movement coding, and this is easier in the absence of spatial reference information. We therefore deliberately reduced egocentric reference information also. Thus, we only used movements that crossed the body midline, so that the beginnings and ends of movements could not be aligned to egocentric anchor points.

The findings showed that movements can indeed be imagined by quite young children, and have effects on performance. They also suggested that 'mental practice' effects can be obtained when spatial reference information is absent, or at best minimal. The interpolated movements biased recall by these young children significantly, even when they had only been imagined, although actual interpolations produced slightly larger errors than purely imagined ones.

A second study, also reported in that paper (Millar & Ittyerah 1991) showed further that imagined movements can also bias recall by congenitally totally blind children. This has considerable practical interest, because linear positioning movements are involved in many activities for them, including reading lines of braille text.

Bias from imaginary movements thus clearly demonstrated movement imagery. But cognitive skill was also involved, at least for reducing overall error and variability by blind children. That was not due to recoding into speech. Articulatory suppression (mouthing an irrelevant syllable) had no effect.

More importantly, we also used a condition in which the interpolation consisted of rehearsing the target length, either by repeatedly executing it or by merely imagining doing so. The blindfolded sighted children showed a significant improvement from both types of rehearsal. In the data for the blind, mental age related to the 'rehearsal' condition. The blind with higher mental ages performed more like the sighted. The mentally younger blind did not, suggesting that cognitive skill was involved also. It thus seems likely that mental practice depends on more than one factor.

No doubt, spatial reference information, adequate feedback on errors, and knowledge of results would improve imagined practice considerably further, as it does actual practice.

The important finding in our (Millar & Ittyerah 1991) study was that imagined or covert movements affected memory for the target distance. The fact that this can be demonstrated in relatively young children, even when spatial information is minimal and vision is absent, supports the view that imagined movements can mediate recall, possibly by acting as retrieval cues (Tulving 1983). Covert movements are thus a credible basis for rehearsable non-verbal mental imagery in the absence of vision (Millar 1990b).

Millar (1981a) argued that the main reason for the small recall spans of young children was not a question of modality-specific coding as such, but of the level of organization of the input. The notion of improved recall with more economical recoding goes back to Miller (1956). But I suggest that modality-specific characteristics can also affect all levels of organization (Millar 1981a, 1986b).

In the case of spatial coding, organization is achieved by using reference information. Spatial coding is 'higher-order' coding in the sense that specifying the location of an object in terms of reference frames reduces the amount of information that needs to be held in mind. But the nature of the symbols or codes that mediate tacit memory for the information are not necessarily identical.

Thus, processing information in spatial tasks is disturbed by difficult secondary tasks to the extent that the main task requires effort, or demands attention or preempts processing requirements. Effects from modality-specific aspects of the input, and from symbolic imagery retrieved from longer-term memory, would be additional to disturbance by cognitively difficult secondary tasks. The hypothesis requires further testing, but the predictions are quite clear.

VIII   Summary: non-verbal representation and temporary memory

The view which is proposed here is that images which relate lawfully to modes of output as well as input can function as symbols to mediate non-verbal memory.

It should be noted that I am not proposing that all mental imagery is movement-based, nor that all forms of representation involve imagery, let alone that imagery is an explanation of thinking. The choice of explanatory models was distinguished explicitly from empirical questions about the nature of coding.

Findings on covert verbal coding show the importance of output factors for demonstrating modality effects. Input mode effects are easier to demonstrate and can be shown to be more effective in mediating recall when they are organized in terms of output factors. It was argued that this is the case also for non-verbal imagery.

Figure and map drawing by blind and sighted children showed how non-verbal symbol systems can develop. It was suggested that covert representation develops in a similar manner, and may indeed be based initially on overt means of representation.

Evidence that movement imagery can affect recall further supported the notion that movement-based spatial coding can be used as an alternative to visuospatial coding in blind conditions. It was argued that cognitive skill and modality effects on coding are not mutually exclusive factors. Both are involved in the use of non-verbal mental representations to mediate temporary memory and for problem-solving.

The analogy of cognitive with actual mapping, like the analogy of imagery with actual representation by drawing, illuminates the differences between covert coding of 'where' and 'what' aspects of information. It is the aspects that are abstracted for coding which differ, rather than the level of abstraction.

The findings also suggest that the invention and discovery of means of representation do not necessarily depend on a long process of associative learning. A connection, seen once, is often sufficient. The wider the knowledge base, the more likely that is to occur.

The findings suggest that cognitive and modality-specific aspects of information are not mutually exclusive aspects of information processing.

Sustained temporary memory seems to depend on organizing input characteristics in terms of output factors by which they can be represented. Organization of inputs for covert (symbolic) action sustains that information in temporary memory. That applies also to organization in terms of references. Models of sustained temporary spatial memory have to include both factors.

9

Some practical implications

The practical implications for the blind of the findings that have been reviewed differ in several respects from some previous descriptions, because they suggest that vision is not necessary for spatial coding but, at the same time, that it is far from irrelevant.

The relevance of vision depends on quite specific, rather than general effects. One effect has to do with the aspects of information which vision is specialized to analyse. The other concerns the reduction in the redundancy of information which the overlap between vision and other modalities normally provides.

The implications for substitute information that follow from the specialization of vision turn particularly on the need for information about the relation between external surfaces to each other. Some reduction in general information about the environment does, of course, occur in the total absence of a major sensory source, and needs to be restored. But the information that mainly requires to be brought to the child's attention concerns the relation of external surfaces to each other and to the child. That is not a question of spatial ability or inability. The point is that this information is not easily obtained or inferred spontaneously in congenital total blindness, because external cues tend to be less reliable. It is therefore necessary to ensure that the specifically relevant information is supplemented adequately.

The evidence also implies that inputs through alternative channels need to be made to converge and to overlap with existing reference cues from other modalities, in order to restore redundancy.

There are pointers about how that may be achieved. The fact that hearing is the other main source for distance information has rightly made it the main substitute information. Touch has also been used in providing alternative sources. But it is much less often realized that haptics (touch and movement) are actually the best complementary source for information about the relation between surfaces. Haptics provide much of the inputs that are relevant to the use of body-centred references. But haptics can be put to important use in conveying the relation between surfaces, and in restoring informational redundancy. The normal convergence between visually-perceived external cues and body-centred reference cues may be substituted by emphasizing convergence and overlap between body-centred information and auditory distance cues.

A further practical point follows from the demonstration that spatial imagery can be derived from movement organization. The assumption that spatial coding is either visual or abstract suggests that congenitally totally blind people can only rely on abstract geometric descriptions. That is by no means so. In principle, movement imagery can provide the basis for an additional non-verbal, non-visual means of coding information in temporary memory.

There are also implications for the sighted. First, for young sighted children, the findings imply that they need informational redundancy in most aspects of tasks, as well as assisted learning.

The second point relates to the use of non-verbal symbol systems. There is a temptation to regard maps, graphs and drawings as totally transparent for sighted children, because there is a 'resemblance' between the symbols used in maps, drawings and graphs, and the aspects of information that they symbolize.

It is rarely recognized sufficiently that maps, graphs, and drawings contain non-verbal symbols that are not necessarily understood immediately. The perceptual similarity of these modes of representation can be as misleading for the sighted as for the blind, or more so.

I want to preface my suggestions, by emphasizing that they are not necessarily applicable in all conditions. The practical implications of research findings have to be seen in the quite specific conditions of individuals and their environment. Experimental findings are necessarily based on results from more than one person. But no individual is precisely the same as another, nor has precisely the same needs as another.

Further, questions that arise in real-life situations are rarely simple. They usually involve a large number of factors which cannot all be studied at once. Indeed, they are not all obvious. A whole host of potentially important conditions therefore have to be temporarily set aside in order to study the most immediately relevant ones sufficiently to get reasonable evidence on these.

In asking about the role of vision and haptics in spatial representation and thinking, I have left out the whole area of the social and emotional context of learning and teaching. That is not because these factors are unimportant. Quite the contrary. As parents, helpers, educators, or even by-standers our expectations of success and failure influence how far we can keep the requisite balance between the necessary encouragement and overambitious expectation that may issue in damaging failures. But it would need a different line of enquiry, and a different book, to do justice to these factors. In the final resort, what is feasible and what works best with an individual child depends on the skill, and inventiveness of teachers, parents, and others in providing what is needed. It is to be hoped that the educational climate will allow them to exercise these.

In the practical domain, the role of this book is limited to pointing out some implications of the findings which may be applicable in practice.

I   Infants without sight

The view that complementary inputs from the sense modalities converge and partially overlap is not the same as saying that the modalities inter-relate. The view implies that it is the redundancy of information which results from the convergence and overlap of information which is import-ant in development. My point is that it is essential to restore the partial overlap which has been lost. Such 'bridging' does not necessarily occur without active help, especially in the case of younger and/or less cognitively efficient children.

Sensory substitution has been the main aim of many intervention pro-grammes. Such substitution is essential. But substitute information alone is not enough, even if it is made sufficiently redundant. It is essential also to ensure that what is substituted does, in fact, converge with existing infor-mation, that it not only complements it, but also overlaps sufficiently to restore redundancy.

An instance is the echo-location device for blind babies that was dis-cussed in Chapter 3. The advantages for eliciting earlier reaching and sitting up are important, although it may be necessary to ensure that the devices do not interfere with unassisted auditory processing. In the view put forward here, it is even more important to ensure that inputs from the device are related consistently to the baby's information from touch and movement. That is likely to require at least some assistance from the caretaker. It is not yet clear from reports, for instance, how adults convey to young babies why their auditory world changes when the device is taken off. Without such knowledge, the difference in the relation between move-ment and sound when the device is not worn may be confusing. Interactive play may be used to convey that even before the baby understands much speech.

Similarly, echo-location alone does not tell the baby that, or how, the sounds which emanate from an object beyond reach relate to the feel or identity of the object when it is close, nor why moving her head, but not her hand or foot, alters the intensity of sounds from the external world. With constant attention and monitoring by the adult, it should be possible to overcome such potential confusions. But the means whereby that is achieved have to be analysed and taken seriously as a part of the process of re-routing information from one modality to another.

If we go by the relation between sight and movement (Chapter 3), it seems reasonable to suppose that, when sound is the main remaining source of external (beyond reach) information, what is needed at least initially is some means whereby sounds can be systematically connected with more than one other source of information. That probably has to be specifically provided, at least at first. Once it is realized that simply substituting a sound 'lure' for the sights that seem to attract the attention of normal babies is not enough, there is no reason, in principle, why systematically correlated experiences cannot be given to blind babies, even before they sit up.

Similarly, the normal process, whereby young babies' eyes follow the movements of their hands before they start to reach spontaneously for objects, does not obtain for babies without sight. But there are some clever arrangements that may encourage reaching. Limbs can be connected to pulleys so that the baby can produce sounds by moving; objects that make noises when touched can be placed within reach. It requires time, patience and invention to supplement hearing so that it connects with reaching in the way in which vision connects with reaching. Some practitioners try to do that already. The point here is that there seem to be good reasons for that principle to be followed systematically.

The principle of restoring overlap of information also applies to personal contact with the infant and toddler. It has been noted that parents tend to avoid body contact with young blind children when playing or teaching them. As language develops the young blind child tends to be 'talked at'. Even when objects are being named, the child is given the object and told the name.

Vygotsky (1962) suggested that the parent provides the child with advance information about objects and features of the environment by pointing to objects, or looking at them so that the child can follow the line of sight, or by handling the object in a way which shows the child what features may be critical for a given task. The parent is much more likely to point to specific features of new objects while labelling them in sighted conditions. Parents are rarely explicitly aware of doing this.

The parent of the blind child has to deliberately find ways of substituting for the looking, pointing, and other apparently quite trivial visual means of getting and keeping the child's attention, and demonstrating objects and features in the environment.

It is less often recognized that such substitution needs to be supplemented by deliberately producing the coincidence (in space and time) of different forms of the 'same' information (touch, movement, sound and explanation). That knowledge needs to be made available to parents of very young blind children.

II   Relating body-centred and external reference and movement

Movement coding, and coding in terms of body-centred references, are often talked about as if they were inferior forms of representation. That is not so. On the contrary, they can be an important basis for understanding external relations, especially, but not necessarily only, in blind conditions.

As we saw earlier, the evidence does not really support the notion that egocentric coding is confined to very young children, and that this is developmentally superseded by allocentric or Euclidean representation.

Sighted children tend to use external visual cues for reference. That is so also for infants and very young children, unless the external cues are too far away or too inconspicuous to catch their attention. Younger children are less accurate and slower than older children in almost all tasks. That usually means that they require more, and more redundant and familiar information before they make use of it, not that they need different information than older children. The reason why it is sometimes concluded that infants cannot use external references is that conditions of testing often disrupt the normal coincidence of body-centred and external cues. That may be necessary to answer questions about the nature of coding. But it produces an ambiguous situation (Butterworth 1977). Young children require informational redundancy. Which aspect of the ambiguous information wins out thus depends very much on the relative salience of current cues, the degree of mental work that is needed to solve the problem, and the amount of previous knowledge and experience the child has.

A major difference between younger and older children is the amount of knowledge and experience they have had, and the speed and efficiency of cognitive processing that is possible.

Blind conditions are not the same as conditions for a younger child. There is no reason whatsoever to believe that absence of sight, as such, produces lower speed or efficiency of cognitive processing. On the contrary, congenitally blind children usually need to be cognitively more efficient than the sighted.

Although complete absence of sight does reduce the total amount of available information, it is important to stress, because it is less often recognized, that the main information that is missing is quite specific. Thus, body-centred reference cues are available as much to the blind as to the sighted. In conditions of congenital total blindness, movement and body-centred information tends to be more salient and reliable than information about external planes. It consequently provides a better basis for coding. The advantage of sighted conditions is that external and body-centred inputs coincide. The gravitational vertical for objects in the environment is congruent with information about the gravitational vertical from proprioceptive inputs. Absence of sight disrupts the balance between body-centred and externally based information.

It is thus not because they are developmentally delayed that blind children tend to use body-centred and movement coding, but because their proprioceptive and kinaesthetic information is normally a far more reliable source of orientation and reference in relation to spatial planes than external cues. It thus tends to outweigh information and knowledge based on external sources, and produces a bias towards body-centred coding.

It should be recognized that, far from being a hindrance, movement and body-centred information are potentially an enormously important basis for providing precisely the type of information that is missing in the total absence of sight. But this too requires assisted learning (e.g. Cratty & Sams 1968; Rieser & Heiman 1982). What the blind child needs to understand above all is the analogy between the relation between the planes or surfaces of his body and planes in the external environment. Distant cues are not enough.

The training programme developed by Cratty and Sams (1968) exemplifies that point particularly well. They argue that a well developed body image is an essential basis for learning to structure external space. They also emphasize the importance of multimodal information, and argue that such experiences should be given simultaneously.

The notion of a body image, as used by Cratty and Sams (1968), covers the forms of representation to which I have referred as body-centred or self-referent coding, and also applies to movement coding. The body image to which they refer includes the child's knowledge of his own body parts and the relation of the parts to each other, as well as the relation of the body to other objects, and finally the relation also of the body-centred knowledge to another person's reference system.

Cratty and Sams (1968) and Cratty (1971) produced training programmes which actually implement these principles very effectively. Their earliest phase in training has to do with teaching the child how his body planes relate to each other. A number of other training programmes also incorporate teaching which relates some bodily extents to those in the outside world (for review see Warren 1977).

Two unwarranted assumptions have to be discarded. One is that knowledge about body planes necessarily precedes knowledge about external planes. What is needed is information about how body planes relate to external planes. In practice, it is usually assumed that the child has already had 'body image' training by the time she enters school. Mobility training in school tends to concentrate on teaching the child to attend to distance cues, and the connection between these and body-centred knowledge is not made explicit. In order to use knowledge about body planes as a basis for understanding the relation between external planes, assisted learning in coordinating these should be simultaneous and coextensive.

Another assumption that needs to be modified is that independent exploration is the best means of gaining access to spatial knowledge. There is certainly anecdotal evidence that blind children who are good spatially are those whose parents have allowed them to explore early, without overprotecting them. But there is, in fact, no reason to think that independent exploration and assisted discovery are mutually incompatible.

The adult should not assume that the congenitally totally blind school child is necessarily aware, for instance, of the potential identity of angles of her outstretched arm to her body, or of the angle made by her upper to lower trunk when sitting, with the right angle between the wall and floor. In principle, such knowledge could largely be derived from unassisted experience of relating body postures with planes in the external surround. If so, there would be no reason for the adult to intervene.

But the evidence reviewed earlier suggests that rather few of the totally congenitally blind received sufficient training, or derived knowledge about the relation between external planes by spontaneous inference from body contact with the environment. It is well known, of course, that children who lack an important sensory source have to be much more intelligent in practice, to compensate unaided by cognitive strategies.

III   Orientation and mobility aids

Once a child without sight is independently mobile, three types of information are crucial for getting around in the environment. One is advance information about what lies ahead, to avoid obstacles. The other is to obtain information from as many fixed sources as possible in the external environment. These are needed to orient oneself in relation to a fixed location. They are also important in updating cues for moving around the environment, and getting to the destination. The third is about the relation between different reference frames.

Most mobility training schemes are geared to at least the first two of these requirements (Welsh & Blash 1980), although there are often major practical (time and money) problems in implementing such training for individual children.

Most programmes are intended to get the children to attend to external cues. Sounds, smells, changes in temperature, air flow, and changes in the terrain underfoot, both in terms of materials and gradients, are all cues which can be used as cues to orientation. Children are alerted to the significance of signals in the environment, and to variations in these signals. It is often taken for granted that young children then use these external (usually auditory) cues as reference points. But young children may need help in appreciating how to orient not only heads but also to point their feet in relation to these points, and what effects that has on reaching to target.

Most mobility methods train blind children to move in right-angled turns. This is a useful means of retaining memory for body orientations.

Moreover, it means that the number of turns can, in principle, be used as updating cues, for instance, in returning to the original location.

What is often neglected is to assist the child in making the connection between right-angled body turns and right-angled turns in external three-dimensional contexts (e.g. wall to floor), but also with right-angled hand movements, and right angles in two-dimensional objects and shapes. These connections are not as obvious in touch as in vision. Older, more able and more experienced children will come to make these connections spontaneously. As we saw earlier, alerting children to such connections is often all that is required. But it is usually needed if the congenitally totally blind are to make these connections early.

Distance information is usually easier to convey. A wide variety of techniques have been developed, based on variations in stimulus intensity or counting (e.g. number of revolutions of wheels containing bells). Similarly, games with balls that contain bells provide a means to track the trajectory of moving objects. Other exercises are geared to judging distances by correlating sounds with movements, such as running while steering a wheel with an attached bell that sounds at every rotation. This allows the subject to gauge distance by counting the number of revolutions.

The extent to which blind children actually have access to systematic mobility training varies considerably in practice. That has more to do with financial priorities, and whether the need for training is perceived by the, usually quite remote, authorities.

Most blind children have some residual sight, or have had early visual experience of some kind. They are thus often reasonably adept at getting around, and it is possible that this explains to some extent why the need for mobility training is often given a low priority. Nevertheless, even when children have residual sight, specific training in how to make the best use of the residual information would be useful. But it is rarely made part of the normal school curriculum, probably for financial reasons. Even for blind children, mobility training is usually considered an extracurricular activity and tends to be confined very largely to familiarizing them with the school environment, and training in looking for external sensory cues to guide locomotion. Both of these are important, but often not sufficient, especially for less able children.

Broadly, training procedures can be divided into those that are geared to making use of residual sources of information about external cues, and training in the use of special mobility aids.

Mobility aids range from very simple tools, such as the 'long cane', to highly sophisticated electronic devices. In principle, these can provide important information for orienting oneself and for moving around in the environment without sight.

The 'long cane' is a long white stick. There is also a version which can be folded up for ease of carrying, and unfolded when it is needed. The user is trained to move it systematically from side to side in front of herself or himself. That makes it possible, for instance, to detect obstacles, and to obtain advance information with the tip of the cane, to detect steps and bends in the path. For obvious reasons of danger to other people, it is less useful for detecting overhead obstacles. Training in its use is rarely provided for young children. It may be that the main reason behind that is that the children may inadvertently (or advertently, for that matter) hurt each other. But it may also be that people imagine that young blind children could not be trained to use the long cane (scaled to size) effectively. That assumption is probably incorrect.

There are now a growing number of sophisticated electronic mobility aids. The laser cane, for instance, projects weak infra-red beams which are neither visible nor harmful, and can be beamed at three angles (up, down and in front). The return signals, when detecting objects, cause the three channels to activate high- medium-, and low-pitched tones respectively. Overhead, as well as low-lying, obstacles can thus be detected. Even school children, trained on the device, show greater confidence when equipped with laser canes. The 'sonic guides' are spectacle frames which emit ultrasound, rather than light, signals and also have receivers on the frame. The sounds that return are converted into audible sounds fed into the ears by small tubes, and which apparently do not interfere with normal hearing. There are a number of reviews of mobility aids (e.g. Hollins 1989; Jansson 1991; Welsh & Blash 1980), and it is not intended to replicate these here. New devices are being developed all the time.

The question for us is rather why many excellent technological devices are actually not used by the majority of those for whom they are intended, despite the fact that they provide substitute information from an intact modality. No doubt, the devices often have specific features that could be changed to make them more 'user-friendly'. But the neglect of quite diverse sensory aids by visually handicapped people is too general for that to be the answer. Hollins (1989) rightly suggests that training programmes are probably not sufficiently long. However, it is not always obvious what aspects of information needs to be substituted.

The evidence reviewed in this book suggests that the most pressing problem for sensory substitution systems and training is that they are not generally geared to overlap specifically with the remaining sources of information which a person has. Extremely able and knowledgeable blind users can make the links themselves. But for most people, the link between devices which substitute, rather than complement existing information and means of coping, needs to be made obvious (Millar 1990c).

What type of informational link a user may need is likely to vary between individuals and the task. For instance, using three channels of inputs from a sonic device is fine, provided that the user has an adequate notion of the external relation between the three dimensions that are being simulated. Such knowledge can, of course, be obtained by the blind child. But it must not be assumed that the blind user necessarily has that knowledge, as a matter of course. It is not irrelevant that familiarity with the layout is a major factor in most spatial performance. It should also be borne in mind that going about in an unfamiliar environment is likely to be much more stressful in blind conditions (e.g. Peake & Leonard 1971; Shingledecker 1978; Shingledecker & Foulke 1978; Wycherly & Nicklin 1970).

It seems to me that, in principle, electronic sensing devices could also help young blind children to orient themselves in the environment, provided that the principle of providing informational overlap is followed. Thus, instead of training children to use the device as a substitute for other means of obtaining information about distant cues, the device needs to be firmly integrated with training in the use of other cues in such a way that the child is aware of the relation in space and time between cues from the device and natural sounds, smells and changes in air temperature, changes in the ground underfoot, and the like.

I have concentrated on the principle of restoring overlap of information even when the intention is merely to provide cues for avoiding obstacles when walking, and updating cues for locomotion. The overlap is, of course, needed more in new environments and in conditions of uncertainty.

Above all, it is equally important to avoid assuming, on the one hand, that a child is unable to acquire adequate knowledge about external reference frames and, on the other, to assume that she has it already. It cannot be presumed either that all children can derive adequate knowledge of the relation between external surfaces from learning how to orient to sounds or other distant cues. In many cases, such knowledge requires assistance in learning. Children, like adults, go beyond the information that is actually presented to them at any one time. But making inferences and analogies is easier when conditions are familiar.

IV   Language and environmental knowledge

The fact that verbal communication is important, and that this is so especially in the absence of sight, is obvious. As we saw earlier, language conveys a good deal of semantic information, even about purely visual concepts such as colour. There is thus no need for verbal coding to be considered empty of meaning, simply because a particular perceptual feature, such as colour, is not directly experienced. At the same time, language can be misleading. Unsupported verbal information does not necessarily convey accurate impressions about the environment (Chapter 7).

Normal discourse about the environment is not, of course, specifically geared to teaching the child about directions or distances. The interesting novelties are about events: what happened to this or that person. Where Auntie Flo lives or how to get to the sweet shop becomes interesting only if one wants to go there.

Language acquisition may be thought of as having two main uses in spatial coding. One is the communication by other people of spatial information that is not within the child's reach, or is not available through experience to the child. The other is the (covert) use of language for memory and recall by the person. Verbal memory, and particularly means of covertly rehearsing information over the short term, improves with age. Memory for sounds is usually particularly good in young blind children, because they necessarily attend to sounds more, and are, at best, also trained to do so.

The main practical implication, for young sighted children as well as for the blind, is that verbal description and spatial demonstrations should not be treated as incompatible alternatives. They need to be linked. The older, more intelligent and more knowledgeable will educe the links spontaneously. For the younger, less knowledgeable child, and in conditions in which spatial information is reduced, the link should be made explicit and obvious. Means of doing so for the use of covert coding will be considered next.

V   Scale models, drawings, maps, and graphs as aids

Small-scale replicas of real objects and scenes are common as toys for sighted children. No one doubts that the young child recognizes toy houses, trees and furniture as replicas of the real thing, or thinks that this needs to be explained. That is usually quite correct. Toy farmyards, zoos, villages and road systems can be a useful means of imparting environmental knowledge. But this is much less so for the blind child.

The fact that shapes can be recognized by touch as well as by vision can be misleading. In the section on haptic coding, I suggested that haptic information differs with the size and depth of objects. It is often not sufficiently appreciated that, unlike vision, it is difficult to recognize small toys as replicas of real objects, by unaided touch. For instance, miniature (toy) landscapes are sometimes used as reading aids for blind children. The houses and lawns and flowers, roads and pavements are certainly easy to recognize by sight. But green painted patches that look like grass do not feel like grass, even if the patch is of a different texture than the grey road. Small shapes that have the same look as real shapes are not similar in feel. The exploratory movements which enable the blind child to recognize full-size chairs and tables are quite different from those needed in exploring small toy chairs. The identification of a toy replica with the 'real thing' is thus much less automatic, and may need assistance.

Such assisted learning may consist in demonstrating that the replica and the real object function in the same way, or by demonstrating similarities in shape, or both. There is more than one reason for assistance. For instance, one way of demonstrating the similarity between a toy and a real chair is to show that toy figures can sit on them. But the young child is likely to displace the toy figure from the chair during unassisted exploration. It is not that children will not be able to learn the layout eventually by independent exploration. But assisted exploration is likely to make that process faster.

The fact that toy layouts may need assisted learning is no reason for not using them. On the contrary, it is even more important for small-scale toy models of urban environments, with houses, roads, traffic signals, toy figures and cars, to form part of the play environment for young blind children. Provided that automatic recognition of the similarity to real objects and scenes is not assumed, the toy scenes can be used to teach relative sizes and uses of objects that are out of normal reach of full tactual exploration.

It is also possible, in principle, to use two-dimensional, raised-line drawings as a means of teaching otherwise difficult concepts to congenitally totally blind children (Millar 1975e). At the time, I suggested this simply on the basis of finding that blind children produced quite acceptable two-dimensional schematic representations of three-dimensional objects. Further findings on drawing 'maps' (see Chapter 8) suggested that a useful means of doing that successfully is to specifically alert the child to the similarity between small-scale exploratory movement and locomotory or larger scale movement.

Further, the type of hand movements which may symbolize the three-dimensional environment also depends on the task. Not all symbol systems are the same. It is probably easier to think of a circle as the symbol for three-dimensional heads, in touch as well as vision, than to think of a right-angled hand movement as a representation for a right-angled bodily turn. It may be that such symbolic substitution needs to be cued by other people, in the first instance. Nevertheless, it is certainly possible to do so.

It is often suggested by teachers and others (e.g. Hatwell 1985, p. 66) that congenitally totally blind children have difficulties with geometry because there is no adequate process by which blind students can correctly and easily draw the figures to which their reasoning apply. The findings on maps and drawing discussed in Chapter 8 suggest that these can be used quite early as means of teaching.

Interestingly enough, Cratty (1967) used haptic (touch and movement) feedback for training blind children between the ages of seven and fourteen years on a spatial inference task. The children were trained to walk along the two (A to B and B to C) sides of a triangular layout and had to infer the direct (A to C) path. Subjects obtained feedback for their actual movement path, by using hand movements to trace the same path (and turns) on a small wire replica. The possibility of demonstrating spatial relations with small-scale layouts, and obtaining knowledge of results by these means, is thus present for the blind as well as the sighted.

There are embossed maps for use by the blind. It is more generally recognized that the symbols have to be learned for maps, because they are in general purely arbitrary simple signs with clearer lines and less 'clutter' than visual maps (Armstrong 1978; Gill 1973; James 1982; James & Gill 1974). The connection between the symbols and actual environments is usually made sufficiently explicit to the newly blind. They are used less often with very young children. But the study by Landau and her colleagues (1984) demonstrates nicely that maps can be used by very young children.

Pretending, and substituting one object for another, occurs very early, and is no doubt a precursor. It is generally very easy to get young children to agree to pretend that a blob on the corner of a piece of paper is a chair in the corner of a room, and this shows that they can use symbols easily. It is all the more important to realize that maps and graphs depend on quite specific symbol systems. The fact that older children and even adults often have trouble with map-reading suggests that the meaning of the symbols does require to be pointed out. Such learning is not necessarily a long slow process of reinforced association.

The question of using tactual icons and 'windows' has become topical for blind users of personal computers. There is now a whole new controversy as to whether spatial displays, icons and 'windows' are useful time-savers for blind computer users, or merely waste time that could be saved more easily by adequate systems for translating between braille and print, which use purely verbal word-processing devices.

In my view, the answer depends on task requirements. There is no reason, in principle, why graphic displays should not be haptic rather than visual (Millar 1985c, 1988b, 1989a). However, three considerations are necessary. One is that tactile displays easily become 'cluttered', and have to be kept simple. Second, haptic graphics need easily-felt coordinates or reference frames. Without these, it becomes extremely difficult to locate individual 'windows' or icons. Third, it is necessary to distinguish between 'icons' that are relatively arbitrary symbols, and graphic displays that have lawful relationships to some aspect of the information to be displayed. Arbitrary icons simply need to be learned associatively. But, even when graphic displays have lawful relations to the information to be displayed, it is necessary to make quite explicit what that relation is and how the symbol system is being used in the display.

For blind users, symbol systems for graphic displays may be less 'transparent' than for sighted users, or it may simply take longer to scan a haptic than a visual display. The answers depend on further empirical study.

The essential point about haptic displays for blind children is that they can provide configurational information, based on active movement. That makes it possible to use small graphic displays to make the relation between external locations and reference frames more salient. Used in conjunction with other forms of input, this adds informational redundancy. That is particularly important in the early stages of learning. It has been argued that making such connections salient does not necessarily demand a long period of associated learning.

Taken together, these conditions can account for the otherwise puzzling age gap in spatial performance that is sometimes found for congenitally totally blind children, but has no obvious parallel for the sighted (e.g. Gomulicki 1961; Hatwell 1978; Millar 1975e, 1991). Absence of sight does, of course, also reduce general knowledge of the environment as well as specific external reference information. That means that the young blind child is likely to be less familiar and less practised in what, for the sighted, are routine procedures by the time they go to school.

Spatial tasks are also likely to be more stressful for the young blind child than for the sighted. By the end of the primary years and beginning of adolescence, many of these routines have become established, and tasks and environments have become more familiar and less daunting. If the present analysis is correct, the age gap should not occur if there is sufficient assisted learning.

A broader knowledge base as well as the provision of specific information which makes it possible to infer and use objective reference frames should reduce the stress of spatial problems, and increase the incentive to engage in such problems, even for young children.

The link between instruction and action, assisted performance and encouraging independent problem-solving can only be solved in the individual case. There is no general prescription that can tell the parent, teacher, or helper when to provide informational overlap, and when a 'nudge' in the right direction is sufficient for children to make the crucial connection, analogy or inference that is needed for them to proceed from knowing 'that' to knowing 'how', from orienting themselves in space to representing that space on paper or mentally.

VI Sighted children

It is rarely thought necessary to assist sighted children with spatial coding. However, the evidence reviewed here suggests that there are two main conditions for younger children's success at spatial tasks. One is that they need greater familiarity with all aspects of tasks, and also greater redundancy of the relevant information. The other related condition is greater saliency of cues or assistance from others in drawing their attention to these.

Although very little, if any, spatial training is generally considered necessary for the sighted child, helping them to use directions and distances in egocentric as well as geographical space explicitly could facilitate their understanding of the two-dimensional symbol (map and graph) systems more easily also.

Map reading and using graphs as geometrical representation are actually often difficult even for sighted adults. Nevertheless, maps and graphs are used as aids to understanding the relevant subject matter. It is simply assumed that people already know the meaning of the symbols, and are merely poor at applying them to problem tasks. These symbol systems are not completely transparent, despite the fact that the symbols are supposed to resemble the subject matter.

The use of graphs is another case in point. As visual displays they are supposed to be easier to scan 'at a glance'. But that can happen only if the user is fully aware of the meaning of symbolic representations, for instance of the meaning of height in bar graphs, or the slope of lines in depicting the relation between terms in an equation.

It is therefore likely that there is a role for explicit and assisted learning of the relevant symbol systems also for the sighted. But that requires further study.

10

A theory of spatial understanding and development

My question concerned the role of the sensory systems in spatial representation. I looked particularly at the effects of visual and haptic information on the nature and development of coding in spatial tasks.

Three main strands of evidence were considered. One concerned the relation between the modalities in spatial coding. The second looked at factors in development. The third considered the nature of coding in the total absence of vision. I shall follow that order in setting out the theory that seems to me to provide the best working hypotheses at present.

I The modalities and spatial coding

I started from the assumption that the specialized functions of the sense modalities complement each other, and that the information they process converges, and partially overlaps. The behavioural findings and the neuro-psychological evidence support that description.

In the model of spatial coding proposed here I want to suggest further that the convergence and integration of inputs both from the current task, and from longer-term knowledge underlies the nature of coding in spatial tasks. This assumption implies that the convergence and integration of more than one input is necessary, if not sufficient, for spatial coding; that is to say, for coding in terms of reference frames.

The evidence comes from behavioural studies on crossmodal and bimodal coding (Chapters 2 & 3), and from neuropsychological studies which suggest that outputs from the modality systems combine and converge on a number of different areas (Chapter 4).

It is no accident that the cortical areas that are important in spatial coding are also the areas on which multimodal inputs converge. Spatial coding demands references in order to specify locations and direction. The neuropsychological findings provide a credible substrate for the behavioural evidence. The more central areas are here assumed to have a special role in integrating multimodal inputs in terms of reference frames. Which mode and facet of previous or current inputs is dominant in the new integration depends on the task as well as on current and longer-term conditions.

This view implies that the nature of spatial coding is influenced by the sense modalities and by the information that is available to the subject from longer-term knowledge. Previous evaluations and organization of converging multisensory inputs are stored, and this influences the analysis, integration, and evaluation of new incoming inputs that depend on the information that is available in current task conditions (Chapters 3, 6, 7 & 8). This description at the behavioural level is consistent with the neuropsychological and physiological evidence (Chapter 4). Changes in synaptic connections of neurones, as impulses travel from peripheral sense organs to a number of (interconnecting) areas in the cortex via subcortical regions, affect processing of new incoming inputs. Processing depends on interconnections and convergence.

The fact that different sense modalities normally provide complementary and converging information, means that general descriptions of shapes and spaces can be couched in the same terms and have the same ostensive references. But, when a sensory source is completely absent, this also means that the characteristics of the other modalities or forms of analysing inputs become more prominent, and this has to be taken into account. There is considerable overlap in information between touch and vision. Nevertheless, touch differs in ways that can become extremely important in the absence of vision.

The analysis of tactual shape perception (Chapter 5) showed that the complementary information that is needed to perceive objects differs in important respects according to the size, depth and composition of the shapes in question. The analysis revealed that the extent to which their recognition involves parameters of tactual acuity, or of active, exploratory movements, and the availability of reference cues depends crucially on the size and type of objects even if they have the same shape. Although acuity and proprioceptive information are also important in vision (Chapter 3), the visual system is very highly organized for detailed analyses. In touch without vision the possibility of using reference information is much less. The fact that information differs with the size, depth and material of tactual objects does not preclude generalization across shapes. But it does suggest that, in models of spatial coding, the theoretical description of haptic perception has to specify parameters of acuity, movement and reference information separately for different types of object.

Another factor which needs to be included in any model of spatial coding is the nature of the task itself. Solving a spatial problem demands the integration and organization of information for a specific purpose. Task effects cannot be dismissed as irrelevant chance variations. The view proposed here is, on the contrary, that task demands and conditions are crucial in eliciting the retrieval of information from memory, and contribute importantly to how the information is organized for output, and for further longer-term storage. The behavioural evidence showed that relatively small differences in task demands and/or conditions can alter performance drastically. The manner in which a task is accomplished depends on the available information. But the demands of the task, and how they are perceived, influence the selection and salience of current inputs, and retrieval from longer-term knowledge. That in turn affects longer-term storage.

The pre-eminence of coding by reference frames based on vertical (upright) and horizontal (prone) directions is assumed here to be due to our being part of a gravitationally-oriented, three-dimensional environment. We are anatomically and physiologically constituted to receive gravitational and three-dimensional information (body and object orientation) through a number of convergent channels, centred both on external objects and on the body. The substrates for integrating and organizing the convergent inputs in terms of reference frames are assumed to be the areas identified by physiological and neuropsychological studies as crucial for spatial processing (Chapter 4). To say that is not the same as assuming the *a priori* existence of spatial concepts.

There is more than one form of spatial coding. The most convenient classification of forms of reference is in terms of their origin. We talk of body-centred reference when the inputs for it arise from within (proprioception) the body. We talk of external ('allocentric') frames when the inputs for them are perceived (exteroception) to arise outside the body. But these are not exhaustive categories (e.g. Howard & Templeton 1966).

Different forms of reference (e.g. external, body-centred) interrelate in normal conditions. But they can be distinguished experimentally from each other, and from coding in terms of movements (Chapters 6 & 7).

Coding in terms of self-referent (egocentric) frames may be centred on the eye (Rock 1984), or on the body midline in blind conditions (e.g. Colley & Colley 1981; Millar 1981b, 1985b). It could also be centred on the hand (e.g. for grasping an object), or on the finger (e.g. for haptic coding of a small pattern).

In principle, any part of the body can be used to specify the location of an object or of another body part. The specification may be incomplete, or may be in terms of coordinates that are centred on the body midaxis or the head. Similarly, the location of external objects may be specified relative to each other, or by reference to coordinate frames based on cues in the external environment, or coding can be object-centred. In this case, the outline configuration of an object can be used to specify locations within it, or shape features may be specified relative to each other.

Further, tasks that are designated as spatial do not necessarily elicit coding by means of spatial reference. Forms of coding are partly determined by the type and level of the task to be performed. Coding in terms of movement sequences is experimentally distinguishable from self-referent spatial coding. It occurs particularly in conditions in which reference information is made unreliable (Chapters 6 & 7). Distance can be coded in terms of time counts, or number of events, or level of fatigue during locomotion, or it can be more strictly defined in terms of arbitrary units.

To avoid theoretical confusions it is important to distinguish between spatial coding which depends on logical inference from Euclidean principles, and spatial coding based on probabilistic evaluation of the available information. Inference from Euclidean geometry has sometimes been considered to be the only rational (adult) form of spatial coding (e.g. Piaget, Chapter 2). The view here is that heuristics based on contingent perceptual experience are no less rational. The evidence (Chapters 3, 6, 7 & 8) suggests that spatial coding even by adults depends more usually on probabilistic (fuzzy logical) evaluation of reference cues. Inference from geometric propositions and probabilisitic heuristics are equally reasonable. But they are not the same, and are not equally appropriate or accurate for all tasks.

The assumption is therefore that the spatial character of coding is determined by the fact that the information is organized in terms of references, but that the nature of coding depends on the available information and the type of symbol system or representation that is used. Not all non-verbal symbol systems used for representation are of the same kind. There are differences between representations that are derived from short-term and longer-term (gravitationally based) information, and symbol systems that embody geometrical propositions with precisely defined orthogonal coordinates.

Spatial problems in the real world are usually contingent in nature. Solutions depend on the available (prior and/or current) evidence, and not on self-evidently true propositions. Spatial reference organization of convergent information from complementary, gravitationally oriented-internal and external sources appears to be the main means of spatial orientation and coding by adults as well as children (Chapter 6). Problem-solving based on covert coding in terms of imagined visual, auditory or movement reference frames, of the kind discussed earlier (Chapter 8), is usually quite adequate for practical purposes, provided that inputs are correctly updated after moving.

Euclidean geometrical principles certainly can be, and are, applied to the real three-dimensional world. But the principles are not probabilistic in nature. The propositions they embody are true by definition. Location, distance and angular direction are accurately determined by orthogonal coordinate reference axes, specified in terms of arbitrarily defined units. To solve a spatial problem by Euclidean geometry means using the self-evident propositions that derive from the definitions.

In my view, knowing that geometrical propositions can be substituted for each other is not as such a matter of learning. Identities between propositions are obvious from definitions. They can be demonstrated by substituting propositions. But once demonstrated, identities and differences are obvious. Difficulties in geometrical reasoning arise when problems demand the use of too many propositions, or if they are couched in terms that are too complex to be transparent initially. They have to be unravelled by propositional substitution before they can be seen to follow necessarily from the initial assumptions.

When procedures strictly follow geometrical principles, they necessarily lead to correct decisions. Calculations that apply geometrical principles and determine locations strictly in terms of orthogonal coordinates are more useful for solving problems that demand mental spatial reorganization, than heuristics based on less precisely determined forms of reference.

However, what form of coding is most useful depends on the type of task. For some problems, vector calculations or algebraic representations may be more appropriate. In other tasks, the best symbol system to use may be quite different. Verbal descriptions are needed, for instance, for communicating spatial information to other people in some conditions. I assume that the most common form of spatial coding is based on probabilistic estimates of all sources of contingent information. The fact that we live in a gravitationally patterned environment means that most sources of information provide overlapping and redundant information about gravitational directions, and these form the 'natural' categories of classification.

I am using the metaphor of 'interrelated networks' as a useful phrase to include all the systems which contribute to the processing and coding of information in spatial tasks. I propose that this description could properly be applied to the behavioural as well as to the neuropsychological data.

II Factors in development and acquisition

The developmental evidence requires the notion of predisposed, but nevertheless constantly changing, interrelated systems.

The potential for selecting, representing and storing information must be present from birth and before. But actual processing by the neonate or infant requires environmental input. The structures that are in place need stimulation from the environment to function and develop and to be maintained. Changes result from lack of inputs and from differences in inputs (Chapter 4).

The implication is that, in the developing infant and child, the processing and storing of incoming information is changed by changes in internal, endogenous factors, and also affects these factors.

The disposition to code spatially means the disposition to use and to code reference information. Converging inputs from the sense modalities are received from birth. The potential for integrating convergent outputs from modality-specific processing is present. Furthermore, some forms of convergence are privileged. One instance is the privileged connection between vision and movement in reaching and locomotion, which is apparently not paralleled initially in precisely the same way by a convergence between audition and movement (Chapter 3). But immature structures are less insulated, and by no means all pathways (synaptic connections) are fixed.

The neuropsychological evidence we have so far suggests that the central regions which integrate converging inputs and underlie specifically spatial (reference) coding (e.g. the posterior parietal, prefrontal, and hippocampal areas) are initially less mature (Chapter 4). The combination of better endogenously established (e.g. well myelinated) factors with processing and storage of new inputs from the environment is important. We do not know as yet whether this makes processing more or less malleable.

In the view presented here, greater early susceptibility to extraneous factors would be predicted. Such susceptibility interacts with the quality, mode and type of information to which the infant is exposed.

The combination of immaturity and lack of knowledge of all kinds produces conditions of uncertainty. These require more informational redundancy than conditions that do not produce uncertainty. Informational redundancy, as conceived here, includes greater familiarity with all aspects of the task, more repetition of inputs, more salient cues, and greater prominence of the relevant perceptual inputs.

This view implies that it is the convergence and overlap of information which is important in development both of infants and young children. Differences in spatial coding during development can be explained completely by the need for greater informational redundancy.

The evidence supports that view. Typically, infants and young children require more familiarity in all aspects of tasks, more repetition, more salience (attention-getting characteristics) of cues, and more redundancy generally than required by older children and adults. When three-to-four year old children get the same task information as older ones, their performance is typically less accurate, slower and more variable. But patterns of responses do not differ with age, provided that the need for greater salience and redundancy of information is taken into account (Chapters 3, 5, 6 & 7).

The combination of increasing maturity, and increasing changes in longer-term storage of previous information and procedures, with further incoming information means that progressively less redundancy of information is needed by the organism.

The younger child's need for greater informational redundancy also means that ambiguities and disparities in information disrupt processing or reduce efficiency more. Relevant cues are ignored if they are relatively unfamiliar, or faint, or far away, or fail to attract attention automatically. Which aspect of competing information wins out in ambiguous situations thus depends very much on the relative salience of current cues, the degree of mental work that is needed to solve the problem, and the amount of previous knowledge and experience the child has.

The conditions that obtain for very young infants exemplify this. Infants cannot initially maintain an upright posture by themselves. Upright conditions are experienced much more intermittently (e.g. by being carried about). In consequence, they have less redundant information initially about the main gravitational axis.

Once children can sit or stand upright independently, they have congruent and redundant information about the vertical axis from their own body (head and eye as well as trunk position), and also from perception of the three-dimensional environment. Body-centred and external cues coincide, in reaching, sitting, standing and locomotion. The important gravitational information which specifies the body midaxis and the position of the head also specifies the top and bottom of objects and planes in the environmental surround.

'Egocentric' coding by young children is not a developmental stage. Conditions that promote such coding are typically those in which inputs that are normally correlated are disrupted, or opposed to each other. Thus self-referent coding predominates when external cues fail to elicit attention because they are not sufficiently prominent—too far away or part of the background rather than foreground—or are totally excluded. It is not a developmental stage, but the consequence of the young child's need for more prominent and more redundant information. In conditions of uncertainty about external cues, adults also tend to rely on body-centred cues.

The fact that the human infant is immature and lacks knowledge has to be taken seriously. On biological grounds alone, it seems likely that the immaturity of an organism has advantages. That advantage presumably lies in ensuring flexibility in adapting to the environment. Changes in the system with environmental changes may be assumed to occur from conception onwards. The uterine environment is relatively stable, and the relevant systems are very immature. But the behavioural findings show that some form of information storage takes place from birth.

It is clear from the evidence that neonates remember what they have seen, even though it may only show in habituation to repeated inputs and dishabituation when new stimuli are presented (Chapter 2). But it is important for the assumption that immaturity has adaptive functions. The findings on neonates suggest that they both learn and store what has been learned. That implies some form of coding from the start. Processing is likely to be more uncertain, fuzzy and slower in the newborn. But it is not absent.

I assume, therefore, that mental representation is not a special condition which arises suddenly at a particular period in the child's life. It is simply a label for the fact that inputs require some form of coding for memory to occur at all. In principle, the normal convergence and overlap of modality inputs amounts to a redundancy of inputs that can be used to organize information in terms of references. Simple forms of spatial coding are relatively easy for young children for that reason.

Frame information need not be complete or accurate to serve as a reference. Indeed, in everyday experience, reference information is rarely quite precise, and perceptual 'eye-ball test' strategies of judging distance and direction are usually adequate for adults as well as children. Younger children tend to be less accurate and slower than adults with strategies like these. It is the use of orientational information to specify locations and directions which constitutes spatial coding.

Predispositions must be assumed for acquiring all forms of coding. That applies to the principles of Euclidean geometry as well as to acquiring verbal, multidimensional, algebraic, and vector symbol systems. Innate predispositions to code spatially are not synonymous with innate knowledge of Euclidean principles. What can be assumed is that perceptual identity and difference can be recognized from the outset, if and when this information is provided. It can also be assumed that infants have a predisposition to acquire relevant symbol systems in which Euclidean propositions can be demonstrated. As was suggested above, once a relevant symbol system is sufficiently developed, equalities between simple geometric propositions must be obvious. However, young children are likely to need more redundancy in information to hold equivalences in temporary memory, especially for complex mental manipulations, and are likely to have more difficulties than older children in retranslating and substituting the relevant propositions.

Adults as well as children sometimes make errors by using contingent procedures inappropriately in geometrical tasks. Children make such errors more often. But adults make them too. The evidence does not support the Piagetian assumption that Euclidean geometry is necessarily achieved only in late childhood and developmentally supersedes coding based on perceptual cues.

The evidence can be explained sufficiently by assuming that young children need more unequivocal and more prominent information of all kinds. This includes facility in using a symbol system that represents propositional definition and substitutions, and knowing when these procedures need to be applied.

The nature of coding does not depend on age as such. Processing is determined by the combination of the (changing) maturity of the system with task demands, the longer-term information that is available, and the salience, redundancy and reliability of the available current reference information.

The theoretical implication is that the relation between perception and representation cannot be modelled as either totally peripherally driven or as a totally 'top–down' system in which the essential principles are specified and merely need to be uncovered.

III Absence of sight and the nature of coding

Findings in conditions of complete absence of sight provide further evidence about the nature of spatial coding.

No sensory modality is necessary or sufficient, by itself, for spatial coding. But absence of a sense modality creates an imbalance between inputs that normally converge. This tends to bias coding by giving a normally contributory source undue prominence. It also reduces the overlap between inputs that is needed to organize inputs in terms of reference frames.

Complete absence of sight has two quite specific main effects. One is a loss of information about external surfaces which vision is geared to process. The other is a loss of overlap with the remaining information.

The finding that complete absence of sight tends to elicit more body-centred and movement coding (Chapters 6 & 7) does not indicate a general developmental 'lag'. There is some reduction in the amount of general knowledge. But the difference in coding occurs because, in the absence of sight, proprioceptive and kinaesthetic inputs to the integrating systems are more prominent and reliable than external cues.

Other sources of distance (e.g. auditory) cues are less specialized than vision for information about the relation of external surfaces to each other, and inputs from external and body-centred sources converge less reliably. Unless these aspects are adequately substituted, the imbalance will influence longer-term reference organization, and in turn bias the nature of coding the incoming information towards the characteristics of inputs from the remaining sources.

The implication is that the missing information can be supplemented through other routes, provided that it is made to converge with information from the remaining sources, so as to restore normal redundancy and overlap.

Perhaps paradoxically, organization in terms of externally based reference frames is probably best supplemented by means of body-centred information.

Proprioceptive, vestibular and touch and movement inputs tend to be organized in terms of body-centred references that determine the locations of body parts relative to each other and to external objects (e.g. those touched by hand). That does, however, include information about the relation between surface areas. In principle, enhancing a convergence between that information and inputs from the remaining sources of distance cues could restore reliance on external cues as means of reference.

A further important point is that outputs from movement, and particularly from hand movements, can serve as an alternative basis for coding spatial configurations and for non-verbal spatial imagery (Chapter 8).

These alternative non-verbal means of covert spatial representation can mediate temporary memory (Chapter 8). In principle, representations derived from movement-based configurations thus provide a powerful means of information about external relations in blind conditions.

The theoretical implication is that the nature of spatial coding is influenced by a long-term imbalance between reference cues from egocentric and from external sources. At the same time, it is also possible for this organization to become the basis for alternative means of representation, which can serve to acquire the missing information.

It should be noted that the assumption that movement information can be used as a basis for mental representation of shape and spatial layouts is not the same as a motor theory of perception, and is not identical with outflow theories (e.g. Jones 1974). It is assumed rather that inputs and outputs are not alternative bases of coding (Notterman & Tufano 1980). The idea is rather that the relation between these provides the best basis for coding in short-term memory (Chapter 8). However, when unsupported haptic information is in question, movement output can be used as an important alternative basis for coding.

IV   The nature of learning and connectionist modelling

The nature of learning becomes an important issue if we want to translate descriptions into a form suitable for computational modelling.

The advantage of computational approaches is that they make theories and predictions more precise, and therefore more easily testable. In principle, computational modelling would also harmonize descriptions at behavioural and neural processing levels. I shall therefore consider briefly what factors in the theory that I am proposing would need to be incorporated into a computational model.

Connectionist modelling of neural networks seems particularly suitable, because it proposes artificial networks that attempt to simulate real neural and brain processes (Crick 1989). Neural network models assume that processing is distributed over a number of networks that work in parallel. The networks consist of several layers of units ranging from input to output layers. The layers represent different types of input features. Activation of input units activates units in other layers. Patterns of incremental activation eventually connect different combinations of units for output.

The incremental learning algorithms originally derived from traditional (e.g. Hebb 1949) views of learning as a slow process of associating unrelated items. These result in larger, connected assemblies which can then become the basis of more rapid processing. Rote learning, and acquiring skills, like playing tennis or following a route, as well as category learning, can be modelled by including feedback about errors (through back propagation). Connectionist modelling has been applied to complex processes like reading and its breakdown in dyslexia (Hinton & Shallice 1991). That requires the assumption of 'hidden units.' Unlike other units which produce weighted averages of inputs, hidden units do not represent features of the input. They are needed to allow the network to discover how to implement arbitrary mappings: for instance, in the case of reading, between print letters and semantic features of texts, and between semantics and sound (McLeod 1993). In principle, connectionist modelling can account for learning categories and rules, without having to assume that these are innately given.

The question is how such networks might model what we know about developmental processes. It has been argued that connectionist modelling of developmental data is possible and predictive without the need to assume a formal *a priori* (e.g. syntactic) system (Plunkett & Sinha 1991). The need for connectionist models to incorporate developmental factors was recently argued by Karmiloff-Smith (1992). However, I wish to offer a view of what these requirements would be which differs in several respects.

Karmiloff-Smith (1992) assumes that infants have innate procedural knowledge, and that innately given, reiterative processes produce constant redescriptions of information into ever more abstract representations. I would certainly agree about the importance of symbolic coding, and the fact that we are dealing with a constantly active system that uses reiterative (feedback and feedforward) processes. But I think that the idea that with development representations become progressively more abstract does not allow for the fact that representations can also become more specific. Indeed, in some respects, infants and young children code more general or abstract (sparser and more general) features of inputs (Chapters 2 & 3) than do older subjects.

Further, the flow of information in longer-term learning does not necessarily proceed in a single direction, that is only from the periphery to higher-order cognitive processing. Nor does it proceed from prior knowledge to input. There is no evidence that babies have innate knowledge of procedures, any more than that they have innate declarative knowledge.

All that is necessary, and sufficient, is to assume that they have *predispositions* for perceptual selection, analysis and coding.

Moreover, coding is seen here as an integral part of memory processes. There is now evidence that learning is present from the start (e.g. Bushnell *et al.* 1989; De Caspar *et al.* 1980), albeit initially memory processes may be rather 'noisy' in the sense of being prone to interference. The nature of coding in spatial tasks derives from the interaction of inputs from a number of (internal and external) sources, and is not the same in all conditions or tasks. Initially, spatial coding will need more unequivocal reference cues. In principle, therefore, the notion of interrelated networks is a useful description of the factors which contribute to the processing and coding of information in spatial tasks.

The first requisite is that the networks should not initially be equipotential. The notion that particular areas are biased by endogenous factors towards selecting and processing some aspects of information more than others could be implemented by assigning differential weights to units at input, and at intermediate levels in different parts of the network.

The networks would have to be conceived as constantly active. Although the overall organization ('architecture') is fairly constant, there can be changes in the networks themselves, especially in the initial, postnatal state of the organism, but to some extent throughout childhood.

In order to model convergence, some portions of the network may have to be biased from the outset to receive specific patterns of activation from a number of different channels that converge on them.

But greater initial flexibility of pathways between nodes has to be modelled also, to simulate endogenous changes and connections between nodes that are less well specified as yet by prior processing and storage. The two requirements are not independent of each other. Indeed, some parts of the system may cease to function altogether when they receive no inputs over a period of time, or there may be some reorganization of pathways.

A computational implementation of the developmental assumptions may therefore be complicated. Threshold values would need constant adjustment, not merely with increased stimulus input but also with changes that are endogenous to the network systems. The balance of weights would have to be made to change as a result of the combined effect of endogenous changes and previous weighting.

The assumption of layers of hidden units could accommodate changes in symbolic representation. But, according to my theory, it would have to be assumed that there are reciprocal connections between layers, and that output factors could feed back into the arrangement of hidden units. Cross-domain connections should be possible without having to assume that these can only occur when coding becomes highly abstract.

The main problem is how single-trial learning, or sudden jumps in learning can be represented in connectionist networks. The main computational assumptions about learning in the networks are associationist in character. The learning algorithm gradually changes the strength of connections (many to one in various combinations) until the output simulates actual behaviour (McLeod 1993).

Some forms of learning and skill acquisition clearly conform to that description. Prima facie, the description is less convincing for learning by observation, or discovering a resemblance, or connection, or a rule from a relation between patterns. Such behaviour is shown by children as well as adults. Learning can occur in a single trial.

For instance, a single cue may draw attention to seeing a connection, or analogy, or a new means of representation, as in the example of the blind child who was simply told to represent a body movement on the page, and realized that this could be done by using a hand movement (Chapter 8).

I have emphasized informational redundancy as a major developmental factor. But the redundancy could result from informational overlap, rather than from long-term knowledge, from conditions in which relevant cues are prominent, and which demand minimal attention to other aspects of tasks.

Sudden reorganization of information could be modelled, for instance, by setting a ceiling beyond which additional stimulation would fail to activate the units. Once that ceiling is reached, further activation to the lowest layer would pass across the middle layers without involving them. In these conditions, hidden units may be free to map across arbitrary connections. That would have to be tried to see whether it works.

However, it is also possible that a learning algorithm based on gradual increments is inappropriate. Learning and memory may depend primarily on trying to make sense of events (Bartlett 1932). Jumping to conclusions on insufficient evidence may be the basic process. Bruner's (1957) pregnant phrase of 'going beyond the given information' characterizes most of our everyday thinking. Learning may consist of searching for evidence to support these jumps. Such behaviour clearly occurs, but we do not know as yet how it is implemented in actual neural processes. Indeed, not all the assumptions that have been found necessary for computational models to simulate actual behaviour have obvious counterparts in actual neural networks (Crick 1989).

The notion of widely distributed convergent active processing in interrelated networks (CAPIN, for short) at several levels, nevertheless, seems to me to be a useful initial description of the neuropsychological and behavioural findings on spatial coding. I am therefore using the notion of convergent active processes in interrelated networks (CAPIN) as a useful metaphor for the theory I am proposing.

V   Convergent active processing in interrelated networks: summary and predictions

Spatial coding depends on relating inputs to reference cues or frames. The perceptual modalities affect coding in two ways. The convergence and overlap of specialized inputs from several sources produces the redundancy needed for organizing inputs in terms of references. The fact that gravitational information from external and internal sources normally coincides highlights vertical orientations, and facilitates spatial organization in relation to these.

The other influence of modalities is on the nature of non-verbal coding in temporary memory. Coding is assumed to be an integral part of memory processes. Moreover, humans are geared to acquire more than one type of symbol system. The symbols can represent tacit (longer-term) knowledge, as well as new inputs in temporary memory. Non-verbal codes can be derived from re-presenting input modes. However, input codes alone sustain relatively few items in temporary memory because they cannot be rehearsed. This results in relatively small memory spans, although that may vary with the modality of origin (e.g. sound, sight, touch and proprioception).

Non-verbal codes that organize input symbols in terms of overt or covert output can sustain temporary memory for more items, and result in larger memory spans. Such organization depends on reciprocal effects between temporary coding and longer-term memory. Visuospatial coding is not the only form of spatial imagery. Imagery based on covert movements can also mediate short-term recall.

Developmental effects result from the need for more salient and redundant information because convergent paths between contributing systems are less well established by endogenous factors and/or prior experience. Simple spatial coding by external cues occurs early in visual conditions, provided that salient external cues coincide with body centred information.

Complex spatial tasks that demand reorganization, or translating between sequential and configurational forms of coding, require attention to more than one thing at a time. They are solved most easily if other task constituents are familiar and demand minimal attention, and if coding is in terms of symbols that can be manipulated (covertly) to sustain inputs in temporary memory.

Complete absence of vision reduces information about external reference cues and informational redundancy. Coding in terms of proprioceptive and body-centred cues is thus more reliable, but less easy to use for complex spatial reorganization. Ways of restoring external reference and redundancy were considered earlier (Chapter 9), including the use of spatial organization based on organized movements.

The theory makes several predictions. The first derives from the assumption that neural connections are initially more labile. The model predicts that if, in conditions of congenital total absence of sight, haptic and movement inputs are deliberately encouraged and coordinated with hearing, future neurophysiological investigations should discover an increase in synaptic connections between posterior parietal, auditory and movement control systems. In principle, there is no physiological reason against the notion that learning can 'strengthen' or alter (chemically) synaptic connections between neurones that connect to different areas of the central nervous system.

At the behavioural level, predictions about the role of familiarity and informational redundancy need testing in relation to age effects and in the absence of sight. If the model is correct, making all constituents of a spatial task thoroughly familiar should significantly increase the probability of making inferences, or solving a problem by analogy.

Blind subjects should be significantly more affected by increases and reductions in familiarity than sighted subjects tested blindfolded; this should also hold in tasks that require spatial reorganization. Similarly, increasing the salience (intensity, significance of a given external cue should make it more probable that it will be used as a reference in recall.

A further prediction is that additional redundancy of information about external frames has relatively little effect on coding in sighted conditions. But it should increase accuracy in spatial reorganization in the absence of sight. The corollary is that mental spatial reorganization of actual locations should be more difficult, even for adults, if visual cues are excluded in conditions of weightlessness. But that should be irrelevant to solving geometrical tasks by means of Euclidean principles.

The CAPIN theory proposes that spatial coding depends on convergent active (dynamic) processing in interrelated networks. This produces redundancy or balance of information from external and internal sources for coding in terms of reference frames. The theory suggests that the same assumptions which explain findings in conditions of total deprivation of sight can also explain the developmental evidence about the relation between perceptual modalities and spatial understanding and representation.

References

Abravanel, E. (1981). Integrating the information from eyes and hands: A developmental account. In R. D. Walk & H. L. Pick, Jr (ed.) *Intersensory Perception and Sensory Integration*. New York: Plenum Press.

Acredolo, L. P. (1976). Frames of reference used by children for orientation in unfamiliar spaces. In G. T. Moore & R. G. Golledge (ed.) *Environmental Knowing*. Stroudsburg, Pennsylvania: Hutchinson & Ross.

Acredolo, L. P. (1977). Developmental changes in the ability to coordinate perspectives of a large-scale space. *Developmental Psychology*, **13**, 1–8.

Acredolo, L. P. (1978). Development of spatial orientation in infancy. *Developmental Psychology*, **14**, 224–34.

Acredolo, L. P. (1981). Small and large-scale spatial concepts in infancy and childhood. In L. S. Liben, A. H. Patterson & N. Newcombe (ed.) *Spatial Representation Across The Life-Span*. London: Academic Press.

Acredolo, L. P. (1988a). Infant mobility and spatial development. In J. Stiles-Davis, M. Kritchevsky, & U. Bellugi (ed.) *Spatial Cognition. Brain Bases and Development*. Hillsdale, New Jersey: Lawrence Erlbaum Associates, pp. 157–66.

Acredolo, L. (1988b). From signal to symbol: The development of landmark knowledge from 9 to 13 months. *British Journal of Developmental Psychology*, **6**, 369–93.

Adams, J. A. & Dijkstra, S. (1966). Short-term memory for motor responses. *Journal of Experimental Psychology*, **71**, 314–18.

Adams, J. A., Gopher, D. & Lintern, G. (1977). The effect of visual and proprioceptive feedback on motor learning. *Journal of Motor Behavior*, **9**, 11–32.

Adams, J. A., Bodis-Wollner, I., Enoch, J. M., Jeannerod, M. & Mitchell, D. E. (1990). Normal and abnormal mechanisms of vision: Visual disorders and visual deprivation. In L. Spillmann & J. S. Werner (ed.) *Visual Perception: The Neurophysiological Foundations*. New York: Academic Press.

Adelson, E. & Fraiberg, S. (1974). Gross motor development in infants blind from birth. *Child Development*, **45**, 114–26.

Akbarin, S., Berndl, K., Gruesser, O. J., Guldin, W. O., Pause, M. & Schreiter, U. (1988). Responses of single neurons in the parietoinsular vestibular cortext of primates. *Annals of the New York Academy of Sciences*, **545**, 187–202.

Allen, G. L. & Kirasic, K. C. (1988). Young children's spontaneous use of spatial frames of reference in a learning task. *British Journal of Developmental Psychology*, **6**, 125–35.

Allen, G. L., Siegel, A. W. & Rosinski, R. R. (1978). The role of perceptual context in structuring spatial knowledge. *Journal of Experimental Psychology: Human Learning and Memory*, **4**, 617–30.

Allen, G. L., Kirasic, K. C., Siegel, A. W. & Herman, J. F. (1979a). Developmental issues in cognitive mapping: the selection and utilization of environmental landmarks. *Child Development*, **50**, 1062–70.

Allport, D. A. (1979). Word recognition in reading (Tutorial paper). In P. A. Kolers, M. E. Wolstad & H. Bouma (ed.) *Processing Visible Language*. New York: Plenum Press.

Alvis, G. R., Ward, J. P. & Dodson, D. L. (1989). Equivalence of male and female performance on a tactuo-spatial maze. *Bulletin of the Psychonomic Society*, **27**, 29–30.

Anderson, R. A. (1987). Inferior parietal lobule function in spatial perception and visuomotor integration. In F. Plum & V. B. Mountcastle (ed.) *Handbook of Physiology*. Rockville, Maryland: American Physiological Society.

Annett, M. (1985). *Left, Right, Hand and Brain: The Right Shift Theory*. Hillsdale, New York: Lawrence Erlbaum Associates.

Annett, J. (1985). Motor learning: a review. In H. Heuer, V. Kleinbeck & K-H. Schmidt (ed.) *Motor Behavior: Programming, Control and Acquisition*. Berlin: Springer Verlag.

Anooshian, L. J. & Young, D. (1981). Developmental changes in cognitive maps of a familiar neighbourhood. *Child Development*, **52**, 341–8.

Anooshian, L. J., Pascal, V. U. & McCreath, H. (1984). Problem mapping before problem solving. Young children's cognitive maps and search strategies. Strategies in large scale environments. *Child Development*, **55**, 1820–34.

Apkarian-Stielau, P. & Loomis, J. M. (1975). A comparison of tactile and blurred visual form perception. *Perception & Psychophysics*, **18**, 362–8.

Appelle, S. & Countryman, M. (1986). Eliminating the haptic oblique effect: Influence of scanning incongruity and prior knowledge of the standard. *Perception*, **15**, 325–9.

Appelle, S., Gravetter, F. G. & Davidson, P. W. (1980). Proportion judgments in haptic and visual form perception. *Canadian Journal of Psychology*, **34**, 161–74.

Arbib, M. (1991). Interaction of multiple representations of space in the brain. In J. Paillard (ed.) *Brain and Space*. Oxford: Oxford University Press.

Arditi, A., Holtzman, J. D. & Kosslyn, S. M. (1988). Mental imagery and sensory experience in congenital blindness. *Neuropsychologica*, **26**, 1–12.

Armstrong, J. D. (1978). The development of tactual maps for the visually handicapped. In G. Gordon (ed.) *Active Touch. The Mechanisms of Recognition of Objects by Manipulation: A multidisciplinary approach*. Oxford: Pergamon Press.

Arnheim, R. (1969). *Visual Thinking*. Berkeley: University of California Press.

Ashmead, D. H. & McCarty, M. E. (1991). Postural sway of human infants while standing in light and dark. *Child Development*, **62**, 1276–87.

Ashton, H. (1992). *Brain Function and Psychotropic Drugs*. Oxford: Oxford University Press.

Assaiante, C. & Amblard, B. (1992). Head–trunk coordination and locomotor equilibrium in 3- to 8-year-old children. In A. Berthoz, P. P. Vidal & W. Graf (ed.) *The Head–Neck Sensory Motor System*, pp. 121–34. Oxford: Oxford University Press.

Atkinson, R. C. & Shiffrin, R. M. (1968). Human memory: A proposed system and its control processes. In K. Spence & J. T. Spence (ed.) *The Psychology of Learning and Motivation*, Vol. 2. London: Academic Press.

Attneave, F. & Arnoult, M. D. (1956). The quantitative study of shape and pattern recognition. *Psychological Bulletin*, **53**, 452–71.

Atwood, G. (1971). An experimental study of visual imagination and memory. *Cognitive Psychology*, **2**, 290–9.

Austen, J. (1813). *Pride and Prejudice*. In R. W. Chapman (ed.) (1987) *The Novels of Jane Austen*. Oxford: Oxford University Press.

Axelrod, S. (1959). *Effects of Early Blindness*. New York: American Foundation for the Blind.

Bach-y-Rita, P. (1972). *Brain Mechanisms in Sensory Substitution*. New York: Academic Press.

Baddeley, A. D. (1986). *Working Memory*. Oxford: The Clarendon Press.

Baddeley, A. D. (1990). *Human Memory: Theory and Practice*. Hillsdale, New Jersey: Lawrence Erlbaum Associates.

Baddeley, A. D. & Hitch, G. (1974). Working Memory. In G. Bower (ed.) *The Psychology of Learning and Motivation*, Vol. VIII, pp. 47–89. New York: Academic Press.

Bai, D. L. & Bertenthal, B. I. (1992). Locomotor status and the development of spatial search skills. *Child Development*, **63**, 215–26.

Baillargeon, R. (1986). Representing existence and location of objects: Object permanence in 6- and 8-month-old infants. *Cognition*, **23**, 21–41.

Baillargeon, R. (1987). Object permanence in 3.5- and 4.5-month-old infants. *Developmental Psychology*, **23**, 655–64.

Baillargeon, M. & Graber, M. (1987). Where's the rabbit? 5.5-month-old infants' representation of the height of a hidden object. *Cognitive Development*, **2**, 375–92.

Baillargeon, R., Graber, M., Devos, J. & Black, J. (1990). Why do young children fail to search for hidden objects? *Cognition*, **36**, 255–84.

Bakan, P. (1978). Why lefthandedness? *Behavioral and Brain Sciences*, **2**, 279–80.

Barlow, H. B. (1975). Visual experience and cortical development. *Nature*, **258**, 199–204.

Bartlett, F. C. (1932). *Remembering*. Cambridge: Cambridge University Press.

Berlá, E. P. & Butterfield, L. H. Jr (1977). Tactual distinctive feature analysis: Training blind students in shape recognition and in locating shapes on a map. *Journal of Special Education*, **11**, 336–46.

Berlá, E. P. & Murr, M. J. (1975). Psychophysical function for active tactual discrimination of line width by blind children. *Perception & Psychophysics*, **17**, 607–12.

Berry, D. C. & Broadbent, D. E. (1984). On the relationship between task performance and associated verbalizable knowledge. *Quarterly Journal of Experimental Psychology*, **36A**, 209–31.

Berry, J. W. (1966). Temne and Eskimo perceptual skills. *International Journal of Psychology*, **1**, 207–29.

Bertenthal, B. I. & Bai, D. L. (1989). Infants's sensitivity to optical flow controlling posture. *Developmental Psychology*, **25**, 936–45.

Bertenthal, B. I., Campos, J. J. & Barrett, K. C. (1984). Self-produced locomotion: An organizer of emotional, cognitive and social development in Infancy. In R. Emde & R. Harmon (ed.) *Continuities and Discontinuities in Development*. New York: Plenum

Berthoz, A. (1991). Reference frames for the perception and control of movement. In J. Paillard (ed.) *Brain and Space*. Oxford: Oxford University Press.

Besner, D. (1987). Phonology, lexical access, in reading, and articulatory suppression: A critical review. *Quarterly Journal of Experimental Psychology*, **39A**, 467–77.

Bever, T. G. & Chirrillo, R. C. (1974). Cerebral dominance in musicians and non-musicians. *Science*, **185**, 537.

Bierwisch, M. (1967). Some semantic universals of German adjectivals. *Foundations of Language*, **3**, 1–36.

Bigelow, A. (1986). The development of reaching in blind children. *British Journal of Developmental Psychology*, **4**, 355–66.

Binet, A. & Simon, Th. (1908). Le dévelopment de l'intelligence chez les enfants. *Année Psychologique*, **14**, 1–94.

Bisiach, E., Capitani, E., Luzzatti, C. & Perani, D. (1981). Brain and conscious representation of outside reality. *Neuropsychologica*, **19**, 543–51.

Bishop, D. (1990). *Handedness and Developmental Disorder*. Oxford: Blackwell.

Bjork, E. L. & Cummings, E. M. (1984). Infant search errors: Concept development or stage of memory development? *Memory & Cognition*, **12**, 1–19.

Bliss, J. C. (1978). Reading machines for the blind. In G. Gordon (ed.) *Active Touch. The Mechanism of Recognition of Objects by Manipulation: A multidisciplinary approach*. Oxford: Pergamon Press.

Bluestein, N. & Acredolo, L. (1979). Developmental changes in map reading skills. *Child Development*, **50**, 691–7.

Boles, D. B. (1980). X-linkage of spatial ability: a critical review. *Child Development*, **51**, 625–35.

Bower, T. G. R. (1967). The development of object-permanence: Some studies of existence constancy. *Perception & Psychophysics*, **2**, 411–18.

Bower, T. G. R. (1974). *Development in Infancy*. San Francisco: W. H. Freeman & Co.

Bower, T. G. R. (1977). Blind babies see with their ears. *New Scientist*, **74**, 712–14.

Bower, T. G. R. (1989). The perceptual world of the newborn child. In A. Slater & G. Bremner (ed.) *Infant Development*. Hillsdale, New Jersey: Lawrence Erlbaum Associates.

Bower, T. G. R., Broughton, J. M. & Moore, M. K. (1970). Demonstrations of intention in the reaching behaviour of neonate humans. *Nature*, **228**, 679–81.

Brabyn, J. A. & Strelow, E. R. (1977). Computer-analyzed measures of characteristics of human locomotion and mobility. *Behavior Research Methods and Instrumentation*, **9**, 456–62.

Bradshaw, J. L., Nettelton, N. C. & Spoehr, K. (1982). Braille reading and left and right hemispace. *Neuropsychologica*, **20**, 493–500.

Braine, D. L. G., Ghent, L. & Fisher, C. B. (1988). Context effects in left–right shape discrimination. *Developmental Psychology*, **24** (2), 183–9.

Bremner, J. G. (1978). Spatial errors made by infants: Inadequate spatial cues or evidence of egocentrism? *British Journal of Psychology*, **69**, 77–84.

Bresard, B. (1988). Primate cognition of space and shape. In L. Weiskrantz (ed.) *Thought without Language*, A Symposium of the Fyssen Foundation.

Briggs, R. (1973). Urban cognitive distance. In R. Downs & D. Stea (ed.) *Image and Environment*. Chicago: Aldine.

Brittain, W. L. (1979). *Creativity, Art, and the Young Child*. New York: Macmillan.

Broadbent, D. E. (1984). The maltese cross: A new simplistic model for memory. *Behavioral & Brain Sciences*, **7**, 55–94.

Broadbent, D. E. & Broadbent, M. H. P. (1980). Priming and the passive/active model of word recognition. In R. S. Nickerson (ed.) *Attention & Performance*. Hillsdale, New Jersey: Lawrence Erlbaum Associates.

Broadbent, D. E., Fitzgerald, P. & Broadbent, M. H. (1986). Implicit and explicit knowledge in the control of complex systems. *British Journal of Psychology*, **77**, 33–50.

Brooks, L. R. (1967). The suppression of visualization during reading. *Journal of Experimental Psychology*, **19**, 289–99.

Brooks, L. R. (1968). Spatial and verbal components in the act of recall. *Canadian Journal of Psychology*, **22**, 349–68.

Brouchon, M. & Hay, L. (1970). Information visuelle, information proprioceptive et controle des positions due corps propre. *Psychologie Française*, **15** (2), 205–12.

Brown, A. L. (1975). The development of memory: knowing, knowing about knowing, and knowing how to know. In H. W. Reese (ed.) *Advances in Child Development & Behavior*, Vol. 10. London: Academic Press.

Brown, J. A. (1958). Some tests of the decay theory of immediate memory. *Quarterly Journal of Experimental Psychology*, **10**, 12–21.

Bruner, J. S. (1957). Going beyond information given. In *Contemporary approaches to Cognition: A symposium held at the University of Colorado*. Cambridge, Massachusetts: Harvard University Press.

Bruner, J., Olver, R. R. & Greenfield, P. M. (1966). *Studies in Cognitive Growth*. New York: John Wiley.

Bryant, P. E. (1973). Discrimination of mirror images by children. *Journal of Comparative and Physiological Psychology*, **82**, 415–25.

Bryant P. E. & Somerville, S. C. (1986). The spatial demands of graphs. *British Journal of Psychology*, **77**, 187–97.

Bryant, P. E., Jones, P., Claxton, V. & Perkins, G. M. (1972). Recognition of shapes across modalities by infants. *Nature*, **240**, 303–4.

Bryden, M. P. (1982). *Laterality: Functional Asymmetry in the Intact Brain*. New York: Academic Press.

Buffery, A. W. H. & Gray, J. A. (1971). Sex differences in the development of hemispheric asymmetry of function in the human brain. *Brain*, **31**, 364–5.

Burnod, Y. & Dufosse, M. (1991). A model for the cooperation between cerebral cortex and cerebellar cortex in movement learning. In J. Paillard (ed.) *Brain and Space*. Oxford: Oxford University Press.

Bushnell, E. W. (1986). Cross-modal functioning in infancy: The basis of infant visual-tactual functioning: Amodal dimensions or multimodal compounds? In C. Rovee-Collier & L. P. Lipsitt (ed.) *Advances in Infancy Research*, Vol. 4, Norwood, N.J.: Ablex Publishing Corporation.

Bushnell, E. W., Sai, F., & Mullin, J. T. (1989). Neonatal recognition of the mother's face. *British Journal of Developmental Psychology*, **7**, 3–15.

Butterworth, G. (1977). Object disappearance and error in Piaget's Stage IV task. *Journal of Experimental Child Psychology*, **23**, 291–401.

Butterworth, G. & Hicks, L. (1977). Visual, proprioceptive and postural stability in infancy: A developmental study. *Perception*, **6**, 255–62.

Butterworth, G., Jarrett, N. L. M. & Hicks, L. (1982). Spatio-temporal identity in infancy: perceptual competence or conceptual deficit? *Developmental Psychologt*, **18** (3), 435–49.

Byrne, R. W. (1979). Memory for urban geography. *Quarterly Journal of Experimental Psychology*, **31** 147–54.

Byrne, R. W. & Salter, E. (1983). Distances and directions in cognitive maps of the blind. *Canadian Journal of Psychology*, **37**, 293–9.

Canter, D. (1977). *The Psychology of Place*. London: The Architectural Press Ltd.

Carpenter, P. A. & Eisenberg, P. (1978). Mental rotation and the frame of reference in blind and sighted individuals. *Perception and Psychophysics*, **23**, 117–24.

Carreiras, M. & Gärling, T. (1990). Discrimination of cardinal compass directions. *Acta Psychologica*, **73**, 3–11.

Casey, S. M. (1978). Cognitive mapping by the blind. *Journal of Visual Impairment & Blindness*, **72**, 297–301.

Casey, M. B. & Brabeck, M. M. (1989). Exceptions to the male advantage on a spatial task: Family handedness and college major as factors in identifying women who excel. *Neuropsychologica*, **27**, 689–96.

Chapman, E. K., Tobin, M. J., Tooze, S. & Moss, S. (1989). *Look and Think: A Handbook for Teachers*. London: RNIB.

Chase, W. G. & Calfee, R. C. (1969). Modality and similarity effects in short-term recognition memory. *Journal of Experimental Psychology*, **81**, 510–14.

Chi, M.T.H. (1976). Short-term memory limitations in children: Capacity limitations or processing deficits? *Memory & Cognition*, **4**, 559–72.

Chi, M. T. H. (1977). Age differences in memory span. *Journal of Experimental Child Psychology*, **23**, 266–81.

Cholewiak, R. W. & Sherrick, C. E. (1986). Tracking skill of a deaf person with long-term tactile aid experience. *Journal of Rehabilitation Research and Development*, **23**, 20–6.

Chomsky, N. (1957). *Syntactic Structures*. The Hague: Mouton.

Chomsky, N. (1965). *Aspects of the Theory of Syntax*. Cambridge, Massachusetts: MIT Press.

Chow, K. L., Riesen, A. H. & Newell, F. W. (1957). Degeneration of ganglion cells in infant chimpanzees reared in darkness. *Journal of Comparative Neurology*, **107**, 27–42.

Clark, E. V. (1971). On the child's acquisition of antonyms in two semantic fields. *Journal of Verbal Learning & Verbal Behavior*, **11**, 750–8.

Clark, E. V. & Garnica, O. K. (1974). Is he coming or going? On the acquisition of deictic verbs. *Journal of Verbal Learning & Verbal Behavior*, **13**, 559–72.

Clark, E. V. & Clark, H. H. (1977). *The Psychology of Language*. New York: Harcourt Brace Jovanovich, Inc.

Clark, H. H., Carpenter, P. A. & Just, M. A. (1973). On the meeting of semantics and perception. In W. Chase (ed.) *Visual Information Processing*. New York: Academic Press.

Cohen, L. A. (1961). The role of eye and neck proprioceptive mechanisms in body orientation and motor coordination. *Journal of Neurophysiology*, **24**, 1–11.

Cohen, H. & Levy, J. (1986). Cerebral and sex differences in the categorization of haptic information. *Cortex*, **22**, 253–9.

Cohen, R. & Weatherford, D. L. (1980). Effects of route travelled on the distance estimates of children and adults. *Journal of Experimental Child Psychology*, **29**, 403–12.

Colburn, C. J. (1978). Can laterality be measured? *Neuropsychologica*, **16**, 283–9.

Colley, A. & Colley, M. (1981). Reproduction of endlocation and distance of movement in early and later blind subjects. *Journal of Motor Behavior*, **13**, 102–9.

Colley, A. & Pritchard, S. (1984). Reproduction of complex two-dimensional movements as a function of mode of presentation. *British Journal of Psychology*, **75**, 267–73.

Coltheart, M. (1987). Functional architecture of the language-processing system. In M. Coltheart, G. Sartori & R. Job (ed.) *The Cognitive Neuropsychology of Language*. Hillsdale, New Jersey: Lawrence Erlbaum Associates.

Coltheart, M., Sartori, G. & Job, R. (ed.) (1987). *The Cognitive Neuropsychology of Language*. Hillsdale, New Jersey: Lawrence Erlbaum Associates.

Connolly, K. & Jones, B. (1970). A developmental study of afferent–efferent integration. *British Journal of Psychology*, **61**, 259–66.

Conrad, R. (1964). Acoustic confusions in immediate memory. *British Journal of Psychology*, **55**, 75–84.

Conrad, R. (1971). The chronology of the development of covert speech in children. *Developmental Psychology*, **5**, 398–405.

Conrad, R. (1972). Short-term memory in the deaf: A test for speech coding. *British Journal of Psychology*, **63**, 173–80.

Corballis, M. C. & Beale, I. L. (1976). *The Psychology of Left and Right*. Hillsdale, New Jersey: Lawrence Erlbaum Associates.

Corballis, M. C. & Zalik, M. C. (1977). Why do children confuse mirror image obliques? *Journal of Experimental Child Psychology*, **24**, 516–23.

Cousins, J. F., Siegel, A. W. & Maxwell, S. E. (1983). Way finding and cognitive mapping in large scale environments: A test of a developmental model. *Journal of Experimental Child Psychology*, **35**, 1–20.

Cowey, A. (1992). Communication at the E.P.S. (April) meeting on neurological mechanisms of blindsight. Oxford.

Cox, M. V. (1986). *The Child's Point of View. The Development of Language and Cognition*. London: Harvester Press.

Craig, J. C. (1976). Vibrotactile letter recognition. The effect of a masking stimulus. *Perception & Psychophysics*, **20**, 317–26.

Craig, J. C. (1977). Vibrotactile pattern perception: extraordinary observers. *Science*, **196**, 450–2.

Craig, J. C. (1982). Temporal integration of vibrotactile patterns. *Perception & Psychophysics*, **32**, 219–29.

Craig, J. C. (1989). Interference in localizing stimuli. *Perception & Psychophysics*, **45**, 343–55.

Craig, J. C. & Sherrick, C. E. (1982). Dynamic tactile displays. In W. Shiff & E. Foulke (ed.) *Tactual Perception: A Sourcebook*. Cambridge: Cambridge University Press.

Cratty, B. J. (1967). The perception of gradient and the veering tendency while walking without vision. *American Foundation for the Blind Research Bulletin*, **14**, 31–51.

Cratty, B. J. (1971). *Movement and Spatial Awareness in Blind Children and Youth*. Springfield, Illinois: Charles Thomas.

Cratty, B. J. & Sams, T. A. (1968). *The Body-image of Blind Children*. New York: A.F.B. Publications.

Crick, F. (1989). The recent excitement about neural networks. *Nature*, **337**, 129–32.

Crowder, R. G. (1974). Inferential problems in echoic memory. In P. M. A. Rabbitt and S. Dornic (ed.) *Attention and Performance*, Vol. V. London: Academic Press.

Cummings, E. M. & Bjork, E. L. (1983). Search behavior on a multi-choice hiding task: Evidence for an objective conception of space in infancy. *International Journal of Behavioral Development*, **1**, 71–88.

Cutting, J. (1990). *The Right Cerebral Hemisphere and Psychiatric Disorders*. Oxford: Oxford University Press.

Davenport, R. K. & Rogers, C. M. (1970). Intermodal equivalence of stimulation in apes. *Science*, **168**, 279–80.

Davenport, R. K., Rogers, C. M. & Russell, I. S. (1973). Cross-modal perception in apes. *Neuropsychologica*, **11**, 21–8.

Davidson, P. W. (1972). The role of exploratory activity in haptic perception: Some issues, data and hypotheses. *Research Bulletin, American Foundation for the Blind*, **24**, 21–8.

DeCaspar, A. J. & Fifer, W. P. (1980). Of human bonding: Newborn prefer their Mother's voices. *Science*, **208**, 1174–6.

DeLoache, J. (1989). The development of representation in young children. In H. W. Reese (ed.) *Advances in Child Development and Behavior*. New York: Academic Press.

Dempster, F. N. (1981). Memory span: sources of individual and developmental differences. *Psychological Bulletin*, **89**, 63–100.

De Renzi, E. (1978). Hemisphere asymmetry as evidenced by spatial disorders. In M. Kinsbourne (ed.). *Asymmetrical Functions of the Brain*. Cambridge: Cambridge University Press.

De Renzi, E. (1982). *Disorders of Space Exploration and Cognition*. New York: John Wiley & Sons.

De Renzi, E., Faglioni, P. & Villa, P. (1977). Topographical amnesia. *Journal of Neurology, Neurosurgery & Psychiatry*, **40**, 498–505.

De Renzi, E., Faglioni, P. & Ferrari, P. (1980). The influence of age and sex on the incidence and type of aphasia. *Cortex*, **16**, 627–30.

Desmedt, J. E., Brunko, E. & Debecker, J. (1976). Maturation of the somato-sensory evoked potential in normal infants and children, with special reference to the early N1 component. *Electroencephalography and Clinical Neurophysiology*, **40**, 43–58.

DeValois, R. L. & DeValois, K. K. (1988). *Spatial Vision*. New York: Oxford University Press.

De Vries, J. I. P., Visser, G. H. A. & Prechtl, H. F. R. (1984). Fetal motility in the first half of pregnancy. In H. F. R. Prechtl (ed.) *Continuity of Neural Functions from Prenatal to Postnatal Life. Clinics in Developmental Medicine*, No. 94, pp. 46–64. Oxford: Spastics International Medical Publications.

Diamond, A. (1985). Development of the ability to use recall to guide action, as indicated by infants' performance on AB. *Child Development*, **56**, 868–83.

Diamond, A. (1991). Guidelines for the study of brain–behavior relationship during development. In H. S. Levin, H. M. Eisenberg & A. L. Benton (ed.) *Frontal Lobe Function and Dysfunction*. Oxford: Oxford University Press.

Diewert, G. L. & Stelmach, G. E. (1978). Perceptual organization in motor learning. In G. E. Stelmach (ed.) *Information Processing in Motor Control and Learning*. New York: Academic Press.

Dobson, V. & Teller, D. Y. (1978). Visual acuity in human infants: a review and comparison of behavioural and electrophysiological studies. *Vision Research*, **18**, 1469–83.

Dodd, B. (1977). The role of vision in the perception of speech. *Perception*, **6**, 31–40.

Dodd, B. (1983). The visual and auditory modalities in phonological acquisition. In A. E. Mills (ed.) *Language Acquisition in the Blind Child*. London: Croom Helm.

Dodd, B. & Campbell, R. (ed.) (1987). *Hearing by Eye: The Psychology of Lip-Reading*. London: Erlbaum.

Dodds, A. (1978). A hemispheric difference in tactuo-spatial processing. *Neuro-psychologica*, **60**, 335–49.

Dodds, A., Howarth, C. & Carter, D. (1982). The mental maps of the blind: The role of previous visual experience. *Journal of Visual Impairment & Blindness*, **76**, 5–12.

Duhamel, J.-R., Colby, C. L. & Goldberg, M. E. (1991). Congruent representations of visual somatosensory space in single neurons of the monkey ventral intra-parietal cortex (Area VIP). In J. Paillard (ed.) *Brain and Space*. Oxford: Oxford University Press.

Eaves, L. J., Last, K., Marting, N. G. & Links, J. L. (1977). A progressive approach to non-additivity and genotype-environmental covariance in the analysis of human differences. *British Journal of Statistical Psychology*, **30**, 1–42.

Ellis, A. W. (1987). Intimations of modularity, or the modularity of mind: Doing cognitive neuropsychology without syndromes. In M. Coltheart, G. Sartori & R. Job (ed.) *The Cognitive Neuropsychology of Language*. Hillsdale, New Jersey: Lawrence Erlbaum Associates.

Eme, D. R. F. (1979). Sex differences in childhood pathology: A review. *Psychological Bulletin*, **86**, 574–95.

Ettlinger, G. (1967). Analysis of cross-modal effects and their relationship to language. In F. L. Darley & C. H. Millikan (ed.) *Brain Mechanisms Underlying Speech and Language*. New York: Grune and Stratton.

Evans, G. (1985). *Collected Papers*. Oxford: Clarendon Press.

Evarts, E. V. (1973). Brain mechanisms in movement. *Scientific American*, **229**, 96–103.

Evarts, E. V., Bizzi, E., Burke, R. E., DeLong, M. & Thatch, W. T. Jr (1971). Central control of movement. *Neuroscience Research Bulletin*, **9**, 1–169.

Fairweather, H. (1976). Sex differences in cognition. *Cognition*, **4**, 231–80.

Fertsch, P. (1947). Hand dominance in reading Braille. *American Journal of Psychology*, **60**, 335–49.

Fessard, A. (1961). The role of neuronal networks in sensory communication within the brain. In W. A. Rosenblith (ed.) *Sensory Communication*. Cambridge, Massachusetts: The MIT Press.

Finke, R. A. (1979). The functional equivalence of mental images and errors of movement. *Cognitive Psychology*, **11**, 235–64.

Fishbein, J. D., Lewis, S. & Keiffer, K. (1972). Children's understanding of spatial relations: Coordination and perspective. *Developmental Psychology*, **7**, 21–33.

Fisher, C. B. (1979). Children's memory for line orientation in the absence of external cues. *Child Development*, **50**, 1088–92.

Fisher, C. B. & Braine, L. G. (1982). Left–right coding in children: Implications for adult performance. *Bulletin of the Psychonomic Society*, **20**(6), 305–7.

Fitts, P. M. (1958). Engineering psychology and equipment design. In S. S. Stevens (ed.) *Handbook of Experimental Psychology*, pp. 1287–340. New York: John Wiley and Sons, Inc.

Flavell, J. H. (1963). *The Psychology of Jean Piaget*. Princeton, New Jersey: Van Nostrand.

Flavell, J. H. (1988). The development of children's knowledge about mind: from cognitive connections to mental representations. In J. W. Astington, P. L. Harris & D. R. Olson (ed.) *Developing Theories of Mind*. Cambridge: Cambridge University Press.

Folstein, M. F., Maiberger, R. & McHugh, P. R. (1977). Mood disorder as a specific complication of stroke. *Journal of Neurology, Neurosurgery & Psychiatry*, **40**, 1018–20.

Fodor, J. (1983). *The Modularity of Mind: An Essay on Faculty Psychology*. Cambridge, Massachusetts: MIT Press.

Foreman, N., Foreman, D., Cummings, A. & Owens, S. (1990). Locomotion, active choice and spatial memory in children. *Journal of General Psychology*, **117**, 215–32.

Forssberg, H. (1985). Ontogeny of human motor control. I. Infant stepping supported locomotion and transition to independent locomotion. *Journal of Neurophysiology*, **42**, 936–53.

Forssberg, H., Hirschfeld, H. & Stokes, V. P. (1991). Development of human locomotor mechanisms. In D. M. Armstrong & B. M. H. Bush (ed.) *Locomotor Neural Mechanisms in Arthropods and Vertebrates*, pp. 313–31. Manchester: Manchester University Press.

Foulke, E. (1982). Reading Braille. In W. Schiff & E. Foulke (ed.) *Tactual Perception: A Source Book*. Cambridge: Cambridge University Press.

Foulke, E. & Warm, J. (1967). Effects of complexity and redundancy on the tactual recognition of metric figures. *Perceptual and Motor Skills*, **25**, 77–187.

Fraiberg, S. (1971). Intervention in infancy: A programme for blind infants. *Journal of the American Academy of Child Psychiatry*, **10** (3), 40–62.

Fraiberg, S. & Fraiberg, L. (1977). *Insights from the Blind*, Human Science Series. London: Souvenir Press.

Freeman, N. H. (1980). *Strategies of Representation in Young Children: Analysis of Spatial Skills and Drawing Processes*. London: Academic Press.

Freeman, N. H. & Cox, M. V. (ed.) (1985). *Visual Order: The Nature and Development of Visual Representation*. Cambridge: Cambridge University Press.

Gärling, T., Böök, A. & Ergezen, N. (1982). Memory for the spatial lay-out of the everyday physical environment. Differential rates of acquisition of different types of information. *Scandinavian Journal of Psychology*, **25**, 23–35.

Gärling, T., Lindberg, E., Carreiras, M. & Böök, A. (1986). Reference systems in cognitive maps. *Journal of Environmental Psychology*, **6**, 1–18.

Galaburda, A. M., Corsiglia, J., Rosen, G. D. & Sherman, G. F. (1987). Planum Temporale asymmetry, reappraisal since Geschwind & Levitzki. *Neuropsychologica*, **25**, 853–68.

Garner, W. R. (1974). *The Processing of Information and Structure*. New York: John Wiley.

Gazzaniga, M. S. (1988). The dynamics of cerebral specialization and modular interactions. In L. Weiskrantz (ed.) *Thought without Language*. Oxford: Clarendon Press.

Gazzaniga, M. S. & Ledoux, J. E. (1978). *The Integrated Mind*. New York: Plenum Press.

Geary, D. & Gilger, J. W. (1989). Age of sexual maturation and adult spatial ability. *Bulletin of the Psychonomic Society*, **27** (3), 241–4.

Geschwind, N. (1972). Language and the brain. *Scientific American*, **226**, 76–83.

Geschwind, N. & Levitzky, W. (1968). Human brain: Left–right asymmetries in temporal speech region. *Science*, **161**, 186–7.

Gesell, A. (1940). *The First Five Years of Life; a Guide to the Study of the Pre-school Child*, The Yale Clinic of Child Development. New York: Harper & Row.

Gesell, A., Thompson, H. & Amatruda, C. S. (1934). *Infant Behavior: Its Genesis and Growth*. New York: McGraw-Hill.

Ghent, L. (1960). Recognition by children of realistic figures presented in various orientations. *Canadian Journal of Psychology*, **14**, 249–56.

Ghent, L. & Bernstein, L. (1961). Effect of orientation on geometric forms and their recognition by children. *Perceptual & Motor Skills*, **12**, 95–101.

Gibson, E. J. (1969). *Principles of Perceptual Learning and Development*. New York: Appleton Century Crofts.

Gibson, E. J. & Gibson, J. J. (1955). Perceptual learning: Differentiation or enrichment? *Psychological Review*, **62**, 32–41.

Gibson, E. J. & Spelke, E. S. (1983). The development of perception. In P. H. Mussen (series ed.); J. H. Flavell & E. M. Markman (Vol. ed.) *Handbook of Child Psychology: Cognitive Development*, Vol. III, pp. 2–76. New York: John Wiley.

Gibson, J. J. (1962). Observations on active touch. *Psychological Review*, **69**, 477–91.

Gibson, J. J. (1966). *The Senses Considered as Perceptual Systems*. Boston: Houghton Mifflin.

Gibson, J. J. (1971). The information available in pictures. *Leonardo*, **4**, 27–35.

Gibson, J. J. (1979). *The Ecological Approach to Visual Perception*. Boston: Houghton Mifflin.

Gilhooley, K. J., Wood, M., Kinnear, P. R. & Green, C. (1988). Skill in map reading and memory for maps. *Quarterly Journal of Experimental Psychology*, **40**, 87–107.

Gill, J. M. (1973). Design, production and evaluation of tactual maps for the blind. Doctoral thesis, University of Warwick.

Gilson, E. Q. & Baddeley, A. D. (1969). Tactile short-term memory. *Quarterly Journal of Experimental Psychology*, **21**, 180–9.

Goethe, W. von (1808). *Faust*. In A. Stern (ed.) *Goethes Werke*, Dritter Band. Leipzig: Verlag von C. Grumbach.

Goldenberg, G., Podreka I. & Steiner, M. (1990). The cerebral localization of visual imagery: evidence from emission computerized tomography of cerebral blood flow. In P. J. Hampson, D. Marks & J. T. E. Richardson (ed.) *Imagery: Current Developments*. London: Routledge.

Goldman-Rakic, P. S. & Friedman, H. R. (1991). The circuitry of working memory revealed by anatomy and metabolic imaging. In H. S. Levin, H. M. Eisenberg & A. L. Benton (ed.) *Frontal Lobe Function and Dysfunction*. Oxford: Oxford University Press.

Golledge, R. G. & Zannaras, G. (1973). Cognitive approaches to the analysis of human spatial behavior. In W. H. Ittelson (ed.) *Environmental Cognition*. New York: Seminar Press.

Gollin, E. S. (1960). Developmental studies of visual recognition of incomplete objects. *Perceptual & Motor Skills*, **11**, 289–98.

Gomulicki, B. R. (1961). The development of perception and learning in blind children. Private publication, Psychology Laboratory, Cambridge University.

Goodenough, F. (1926). *The Measurement of Intelligence by Drawing*. Yonkers, New York: World Books.

Goodnow, J. J. (1971). Eye and hand: Differential memory and its effect on matching. *Neuropsychologica*, **42**, 1187–201.

Goodnow, J. J. (1977). *Children's Drawing*. London: Fontana/Open Books.

Goodnow, J. J. (1978). Visible thinking: Cognitive aspects of change in drawing. *Child Development*, **49**, 637–41.

Goodnow, J. J. & Levine, R. (1973). The grammar of action: Sequence and syntax in children's copying of simple shapes. *Cognitive Psychology*, **4**, 82–98.

Gopher, D. (1984). The contribution of vision-based imagery. In W. Prinz & A. F. Saunders (ed.) *Cognitive and Motor Processes*. Berlin: Springer-Verlag.

Gordon, H. W. (1978). Hemisphere asymmetry for dichotically presented chords in musicians and nonmusicians, males and females. *Acta Psychologica*, **42**, 382–95.

Goswami, U. (1988). Orthographic analogies and reading development. *Quarterly Journal of Experimental Psychology*, **40A**, 239–68.

Granrud, C. E. (1986). Binocular vision and spatial perception in 4- and 5-month-old infants. *Journal of Experimental Psychology: Human Perception and Performance*, **12**, 36–49.

Gray, J. A. (1971). Sex differences in emotional behaviour in mammals including man. *Acta Psychologica*, **35**, 29–48.

Gray, J. A. & Buffery, A. W. H. (1971). Sex differences in emotional and cognitive behaviour in mammals including man: Adaptive and Neural bases. *Acta Psychologica*, **35**, 89–111.

Gregory, R. L. (1966). *Eye and Brain: The Psychology of Seeing*. London: Weidenfeld & Nicolson.

Gregory, R. L. & Wallace, J. C. (1963). *Recovery from Blindness: A case study*, Experimental Psychology Society Monograph, No. 2. Cambridge: Cambridge University Press.

Grunewald, A. P. (1966). A braille reading machine. *Science*, **154**, 144–6.

Gurfinkel, V. S. & Levick, Yu. S. (1991). Perceptual and automatic aspects of the postural body scheme. In J. Paillard (ed.) *Brain and Space*. Oxford: Oxford University Press.

Guttman, R. (1974). Genetic analysis of Raven's progressive matrices. *Behavior Genetics*, **4**, 273–84.

Haber, R. N. & Haber, R. B. (1964). Eidetic imagery: I. Frequency. *Perceptual and Motor Skills*, **19**, 131–8.

Halverson, H. M. (1932). An experimental study of prehension in infants by means of systematic cinema records. *Genetic Psychology Monographs*, **10**, 110–286.

Hardwyk, D. A., McIntyre, C. W. & Pick, H. L. (1976). The content and manipulation of cognitive maps in children and adults. *Monographs of the Society of Research in Child Development*, **41** (166), 1–55.

Harlow, H. F. (1949). The formation of learning sets. *Psychological Review*, **56**, 51–65.

Harris, D. B. (1963). *Children's Drawings as Measures of Intellectual Maturity*. New York: Harcourt, Brace and World.

Harris, L. J. (1981). Sex related variations in spatial skill. In L. S. Liben, A. H. Patterson & N. Newcombe (ed.) *Spatial Representation and Behavior across the Life Span*. New York: Academic Press.

Harris, L. J., Hanley, C. & Best, T. C. (1975). Conservation of horizontality: Sex differences in six graders and college students. Paper presented at Biennial Meeting of the Society for Research in Child Development, Denver, Colorado.

Harris, P. L. (1973). Perseverative errors in search by young children. *Child Development*, **44**, 28–33.

Harris, P. L. (1983). Infant cognition. In M. M. Haith & J. J. Campos (ed.) *Handbook of Child Psychology: Infancy and Developmental Psychology*, Vol. 2. New York: John Wiley.

Hart, R. A. & Moore, G. T. (1973). The development of spatial cognition: a review. In R. M. Downs & D. Stea (ed.) *Image and Environment: Cognitive Mapping and Spatial Behavior*. Chicago: Aldine.

Hartlage, L. C. (1970). Sex-linked inheritance of spatial ability. *Perceptual and Motor Skills*, **31**, 610.

Hatwell, Y. (1985). *Piagetian Reasoning and the Blind*. New York: American Foundation for the Blind.

Hatwell, Y. (1978). Form perception and related issues in blind humans. In R.

Held, H. W. Leibowitz & H. L. Teuber (ed.) *Handbook of Sensory Physiology*. Berlin: Springer-Verlag.

Hazen, N. L., Lockman, J., Pick, H. L. Jr (1978). The development of children's representations of large-scale environments. *Child Development*, **49**, 623–36.

Hebb, D. O. (1949). *The Organization of Behavior*. New York: John Wiley.

Hein, A. & Jeannerod, M. (ed.) (1982). *Spatially Oriented Behavior*. New York Springer-Verlag.

Held, R. (1963). Plasticity in human sensori-motor control. *Science*, **142**, 455–62.

Held, R. (1965). Plasticity in sensory-motor systems. *Scientific American*, **213**, 84–94.

Held, R. & Bauer, J. A. (1967). Visually guided reaching in infant monkeys after restricted rearing. *Science*, **155**, 718–20.

Held, R. & Hein, A. (1963). Movement produced stimulation in the development of visually guided behavior. *Journal of Comparative Physiology and Psychology*, **56**, 872–6.

Heller, M. A. (1989). Tactile memory in sighted and blind observers: the influence of orientation and rate of presentation. *Perception*, **18**, 121–33.

Henry, L. & Millar, S. (1991). Memory span increase with age. A test of two hypotheses. *Journal of Experimental Child Psychology*, **51**, 459–84.

Henry, L. & Millar, S. (1993). Why does memory span improve with age? A review of the evidence for two current hypotheses. *European Journal of Cognitive Psychology*, **5**, 241–87.

Herman, J. F. (1980). Children's cognitive maps of large scale spaces: Effects of exploration, direction, and repeated experience. *Journal of Experimental Child Psychology*, **29**, 126–43.

Herman, J. F. & Siegel, A. W. (1978). The development of cognitive mapping of large-scale spatial environments. *Journal of Experimental Child Psychology*, **26**, 389–406.

Herman, J. F., Chatman S. P. & Roth, S. F. (1983a). Cognitive mapping in blind people: Acquisition of spatial relationships in a large-scale environment. *Journal of Visual Impairment & Blindness*, **77**, 161–6.

Herman, J. F., Herman, T. G. & Chatman, S. P. (1983b). Constructing cognitive maps from partial information: A demonstrative study with congenitally blind subjects. *Journal of Visual Impairment and Blindness*, **77**, 195–8.

Herman, J. F., Norton, L. M. & Roth, S. F. (1983). Children and adults' distance estimation in a large-scale environment: effects of time and clutter. *Journal of Experimental Child Psychology*, **36**, 453–70.

Herman, J. F., Blouquist, S. L. & Klein, C. A. (1987). Children's and adults cognitive maps of very large unfamiliar environments, *British Journal of Developmental Psychology*, **5**, 61–72.

Hermelin, B. & O'Connor, N. (1971). Functional asymmetry in the reading of braille. *Neuropsychologica*, **9**, 431–5.

Hermelin, B. & O'Connor, N. (1975). Location and distance estimates by blind and sighted children. *Quarterly Journal of Experimental Psychology*, **27**, 295–301.

Hinton, G. E. & Shallice, T. (1991). Lesioning an attractor network: Investigations of acquired dyslexia. *Psychological Review*, **98**, 74–95.

Hirtle, S. C. & Mascolo, M. F. (1986). Effects of semantic clustering on the memory of spatial locations. *Journal of Experimental Psychology: Learning, Memory and Cognition*, **12**, 182–9.

Hiscock, M. & Kinsbourne, M. (1978). Ontogeny of cerebral dominance: Evidence from time-sharing asymmetry in children. *Developmental Psychology*, **14**, 321–92.

Hitch, G. J. & Halliday, M. S. (1983). Working memory in children. *Philosophical Transactions of the Royal Society of London*, **B302**, 325–40.

Hitch, G. J., Halliday, M. S., Dodd. A. & Littler, J. E. (1989). Development of rehearsal in short-term memory: Differences between pictorial and spoken stimuli. *British Journal of Developmental Psychology*, **7**, 347–62.

Hollins, M. (1989). *Understanding Blindness*. Hillsdale, New Jersey: Lawrence Erlbaum Associates.

Hollins, M. (1989). Mental haptic rotation: More consistent in blind subjects? *Journal of Visual Impairment and Blindness*, **80**, 950–2.

Hollyfield, R. L. & Foulke, E. (1983). The spatial cognition of blind pedestrians. *Journal of Visual Impairment and Blindness*, **77**, 204–10.

Holyoak, K. J. (1974). The role of imagery in the evaluation of sentences: Imagery or semantic factors. *Journal of Verbal Learning and Verbal Behavior*, **13**, 163–6.

Homer, D. T. & Craig, J. C. (1989). A comparison of discrimination and identification of vibrotactile patterns. *Perception & Psychophysics*. **45**, 21–30.

Hood, B. & Willats, P. (1986). Reaching in the dark to an object's remembered position: Evidence for object permanence in 5-month-old infants. *British Journal of Developmental Psychology*, **4**, 57–65.

Howard, I. P. & Templeton, W. B. (1966). *Human Spatial Orientation*. New York: John Wiley.

Howard, I. P., Bergstroem, S. S. & Ohmi, M. (1990). Shape from shading in different frames of reference. *Perception*, **19**, 523–30.

Hubel, D. H. & Wiesel, T. N. (1963). Receptive fields of cells in striate cortex of very young, visually inexperienced kittens. *Journal of Neurophysiology*, **26**, 994–1002.

Hubel, D. H. & Wiesel, T. N. (1965). Receptive fields and functional architecture in two nonstriated visual areas (18 and 19) of the cat. *Journal of Neurophysiology*, **28**, 229–89.

Hubel, D. H. & Wiesel, T. N. (1977). Functional architecture of macaque visual cortex. *Proceedings of the Royal Society London*, **B198**, 1–59.

Hughes, S., Epstein, W., Schneider, S. D. & Dudcock, A. (1990). An asymmetry in transmodal perceptual learning. *Perception & Psychophysics*, **48**, 143–50.

Hulme, C. & Tordoff, V. (1989). Working memory development: The effects of speech rate, word length, and acoustic similarity on serial recall. *Journal of Experimental Child Psychology*, **47**, 72–87.

Humphrey, G. K. & Humphrey, D. E. (1985). The use of binaural sensory aids by blind infants and children: Theoretical and Applied Issues. In F. Morrison & C. Lord (ed.) *Applied Developmental Psychology*, Vol. 2. New York: Academic Press.

Humphrey, N. & Weiskrantz, L. (1967). Vision in monkeys after removal of the striate cortex. *Nature*, **215**, 595–7.

Hunter, W. S. (1912). The delayed reaction in animals and children. *Behavior Monographs*, **2** (1), 1–86.

Huttenlocher, J. (1967). Discrimination of figure orientation: Effects of relative position. *Journal of Comparative and Physiological Psychology*, **63**, 359–61.

Huttenlocher, J. & Presson, C. (1973). Mental rotation and the perspective problem. *Cognitive Psychology*, **4**, 277–99.

Huttenlocher, J. & Presson, C. (1979). The coding and transformation of spatial information. *Cognitive Psychology*, **11**, 375–94.

Hyvärinen, J. & Poranen, A. (1978). Receptive field integration and submodality convergence in the hand area of the post-central gyrus of the alert monkey. *Journal of Physiology*, **283**, 539–56.

Hyvärinen, J., Carlson, S. & Hyvärinen, L. (1981). Early visual deprivation alters modality of neuronal responses in area 19 of the monkey cortex. *Neuroscience Letters*, **26**, 239.

Ibbotson, A. & Bryant, P. E. (1976). The perpendicular error and the vertical effect in children's drawing. *Perception*, **5**, 319–26.

Imanaka, K. & Abernethy, B. (1992). Cognitive strategies and short-term memory for movement distance and location. *Quarterly Journal of Experimental Psychology*, **45a**, 669–700.

Ingle, D. J., Jeannerod, M. & Lee, D. N. (1985). *Brain Mechanisms and Spatial Vision*. Dordrecht: Martinus Nijhoff Publishers.

Inglis, J. & Lawson, J. S. (1982). Sex differences in the effects of unilateral brain damage on intelligence. *Science*, **212**, 693–5.

Ittelson, W. H. (1973). *Environment and Cognition*. New York: Seminar Press.

James, G. A. (1982). Mobility maps. In W. Schiff & E. Foulke (ed.) *Tactual Perception: A Source Book*. Cambridge: Cambridge University Press.

James, G. A. & Gill, J. M. (1974). Mobility maps for the visually handicapped: A study of learning and retention of raised symbols. *Research Bulletin of the American Foundation for the Blind*, **27**, 187–98.

Jancke, L., Steinmetz, H. & Volkmann, J. (1992). Dichotic listening: What does it measure? *Neuropsychologica*, **30**, 941–50.

Jansson, G. (1991). The control of locomotion when vision is reduced or missing. In A. E. Patla (ed.) *Adaptability of Human Gait*. Amsterdam: Elsevier Science Publishers, North-Holland.

Jastrow, J. (1886). The perception of space by disparate senses. *Mind*, **11**, 539–54.

Jeannerod, M. (1988). *The Neural and Behavioural Organization of Goal-Directed Movements*. Oxford: Clarendon Press.

Jeannerod, M. (1991). A neurophysiological model for the directional coding of reaching movements. In J. Paillard (ed.) *Brain and Space*. Oxford: Oxford University Press.

Johnson, P. (1982). The functional equivalence of imagery and movement. *Quarterly Journal of Experimental Psychology*, **34A**, 349–65.

Johnson-Laird, P. N. (1983). *Mental Models: Towards a Cognitive Science of Language and Consciousness*. London: Cambridge University Press.

Jones, B. (1974). Role of central monitoring of efference in short-term memory for movements. *Journal of Experimental Psychology*, **102**, 37–43.

Jones, B. (1981). The developmental significance of cross-modal matching. In

R. D. Walk & H. L. Pick, Jr (ed.) *Intersensory Perception and Sensory Integration*. New York: Plenum Press.

Juurmaa, J. & Suonio, K. (1975). The role of audition and motion in the spatial orientation of the blind and sighted. *Scandinavian Journal of Psychology*, **16**, 209–16.

Kail, R. & Park, Y-S. (1990). Impact of practice on speed of mental rotation. *Journal of Experimental Child Psychology*, **49**, 227–44.

Kandel, E. R. & Hawkins, R. D. (1992). The biological basis of learning and individuality. *Scientific American*, **267**, 79–86.

Kant, I. (1781). *Kritik der Reinen Vernunft* (Raymund Schmidt (ed.)). Hamburg: Felix Meiner Verlag (1956).

Karmiloff-Smith, A. (1992). *Beyond Modularity: A Developmental Perspective on Cognitive Science*. Cambridge, Massachusetts: MIT Press.

Katz, D. (1925). *Der Aufbau der Tastwelt*. Leipzig: Barth.

Kay, L. (1974). A sonar aid to enhance spatial perception by the blind: Engineering and evaluation. *The Radio & Electronic Engineer*, **44**, 605–26.

Keele, S. W. (1968). Movement control in skilled motor performance. *Psychological Bulletin*, **70**, 387–403.

Keele, S. W. & Boies, S. J. (1973). Processing demands of sequential information. *Memory & Cognition*, **1**, 85–90.

Keller, H. (1905). *The Story of My Life*. J. A. Macey (ed.) New York: Grosset & Dunlap.

Kelso, J. A. S. & Wallace, S. A. (1978). Conscious mechanisms in movement. In G. E. Stelmach (ed.) *Information Processing in Motor Control and Learning*. New York: Academic Press.

Kelso, J. A. S. & Clarke, J. E. (1982). *The Development of Movement Control*. New York: John Wiley.

Kendler, H. H. & Kendler, T. S. (1962). Vertical and horizontal processes in problem solving. *Psychological Review*, **69**, 1–16.

Kennedy, J. M. (1982). Haptic pictures. In W. Shiff & E. Foulke (ed.) *Tactual Perception*: A Source Book. Cambridge: Cambridge University Press.

Kennedy, J. M. & Gabias, P. (1985). Metaphoric devices in drawings of motion mean the same to the blind and sighted. *Perception*, **14**, 189–95.

Kerr, N. H. (1983). The role of vision in visual imagery experiments: evidence from the congenitally blind. *Journal of Experimental Psychology: General*, **112**, 265–77.

Kimura, D. (1963). Speech lateralization by children. *Journal of Comparative Psychology and Physiology*, **56**, 899–902.

Kimura, D. (1964). Right–left differences in the perception of melodies. *Quarterly Journal of Experimental Psychology*, **16**, 355–9.

Kimura, D. (1967). Functional asymmetry of the brain in dichotic listening. *Cortex*, **3**, 163–78.

Kimura, D. (1973). Manual activity during speaking. I. Right handers. *Neuropsychologica*, **11**, 45–50.

Kimura, D. (1992). Sex differences in the brain. *Scientific American*, **267** (3), 119–25.

Kimura, D. & Vanderwolf, C. H. (1970). The relation between hand preference and the performance of individual finger movements by the left and right hands. *Brain*, **93**, 769–74.

Kintsch, W. (1977). *Memory and Cognition*. New York: John Wiley.

Kirasic, K. C., Siegel, A. W. & Allen, G. L. (1980). Developmental changes in recognition in context memory. *Child Development*, **51**, 302–5.

Kitcher, P. (1990). *Kant's Transcendental Psychology*. Oxford: Oxford University Press.

Klein, W. (1983). Deixis and spatial orientation in route directions. In H. L. Pick, Jr & L. P. Acredolo (ed.) *Spatial Orientation: Theory, Research and Application*. New York: Plenum Press.

Knox, C. & Kimura, D. (1970). Cerebral processing of nonverbal sounds in boys and girls. *Neuropsychologica*, **8**, 227–37.

Kornhuber, H. H. (1984). Mechanisms of voluntary movement. In W. Prinz & A. F. Saunders (ed.) *Cognitive and Motor Processes*. Berlin: Springer-Verlag.

Kosslyn, S. M. (1980). *Image and Mind*. Cambridge, Massachusetts: Harvard University Press.

Kosslyn, S. M. (1981). The medium and the message in mental imagery: A theory. *Psychological Review*, **88**, 46–66.

Kosslyn, S. M. (1987). Seeing and imaging in the two hemispheres. *Psychological Review*, **94**, 148–75.

Kosslyn, S. M., Heldmeyer, K. H. & Locklear, E. P. (1977). Children's drawings as data about internal representations. *Journal of Experimental Child Psychology*, **23**, 191–211.

Kosslyn, S. M., Ball, T. M. & Reiser, B. J. (1978). Visual images preserve metric spatial information: Evidence from studies of image scanning. *Journal of Experimental Psychology: Human Perception and Performance*, **4**, 47–60.

Krasnoff, A. G., Walker, J. T. & Howard, M. (1989). Early sex-linked activities and interests related to spatial abilities. *Personality and Individual Differences*, **10**, 81–5.

Krauthammer, G. (1968). Form perception across sensory modalities. *Neuropsychologica*, **6**, 105–13.

Kress, G. & Cross, J. (1969). Visual and tactual interaction in judgements of the vertical. *Psychonomic Science*, **14**, 165–6.

Kumar, S. (1977). Short-term memory for a non-verbal tactual task after cerebral commissurotomy. *Cortex*, **13**, 55–61.

Kusajima, T. (1974). *Visual Reading and Braille Reading: An Experimental Investigation of the Physiology and Psychology of Tactual Reading*. New York: American Foundation for the Blind.

Laabs, G. L. (1973). Retention characteristics of different reproduction cues in short-term memory. *Journal of Experimental Psychology*, **100**, 168–77.

Laabs, G. L. & Simmons, R. W. (1981). Motor memory. In D. Holding (ed.) *Human Skills*. New York: Wiley.

Lake, D. A. & Bryden, M. P. (1976). Handedness and sex differences in hemisphere asymmetry. *Brain and Language*, **3**, 266–82.

Landau, B. (1983). Blind children's language is not 'meaningless'. In A. E. Mills (ed.) *Language Acquisition in the Blind Normal and Deficient*. London: Croom Helm.

Landau, B. (1986). Early map use as an unlearned ability. *Cognition*, **22**, 201–23.

Landau, B. & Jackendoff, R. (1993). "What" and "where" in spatial language and spatial cognition. *Behavioral & Brain Sciences*, **16**, 217–65.

Landau, B., Gleitman, H. & Spelke, E. (1981). Spatial knowledge and geometric representation in a child blind from birth. *Science*, **213**, 1275–8.

Landau, B., Spelke, E. & Gleitman, H. (1984). Spatial knowledge in a young blind child. *Cognition*, **16**, 225–60.

Lansdell, H. (1962). A sex difference in the effect of temporal-lobe neurosurgery on design preference. *Nature*, **196**, 852–4.

Larish, D. D., Volp, C. M. & Wallace, S. A. (1984). An empirical note on attaining a spatial target after distorting initial conditions of movement after muscle vibration. *Journal of Motor Behavior*, **16**, 76–83.

Laurendeau, M. & Pinard, A. (1970). *The Development of the Concept of Space in the Child*. York: International Universities Press.

Lechelt, E. C. & Verenka, A. (1980). Spatial anisotropy in intramodal and cross-modal judgments of stimulus orientation. *Perception*, **9**, 581–7.

Lederman, S. J. & Klatzky, R. L. (1990). Haptic object classification: knowledge driven exploration. *Cognitive Psychology*, **22**, 421–59.

Lee, D. N. (1980). The optic flow field. *Philosophical Transactions of the Royal Society*, **B290**, 167–79.

Lee, D. N. & Aronson, E. (1974). Visual proprioceptive control of standing in human infants. *Perception & Psychophysics*, **15**, 529–32.

Lee, D. N. & Lishman, J. R. (1975). Visual proprioceptive control of stance. *Journal of Human Movement Studies*, **1**, 87–95.

Lee, D. N., Young, D. S., Reddish, P. E., Lough, S. & Clayton, T. M. H. (1983). Visual timing in hitting an accelerating ball. *Quarterly Journal of Experimental Psychology*, **35A**, 333–46.

Lee, T. D., Wulf, G. & Schmidt, R. A. (1992). Contextual interference in motor learning: Dissociated effects due to the nature of task variations. *Quarterly Journal of Experimental Psychology*, **44A**, 627–44.

Lee, T. R. (1970). Perceived distance as a function of direction in the city. *Environment & Behavior*, **2**, 40–51.

Legge, D. (1965). Visual and proprioceptive components of motor skill. *British Journal of Psychology*, **56**, 243–54.

Leinonen, L., Hyvärinen, J., Nyman, G. & Linnankoski, I. (1979). Functional properties of neurons, in lateral part of associative area 7 in awake monkeys. *Experimental Brain Research*, **34**, 299–320.

Leonard, J. A. & Newman, R. C. (1967). Spatial orientation in the blind. *Nature*, **215**, 1413–14.

Leonard, J. A. & Newman, R. C. (1970). Three types of maps for blind travel. *Ergonomics*, **13**, 165–79.

Levin, H. S., Eisenberg, H. M. & Benton, A. L. (ed.) (1991). *Frontal Lobe Function and Dysfunction*. Oxford: Oxford University Press.

Liben, L. S. (1991). Environmental cognition through direct and representational experiences: A life-span perspective. In T. Garling & G. W. Evans (ed.) *Environment, Cognition, and Action: An Integrated Approach*. Oxford: Oxford University Press.

Liben, L. S. (1982). Children's Large Scale Spatial Cognition. In R. Cohen (ed.) *New Directions for Child Development: Children's Conceptions of Spatial Relationships*, Vol. 15. San Francisco: Jossey-Bass.

Liben, L. S. (1988). Conceptual issues in the development of spatial cognition. In J. Stiles-Davis, M. Kritchevsky, & U. Bellugi (ed.) *Spatial Cognition*. Hillsdale, New Jersey: Lawrence Erlbaum Associates.

Liben, L. S. & Downs, R. M. (1989). Understanding maps as symbols: The development of map concepts in children. In W. H. Reese (ed.) *Advances in Child Development and Behavior*, Vol. 22. New York: Academic Press.

Liben, L. S. & Golbeck, L. S. (1984). Performance on Piagetian horizontality and verticality tasks: Sex-related differences in knowledge of relevant physical phenomena. *Developmental Psychology*, **20**, 595–606.

Locher, P. J. & Simmons, R. W. (1978). Influence of stimulus symmetry and complexity upon haptic scanning strategies during detection, learning and recognition tasks. *Perception & Psychophysics*, **23**, 110–16.

Locke, J. (first publ. 1689). *An Essay Concerning Human Understanding*. London: Routledge & Sons.

Locke, J. L. (1970). Short-term memory encoding strategies of the deaf. *Psychonomic Science*, **18**, 233–4.

Logie, R. H. (1986). Visuo-spatial processing in working memory. *Quarterly Journal of Experimental Psychology*, **38A**, 229–47.

Logie, R. H. & Baddeley, A. D. (1990). Imagery and working memory. In P. J. Hampson, D. F. Marks & J. T. E. Richardson (ed.) *Imagery: Current Developments*. London: Routledge.

Logie, R. H., Zucco, G. M. & Baddeley, A. D. (1990). Interference with visual short-term memory. *Acta Psychologica*, **75**, 55–74.

Loomis, J. (1981). Tactile pattern perception. *Perception*, **10**, 5–27.

Loomis, J. M. (1990). A model of character recognition and legibility. *Journal of Experimental Psychology: Human Perception & Performance*, **16**, 106–20.

Loomis, J. M. (1993). Counterexample to the hypothesis of functional similarity between tactual and visual pattern perception. *Perception & Psychophysics*, **54**, 179–84.

Luquet, G. H. (1927). *Le Dessin Enfantin*. Paris: Alcan.

Luria, A. R. (1961). *The Role of Speech in the Regulation of Normal and Abnormal Behavior*. New York: Liveright.

Luria, A. R. (1968). *The Mind of a Mnemonist*. New York: Basic Books.

Lynch, K. (1960). *The Image of the City*. Cambridge, Massachusetts: MIT Press.

Maccoby, E. E. & Bee, H. L. (1965). Some speculations concerning the lag between perceiving and performing. *Child Development*, **36**, 367–77.

Maccoby, E. E. & Jacklin, C. N. (1974). *The Psychology of Sex Differences*. Stanford: Stanford University Press.

Mach, E. (1897). *The Analysis of Sensation*. Chicago: Pen Court Publishing.

MacDonald, J. & McGurk, H. (1978). Visual influence on speech perception processes. *Perception & Psychophysics*, **24**, 253–7.

MacLeod, C. M. (1991). Half a century of stroop. *Psychological Bulletin*, **109**, 162–223.

Maki, R. H. & Ghent Braine, L. (1985). The role of verbal labels in the judgment of orientation and location. *Perception*, **14**, 67–80.

Maki, R. H., Maki, W. S. & Marsh, L. G. (1977). Processing locational and orientational information. *Memory & Cognition*, **5**, 602–12.

Maki, R. H., Grandy, C. A. & Hauge, G. (1979). Why is telling left from right more difficult than telling above from below? *Journal of Experimental Psychology: Human Perception and Performance*, **5**, 52–67.

Marmor, G. S. & Strauss, G. (1975). Development of kinetic images: When does the child first represent movement in mental images? *Cognitive Psychology*, **7**, 548–59.

Marmor, G. S. & Zaback, L. A. (1976). Mental rotation by the blind: Does mental rotation depend on visual imagery? *Journal of Experimental Psychology: Human Perception & Performance*, **2**, 515–21.

Marr, D. (1982). *Vision*. San Francisco: Freeman.

Marteniuk, R. G. (1978). The role of eye and head position in slow movement execution. In G. E. Stelmach (ed.) *Information Processing in Motor Control and Learning*. New York: Academic Press.

Martinez, F. (1971). Comparison of two types of tactile exploration in a task of mirror-image recognition. *Psychonomic Science*, **22**, 124–5.

Marzi, C. A., Grabonska, A., Tressoldi, P. & Bisiachi, P. S. (1988). Left hemisphere superiority for visuospatial functions in lefthanders. *Behavioral Brain Research*, **30**, 183–92.

Massaro, D. W. (1989). Review of speech perception by ear and eye: A paradigm for psychological enquiry. *Behavioral & Brain Sciences*, **12**, 741–55.

Massaro, D. W. & Friedman, D. (1990). Models of integration given multiple sources of information. *Psychological Review*, **97**, 225–52.

Massaro, D. W., Cohen, M. M. & Gesi, A. T. (1993). Long-term training, transfer and retention in learning to lipread. *Perception & Psychophysics*, **53**, 549–62.

McArthur, R. (1967). Sex differences in field dependence for the Eskimo: A replication of Berry's findings. *International Journal of Psychology*, **2**, 139–40.

McCarthy, D. (1954). Language development in children. In L. Carmichael (ed.) *Manual of Child Psychology*. New York: John Wiley.

McClosky, D. I. & Gandevia, S. G. (1978). Role of inputs from skin, joints and muscles and of corollary discharges, in human discrimination tasks. In G. Gordon (ed.) *Active Touch The Mechanism of Recognition of Objects by Manipulation: A Multi-disciplinary Approach*. Oxford: Pergamon Press.

McGee, M. G. (1979). Human Spatial Abilities: Psychometric studies and environmental, genetic, hormonal and neurological influences. *Psychological Bulletin*, **86**, 889–918.

McGlone, J. (1980). Sex differences in human brain asymmetry: A critical survey. *Brain and Behavioral Science*, **3**, 215–27.

McGlone, J. & Davidson, W. (1973). The relation between cerebral speech laterality and spatial ability with special reference to sex and hand preference. *Neuropsychologica*, **11**, 105–13.

McGurk, H. (1972). Infant discrimination of orientation. *Journal of Experimental Child Psychology*, **14**, 151–64.

McGurk H. & MacDonald, J. (1976). Hearing lips and seeing voices. *Nature*, **264**, 746–8.

McKenzie, B. E., Day, R. H. & Ihsen, R. (1984). Localization of events in space. Young children are not always egocentric. *British Journal of Developmental Psychology*, **2**, 1–9.

McLeod, P. (1993). Dyslexic neural networks. *Current Biology*, **3**, 300–2.

McNamara, T. P. & LeSueur, L. L. (1989). Mental representation of spatial and nonspatial relations. *Quarterly Journal of Experimental Psychology*, **41A** (2), 215–33.

Mehta, Z. & Newcombe, F. (1991). A role for the left hemisphere in spatial processing. *Cortex*, **27**, 153–67.

Meltzoff, A. N. & Borton, R. W. (1979). Intermodal matching by human neonates. *Nature*, **282**, 403–4.

Meuwissen, I. & McKenzie, B. E. (1987). Localization of an event by young children: The effect of visual and body movement information. *British Journal of Developmental Psychology*, **5**, 1–8.

Millar, S. (1968). *The Psychology of Play*. London: Penguin Books.

Millar, S. (1971). Visual and haptic cue utilization by preschool children: The recognition of visual and haptic stimuli presented separately and together. *Journal of Experimental Child Psychology*, **12**, 88–94.

Millar, S. (1972a). The effects of interpolated tasks on latency and accuracy of intramodal and crossmodal shape recognition by children. *Journal of Experimental Child Psychology*, **96**, 170–5.

Millar, S. (1972b). The development of visual and kinaesthetic judgements of distance. *British Journal of Psychology*, **63**, 271–82.

Millar, S. (1972c). Effects of instructions to visualise stimuli during delay on visual recognition by preschool children. *Child Development*, **43**, 1073–5.

Millar, S. (1974). Tactile short-term memory by blind and sighted children. *British Journal of Psychology*, **65**, 253–63.

Millar, S. (1975a). Effects of input variables on visual and kinaesthetic matching by children within and across modalities. *Journal of Experimental Child Psychology*, **19**, 63–78.

Millar, S. (1975b). Effects of tactual and phonological similarity on the recall of braille letters by blind children. *British Journal of Psychology*, **66**, 193–201.

Millar, S. (1975c). Effects of phonological and tactual similarity on serial object recall by blind and sighted children. *Cortex*, **11**, 170–80.

Millar, S. (1975d). Spatial memory by blind and sighted children. *British Journal of Psychology*, **66**, 449–59.

Millar, S. (1975e). Translation rules or visual experience? Drawing the human figure by blind and sighted children. *Perception*, **4**, 363–71.

Millar, S. (1976). Spatial representation by blind and sighted children. *Journal of Experimental Child Psychology*, **21**, 460–79.

Millar, S. (1977a). Early stages of tactual matching. *Perception*, **6**, 333–43.

Millar, S. (1977b). Tactual and name matching by blind children. *British Journal of Psychology*, **68**, 377–87.

Millar, S. (1977c). Spatial representation by blind and sighted children. In G. Butterworth (ed.) *The Child's Representation of the World*. London: Plenum Press.

Millar, S. (1978a). Aspects of information from touch and movement. In G. Gordon (ed.) *Active Touch*. New York: Pergamon Press.

Millar, S. (1978b). Short-term serial tactual recall: Effects of grouping tactually probed recall of Braille letters and nonsense shapes by blind children. *British Journal of Psychology*, **69**, 17–24.

Millar, S. (1979). Utilization of shape and movement cues in simple spatial tasks by blind and sighted children. *Perception*, **8**, 11–20.

Millar, S. (1981a). Crossmodal and intersensory perception and the blind. In R. D. Walk & H. L. Pick, Jr (ed.) *Intersensory Perception and Sensory Integration*. New York: Plenum Press.

Millar, S. (1981b). Self-referent and movement cues in coding spatial location by blind and sighted children. *Perception*, **10**, 255–64.

Millar, S. (1982a). Studies on the deaf and blind. In A. Burton (ed.) *The Pathology and Psychology of Cognition*. London: Methuen.

Millar, S. (1982b). The problem of imagery and spatial development in the blind. In B. de Gelder (ed.) *Knowledge and Representation*. London: Routledge & Kegan Paul.

Millar, S. (1983). Language and active touch. In A. E. Mills (ed.) *Language and Communication in the Blind Child*. London: Croom Helm.

Millar, S. (1984a). Is there a 'best hand' for braille? *Cortex*, **13**, 567–79.

Millar, S. (1984b). Strategy choices by young Braille readers. *Perception*, **3**, 567–79.

Millar, S. (1985a). The perception of complex patterns by touch. *Perception*, **14**, 293–303.

Millar, S. (1985b). Movement cues and body orientation in recall of locations of blind and sighted children. *Quarterly Journal of Experimental Psychology*, **37A**, 257–79.

Millar, S. (1985c). Drawing as representation and image in blind children. Paper presented at The Second International Imagery Conference, University College of Swansea. Abstract in *International Imagery Bulletin*, **2**, 45.

Millar, S. (1986a). Aspects of size, shape and texture in touch: Redundancy and interference in children's discrimination of raised dot patterns. *Journal of Child Psychology and Psychiatry*, **27**, 367–81.

Millar, S. (1986b). Drawing as image and representation in blind children. In D. G. Russell, D. Marks & T. E. Richardson (ed.) *Image 2*. Dunedin, New Zealand: Human Performance Associates.

Millar, S. (1986c). Studies on touch and movement: Their role in spatial skills and Braille. *British Journal of Visual Impairment and Blindness*, **IV**, 4–6.

Millar, S. (1987a). The perceptual 'window' in two-handed braille: Do the left and right hands process text simultaneously? *Cortex*, **23**, 111–222.

Millar, S. (1987b). Perceptual and task factors in fluent braille. *Perception*, **16**, 521–36.

Millar, S. (1988a). Models of sensory deprivation: The nature/nurture dichotomy and spatial representation in the blind. *International Journal of Behavioural Development*, **11**, 69–87.

Millar, S. (1988b). Perceptual and conceptual skills under visual handicap: Perceptual and task factors in understanding braille and tactual graphs. Workshop on Access to Computers and Electronic Devices by Blind Individuals, Trace Center, University of Wisconsin, Madison, October 1988.

Millar, S. (1988c). Prose reading by touch: The role of stimulus quality, orthography and context. *British Journal of Psychology*, **79**, 87–103.

Millar, S. (1988d). An apparatus for recording handmovements. *British Journal of Visual Impairment and Blindness*, **VI**, 87–90.

Millar, S. (1989a). Perception by touch. Conference on Reading Images by Touch, convened by F. Deconinck, Frije Universiteit, Brussels.

Millar, S. (1989b). Studies in Braille. In R. F. V. Witte (ed.) *Production of Hard Copy Materials for the Blind*. Marburg Lahn: Verlag der Deutschen Blindenstudien-anstalt e.v.

Millar, S. (1990a). Articulatory coding in prose reading: Evidence from braille on changes with skill. *British Journal of Psychology*, **81**, 205–19.

Millar, S. (1990b). Imagery and blindness. In P. Hampson, D. F. Marks & J. T. E. Richardson (ed.) *Imagery: Current Developments*. London: Routledge & Kegan Paul.

Millar, S. (1990c). Research on braille and graphics. In P. L. Emiliani (ed.) *Techniques and Devices for the Blind, Medical and Health Research Programme of the European Community*. Brussels: Commission of European Communities.

Millar, S. (1991). A reverse lag in the recognition and production of tactual drawings: Theoretical implications for haptic coding. In M. Heller & W. Schiff (ed.) *The Psychology of Touch*. Hillsdale, New Jersey: Lawrence Erlbaum Associates.

Millar, S. & Ittyerah, M. (1991). Movement imagery in young and congenitally blind children: Mental practice without visuo-spatial information. *International Journal for the Study of Behavioral Development*, **15** (1), 125–46.

Miller, G. A. (1956). The magical number seven plus or minus two: Some limits on capacity for processing information. *Psychological Review*, **63**, 81–7.

Milner, B. & Taylor, L. (1972). Right hemisphere superiority in tactile pattern recognition after cerebral commissurotomy. *Neuropsychologica*, **10**, 1–15.

Moar, I. & Bower, G. H. (1983). Inconsistency in spatial knowledge. *Memory & Cognition*, **11**, 107–13.

Moar, I. & Carleton, L. R. (1982). Memory for routes. *Quarterly Journal of Experimental Psychology*, **34A**, 381–94.

Molfese, D. L. & Molfese, V. J. (1979). Hemispheric and stimulus differences as reflected in cortical responses of newborn infants. *Developmental Psychology*, **15**, 505–11.

Monsell, S. (1987). On the relation between lexical input and output pathways for speech. In A. Allport, D. G. Mackay, W. Prinz, & E. Scheerer (ed.) *Language Perception and Production: Relations between Listening, Speaking, Reading and Writing*. London: Academic Press.

Morgan, M. J. (1977). *Molineux's Question: Vision, Touch and Philosophy of Perception*. Cambridge: Cambridge University Press.

Morris, R. G. M. (1989). Does synaptic plasticity play a role in information storage in the vertebrate brain? In R. G. M. Morris (ed.) *Parallel Distributed Processing: Implications for Psychology and Neurobiology*. Oxford: Clarendon Press.

Muller, R. U., Kubie, J. L., Bostock, E. M., Taube, J. S. & Quirk, G. J. (1991). Spatial firing correlates of neurons in the hippocampal formation of freely moving rats. In J. Paillard (ed.) *Brain and Space*. Oxford: Oxford University Press.

Munsinger, H. (1967). Developing perception and memory for stimulus redundancy. *Journal of Experimental Child Psychology*, **5**, 39–49.

Neisser, U. & Kerr, N. (1973). Spatial and mnemonic properties of visual images. *Cognitive Psychology*, **5**, 138–50.

Newcombe, N. & Huttenlocher, J. (1992). Children's early ability to solve perspective-taking problems. *Developmental Psychology*, **28**, 635–43.

Newcombe, N. & Liben, L. S. (1982). Barrier effects in the cognitive maps of children and adults. *Journal of Experimental Child Psychology*, **34**, 46–58.

Nolan, C. Y. & Kederis, C. J. (1969). *Perceptual Factors in Braille Word Recognition*, American Foundation for the Blind Research Series, No. 20. New York: American Foundation for the Blind.

Norris, M., Spaulding, P., & Brodie, F. (1957). *Blindness in Children*. Chicago: University of Chicago Press.

Notterman, J. M. & Tufano, D. R. (1980). Variables influencing outflow–inflow interpretations of tracking performance: predictability of target motion, transfer function and practice. *Journal of Experimental Psychology: Human Perception and Performance*, **6**, 85–8.

Novikova, L. A. (1973). *Blindness and the Electrical Activity of the Brain*, American Foundation for the Blind Research Series, No. 23. New York: American Foundation for the Blind.

O'Connor, N. & Hermelin, B. (1975). Modality-specific spatial coordinates. *Perception & Psychophysics*, **17**, 213–17.

O'Keefe, J. (1991). The hippocampal cognitive map and navigational strategies. In J. Paillard (ed.) *Brain and Space*. Oxford: Oxford University Press.

O'Keefe, J. & Nadel, L. (1978). *The Hippocampus as a Cognitive Map*. Oxford: Clarendon Press.

Olson, D. R. & Bialystok, E. (1983). *Spatial Cognition*. Hillsdale, New Jersey: Lawrence Erlbaum Associates.

Olton, D. S. & Papas, B. (1979). Spatial memory and hippocampal function. *Neuropsychology*, **17**, 669–82.

Olton, D. S., Becker, J. T. & Handelmann, G. E. (1979). Hippocampus, space and memory. *Behavioral & Brain Sciences*, **2**, 213–322.

Over, R. & Over, J. (1967a). Detection and recognition of mirror-image obliques by young children. *Journal of Comparative and Physiological Psychology*, **64**, 467–70.

Over, R. & Over, J. (1967b). Kinaesthetic judgments of direction of line by young children. *Quarterly Journal of Experimental Psychology*, **XIX**, 337–40.

Paillard, J. (1971). Les déterminants moteur de l'organisation spatiale. *Cahiers de Psychologie*, **14**, 261–316.

Paillard, J. (1991). Motor and representational framing of space. In J. Paillard (ed.) *Brain and Space*. Oxford: Oxford University Press.

Paillard, J., Michel, F. & Stelmach, G. (1983). Localization without content: A tactile analogue of "blind sight". *Archives of Neurology*, **40**, 548–51.

Paivio, A. (1971). *Imagery and Verbal Processes*. New York: Holt, Rinehart & Winston.

Pascual-Leone, J. A. (1970). A mathematical model for the transition rule in Piaget's developmental stages. *Acta Psychologica*, **32**, 301–45.

Peake, P. & Leonard, J. A. (1971). The use of heart rate as an index of stress in blind pedestrians. *Ergonomics*, **14**, 189–204.

Pepper, R. & Herman, L. M. (1970). Decay and interference in the short-term retention of a discrete motor act. *Journal of Experimental Psychology, Monograph Series*, **83**, No. II.

Peterson, L. R. & Peterson, M. J. (1959). Short-term retention of individual verbal items. *Journal of Experimental Psychology*, **58**, 193–8.

Piaget, J. (1954). *The Construction of Reality in the Child*. New York: Basic Books.

Piaget, J. (1953). *Logic and Psychology*. Manchester: Manchester University Press.

Piaget, J. & Inhelder, B. (1948). *La représentation de l'Espace chez l'Enfant*. Paris: Presses Universitaires de France.

Piaget, J. & Inhelder, B. (1956). *The Child's Conception of Space*. London: Routledge & Kegan Paul.

Pick, A. D. & Pick, H. L. (1966). A developmental study of tactual discrimination in blind children, sighted children and adults. *Psychonomic Science*, **6**, 367–8.

Pick, H. L. Jr (1988). Perceptual aspects of spatial cognitive development. In J. Stiles-Davis, M. Kritchevsky & U. Bellugi (ed.) *Spatial Cognition: Brain bases and development*. Hillsdale, New Jersey: Lawrence Erlbaum Associates.

Pick, H. L. Jr & Acredolo, L. P. (1983). *Spatial Orientation: Theory Research and Application*. New York: Plenum Press.

Pick, H. L. Jr & Lockman, J. J. (1981). From frames of reference to spatial representations. In K. S. Liben, A. H. Patterson & N. Newcombe (ed.) *Spatial Representation and Behavior across the Life Span*. New York: Academic Press.

Pick, H. L. Jr & Lockman, J. J. (1983). Map reading and spatial cognition: Discussion. In H. L. Pick, Jr & L. P. Acredolo (ed.) *Spatial Orientation*. New York: Plenum Press.

Plunkett, K. & Sinha, Ch. (1991). *Connectionism and Developmental Theory*. Aarhus: Aarhus Universiteit. Psykologikskriftserie.

Polit, A. & Bizzi, E. (1978). Processes controlling arm movement in monkeys. *Science*, **201**, 1235–7.

Posner, M. I. (1967). Characteristics of visual and kinaesthetic memory codes. *Journal of Experimental Psychology*, **75**, 103–7.

Posner, M. I. (1973). Coordination of internal codes. In W. Chase (ed.) *Visual Information Processing*. New York: Academic Press.

Posner, M. I. & Konick, A. F. (1966). Short-term retention of visual and kinaesthetic information. *Organizational Behavior and Human Performance*, **1**, 71–6.

Poulton, E. C. (1979). Models for biases in judging sensory magnitude. *Psychological Bulletin*, **86**, 777–803.

Prechtl, H. F. R. (1961). Neurological sequelae of prenatal and paranatal complications. In B. M. Foss (ed.) *Determinants of Infant Behaviour*. London: Methuen & Co Ltd.

Presson, C. C. (1980). Spatial egocentrism and the effect of an alternative frame of reference. *Journal of Experimental Child Psychology*, **29**, 391–402.

Presson, C. C. (1982). The development of map reading skills. *Child Development*, **53**, 196–9.

Previc, F. H. (1991). A general theory concerning the prenatal origins of cerebral lateralization in humans. *Psychological Review*, **98**, 299–334.

Pring, L. (1988). The 'reverse-generation' effect: A comparison of memory performance between blind and sighted children. *British Journal of Psychology*, **79**, 387–400.

Prinz, W. & Saunders, A. F. (1984). *Cognitive and Motor Processes*. Berlin: Springer-Verlag.

Proskura, E. V. (1976). Egocentrism in the preschooler's conception of spatial relations. *Soviet Psychology*, **14**, 42–50.

Pufall, P. B. & Shaw, R. S. (1973). Analysis of the development of children's reference systems. *Cognitive Psychology*, **5**, 151–75.

Pylyshyn, Z. W. (1973). What the mind's eye tells the mind's brain. *Psychological Bulletin*, **80**, 1–24.

Pylyshyn, Z. W. (1981). The imagery debate: Analogue media versus tacit knowledge. *Psychological Review*, **88**, 16–45.

Rapin, I. (1979). Effects of early blindness and deafness on cognition. In R. Katzman (ed.) *Congenital and Acquired Disorders*, pp. 189–245. New York: Raven Press.

Rasmussen, T. & Milner, B. (1977). The role of early brain damage in determining the lateralization of speech functions. In S. Dimond & D. Blizard (ed.) *Evolution and Lateralization of the Brain*, pp. 355–69. New York: New York Academy of Science.

Ratcliff, G. (1991). Brain and space: some deductions from the clinical evidence. In J. Paillard (ed.) *Brain and Space*. Oxford: Oxford University Press.

Reese, H. W. (1970). Imagery in children's paired associate learning. *Journal of Experimental Child Psychology*, **9**, 174–8.

Reese, H. W. & Parkington, J. J. (1973). Intralist interference and imagery in deaf and hearing children. *Journal of Experimental Child Psychology*, **16**, 165–83.

Revesz, G. (1950). *Psychology and Art of the Blind*. London: Longmans.

Rice, C. (1930). The orientation of plane figures as a factor in their perception. *Child Development*, **1**, 111–43.

Richardson, A. (1967). Mental practice: A review and discussion. *Research Quarterly*, **38** (1), 95–107; **38** (2), 263–73.

Richardson, B. L., Wuillemin, D. B. & Mackintosh, G. J. (1981). *British Journal of Psychology*, **72**, 353–62.

Riesen, A. H. (1947). The development of visual perception in man and chimpanzee. *Science*, **106**, 107–8.

Rieser, J. (1979). Spatial orientation in six-month-old infants. *Child Development*, **50**, 1078–87.

Rieser, J. & Heiman, M. L. (1982). Spatial self-reference systems and shortest route behavior in toddlers. *Child Development*, **53**, 524–33.

Rieser, J., Lockman, J. J. & Pick, H-L. Jr (1980). The role of visual experience in knowledge of spatial lay-out. *Perception & Psychophysics*, **28**, 185–90.

Rieser, J., Guth, D. A. & Hill, E. W. (1986). Sensitivity to perspective structure while walking without vision. *Perception*, **15**, 137–88.

Rieser, J., Ashmead, C. R. T., Taylor, C. R. & Youngquist, G. A. (1990). Visual perception and the guidance of locomotion without vision to previously seen targets. *Perception*, **19**, 675–89.

Roberts, T. D. M. (1978). *Neurophysiology of Postural Mechanisms*. London: Butterworths.

Robin, M. & Pêcheux, M. G. (1976). Problèmes posés par la reproduction de modèles spatiaux chez des enfants aveugles: une étude expérimentale. *Perception*, **5**, 39–49.

Robinson, D. L., Goldberg, M. E. & Stanton, G. B. (1978). Parietal Association cortex in the primate: Sensory mechanisms and behavioral modulation. *Journal of Neurophysiology*, **41**, 910–32.

Rock, I. (1973). *Orientation and Form*. London: Academic Press.

Rock, I. (1984). *Perception*. New York: W. H. Freeman.

Roderiguez, M., Gomez, C., Alonso, J. & Alfonso, D. (1992). Laterality, alternation and perseverative relationships on the T-Maze test. *Behavioral Neuroscience*, **106** (6), 974–80.

Roemer, G., Gresch, H., Ettlinger, G. & Brown, J. V. (1986). Tactile recognition of laterally inverted mirror images by children: intermanual transfer and rotation of the palm. *Perception*, **15**, 303–12.

Rolls, E. T. (1991). Functions of the primate hippocampus in spatial processing and memory. In J. Paillard (ed.) *Brain and Space*. Oxford: Oxford University Press.

Rosch, E. H. (1973). Natural categories. *Cognitive Psychology*, **4**, 328–50.

Rosch, E. R. (1976). Basic objects in natural categories. *Cognitive Psychology*, **8**, 382–439.

Rosch, E. & Mervis, C. B. (1975). Family resemblances: studies in the internal structure of categories. *Cognitive Psychology*, **7**, 573–605.

Rowher, W. D. Jr (1970). Images and pictures in children's learning. *Psychological Bulletin*, **73**, 393–403.

Roy, E. A. & Elliott, D. (1989). Manual asymmetries in aimed movements. *Quarterly Journal of Experimental Psychology*, **41A** (3), 501–16.

Rudel, R. G. & Teuber, H. L. (1963). Discrimination of direction of line in children. *Journal of Comparative and Physiological Psychology*, **56**, 892–8.

Rudel, R. G. & Teuber, H. L. (1964). Crossmodal transfer of shape discrimination by children. *Neuropsychologica*, **2**, 1–8.

Rudel, R. G., Denckla, M. & Hirsch, S. (1977). The development of left hand superiority for discriminating braille configurations. *Neurology*, **27**, 160–4.

Rumelhart, D. E. & McClelland, J. L. (1986). *Parallel Distributed Processing: Explorations in the Microstructure of Cognition*, Vols I & II. Cambridge, Massachusetts: MIT Press.

Runeson, S. (1977). On visual perception of dynamic events. Doctoral dissertation, University of Uppsala (quoted by J. J. Gibson 1979).

Russell, D. G. (1976). Spatial location cues and movement production. In G. E. Stelmach (ed.) *Motor Control: Issues and Trends*. New York: Academic Press.

Ryan, E. D. & Simmons, J. (1981). Cognitive demand, imagery, and frequency of mental rehearsal as factors influencing acquisition of motor skills. *Journal of Sports Psychology*, **3**, 35–45.

Sackett, R. S. (1934). The influence of symbolic rehearsal upon the retention of a maze habit. *Journal of General Psychology*, **10**, 376–9.

Sadalla, E. K., Staplin, L. J. & Burrows, W. J. (1979). Retrieval processes in distance cognition. *Memory and Cognition*, **7**, 291–6.

Sakata, H. & Iwamura, Y. (1978). Cortical processing of tactile information in the first somato-sensory and parietal association areas in the monkey. In G. Gordon (ed.) *Active Touch*. New York: Pergamon.

Salame, P. & Baddeley, A. (1982). Disruption of short-term memory by unattended speech: Implications for the structure of working memory. *Journal of Verbal Learning & Verbal Behavior*, **21**, 150–64.

Salatas, H. & Flavell, J. H. (1976). Perspective taking: The development of two components of knowledge. *Child Development*, **47**, 103–9.

Sandstroem, C. I. (1953). Sex differences in localization and orientation. *Acta Psychologica*, **9**, 82–96.

Schachter, D. & Gollin, E. S. (1979). Spatial perspective taking in young children. *Journal of Experimental Child Psychology*, **27**, 467–78.

Schiff, W. & Foulke, E. (ed.) (1982). *Tactual Perception: A Source Book*. New York: Cambridge University Press.

Schiff, W. & Isikow, H. (1966). Stimulus redundancy in the tactile perception of histograms. *International Journal for the Education of the Blind*, **16**, 1–11.

Schlaegel, T. F. (1953). The dominant method of imagery in blind compared to sighted adolescents. *Journal of Genetic Psychology*, **83**, 265–77.

Schmidt, R. A. (1968). Postural set as a factor in motor memory. *Psychonomic Science*, **13**, 223–4.

Schneider, G. E. (1967). Contrasting visuo-motor functions of tectum and cortex in the golden hamster. *Psychologische Forschungen*, **31**, 52–62.

Scholtz, C. L. & Mann, D. M. A. (1977). Tetraploidy and Blindness. *Neuropathology and Neurobiology*, **3**, 137–40.

Scholtz, C. L., Swettenham, K., Brown, A. & Mann, D. M. A. (1981). A Histoquantitative study of the striate cortex and lateral geniculate body in normal, blind and demented subjects. *Neuropathology and Applied Neurobiology*, **7**, 103–14.

Schuberth, R. E. (1982). The infant's search for objects: Alternatives to Piaget's theory of concept development. In L. P. Lipsitt (ed.) *Advances in Infancy Research*, Vol. 2. Norwood, New Jersey: Ablex Publishing Co.

Schwartz, A. S., Perey, A. J. & Azulay, A. (1975). Further analysis of active and passive touch in pattern discrimination. *Bulletin of the Psychonomic Society*, **6**, 7–9.

Schwartz, M. (1984). The role of sound for space and object perception in the congenitally blind infant. In L. P. Lipsitt & C. Rovee-Collier (ed.) *Advances in Infancy Research*, Vol. 3. Norwood, New Jersey: Ablex Publishing Co.

Segal, S. J. & Fusella, V. (1970). Influence of imaged pictures and sounds on detection of auditory and visual signals. *Journal of Experimental Psychology*, **83**, 458–64.

Semmes, J., Weinstein, S., Ghent, L. & Teuber, H. L. (1963). Correlates of impaired orientation in personal and extra personal space. *Brain*, **86**, 747–72.

Sergent, J. (1988). Face perception and the right hemisphere. In L. Weiskrantz (ed.) *Thought Without Language*. Oxford: Clarendon Press.

Shallice, T. (1988). *From Neuropsychology to Mental Structure*. Cambridge: Cambridge University Press.

Shantz, C. V. & Watson, J. S. (1971). Spatial abilities and spatial egocentrism in the young child. *Child Development*, **42** (1), 171–81.

Shatz, C. J. (1992). The developing brain. *Scientific American*, **267** (3), 61–7.

Shemyakin, F. N. (1962). Orientation in space. In B. G. Anan'yev *et al.* (eds) *Psychological Science in the USSR*, Vol. 1, US Office of Technical Services Report 62-11083. Washington, DC: US Office of Technical Services.

Shepard, R. N. & Cooper, L. A. (1982). *Mental Images and their Transformations*. Cambridge: MIT Press.

Shepard, R. N. & Feng, C. (1972). A chronometric study of mental paperfolding. *Cognitive Psychology*, **3**, 228–43.

Shepard, R. N. & Hurvitz, S. (1984). Mental rotation and discrimination of left and right turns in maps. *Cognition*, **18**, 161–93.

Shepard, R. N. & Metzler, J. (1971). Mental rotation of three-dimensional objects. *Science*, **171**, 701–3.

Sherman, J. A. (1971). Problem of sex differences in space perception and aspects of intellectual functioning. *Psychological Review*, **74**, 290–9.

Sherrick, C. E. (1976). The antagonism of hearing and touch. In S. K. Hirsch, D. H. Eldridge, I. J. Hirsch & S. R. Silverman (ed.) *Hearing and Davis: Essays Honoring Hallowell Davis*. Saint Louis, Missouri: Washington University Press.

Sherrick, C. E. (1984). Basic and applied research on tactile aids for deaf people: progress and prospects. *Journal of the Acoustic Society of America*, **75**, 1325–42.

Sherrick, C. E. (1991). Vibrotactile pattern perception. Some findings and applications. In M. A. Heller & W. Schiff (ed.) *The Psychology of Touch*. Hillsdale, New Jersey: Lawrence Erlbaum Associates.

Sherrick, C. E. (1992). Tactual sound-and-speech analyzing aids for deaf persons. In C. L. Christman & A. N. Albert (ed.) *Cochlear Implants: A Model for the Regulation of Emerging Medical Technologies*. Norwell, Massachusetts: Kluwer Academic Publishers.

Sherrick, C. E. & Cholewiak, R. W. (1986). Cutaneous sensitivity. In K. Boff, L. Kaufman & J. Thomas (ed.) *The Handbook of Perception and Human Performance*, Vol. 1, pp. 1–58. New York: John Wiley.

Sherrick, C. E. & Craig, J. C. (1982). The psychophysics of touch. In W. Schiff & E. Foulke (ed.) *Tactual Perception: A Sourcebook*. New York: American Foundation for the Blind.

Shingledecker, C. A. (1978). The effect of anticipation on performance and processing load in blind mobility. *Ergonomics*, **21**, 355–71.

Shingledecker, C. A. & Foulke, E. (1978). A human factors approach to the assessment of mobility of blind pedestrians. *Human Factors*, **20**, 273–86.

Siegel, A. (1981). The externalization of cognitive maps by children and adults: In search of ways to ask better questions. In L. S. Liben, A. H. Patterson & N. Newcombe (ed.) *Spatial Representation and Behavior across the Life Span*. New York: Academic Press.

Siegel, A. & White, S. H. (1975). The development of spatial representation of large-scale environments. In H. W. Reese (ed.) *Advances in Child Development & Behavior*, Vol. 10. London: Academic Press.

Siegel, A. W. & Schadler, M. (1977). The development of young children's spatial representations of their classrooms. *Child Development*, **48**, 388–94.

Siegel, A. W., Allen, G. L. & Kirasic, K. C. (1979a). Children's ability to make bi-directional distance comparisons. *Developmental Psychology*, **15**, 656–7.

Siegel, A. W., Herman, J. F., Allen, G. L. & Kirasic, K. C. (1979b). The development of cognitive maps of large-scale and small-scale spaces. *Child Development*, **50**, 582–5.

Slator, R. (1982). The Development of Spatial Perception and Understanding in Young Children. D.Phil. thesis, University of Oxford.

Smyth, M. M. & Scholey, K. A. (1992). Determining spatial span: The role of movement time and articulation rate. *Quarterly Journal of Experimental Psychology*, **45A**, 479–501.

Somerville, S. C. & Bryant, P. E. (1985). Young children's use of spatial coordinates. *Child Development*, **56**, 604–13.

Sophian, C. (1985). Understanding the movement of objects: Early developments in spatial cognition. *British Journal of Developmental Psychology*, **3**, 321–33.

Sophian, C. & Wellman, H. (1987). The development of indirect search strategies. *British Journal of Developmental Psychology*, **5**, 9–18.

Spearman, C. (1927). *The Abilities of Man*. New York: Macmillan.

Spelke, E. S. (1979). Perceiving bimodally specified events in infancy. *Developmental Psychology*, **15**, 626–36.

Spence, K. W. (1942). The basis of solution by chimpanzees of the intermediate size problem. *Journal of Experimental Psychology*, **31**, 257–71.

Spencer, C., Blades, M. & Morsley, K. (1989). *The Child in the Physical Environment: The development of spatial knowledge and cognition*. Chichester: Wiley.

Sperling, G. (1963). A model for visual memory tasks. *Human Factors*, **5**, 19–30.

Sperry, R. W., Zaidel, E. & Zaidel, D. (1979). Self recognition and social awareness in the deconnected minor hemisphere. *Neuropsychologica*, **17**, 153–66.

Spreen, O., Tupper, D., Risser, A., Tuoko, H. & Edgell, D. (1984). *Human Developmental Neuropsychology*. Oxford: Oxford University Press.

Springer, S. P. & Sealman, A. (1978). The ontogeny of hemisphere specialization: evidence from dichotic listening in twins. *Neuropsychologica*, **16**, 269–81.

Squire, L. R. (1987). *Memory and Brain*. Oxford: Oxford University Press.

Stafford, R. T. (1961). Sex differences in spatial visualization as evidence of sex-linked inheritance. *Perceptual and Motor Skill*, **13**, 428.

Starkey, P., Spelke, E. S. & Gelman, R. (1983). Detection of intermodal numerical correspondences by human infants. *Science*, **222**, 179–81.

Starkey, P., Spelke, E. S. & Gelman, R. (1990). Numerical abstraction by human infants. *Cognition*, **36**, 97–127.

Stein, J. F. (1991). Space and the parietal association areas. In J. Paillard (ed.) *Brain and Space*. Oxford: Oxford University Press.

Stein, J. F. (1992). The representation of egocentric space in the posterior parietal cortex. *Behavioral and Brain Sciences*, **15**, 691–700.

Stein, J. F., Riddell, P. M. & Fowler, M. S. (1987). Fine binocular control in dyslexic children. *Eye*, **11**, 433–8.

Stelmach, G. E. (1969). Prior positioning responses as a factor in short-term retention of a simple motor task. *Journal of Experimental Psychology*, **81**, 523–6.

Stelmach, G. E. & Larish, D. D. (1980). Egocentric referents in human limb orientation. In G. E. Stelmach & J. Requin (ed.). *Tutorials in Motor Behavior*. Amsterdam: North-Holland Publishing Co.

Stelmach, G. E., Kelso, J. A., Scott & Wallace, S. A. (1975). Pre-selection in short-term motor memory. *Journal of Experimental Psychology: Human Learning and Memory*, **1**, 745–55.

Stiles-Davis, J. (1988). Spatial dysfunction in young children with right hemisphere injury. In J. Stiles-Davis, M. Kritchevsky & U. Bellugi (ed.) *Spatial Cognition: Brain Bases and Development*. Hillsdale, New Jersey: Lawrence Erlbaum Associates.

Stiles-Davis, J., Kritchevsky, M. & Bellugi, U. (ed.) (1988). *Spatial Cognition: Brain Bases and Development*. Hillsdale, New Jersey: Lawrence Erlbaum Associates.

Strawson, P. F. (1989). *The Bounds of Sense: An Essay on Kant's Critique of Pure Reason*. London: Routledge.

Strelow, E. R. & Brabyn, J. A. (1982). Locomotion of the blind controlled by natural sound cues. *Perception*, **11**, 635–40.

Strelow, E. R., Brabyn, J. A. & Clark, G. R. S. (1976). Apparatus for measuring and recording path velocity and direction characteristics of human locomotion. *Behavior Research Methods & Instrumentation*, **8**, 442–6.

Streri, A. (1987). Tactile perception of shape and intermodal transfer in 2- to three-month-old infants. *British Journal of Developmental Psychology*, **5**, 213–20.

Sullivan, M. J. & Turvey, M. T. (1974). Short-term retention of tactile stimulation. *Quarterly Journal of Experimental Psychology*, **24**, 253–61.

Swain, I. V., Zelazo, P. R. & Clifton, R. K. (1993). Newborn infants' memory for speech sounds retained over 24 hours. *Developmental Psychology*, **29**, 312–23.

Talmy, L. (1983). How language structures space. In H. L. Pick, Jr & L. P. Acredolo (ed.) *Spatial Orientation: Theory, Research and Application*. New York: Plenum Press.

Teghtsoonian, M. & Teghtsoonian, R. (1965). Seen and felt length. *Psychonomic Science*, **3**, 465–9.

Teghtsoonian, R. & Teghtsoonian, M. (1970). Two varieties of perceived length. *Perception & Psychophysics*, **8**, 389–92.

Thomson, J. (1983). Is continuous visual monitoring necessary for guided locomotion? *Journal of Experimental Psychology: Human Perception and Performance*, **9**, 427–43.

Thorndyke, P. W. & Hayes-Roth, B. (1982). Differences in spatial knowledge acquired from maps and navigation. *Cognitive Psychology*, **14**, 560–89.

Thorndyke, P. W. & Stasz, C. (1980). Individual differences in procedures for knowledge acquisition from maps. *Cognitive Psychology*, **12**, 137–75.

Tinbergen, N. (1951). *The Study of Instinct*. Oxford: Clarendon Press.

Titchener, E. B. (1909). *Lectures on the Experimental Psychology of Thought*. New York: Macmillan.

Tobin, M. J. & Hill, E. (1984). A moon writer. *The New Beacon*, **LXVIII** (807), 173–6.

Tobin, M. J. & Hill, E. W. (1989). Harnessing the community: moon script, the moon-writer and sighted volunteers. *The British Journal of Visual Impairment*, **VII** (1), 3–5.

Tolman, E. C. (1948). Cognitive maps in rats and men. *Psychological Review*, **40**, 60–70.

Trevarthen, C. B. (1968). Two mechanisms of vision in primates. *Psychologische Forschung*, **31**, 299–337.

Tulving, E. (1983). *Elements of Episodic Memory*. New York: Oxford University Press.

Tversky, B. (1981). Distortion in memory for maps. *Cognitive Psychology*, **13**, 407–33.

Tversky, B. & Schiano, D. J. (1989). Perceptual and conceptual factors in distortions in memory for graphs and maps. *Journal of Experimental Psychology (General)*, **118** (4), 387–98.

Twitchell, T. E. (1965). The automatic grasping responses of infants. *Neuropsychologica*, **7**, 247–59.

Ullich, E. (1967). Some experiments on the functions of mental practice training in the acquisition of motor skills. *Ergonomics*, **10**, 411–19.

Uttal, D. H. & Wellman, H. M. (1989). Young children's representation of spatial information acquired from maps. *Developmental Psychology*, **25**, 128–38.

Vallar, G. & Baddeley, A. D. (1982). Short-term forgetting and the articulatory loop. *Quarterly Journal of Experimental Psychology*, **34A**, 53–60.

Vallbo, A. B. & Johansson, R. S. (1978). The tactile sensory innervation of the glabrous skin of the human hand. In G. Gordon (ed.) *Active Touch. The Mechanism of Recognition of Objects by Manipulation: A Multidisciplinary Approach*. Oxford: Pergamon Press.

Van Sluyters, R. C., Atkinson, J., Banks, M. S., Held, R. M., Hoffmann, K-P. & Shatz, C. J. (1990). The development of vision and visual perception. In L. Spillmann & J. S. Werner (ed.) *Visual Perception: The Neurophysiological Foundations*. New York: Academic Press.

Van Sommers, P. (1984). *Drawing and Cognition: Descriptive and Experimental Studies of Graphic Production Processes*. Cambridge: Cambridge University Press.

von Bekesy, G. (1960). *Experiments on Hearing*. New York: McGraw-Hill.

von Holst, E. & Mittelstaedt, H. (1950). Das Reafferenzprinzip. *Naturwissenschaften*, **37**, 464–76.

von Senden, M. (1932). *Raum und Gestalt: Auffassung bei operierten Blindgeborenen vor und nach der Operation*. Leipzig: Barth.

Vurpillot, E. (1976). *The Visual World of the Child*. London: George Allen & Unwin.

Vygotsky, L. S. (1962). *Thought and Language*. Cambridge, Massachusetts: MIT Press.

Walk, R. D. (1965). Tactual and visual learning of forms differing in degrees of symmetry. *Psychonomic Science*, **2**, 93–4.

Walker, L. D. & Gollin, D. S. (1977). Perspective role taking in young children. *Journal of Experimental Child Psychology*, **24**, 343–57.

Wallace, S. A. (1977). The coding of location: A test of the target hypothesis. *Journal of Motor Behavior*, **9**, 157–69.

Wallace, S. A., Frankeny, J. R. & Larish, D. D. (1982). Effects of initial limb position on the accuracy, reaction time & electromyographic patterns of rapid movements. *Human Movement Science*, **1**, 215–31.

Walsh, W. D. (1981). Memory for preselected and constrained short movements. *Research Quarterly for Exercise & Sport*, **52**, 368–79.

Walsh, W. D., Russell, D. G. & Crassini, B. (1981). Interference effects in recalling movements. *British Journal of Psychology*, **72**, 287–98.

Walton, G. E. & Bower, T. G. R. (1993). Newborns from "proto-types" in less than 1 minute. *Psychological Science*, **4**, 203–5.

Walton, G. E., Bower, N. J. A. & Bower, T. G. R. (1992). Recognition of familiar faces by newborns. *Infant Behavior & Development*, **15**, 265–9.

Wanet, M. C. & Veraart, C. (1985). Processing auditory information by the blind in spatial localization tasks. *Perception & Psychophysics*, **38**, 91–6.

Wapner, S. (1968). Age changes in perception of verticality and of the longitudinal body axis under body tilt. *Journal of Experimental Child Psychology*, **6**, 543–55.

Wapner, S. & Werner, H. (1957). *Perceptual Development: An Investigation within Sensori-tonic Field Theory*. Worcester: Clark University Press.

Warren, D. H. (1974). Early vs late vision: the role of early vision in spatial reference systems. *New Outlook for the Blind*, **68**, 157–62.

Warren, D. H. (1977). *Blindness and Early Childhood Development*. New York: American Foundation for the Blind.

Waugh, N. & Norman, D. A. (1965). Primary memory. *Psychological Review*, **72**, 89–104.

Waxman, W. (1991). *Kant's Model of the Mind: A New Interpretation of Transcendental Idealism*. Oxford: Oxford University Press.

Weber, E. H. (1978). *The Sense of Touch*. (*De Tactu* (1834) translated by H. E. Ross, & *Der Tastsinn und das Gemeingefuhl* (1846) translated by D. J. Murray, for the Experimental Psychology Society). London: Academic Press.

Weiskrantz, L. (1950). An unusual case of after-imagery following fixation of an "imaginary" pattern. *Quarterly Journal of Experimental Psychology*, **2**, 170–5.

Weiskrantz, L. (1963). Contour discrimination in a young monkey with striate cortex ablation. *Neuropsychologica*, **1**, 145–64.

Weiskrantz, L. (1986). *Blindsight: A Case Study and its Implications*. Oxford: Oxford University Press.

Weiskrantz, L. & Cowey, A. (1975). Crossmodal matching in the rhesus monkey using a single pair of stimuli. *Neuropsychologica*, **13**, 257–61.

Welsh, R. A. & Blash, B. B. (1980). *Foundations of Orientation and Mobility*. New York: American Foundation for the Blind.

Werner, H. (1948). *Comparative Psychology of Mental Development*. New York: Follett.

Wertheimer, M. (1961). Psychomotor coordination of auditory and visual space at birth. *Science*, **134**, 1692.

White, B. L. & Held, R. (1966). Plasticity of sensorimotor development in the human infant. In J. Rosenblith & W. Allinsmith (ed.) *The Causes of Behaviour: Readings in Child Development and Educational Psychology*, pp. 60–70. Boston: Allyn & Bacon.

Whorf, B. L. (1956). *Language, Thought and Reality*. New York: John Wiley.

Willats, J. (1977). How children learn to draw. *Quarterly Journal of Experimental Psychology*, **29**, 367–82.

Williams, M. (1956). *Williams Intelligence Test For Children with Defective Vision*. Windsor, England: N.F.E.R. Publishing Co Ltd.

Wilton, R. N. (1977). Knowledge of spatial relations: The determination of the relationship "nearest to". *Quarterly Journal of Experimental Psychology*, **29**, 685–98.

Wilton, R. N. (1989). The structure of memory: Evidence concerning the recall of surface and background colour of shapes. *The Quarterly Journal of Experimental Psychology*, **41A**, 579–98.

Wisehart, J. G. & Bower, T. G. R. (1982). The development of spatial understanding in infancy. *Journal of Experimental Child Psychology*, **33**, 363–85.

Wisehart, J. G. & Bower, T. G. R. (1984). Spatial relations and the object concept: a normative study. In L. P. Lipsitt & C. Rovee-Collier (ed.) *Advances in Infancy Research*, Vol. 3. Norwood, New Jersey: Ablex Publishing Co.

Witelson, S. F. (1976). Sex and the single hemisphere: Specialization of the right hemisphere for spatial processing. *Science*, **193**, 425–7.

Witelson, S. F. & Pallie, W. (1973). Left hemisphere specialization for speech in the newborn: Neuroanatomical evidence of asymmetry. *Brain*, **96**, 641–6.

Wittgenstein, L. (1958). *Philosophical Investigations* (2nd edn.), translated by G. E. M. Anscombe. Oxford: Blackwell.

Witkin, H. A. & Ash, A. E. (1948). Studies in space orientation. Parts I, III & IV. Perception of the upright in the absence of a visual field. *Journal of Experimental Psychology*, **38**, 325–37; 603–14; 762–82.

Witkin, H. A., Dyk, R. B., Faterson, G. E., Goodenough, D. R. & Karp, S. A. (1962). *Psychological Differentiation*. New York: John Wiley.

Witkin, H. A., Goodenough, D. R. & Karp, S. A. (1967). Stability of cognitive style from childhood to adolescence. *Journal of Personality and Social Psychology*, **7**, 291–300.

Woodworth, R. S. (1899). The accuracy of voluntary movement. *Psychological Monographs*, **3**, No. 3.

Worchel, P. (1951). Space perception and orientation in the blind. *Psychological Monographs*, **65**, No. 332.

Wycherly, R. J. & Nicklin, B. H. (1970). The heart rate of blind and sighted pedestrians on a town route. *Ergonomics*, **13**, 181–92.

Zaidel, E. (1985). Language in the right hemisphere. In D. F. Benson & E. Zaidel (ed.) *The Dual Brain*, pp. 205–31. New York: Guilford Press.

Zaporozhets, A. V. (1965). The development of perception in the preschool child. In P. H. Mussen (ed.) European Research in Child Development, *Monographs of the Society for Research in Child Development*, **30**, 82–101.

Zeki, S. (1992). The visual image in mind and brain. *Scientific American*, **267**, 69–76.

Zelazo, P. R. (1983). The development of walking: new findings and old assumptions. *Journal of Motor Behavior*, **15**, 99–137.

Author index

Subject index